QUICK & EASY COOKING

READER'S DIGEST

QUICK & EASY COOKING

Consultant Editor: Anne Ager

Published by The Reader's Digest Association Limited
London   New York

First Edition Copyright © 1988
The Reader's Digest Association Limited,
Berkeley Square House, Berkeley Square,
London W1X 6AB

Second reprint 1989

Copyright © 1988, Reader's Digest Association Far East Limited
Philippines Copyright © 1988, Reader's Digest Association
Far East Ltd

Printed in England

ISBN 0 276 42006 3

CONTENTS

QUICK AND EASY COOKING

Quick and Easy Cooking contains more than 500 carefully tested, delicious recipes, covering every type of meal. All are quick to prepare, simple to cook, and make the most of value-for-money ingredients. Fresh foods are used whenever possible, but dried, canned or frozen products are often suggested as substitutes.

THE RECIPES

The recipes in this book will help you make the most of familiar foods and achieve impressive results with ease and confidence.

• Time spent in the kitchen is kept to a minimum. Over half the recipes in this book can be made in under 30 minutes.

• All the recipes are clearly written, making it simple to check ingredients and follow the numbered, step-by-step methods.

• Three symbols show at a glance how quick and how economical a recipe is, and whether quantities can be reduced:

⊘ *Extra-quick preparation and cooking times*
½ *Ingredients can be halved to feed fewer people*
🐷 *Particularly economical to prepare*

Preparation and Cooking Times

Directly beneath each recipe title are estimated times for preparation and cooking, so that you can see immediately how long it takes to make a particular recipe. You may find you are a little slow the first time you follow a recipe, but become quicker when you repeat it. Preparation time covers such actions as peeling, chopping and mixing, and preliminary cooking stages such as melting butter or frying onions. If one part of a dish can be prepared while the other is cooking, only the longer time is noted.

Servings

Each recipe indicates how many average-sized portions it makes. In a recipe such as a sauce, a liquid measurement is given, such as: Makes **½ pint (285ml)**.

Calories

For those who like to keep an eye on their calorie intake, a rough guide to the number of calories per portion or serving is given, or in the case of sauces and dressings, calories per tablespoon. Where alternative ingredients are given, the calorie count is based on the first choice.

Ingredients

The ingredients are listed in the order in which they are used. Quantities are given in both imperial and metric measurements. Although the equivalent for each is as accurate as possible, it is important to follow just one set of measurements throughout – either metric or imperial – for a successful result.

Method

Clear, step-by-step instructions are given for every recipe. The type of pan is specified; the degree of cooking heat clearly indicated; and if a dish has to be cooked covered, you are told.

The first mention of each ingredient in the cooking method is always in **heavy** lettering, making it easy for you to check whether you have left anything out.

Hints and Tips

Many of the recipes carry helpful suggestions for varying a particular dish or for what to serve with it, hints on advance preparation, or tips on reheating. This makes them more versatile and adaptable to your particular needs. Certain ingredients may be out of season or unavailable; it is reassuring to know what can be used in their place.

Starting Out

When planning to use a recipe, make a list of the exact ingredients you need. Check the store cupboard for non-perishable items – don't forget obvious things such as spices and dried herbs. Check the refrigerator for perishable staples such as butter, eggs and cheese.

Make sure you have all the right equipment too. There is nothing more frustrating than getting halfway through a recipe only to find that you do not have a vital utensil.

Collect all necessary ingredients and equipment before starting. Be organised, follow the book closely, and you really will discover that cooking can be quick, easy and rewarding.

EQUIPMENT

A well-equipped kitchen saves time and money. A good cook can work with surprisingly few, carefully chosen tools, and there is no necessity to buy expensive gadgets. Stick to the utensils you really need and feel confident with and bear in mind that some items of equipment can double up on their uses: a vegetable peeler, for example, will also get the last awkward flakes of cheese from a hard wedge or piece of rind.

There are also ways of substituting for equipment that you do not have. No double saucepan? Just stand a basin on top of a suitably sized saucepan so that the basin rim just overlaps the edge of the pan ... Or instead of an expensive steamer, use a metal colander set over a large saucepan, topped by a lid of the same size.

The following guide to basic kitchen equipment will make cooking easier and more enjoyable, and you will be equipped to follow any of the recipes in this book.

POTS AND PANS

Choose sturdy equipment that will stand up to regular cooking and is relatively easy to keep clean. Top quality copper and stainless steel pans are best, but expensive. Many non-stick pans tend to lose their surface, and unless kept for gentle uses such as boiling milk, do not last long. Enamel-coated pans are often good to cook in, but the coating tends to chip. Solid aluminium, medium-grade stainless steel and cast iron are the best value for money. Remember that some foods discolour aluminium, so the pans should be emptied and cleaned as quickly as possible after cooking. Cast-iron pans are not always easy to keep immaculate, as they rust easily. To prevent rust, 'season' them occasionally – clean and dry them, then rub with cooking oil and (as long as all handles and knobs are ovenproof) bake in a moderately hot oven for 2 hours.

The following equipment should be adequate for the average family.

• **Saucepans:** One small, one medium, one large. Plus one very large pan for pasta, boiling gammon, etc. All should have matching lids.

• **Frying pans:** One large, one medium, preferably with matching lids. A deep-fryer with a wire basket is also useful if you do a lot of deep-frying. Alternatively, use a large saucepan and a perforated spoon for draining.

• **Non-stick pans:** One small, with lip – for boiling milk and making sauces (much easier to clean).

• **Roasting tin:** One large – big enough for large joints. Doubles as *bain marie* or 'water bath' for gently cooking dishes such as baked egg custard.

• **Casseroles:** One 2 pint, one 4 pint (about 1 litre and 2 litres), with lids.

• **Shallow ovenproof or pie dishes:** One large, one medium.

• **Cake tins:** Two round tins, one 7in (180mm), and one 8in (200mm) in diameter. Loose-bottomed tins make turning out easier.

• **Loaf tin:** One, with a capacity of about 2lb (900g).

• **Patty tin:** One standard-sized, 12-patty tin for small pies and tarts, individual Yorkshire puddings, and so on.

• **Baking sheet:** One large, non-stick if preferred.

• **Flan tin:** One tin or dish, 8-9in (200-230mm) in diameter.

• **Mixing bowls:** A set of three – a large one for mixing cakes, and two smaller ones for mixing batters, whipping cream, and so on. Choose ovenglass rather than plastic; it is more versatile, and can also be used for steamed puddings.

• **Measuring jug:** One large glass jug with imperial and metric measurements.

KITCHEN CUTLERY

Good knives are essential for quick and effective chopping, slicing and dicing. They are a worthwhile investment and will last a lifetime if looked after carefully.

Choose knives made of carbon steel or really high quality stainless steel for durability and sharpness, and with blades that extend into the handle for maximum strength, better balance and efficient cutting. Wooden handles are less slippery than plastic ones. Sharpen knives with a steel; electric sharpeners can damage the edge of the blade. *Never* leave knives soaking in water, as this will loosen and ruin the handles. Always wipe the blade immediately after use to prevent discoloration.

Use non-stick utensils if you are using a non-stick baking surface.

• **Cook's knife:** A large, general-purpose knife for cutting meat and chopping vegetables.

• **Vegetable knife:** A small, sharp knife with a slim blade for scraping vegetables and skinning fish.

• **Serrated knife:** For slicing bread.

• **Carving knife:** With a slim blade for carving meat and poultry.

• **Carving fork:** Can also be used for pricking biscuits and pastry lids.

• **Palette knife:** For mixing pastry; finishing icing on a cake; removing baked foods from a baking sheet, and so on.

• **Fish/egg slice:** For turning cooked foods without breaking them up.

• **Spoons:** One large, perforated spoon for draining fried foods, and skimming stocks and soups; wooden spoons for mixing and making sauces; tablespoons and teaspoons for measuring ingredients, or a set of metric measuring spoons.

• **Metal skewers:** Large sizes for kebabs; smaller ones for securing joints or stuffed meat, testing cakes, and so on.

• **Grater:** Choose one that has several grades of cutting surface and that stands rigid and upright on a chopping board.

• **Rolling pin:** Can also be used for battening meat and poultry, crushing biscuits, and so on.

• **Potato masher:** Apart from its obvious use, this is a convenient tool for lifting poached eggs from their cooking water.

• **Flexible spatula:** Either plastic or rubber – for scraping those last bits of mixture from a bowl.

• **Wire whisk:** Useful in addition to electric mixers for recipes with several ingredients which need whisking in separate bowls. Some people find the rotary variety quicker to use, but the balloon type is more flexible.

• **Scissors:** Good quality kitchen scissors for removing bacon rinds, snipping parsley, and so on.

• **Can opener:** A strong, hand model with a shield to the cutting edge is more reliable than a wall-mounted one.

• **Bottle-opener:** A combined bottle-opener and lever corkscrew is the most useful.

• **Pastry tools:** A selection of shapes and sizes of pastry cutter – they can also be used for cutting shaped croutons from bread. Pastry brush.

KITCHEN EXTRAS
These are the miscellaneous items which do not fit readily into any one equipment category:

• **Scales:** Essential for accurate weighing; go for those with both imperial and metric measurements.

• **Chopping boards:** One large, and one smaller, more easily portable size. Choose either a close-grained wood or white polypropylene (which is light to use and easy to clean).

• **Wire rack:** For cooling baked foods; saucepans of cooked food which need chilling cool more quickly standing on a wire rack.

Many other items of kitchen equipment can ease food preparation and cooking, but are by no means essential. Keen cooks, however, may like to have the following:
Salad spinner (for quick drying of washed salad greens)
Flour and/or icing sugar sifter
Bulb baster (for basting roast meats during cooking)
Automatic timer
Wooden or metal tongs
Oven thermometer
Meat thermometer
Kitchen shears (for cutting poultry bones)
Mincer
Garlic press

• **Food processors, electric mixers and liquidisers:** These are major buys, but can transform life in the kitchen. Cakes and puddings can be prepared in a matter of minutes; soups made quickly from fresh or leftover cooked vegetables; and most machines can also cope with the smaller, time-consuming tasks such as making breadcrumbs, grating cheese, shredding carrots, chopping nuts, and so on. A food processor or liquidiser also enables you to turn fresh and over-ripe or canned fruits into thick purées, and to make breakfast drinks and milk-shakes. Many recipes in this book suggest using a food processor, electric mixer or liquidiser for at least part of the preparation.

QUICK AND EASY SHOPPING

To be a successful and efficient cook, you also need to be a skilled shopper. The food bill is one of the largest items in the average family budget, and it is vital to be well prepared before every trip to the local shops to get the best value for your money.

Planning
The first step in buying food wisely is good organisation; and it's essential to plan food shopping and cooking together. Try to plan meals for a week at a time; this reduces the temptation to buy on impulse, eliminates last-minute trips for forgotten items, and certainly saves time and money. All you need is a basic cooking plan – you don't have to stick rigidly to particular meals right down to the last onion.

Checklist
Once you have outlined the week's meals, draw up your shopping list. Check what is in your freezer and store cupboard; if you are going to use up any food from them, will it need to be replaced? If your store cupboard needs to be restocked, use the checklist on page 12.

Where to Shop
Choose your main shopping places carefully. Don't be influenced solely by price – quality and freshness of food, service and checkout waiting time are just as important. It may be worth doing the bulk of your food shopping in a supermarket, and to take advantage of cheaper fresh produce from a good open market. But once you

have found a reliable source of good food, stick with it; shopping around from one store to another, looking for bargains, is unlikely to save money in the long run, and will waste a lot of time. The main motto is: Stick to your list, and don't be led astray by 'supermarket hypnosis' – the seductive lure of soft music, bright lights and carefully positioned, tempting packaging.

Watching Prices

Some items will appear on your shopping list each week; make a note of the cost alongside each item (some supermarkets now make this easy by issuing itemised, priced receipts), so that you can keep a check on how prices fluctuate from week to week and plan your shopping accordingly.

Shopping Guide

Keep the following points in mind to help you get the very best value for your money:

• Make out your shopping list in sections, according to the type of food – dried packet foods, dairy products, fruit and vegetables, and so on. You can then shop methodically, without having to retrace your steps.

• Be flexible! If you have always bought a particular cut of meat or fish, look around for similarly priced alternatives. The same applies to canned and packet foods – it is never worth sticking to a particular brand for the sake of it. Value for money is the thing to look for.

• Buy the amount of food that you know you will use – excess often means wastage.

• Buy seasonal produce whenever possible – out-of-season foods are always more expensive. Although fresh vegetables require more preparation, they are cheaper, tastier and more nutritious than canned or frozen ones.

• Make sure you know exactly what you're getting for your money – check the weight! Over-elaborate packaging can be like an edible pass-the-parcel; by the time you've removed the outer carton and the inner wrapper, the actual food content is minute.

• Choose frozen vegetables in packets rather than in boxes; they are easier to reseal and you can return what you don't use to the freezer. Don't be tempted by added butter or sauces; it is cheaper to buy the plain frozen product and add your own extras.

• Use any reduced price food products quickly – their shelf-life is greatly reduced, and they deteriorate quickly. *Never freeze marked-down meat or fish.*

• When buying just two or three items in a supermarket, do not take a trolley – it is all too easy to fill it with extra goods.

• Always buy a food in the form that suits the particular dish; it will save on preparation time, and may even be cheaper – crushed pineapple, for example, is more economical than chunks, and broken walnuts are cheaper than halves.

• Go for fewer, larger quantities wherever possible. Anticipate ingredients that will be used for more than one meal – if you are using canned tomatoes on two successive days in different recipes, buy one large can rather than two smaller ones. Remember – especially if you are in a country area – that basics such as flour, sugar and rice can be bought in bulk quantities, which will not only work out cheaper, but also save on arduous shopping trips.

STOCKING UP

Keep these foods in store. Replace them well before they run out to avoid last-minute dashes to the shops. This is a checklist, not a shopping list, and most of the items have a long shelf-life. Remember to put the most recent purchase of a particular item to the back of the cupboard, and bring the one already there to the front.

Cereals and grains
Dry biscuits
Dried breadcrumbs
Stuffing mix
Breakfast cereals
Cornmeal or semolina
Rice
Dry pasta
Oatmeal
Plain flour
Wholemeal flour
Self-raising flour
Cornflour
Bulgur (cracked
    wheat)

Sauces, dressings and condiments
Olive oil
Cooking oil
Tomato purée
Vinegar
Worcestershire sauce
Tabasco sauce
Mustard – dry and
    French

Capers
Tomato ketchup
Gherkins
Olives
Soya sauce
Salt
Black pepper
Mayonnaise
Creamed horseradish
Chutney
Anchovy essence

Sugars and preserves
Granulated sugar
Caster sugar
Demerara sugar
Soft brown sugar
Icing sugar
Golden syrup
Treacle
Honey
Assorted jams
Redcurrant jelly

Herbs and spices
Mixed spice
Basil
Bay leaves
Chilli powder
Chives
Cinnamon
Cloves
Cumin
Curry powder
Tarragon
Dill
Ground ginger
Marjoram
Nutmeg
Oregano
Paprika
Cayenne
Rosemary
Sage
Thyme

Canned foods
Anchovy fillets
Tuna
Sardines

Pimentos
Tomatoes
Chickpeas
Kidney beans
Sweetcorn kernels
Baked beans

Miscellaneous
Baking powder
Bicarbonate of soda
Dried yeast
Cocoa powder
Semi-sweet chocolate
Gelatine
Stock cubes
Skimmed milk powder
Coffee
Tea
Almond essence
Vanilla essence
Nuts
Raisins
Sultanas
Currants
Prunes
Packet fruit jellies

EFFICIENT STORAGE

The Freezer

Place already frozen foods in your freezer as soon as possible; if there is an unavoidable delay, wrap them in newspaper and keep them in a cool place. Never re-freeze frozen food which has started to thaw. Food to be frozen should, when possible, be cooled in the refrigerator first to prevent the freezer temperature from falling too drastically with the addition of 'warm' goods.

Wrap meat and poultry in individual portions before freezing so that you can remove exactly what you want as and when you need it. Minced meat should not be frozen in one large chunk; it takes too long to freeze and too long to thaw out. Shape the meat into patties and wrap individually; there will be no need to thaw the meat before grilling or frying.

The freezer temperature is affected every time the lid or door is opened, so do any rearranging or refilling at the same time as you take food out.

Date goods before packing them in the freezer, and always use the 'oldest' first.

Recommended Freezer Storage Times:

Meat and poultry	6 months
Bacon and ham	1 month
Fish and shellfish	2 months
Fruit and vegetables	9 months
Made-up dishes	Best within 3 months

The Refrigerator

The temperature varies from one part of the refrigerator to another – the middle is usually the coldest part, the top shelf is slightly higher in temperature, and the 'warmest' area is at the bottom. If there's a three-star freezer compartment, it can be used for storing commercially frozen food (check the packet for recommended storage times).

Highly perishable foods such as meat and fish should go in the coldest, central part of the refrigerator; dairy products towards the top, and salad greens and vegetables at the bottom – in the 'crisper' drawer if there is one.

All foods should be wrapped or covered adequately to prolong their storage life and prevent different foods affecting each other. A high-acid fruit, for example, can curdle fresh milk if both foods are left exposed.

Wrap cheese in clear food film or foil – polythene tends to make cheese sweat. Fresh fish and meat should be in a foil or clear food film wrapping that is not completely airtight – the food should still be able to 'breathe'. Store salad greens and vegetables unwashed and loosely wrapped in a punctured polythene bag.

Never over-pack your refrigerator – to work efficiently, the air must be able to circulate freely within it. Check occasionally that nothing has dropped into the defrost gully; if the drain-away vent becomes blocked, it can disrupt the refrigerator mechanism.

The refrigerator is *only* for short-term storage. Perishable food must be used while it is still fresh; if there is a 'sell-by' or 'eat-by' date, stick to it!

Recommended Refrigerator Storage Times:

Fresh meat and poultry	2 days
Cooked fresh meat and poultry	3 days
Bacon (unsmoked)	1 week
Bacon (smoked)	10 days
Fresh fish and shellfish	1 day
Fresh milk (unopened)	4 days
Cream	3 days
Yoghurt (unopened)	1 week
Butter	3 weeks
Firm cheeses	1 week
Soft cheeses	4 days
Salad greens	4 days
Soft fruits	3 days
Green vegetables	3 days
Leftovers (containing meat, sauces or, potatoes)	1 day

HELPFUL HINTS

Do-it-yourself

• Avoid convenience food, and ready-prepared meals in particular – unless the saving in time is really worth the extra expense. It is much cheaper to make up your own meals in advance when you have time and freeze them for later use.

• Use leftover bread to make croutons and breadcrumbs. Store in a polythene bag in the refrigerator for 5 days, or freeze.

• Make your own stock – chicken stock is especially nutritious and versatile:

Put a cooked chicken carcass into a large pan with 1 peeled onion, a few peppercorns, a sprig of parsley (or other herbs), 2 bay leaves and enough water to cover completely. Bring to the boil and simmer for 40 minutes. Remove any surface scum. Strain stock and cool very quickly. Chill and use within 2 days, or freeze for up to 6 months. You can also make your own stock 'cubes' by reducing the stock further and pouring into ice-cube trays for freezing.

• You can make fish stock in the same way, but omit the onion and simmer for only 30 minutes. If your fishmonger is preparing the fish for you, don't forget to ask for the bones.

Saving Fuel

• Try and cook at least two dishes in your oven at the same time – it is never really worth putting it on just for one dish.

• When boiling water, always put the lid on the saucepan to make the process as quick as possible.

• You can wrap vegetables in foil parcels and cook a number of different varieties simultaneously in one large saucepan to save using three different cooker rings.

• Match the saucepan to the size of the cooker ring to minimise the amount of heat escaping.

Fruit and Vegetables

• Do not store citrus fruits in the refrigerator – the flesh tightens and dries up.

• Buy under-ripe bananas and keep at room temperature – they tend to go black in the refrigerator.

• Fresh root ginger keeps for months in the freezer; wrap tightly in foil, cutting off pieces as you need them.

• When you need only a few drops of lemon juice, puncture a whole lemon with a toothpick, squeeze out what you need and put the toothpick back in the hole.

• To separate the leaves from a round lettuce, hit the core sharply against the work surface – the core can then be pulled out and the leaves will detach easily.

• Save the nutritious water from cooking vegetables to use in soups, sauces or stocks. Leftover vegetables can be turned into delicious purées. Reheat in a basin over a pan of simmering water, add a knob of butter, and liquidise.
  Alternatively, add enough chicken stock and milk to make a quick soup. Season to taste. Store in the refrigerator and use within 24 hours.

• Frozen parsley is a great standby. Wash and dry thoroughly; chop and freeze.

• To skin tomatoes, make a nick at the stalk end, plunge into boiling water for 40 seconds, run under the cold tap, and peel.

• To remove the slightly bitter skin from peppers, grill them until the skin blisters and chars; it will then slide off easily.

• Shape leftover mashed potato into small flat cakes, coat with beaten egg and dry stuffing mix, and fry until crisp.

• Chopped spring onion tops can be used instead of chives.

Meat

• If you are thawing a frozen chicken in the refrigerator, make a hole in the wrapping and stand the chicken on several layers of absorbent paper on a large plate, to stop thawed juices dripping onto other foods.

• Add soured cream to chopped, cooked meat or poultry; heat gently and use a sauce for cooked pasta.

• Mince cooked meat and use for stuffing peppers, onions and large tomatoes.

• It is much easier to cut thin slices of fresh raw meat if the meat is partially frozen.

• When stuffing a chicken, just fill the neck end; stuffing in the cavity of the chicken tends to result in inadequate cooking.

Fish

• When buying fresh fish, especially in warm weather, check that the fishmonger's counter is well iced.

• Look for whole fish with bright eyes and healthy, moist scales; avoid fish that looks 'tired'. White fish fillets should really look white – yellowing is a sign of poor quality.

• Discard shellfish with broken shells, or with shells that have not opened during cooking.

• Flaked, crab-flavoured sticks can be used instead of the more expensive white crabmeat.

Dairy

• Remove cheese from the refrigerator an hour before it is to be eaten – it needs to be at room temperature to release the full flavour.

• Cream whips faster if the bowl and whisk are chilled beforehand.

• Ordinary cream can be 'soured' by adding a few drops of white vinegar or lemon juice.

EGGS *In 1988, the Government warned that in some recent outbreaks of salmonella food poisoning, eggs were the source of infection. Most infections have caused only a mild stomach upset, but the effects can be more serious in the very young or old, in those already weakened by poor health, and among pregnant women. They should eat only eggs cooked until hard. To other people there is very little risk in cooked eggs; but everyone should avoid raw egg and recipes containing it. Commercial products made with pasteurised egg have not been implicated.*

APPETISERS

Spreads and Dips

Pâtés

Canapés

APPETISERS

Turn a piece of ordinary Cheddar cheese into a special Cocktail Cheese Spread in 8 minutes, or prepare an aromatic Herbed Cream Cheese in 5 minutes. For hot hors d'oeuvres, make Crispy Chicken Titbits or Sausage and Cheese Balls in 30 minutes or less. Eight of these dishes can be made at least a day in advance – and Black Olive Pâté will keep in the refrigerator for up to a month. Keep the ingredients of your favourite recipes on hand – for example, a can of sardines or artichoke hearts so that you can cater for unexpected guests at a moment's notice.

Artichoke Spread

Preparation: **8 min**   Cooking: **20 min**   Serves **4**   Cals per tablespoon: **50**

This spread has a surprising flavour and will have everyone guessing as to what it contains.

1 x 15 oz (425g) can artichoke hearts

3 oz (75g) grated Parmesan cheese

4 fl oz (115ml) mayonnaise

1 large clove garlic, peeled and finely chopped

Salt and black pepper

1. Preheat the oven to 180°C (350°F, gas mark 4). Drain the **artichoke hearts** and chop them coarsely.

2. In a mixing bowl, combine the artichokes, **cheese, mayonnaise** and **garlic.** Add **salt** and **pepper** to taste. Using a rubber spatula, scrape the mixture into a greased small casserole dish and bake for 20 minutes, or until bubbling and slightly browned. Serve hot, warm or chilled, as a spread for savoury biscuits or toast.

> **Tip:** *Use to stuff button mushrooms as a hot starter.*

Black Olive Pâté

Preparation: **10 min**   Cooking: **1 min**   Serves **4**   Cals per tablespoon: **135**

You can store this pâté in a screw-top jar in the refrigerator for up to a month.

6 oz (175g) pitted black olives (Greek or Italian), drained

6 cloves garlic, peeled

4 oz (115g) butter (preferably unsalted), softened

Pinch cayenne pepper

¼ teaspoon salt (optional)

1. Chop the **olives** finely.

2. Bring 8fl oz (225ml) of water to the boil in a small saucepan, add the **garlic,** and cook for 1 minute. Drain the garlic, chop, then grind into a paste.

3. Place the olives, garlic, **butter** and **cayenne pepper** in a mixing bowl, and blend thoroughly. Taste, and add the **salt** if desired.

4. Put the mixture into a bowl. Chill for 10 to 15 minutes if you wish. Serve with thin slices of crusty French or Italian bread.

> **Tip:** *Use a spoonful of the mixture as an unusual topping for grilled steaks.*

Chickpea Spread

Preparation: **15 min**   Serves **4**   Cals per tablespoon: **45**

1 x 15 oz (425g) can chickpeas (garbanzos)

1 or 2 cloves garlic, peeled and chopped

Juice ½ lemon

2 oz (50g) tahini paste

Pinch of ground cumin

Pinch cayenne pepper

¼ teaspoon salt

1 tablespoon olive oil

Canned chickpeas are sometimes known as 'garbanzos'. Tahini paste is readily available in jars at health food shops and delicatessens.

1. Drain the **chickpeas** and reserve the liquid. Mash them, or purée in a blender or food processor.

2. Blend in the **garlic, lemon juice, tahini paste, cumin, cayenne pepper, salt** and **oil.** Add enough of the reserved chickpea liquid to make a smooth, but not runny, purée. Serve at room temperature, or chilled, with pitta bread cut into small triangles.

Tip: *You can make this spread in advance and refrigerate it for 3 to 5 days.*

Cocktail Cheese Spread

Preparation: **8 min**   Serves **4**   Cals per tablespoon: **70**

4 oz (115g) strong Cheddar cheese

3½ oz (90g) cream cheese, softened

1 oz (25g) butter or margarine, softened

1½ oz (40g) chopped walnuts

Salt and black pepper

In a mixing bowl, blend the **Cheddar cheese, cream cheese, butter** and **walnuts.** Add **salt** and **pepper.** Put the spread into a small bowl. Serve at room temperature or slightly chilled as a spread for savoury biscuits or toast.

Herbed Cream Cheese ½

Preparation: **5 min**   Serves **4**   Cals per tablespoon: **75**

Goat cheese is worth trying in this traditional recipe.

8 oz (225g) cream cheese

2 tablespoons olive oil

½ teaspoon dried thyme

½ teaspoon dried rosemary

2 cloves garlic, peeled and crushed

Salt and black pepper

1. Shape the block of **cream cheese** into a disc about ½in (15mm) thick, and put it in a shallow bowl. Prick the cheese all over with a cocktail stick.

2. Pour the **oil** over the cheese, and sprinkle with the **thyme, rosemary** and **garlic.** Season to taste. Serve with slices of French or Italian bread.

Tip: *You can make this spread in advance and refrigerate it for up to 7 days.*

Chicken Liver Pâté ½

Preparation: **10 min**   Cooking: **16 min**   Serves **6**   Cals per tablespoon: **75**

Remove the stringy connective tissues from the chicken livers before they are cooked.

3 oz (75g) butter or margarine

2 medium-sized onions, peeled and coarsely chopped

12 oz (350g) chicken livers, drained

2 tablespoons brandy

1 hard-boiled egg

½ teaspoon salt

Pinch black pepper

1 clove garlic, peeled and crushed

Tip: You can use an electric blender or food processor for blending the mixture, but the consistency will be creamier and have less texture.

1. Melt half the **butter** in a heavy frying pan over moderately low heat. Add the **onions** and cook until soft and golden but not brown – about 10 minutes. Transfer the onions to a mixing bowl and put aside.

2. Raise the heat to moderate. Add half of the remaining butter and the **chicken livers** to the pan, and cook, stirring occasionally, for 5 minutes or until the livers are pink all the way through. Add the livers to the onions.

3. Pour the **brandy** into the pan and boil until only 1 tablespoon remains, scraping up any brown bits stuck to the pan. Add to the onions and livers.

4. Mash and pull the mixture with two forks until fairly smooth. Mix in the yolk of the **egg** along with the remaining butter, and season to taste with the **salt, pepper** and **garlic.** Put the pâté into a small bowl. Chop the egg white and sprinkle on top. Chill until serving, preferably at least 1 hour.

'Caviar Pie' ½

Preparation: **30 min**   Serves **10**   Cals per tablespoon: **30**

This sounds extravagant, but lumpfish roe is relatively inexpensive. Moreover, the pie is always a success. It must be made just before serving, or the roe will discolour the soured cream, but you can save time by cooking and chopping the eggs in advance.

6 hard-boiled eggs, finely chopped

2 tablespoons mayonnaise

Salt and black pepper

1 medium-sized onion, peeled and finely chopped

7 oz (200g) red or black lumpfish roe

12 fl oz (340ml) soured cream

3 tablespoons finely chopped parsley

1. Combine the **eggs** and **mayonnaise** with **salt** and **pepper** to taste, and press the mixture into a buttered 9in (230mm) pie plate.

2. Scatter the **onion** over the mixture, then spread the **roe** evenly over the onion. Spoon the **soured cream** onto the centre of the pie and carefully spread it to the edges so that it completely covers the roe.

3. Decorate the centre and edge of the pie with the **parsley.** Serve as a spread with party-sized dark pumpernickel bread or savoury biscuits.

Tip: You can substitute natural yoghurt for half the amount of soured cream in this recipe and reduce the number of calories per tablespoon to 25.

Sardine Pâté 🐷

Preparation: **30 min**   Serves **4**   Cals per tablespoon: **45**

1 x 4½ oz (130g) can sardines, drained

2 oz (50g) butter or margarine, softened

Juice ½ lemon

2 oz (50g) finely chopped stuffed olives

2 teaspoons creamed horseradish

1 clove garlic, peeled and crushed

½ teaspoon French mustard

½ teaspoon paprika

Pinch black pepper

½ teaspoon Worcestershire sauce

Pinch cayenne pepper

2 tablespoons finely chopped walnuts (optional)

Some sardines are canned without salt while others have a great deal, so be sure to taste this spread for seasoning after you have made it, and add salt only if necessary. Note that the preparation time includes 15 minutes of chilling in the refrigerator.

1. In a mixing bowl, mash the **sardines** with a fork, then blend in the **butter** to make a smooth paste. Add the **lemon juice, olives, horseradish, garlic, mustard, paprika, black pepper, Worcestershire sauce, cayenne pepper,** and the **walnuts** if used. Blend well and taste the mixture for seasoning.

2. Chill for 15 minutes. Serve as a spread for savoury biscuits or toast, or use as a stuffing for celery.

> ***Tips: 1.*** *You can make this spread in advance and refrigerate it for 1 or 2 days.* ***2.*** *Try this with a small can of tuna instead of the sardines.*

Egg Chutney Madras ½

Preparation: **25 min**   Serves **8**   Cals per tablespoon: **55**

4 hard-boiled eggs, chopped

3½ oz (90g) cream cheese, softened

1 tablespoon Worcestershire sauce

1 teaspoon curry powder

Pinch cayenne pepper

3 or 4 drops Tabasco sauce

2 tablespoons mayonnaise

3 tablespoons chopped chutney

¼ teaspoon salt

Pinch black pepper

A mildly spicy, very spreadable egg salad, this recipe is quicker to prepare than it appears – 15 minutes of the preparation time is for cooking the eggs.

1. Mash the **eggs** and **cream cheese** together with a fork. Add the **Worcestershire sauce, curry powder, cayenne pepper, Tabasco sauce, mayonnaise, chutney, salt** and **black pepper** and blend thoroughly.

2. Chill until ready to serve. Serve as a spread for savoury biscuits, or on slices of cucumber or raw courgette.

> ***Tips: 1.*** *Leftovers can be refrigerated for 1 or 2 days.* ***2.*** *This mixture is delicious when used as a sandwich filling.*

Cheese Puffs

Preparation: **5 min**   Cooking: **2 min**   Makes **16** puffs   Cals per puff: **75**

4 oz (115g) mayonnaise

3 oz (75g) grated Parmesan cheese

1 small onion, peeled and finely chopped

2 teaspoons French mustard

Salt and black pepper

4 slices rye bread

1. Preheat grill. Combine **mayonnaise, cheese, onion, mustard, salt** and **pepper** to taste.

2. Place the **bread** on a baking sheet and toast one side lightly under the grill. Spread the cheese mixture over the untoasted sides, then cut each slice into 4 triangles or squares.

3. Grill 6in (150mm) from the heat for 2 minutes, or until the cheese spread is golden-brown and slightly puffed. Serve immediately.

Cheese Wafers

Preparation: **10 min**   Cooking: **12 min**   Makes **12** wafers   Cals per wafer: **85**

These rich and tasty appetisers are sure to disappear fast. You may want to double or even triple the recipe.

2 oz (50g) butter or margarine, softened

4 oz (115g) grated strong Cheddar cheese

1½ oz (40g) unsifted plain flour

Pinch cayenne pepper

Pinch salt

1. Preheat the oven to 180°C (350°F, gas mark 4). In a mixing bowl, combine the **butter** and **cheese** with a fork, then blend in the **flour, cayenne pepper** and **salt.**

2. Roll the mixture into ¾in (20mm) balls, place on a greased baking sheet, and flatten with the heel of your hand until the balls are about ¼in (5mm) thick. Bake for 12 to 15 minutes, or until golden-brown and crisp. Serve warm or at room temperature.

> *Tip: You can make these wafers 1 or 2 days in advance and store them in an airtight container.*

Pimento Cheese Canapés   ½

Preparation: **15 min**   Makes **40** canapés   Cals per canapé: **55**

8 oz (225g) grated strong Cheddar cheese

4 oz (115g) canned pimentos, drained and finely chopped

3 tablespoons mayonnaise or natural yoghurt

Salt and black pepper

10 slices white or wholewheat bread, with crusts removed

This all-time favourite can also be used as a wholesome sandwich filling.

In a mixing bowl, combine **cheese, pimentos** and **mayonnaise.** Season to taste. Spread the mixture evenly over the **bread,** then cut each slice into 4 squares or triangles.

> *Tips: 1. You can make this spread in advance and refrigerate it for up to 4 days. 2. The canapés can be toasted and served warm, if preferred.*

Anchovy Rolls ◎ ½ 🐷

Preparation: **10 min**   Cooking: **6 min**

Makes **32** rolls   Cals per roll: **62**

16 thin bread slices

4½ oz (130g) butter or margarine for spreading

2 tablespoons French mustard

2 x 1¾ oz (45g) jars anchovy paste

3 tablespoons grated Parmesan cheese

Pinch black pepper

1. Preheat oven to 200°C (400°F, gas mark 6). Remove crusts from **bread** and spread each slice with **butter,** a little **French mustard** and **anchovy paste.** Sprinkle with **cheese** and **black pepper** to taste, and roll up.

2. Place the rolls, flap side down, on a buttered baking sheet and dot each one with butter. Bake for 6 minutes, or until the rolls are golden-brown. Cut in half and serve hot.

Crispy Chicken Titbits

Preparation: **15 min**   Cooking: **10 min**

Makes **32** pieces   Cals per piece: **50**

3 oz (75g) butter or margarine

Juice ½ small lemon

1½ lb (700g) boned chicken breast

1½ oz (40g) fine dry breadcrumbs

¼ teaspoon salt

Pinch black pepper

1 teaspoon dried rosemary

3 cloves garlic, peeled and finely chopped

1. Preheat the oven to 200°C (400°F, gas mark 6). Melt the **butter** in a small saucepan, stir in the **lemon juice.** Meanwhile, cut the **chicken** into 32 pieces.

2. Combine the **breadcrumbs, salt, pepper, rosemary** and **garlic** on a plate or a sheet of waxed paper. Dip the chicken into the lemon butter, then roll in the breadcrumb mixture.

3. Place the titbits in one layer in a large greased baking dish, and bake for 10 to 15 minutes, or until the pieces are golden-brown.

Sausage and Cheese Balls 🐷

Preparation: **15 min**   Cooking: **15 min**

Makes **36** balls   Cals per ball: **65**

4 oz (115g) plain flour

¼ teaspoon baking powder

¼ teaspoon salt

9 oz (250g) sausage meat

4 oz (115g) grated strong Cheddar cheese

3 tablespoons butter or margarine, softened

1 tablespoon Worcestershire sauce

Pinch black pepper

1. Preheat the oven to 220°C (425°F, gas mark 7). Combine **flour, baking powder** and **salt** in a large bowl; add **sausage, cheese, butter, Worcestershire sauce** and **pepper.** Blend well with a wooden spoon or with your hands.

2. Roll the mixture into about 36 x ¾in (20mm) balls. Place the balls about ½in (15mm) apart on a greased baking sheet and flatten them slightly with the heel of your hand. Bake for 15 to 20 minutes, or until the balls are golden-brown on the bottom.

SOUPS

SOUPS

Soups often take hours to prepare, but all of these can be made in 45 minutes or less, and many can be served as main courses or one-course meals. Light and hearty soups, hot and cold soups, soups with meat, fish or vegetables; there's something for everyone.

Red Bean Soup ½

Preparation: **10 min**   Cooking: **12 min**   Serves **4**   Cals per portion: **235**

2 tablespoons bacon fat or oil

1 medium-sized onion, peeled and chopped

1 clove garlic, peeled and finely chopped

¼ teaspoon dried thyme

2 x 15 oz (425g) cans red kidney beans, undrained

¾ pint (450ml) beef stock

3 tablespoons dry sherry

Salt and black pepper

1 tablespoon chopped chives

This soup takes minutes to make, yet it is a meal in itself.

1. Heat the **bacon fat** in a large, heavy saucepan over moderate heat. Add the **onion** and **garlic,** and cook for about 5 minutes, until the onion is soft. While the onions are cooking, mash half the **beans.**

2. Add the **thyme,** all the **beans** and their liquid and **beef stock.** Simmer, stirring occasionally, for 10 minutes. Stir in the **sherry,** and simmer 1 or 2 minutes longer. Season to taste. Sprinkle each portion with some of the **chives.**

> **Tip:** *Leftovers can be stored in the refrigerator for up to 3 days.*

Greek Lemon Soup ½

Preparation: **5 min**   Cooking: **15 min**   Serves **4**   Cals per portion: **140**

2 pints (1.1 litres) chicken stock, well seasoned

2 tablespoons rice

2 eggs

Juice 1 lemon

Salt and black pepper

> **Tip:** *The soup is less likely to curdle if heated through in a double saucepan.*

1. Bring the **stock** to the boil in a medium-sized saucepan and add the **rice.** Cook over a moderate heat until the rice is tender, about 15 minutes.

2. Two or three minutes before you are ready to serve the soup, beat the **eggs** in a bowl with a whisk until they are light and frothy, then slowly beat in the **lemon juice.** Stir in, gradually, ⅓ pint (190ml) of the hot soup.

3. Pour the egg and lemon mixture into the rest of the soup and beat well. Season to taste. Heat, but do not boil or the soup will curdle. Serve immediately.

Lentil and Sausage Soup

Preparation: **10 min**   Cooking: **30 min**

Serves **6**   Cals per portion: **650**

3 tablespoons olive oil or vegetable oil

1 medium-sized onion, peeled and chopped

1 clove garlic, peeled and finely chopped

3 medium-sized carrots, peeled and cut into ½ in (15mm) slices

1¼ pints (725ml) beef stock

4½ oz (130g) tomato purée

12 fl oz (340ml) water

1 bay leaf

6 sprigs parsley, tied together

6 oz (175g) dry brown lentils, rinsed and sorted

6 oz (175g) rice

1½ lb (700g) pepperoni sausage, cut into ½ in (15mm) slices

Salt and black pepper

This is a one-dish meal that is rich in vitamins, protein and fibre – even if you omit the sausage.

1. Heat 2 tablespoons of the **oil** in a heavy medium-sized saucepan over moderate heat. Add the **onion, garlic** and **carrots,** and cook for 5 minutes, or until the onion is soft.

2. Add the **beef stock, tomato purée, water, bay leaf, parsley** and **lentils.** Cover, bring to the boil, then reduce the heat and simmer for 10 minutes.

3. Add the **rice** to the soup, cover and simmer for 20 to 30 minutes longer, or until the rice and lentils are tender. Meanwhile, place the remaining oil in a frying pan over moderate heat, add the **pepperoni** slices and cook for 10 minutes, or until browned. Drain on absorbent paper.

4. Add the sausage slices to the soup when it is cooked, and heat them through. Season to taste. Serve with thick, crusty bread and a green salad.

Broccoli Chowder ½

Preparation: **12 min**   Cooking: **4 min**

Serves **4**   Cals per portion: **460**

For a complete meal, serve this nutritious soup with bread and a fresh-fruit dessert.

1 lb 2 oz (500g) broccoli

¾ pint (450ml) chicken stock

¾ pint (450ml) milk

9 oz (250g) diced ham

¼ teaspoon salt

Pinch black pepper

4 fl oz (115ml) double cream or top of the milk

4 tablespoons grated Swiss or mild Cheddar cheese

1. Trim the leaves and coarse stems from the **broccoli,** and cut the stems and florets into bite-sized pieces. Bring the **chicken stock** to the boil in a large saucepan. Add the broccoli and cook for 5 minutes, or until the broccoli is almost tender but still crisp. Using a slotted spoon, remove the broccoli from the saucepan, chop coarsely and put aside.

2. Add the **milk, diced ham, salt** if necessary, and **pepper** to the stock, bring to the boil, then stir in the **cream** and the broccoli. Heat the soup through, but do not boil. Top each serving with a tablespoon of the **cheese.**

Tips: 1. For a smooth soup, purée the cooked broccoli in a blender or food processor before returning it to the saucepan. 2. You can substitute cauliflower for the broccoli. 3. Leftovers can be refrigerated for 3 days.

Carrot Soup ½

Preparation: **10 min**   Cooking: **20 min**   Serves **6**   Cals per portion: **85**

1½ pints (850ml) water

1 teaspoon salt

9 oz (250g) carrots, peeled and cut into ¼ in (5mm) slices

1 large potato, peeled and diced

1 large onion, peeled and chopped

Pinch black pepper

¼ teaspoon dried basil (optional)

¾ oz (20g) butter or margarine, softened

3 oz (75g) croutons (optional) or 2 tablespoons finely chopped parsley

This light and refreshing soup is easy to prepare and economical in any season.

1. Put the **water** and **salt** into a large saucepan, and bring to the boil. Add the **carrots, potato** and **onion,** cover, and simmer for 10 to 15 minutes, or until the vegetables are tender. Purée the vegetables with their cooking liquid in a blender or food processor.

2. Return the purée to the saucepan. Add the **pepper** and the **basil** if used. Reheat the soup. Stir in the **butter** just before serving and garnish with the **croutons** if desired or sprinkle with **parsley.**

> *Tips: 1. As a variation, omit the basil and reheat with 4fl oz (115ml) of single cream and a pinch of ground nutmeg or curry powder. 2. You can make this dish in advance and refrigerate it for 1 or 2 days, but do not add the butter until just before serving.*

Easy Cauliflower Soup ½

Preparation: **10 min**   Cooking: **12 min**   Serves **4**   Cals per portion: **210**

1½ oz (40g) butter or margarine

1 medium-sized onion, peeled and chopped

1 medium cauliflower

1½ pints (850ml) chicken stock

6 fl oz (175ml) single cream

¼ teaspoon salt

Pinch black pepper

2 tablespoons grated Swiss or Jarlsberg cheese (optional)

1. Melt the **butter** in a large saucepan over moderate heat, add the **onion** and cook for 5 minutes, or until soft. Meanwhile, separate the **cauliflower** into florets, then chop the florets into ½in (15mm) pieces.

2. Add the cauliflower and **chicken stock** to the onion in the saucepan. Cover and simmer about 10 minutes, or until the cauliflower is tender.

3. Add the **cream, salt** and **pepper,** and heat until the soup returns to a simmer. Sprinkle each portion with some of the **cheese** if desired.

> *Tips: 1. Leftovers can be refrigerated for 1 or 2 days. You need not reheat; the soup is excellent chilled. 2. For a smooth soup, purée it in a blender or food processor at the end of Step 2, then continue with the recipe. 3. To make a spicy variation, cook 1 teaspoon of curry powder in the butter for 3 or 4 minutes before adding the onion.*

Curried Celery Soup ½ 🐖

Preparation: **14 min** Cooking: **10 min**   Serves **6** Cals per portion: **120**

1½ oz (40g) butter or margarine

4 stems celery, finely chopped

3 tablespoons plain flour

1½ teaspoons curry powder

¾ teaspoon salt

¼ teaspoon black pepper

¾ pint (450ml) milk

1½ pints (850ml) chicken stock

1. Melt the **butter** in a medium-sized saucepan over moderate heat. Add the **celery,** and cook for 5 minutes, stirring occasionally.

2. Remove the pan from the heat, and blend in the **flour, curry powder, salt** and **pepper** to make a paste. Gradually stir in the **milk** and **chicken stock.**

3. Return the mixture to the heat and stir continuously until it comes to the boil. Reduce the heat, cover, and simmer for 10 minutes.

> *Tips:* **1.** *Leftovers can be refrigerated for up to 3 days.* **2.** *For a garnish, top each serving with 1 tablespoon desiccated coconut, chopped walnuts or chopped raisins, or with 1 teaspoon chopped chives.* **3.** *For a richer soup, use half milk, half single cream instead of all milk.*

Sweetcorn Chowder ½

Preparation: **10 min** Cooking: **13 min**   Serves **4** Cals per portion: **305**

4 rashers bacon, cut into ¾ in (20mm) strips

1 medium-sized onion, peeled and chopped

1 medium-sized red or green pepper, halved, seeded and chopped

¾ pint (450ml) water

13 oz (375g) frozen sweetcorn kernels, thawed

12 fl oz (340ml) single cream or milk

2 tablespoons finely chopped parsley

¼ teaspoon salt

Pinch black pepper

1. Cook the **bacon** in a medium-sized saucepan over moderately high heat until crisp – about 5 minutes. Using a slotted spoon, transfer the bacon to absorbent paper to drain. Put aside.

2. Pour off all but 1½ tablespoons of the bacon fat from the saucepan, add the **onion** and **pepper,** and cook for 5 minutes over moderate heat, or until the vegetables are soft. Add the **water** and **sweetcorn,** and simmer, covered, for 10 minutes.

3. Add the **cream** and reheat gently. Do not let the soup boil or it may curdle. Stir in the **parsley, salt** and **black pepper.** Sprinkle each portion with some of the reserved bacon.

> *Tips:* **1.** *You can make this dish in advance and refrigerate it for 1 or 2 days.* **2.** *For an even richer soup, use canned, creamed sweetcorn.*

Cucumber Soup ½

Preparation: 12 min   Cooking: 22 min   **Serves 6   Cals per portion: 120**

¾ oz (20g) butter or margarine

1 small onion, peeled and finely chopped

2 large cucumbers, peeled, seeded and diced

1 tablespoon white wine vinegar or cider vinegar

1 tablespoon plain flour

1½ pints (850ml) chicken stock

¼ teaspoon salt

Pinch black pepper

½ teaspoon dried tarragon, or ½ teaspoon dried dill (optional)

4 fl oz (115ml) soured cream

3 tablespoons finely chopped parsley (optional)

1. Melt the **butter** in a medium-sized saucepan over moderate heat, add the **onion** and cook for 5 minutes, or until soft. Add the **cucumbers** and **vinegar.** Stir in the **flour** and cook, stirring continuously, for 1 or 2 minutes. Gradually stir in the **chicken stock,** then add the **salt, pepper** and the **tarragon** if used.

2. Cover and simmer for 20 minutes, or until the cucumbers are very soft, then purée the mixture in a blender or food processor. Return the mixture to the saucepan and reheat. If you plan to serve the soup cold, chill it in the refrigerator for 1 or 2 hours.

3. Top each portion with a heaped teaspoon of the **soured cream** and a sprinkling of the **parsley** if used.

> *Tips: 1. You can substitute natural yoghurt for the soured cream. 2. This dish can be made in advance and refrigerated for 1 or 2 days.*

Fresh Mushroom Soup ☉ ½

Preparation: 10 min   Cooking: 5 min   **Serves 6   Cals per portion: 190**

2 oz (50g) butter or margarine

13 oz (375g) mushrooms, thinly sliced

1¼ pints (725ml) chicken stock

3 egg yolks

8 fl oz (225ml) single cream

¼ teaspoon salt

Pinch black pepper

> *Tips: 1. If this recipe is halved, use 1 large egg yolk. 2. For a smoother, more elegant soup, set aside 6 mushroom slices, purée the soup in a blender or food processor, and top each serving with a mushroom slice.*

Serve this soup as a first course for dinner for 6, or with sandwiches and a salad for a lunch for 4.

1. Melt the **butter** in a medium-sized saucepan over moderate heat. Reduce the heat, add the **mushrooms,** and cook for 5 minutes, stirring frequently. Add the **chicken stock,** raise the heat, and bring to the boil.

2. Beat the **egg yolks** in a small bowl. Remove the mushroom mixture from the heat. Beat 4fl oz (115ml) of the warm stock into the yolks until the mixture is frothy. Gradually pour this mixture back into the saucepan, stirring to prevent the eggs from curdling.

3. Return the saucepan to a moderate heat, and add the **cream, salt** and **pepper.** Reheat, stirring constantly, but do not let the soup boil.

Onion Soup with Cheese Toast ½ 🐷

Preparation: **17 min**   Cooking: **13 min**   Serves **4**   Cals per portion: **175**

1½ oz (40g) butter or margarine

2 large onions, peeled, halved lengthwise, and cut crosswise into very thin slices

1½ teaspoons plain flour

1½ pints (850ml) beef stock

¼ teaspoon salt

Pinch black pepper

4 slices French bread, about ¾ in (20mm) thick

4 thin slices Gruyère or Swiss cheese

1. Melt the **butter** in a medium-sized saucepan over moderate heat. Reduce the heat, add the **onions,** and cook for 10 minutes, or until golden but not brown, stirring occasionally. Stir in the **flour** and cook for 1 minute.

2. Add the **beef stock, salt** and **pepper,** and simmer, covered, for 10 minutes.

3. While the soup is simmering, top each slice of **bread** with a large enough piece of the **cheese** to completely cover it.

4. Just before serving, place the bread slices briefly under the grill about 3in (80mm) from the heat until the cheese melts. Float one slice in each bowl of soup and serve.

Old-Fashioned Potato Soup ½ 🐷

Preparation: **24 min**   Cooking: **5 min**   Serves **4**   Cals per portion: **300**

4 medium-sized baking potatoes, peeled and cut into ½ in (15mm) slices

1½ oz (40g) butter or margarine

1 small onion, peeled and thinly sliced

1¼ pints (725ml) milk

Pinch celery salt (optional)

¼ teaspoon salt

Pinch cayenne pepper

1 tablespoon finely chopped parsley

1. Put the **potatoes** in a medium-sized saucepan with enough salted water to cover. Cover, and boil for 10 minutes, or until tender.

2. Meanwhile, melt the **butter** in a frying pan over low heat. Add the **onion** and cook for 5 minutes, or until soft. Put aside.

3. When the potatoes are tender, drain them in a colander, then mash them while they are still warm.

4. Return the potatoes to the saucepan, and add the onion and any butter remaining in the pan. Stir in the **milk, celery salt** if used, **salt** and **cayenne pepper.** Stir over a moderate heat until smooth and hot – about 3 minutes. Do not let the soup boil or it will curdle. Sprinkle each serving with some of the **parsley.**

> *Tips:* **1.** *For a cold, thicker soup, substitute single cream for the milk, chill the soup, and top each serving with 2 teaspoons of chopped chives instead of parsley.* **2.** *For a thinner soup, add chicken stock to dilute.*

Bread and Pumpkin Soup ½

Preparation: **12 min**   Cooking: **32 min**   Serves **4**   Cals per portion: **245**

1½ pints (850ml) water or chicken stock

½ teaspoon salt

2¼ lb (1kg) pumpkin, peeled, seeded and diced

8 to 10 cloves garlic, peeled and left whole

2 slices stale white bread, with the crusts removed, diced

¼ teaspoon black pepper

1 teaspoon dried basil

2 fl oz (50ml) olive oil or vegetable oil

2 tablespoons finely chopped parsley

This soup is rich and satisfying, yet it is delicately flavoured because the strong taste of garlic becomes very subdued when it is boiled.

1. Bring salted **water** to the boil in a large saucepan. Add the **pumpkin** and **garlic,** and simmer for 25 minutes, covered, or until the pumpkin is very tender, stirring occasionally.

2. Add the **bread, pepper** and **basil,** reduce the heat and simmer for 2 or 3 minutes longer. Purée the soup in a blender or food processor, then return it to the saucepan and reheat. Stir in the **oil,** and sprinkle each serving with some of the **parsley.**

Tips: 1. You can make this dish in advance and refrigerate it for 1 or 2 days. 2. If you like, substitute squash for the pumpkin. You can also substitute courgettes, but cook them for only 10 to 15 minutes.

Buttermilk Gazpacho ½

Preparation: **23 min**   Serves **4**   Cals per portion: **105**

2 hard-boiled eggs, halved

12 fl oz (340ml) tomato juice or mixed vegetable juice

12 fl oz (340ml) buttermilk

1 medium-sized onion, peeled and chopped

1 stem celery, diced

1 medium-sized green or red pepper, halved, seeded and chopped

¼ teaspoon salt

Pinch black pepper

1 tablespoon snipped fresh dill or ¼ teaspoon dried dill (optional)

1 lime or small lemon, thinly sliced (optional)

Wonderfully quick and cooling, this soup is low in calories and high in Vitamin C. You can reduce the preparation time to 8 minutes if you boil the eggs in advance. Use very cold ingredients for serving immediately, or prepare in advance and chill.

1. Press the yolks of the **eggs** through a sieve into a mixing bowl. Add the **tomato juice, buttermilk, onion, celery, pepper, salt, black pepper** and the **dill** if used. Stir to mix.

2. Chop the egg whites very finely, and divide among 4 mugs or soup bowls. Pour the soup over the whites. Garnish each serving with a slice of **lime** if desired.

Cream of Tomato Soup ½ 🐷

Preparation: **10 min**   Cooking: **20 min**   Serves **6**   Cals per portion: **160**

1½ oz (40g) butter or margarine

1 tablespoon olive oil or vegetable oil

1 large onion, peeled and chopped

5 medium-sized tomatoes, peeled and chopped, or 1 x 15 oz (425g) can tomatoes, chopped, with their juice

2 tablespoons tomato purée

2 tablespoons plain flour

1 pint (570ml) chicken stock

½ teaspoon sugar

¼ teaspoon salt

Pinch black pepper

8 fl oz (225ml) single cream

Save a few minutes' preparation time by peeling and chopping the tomatoes while the onion is cooking.

1. Heat the **butter** with the **oil** in a large saucepan over moderate heat. Add the **onion** and cook, stirring occasionally, for 5 minutes.

2. Stir in the **tomatoes** and **tomato purée**, and cook for 2 or 3 minutes. Blend in the **flour**, then add the **chicken stock, sugar, salt** and **pepper.** Cover and simmer for 15 minutes.

3. Purée the mixture in a blender or food processor, then return the purée to the saucepan and add the **cream.** Reheat gently for 2 or 3 minutes.

Tips: 1. For a richer soup, top each serving with 1 tablespoon of grated Swiss or strong Cheddar cheese, or a few croutons. 2. You can make this dish in advance and refrigerate it for 1 or 2 days. When reheating, do not let the soup boil or it may curdle.

Creamy Watercress Soup ½ 🐷

Preparation: **11 min**   Cooking: **18 min**   Serves **4**   Cals per portion: **370**

1½ oz (40g) butter or margarine

1 medium-sized onion, peeled and chopped

1 medium-sized potato, peeled and diced

8 fl oz (225ml) water

1 bunch watercress

Pinch ground nutmeg

16 fl oz (475ml) chicken stock

8 fl oz (225ml) double cream

½ teaspoon salt

¼ teaspoon black pepper

1. Melt the **butter** in a medium-sized saucepan over moderate heat. Add the **onion** and **potato,** and cook for 5 minutes, or until the onion is soft. Add the **water,** cover, and simmer for 10 to 15 minutes, or until the potato is tender.

2. Meanwhile, cut the stems from the **watercress** and discard them. Wash, drain, and chop the leaves. Purée the watercress with the onion-potato mixture in a blender or food processor.

3. Pour the purée into the saucepan and stir in the **nutmeg, chicken stock** and **cream.** Heat gradually to serving temperature, but do not let the soup boil. Season with the **salt** and **pepper,** and serve hot or cold.

Speedy Cream of Chicken Soup ½

Preparation: **4 min**   Cooking: **3 min**   Serves **4**   Cals per portion: **245**

1½ pints (850ml) chicken stock

1 lb 2 oz (500g) finely chopped
cooked chicken

1 teaspoon Worcestershire sauce

1 clove garlic, peeled and finely
chopped

3 to 4 drops Tabasco sauce

8 fl oz (225ml) single cream

¼ teaspoon salt

Pinch black pepper

In a medium-sized saucepan, mix the **chicken stock, chicken, Worcestershire sauce, garlic, Tabasco sauce** and **cream.** Cook over moderate heat, stirring, for 3 minutes. Taste for seasoning, and add the **salt** and **pepper.**

> ***Tips: 1.*** *Leftovers can be refrigerated for 1 or 2 days or frozen.* ***2.*** *If you like, add leftover cooked vegetables such as sweetcorn, peas, green beans or diced carrots; or add 2 tablespoons of cooked rice.*

Beef and Cabbage Soup ½

Preparation: **15 min**   Cooking: **8 min**   Serves **6**   Cals per portion: **190**

1 small onion, peeled
and chopped

2 large carrots, peeled and diced

2 stems celery, diced

1 small head cabbage (about
13 oz/375g), cored and thinly
sliced

1 bay leaf

6 whole black peppercorns

2 pints (1.1 litres) beef stock

¼ teaspoon salt

¼ teaspoon black pepper

10 oz (275g) diced cooked beef

6 tablespoons soured cream
(optional)

Use leftover roast beef to make this quick, economical and full-flavoured soup. Serve it with thick slices of dark, crusty bread for a light lunch.

1. Put the **onion, carrots, celery, cabbage, bay leaf, peppercorns** and **beef stock** in a large saucepan. Cover and bring to the boil. Reduce the heat and simmer for 8 to 10 minutes, or until the cabbage is almost tender but still crisp. (Cook about 2 minutes longer if you like very soft cabbage.) Add the **salt** and **pepper.**

2. Divide the **beef** equally among 6 soup bowls and ladle the soup over it. Top each serving with 1 tablespoon of the **soured cream** if desired, or serve the soured cream separately.

> ***Tips: 1.*** *You can substitute diced chicken and chicken stock for the beef ingredients.* ***2.*** *Leftovers can be refrigerated for 1 or 2 days or frozen.*

Minced Beef and Vegetable Chowder ½

Preparation: **15 min**   Cooking: **30 min**   Serves **6**   Cals per portion: **350**

6 rashers bacon, cut into ¾ in (20mm) strips

1 lb 2 oz (500g) lean minced beef

1 medium-sized onion, peeled and chopped

2 medium-sized carrots, peeled and diced

1 stem celery, diced

5 medium-sized tomatoes, peeled and chopped, or 1 x 15 oz (425g) can tomatoes, chopped, with their juice

2 oz (50g) rice

2 medium-sized potatoes, scrubbed (but not peeled) and diced

½ teaspoon dried basil or rosemary

2½ pints (1.4 litres) water or beef stock

1 teaspoon salt

¼ teaspoon black pepper

Serve this chowder as a main course with garlic bread and a tossed salad, which you can make while the soup is cooking. Peel and chop the onion and prepare as many of the remaining vegetables as you can while the bacon is browning; finish the chopping while the beef and onion cook.

1. Cook the **bacon** in a large saucepan over moderate heat until golden-brown and crisp – about 5 minutes. Using a slotted spoon, transfer the bacon to absorbent paper to drain. Put aside.

2. Add the **beef** to the bacon fat in the saucepan, and cook, stirring, for 5 minutes. Add the **onion** and cook 5 minutes longer.

3. Add the **carrots, celery, tomatoes, rice, potatoes, basil, water, salt, pepper** and the bacon. Cover and bring to the boil. Reduce the heat and simmer for 25 minutes, or until the rice and potatoes are tender.

Tips: 1. You can stretch this recipe to serve 8 by adding 6oz (175g) frozen peas or sweetcorn kernels during the last 10 minutes of cooking. 2. You can cook this soup in advance and refrigerate it for 1 or 2 days, or freeze it.

Meatball Soup ½

Preparation: **10 min**   Cooking: **19 min**   Serves **6**   Cals per portion: **300**

2½ pints (1.4 litres) beef stock

13 oz (375g) lean minced beef

13 oz (375g) lean minced pork

1 egg, lightly beaten

1½ teaspoons salt

Pinch black pepper

5 medium-sized tomatoes, peeled and chopped, or 1 x 15 oz (425g) can tomatoes, chopped, with their juice

1 x 15 oz (425g) can red kidney beans, drained

4 tablespoons chopped parsley

1. Bring the **beef stock** to the boil in a large saucepan. Meanwhile, combine the **beef, pork, egg, salt** and **pepper** in a mixing bowl. Shape the mixture into ¾in (20mm) meatballs.

2. Reduce the heat, and add the meatballs and **tomatoes** to the stock. Cover and simmer for 15 minutes. Add the **beans** and **parsley,** and simmer until heated through – about 2 minutes.

Tips: 1. You can use all beef instead of the beef and pork, and chickpeas (garbanzos) instead of the kidney beans. 2. This dish can be made in advance and refrigerated for 1 or 2 days, or frozen.

Sausage Soup ½

Preparation: **15 min** Cooking: **10 min**　　　　　Serves **4** Cals per portion: **450**

1 lb (450g) pork sausage meat

1 medium-sized onion, peeled and chopped

5 medium-sized tomatoes, peeled and chopped, or 1 x 15 oz (425g) can tomatoes, chopped, with their juice

1¼ pints (725ml) chicken stock

1 teaspoon dried basil

3 oz (75g) elbow macaroni

¼ teaspoon salt

Pinch black pepper

This main-course soup needs only a salad and good, crusty bread to make a meal.

1. Cook the **sausage meat** in a medium-sized saucepan over moderate heat, using a spoon to break up the meat into small pieces. Cook for 5 minutes.

2. Add the **onion** and continue cooking for 5 minutes, or until the onion is soft. Add the **tomatoes, chicken stock** and **basil,** and bring to the boil. Stir in the **macaroni** and simmer, covered, for 10 minutes, or until tender. Add the **salt** and **pepper** and serve.

Tips: 1. For added richness, top each serving with 2 tablespoons of grated Parmesan cheese. 2. Leftovers can be refrigerated for 1 or 2 days or frozen.

Tuna Chowder ½

Preparation: **16 min** Cooking: **20 min**　　　　　Serves **4** Cals per portion: **260**

2 rashers bacon, diced

1 medium-sized onion, peeled and chopped

3 medium-sized potatoes, peeled and chopped

¾ pint (450ml) water

1 x 7 oz (198g) can tuna

1 tablespoon plain flour

Juice ½ lemon

12 fl oz (340ml) tomato juice

Salt and black pepper

1 tablespoon finely chopped parsley

Tip: For a richer soup, add a swirl of cream to each portion.

1. Cook the **bacon** in a medium-sized saucepan over a moderately high heat until crisp. Using a slotted spoon, transfer the bacon to absorbent paper to drain. Put aside.

2. Reduce the heat to moderate, add the chopped **onion** to the bacon fat and cook for 5 minutes, or until soft.

3. Add the **potatoes** and the **water.** Cover and simmer for 15 minutes, until the potatoes are tender. Meanwhile, drain the liquid from the **tuna.** Remove the bones or skin from the tuna and flake the flesh.

4. Combine the **flour** and the **lemon juice.** Remove the saucepan from the heat and whisk in the flour paste and the **tomato juice.** Cook over a moderate heat until bubbling.

5. Add the flaked tuna, season with **salt** and **pepper** to taste and simmer gently for 5 minutes. Sprinkle each portion with the chopped **parsley** and the reserved crispy bacon.

Haddock Chowder ½

Preparation: **22 min**   Cooking: **15 min**   Serves **6**   Cals per portion: **450**

Serve this chowder as a main course with a lettuce and tomato salad.

2 medium-sized onions, peeled and coarsely chopped

2 large potatoes, peeled and diced

¾ pint (450ml) water

3 rashers bacon, cut into ¾ in (20mm) strips

1½ lb (700g) smoked haddock or cod fillets

¾ pint (450ml) milk

8 fl oz (225ml) double cream

Salt (optional) and black pepper

1. Bring the **onions, potatoes** and **water** to the boil in a medium-sized saucepan. Cover and cook over moderate heat for 15 minutes.

2. Meanwhile, cook the **bacon** in a large saucepan over moderate heat until golden-brown and crisp – about 5 minutes.

3. When the onions and potatoes are tender, add them with their cooking liquid to the bacon and bacon fat; add the **haddock** and the **milk.** Cover, and simmer for 10 to 15 minutes, stirring once or twice until the fish is tender (it will break apart as it cooks).

4. Add the **cream** and season to taste. Reheat gently. Do not let the soup boil or it may curdle.

Purée of Bean Soup

Preparation: **15 min**   Cooking: **15 min**   Serves **4**   Cals per portion: **275**

1 x 15 oz (425g) can butter beans, drained

1½ pints (850ml) chicken stock or water

1½ oz (40g) butter or margarine

1 tablespoon olive oil or vegetable oil

4 slices bread, crusts removed, cut into ½ in (15mm) cubes

1 tablespoon plain flour

Salt and black pepper

1 egg yolk

4 tablespoons single cream or milk

1. Put the **beans** and a quarter of the **stock** into a medium-sized saucepan over a moderate heat and simmer for a few minutes.

2. Meanwhile, heat 1 tablespoon of the **butter** and the **oil** in a large frying pan. Add the **bread cubes** in a single layer so that they soak up the oil evenly. Fry gently and toss frequently until crisp and golden. Transfer the croutons to absorbent paper to drain.

3. Purée the beans and stock in a blender or food processor. Melt the remaining butter, add the **flour** and mix well. Gradually blend in the rest of the stock, stirring until the mixture boils and is quite smooth. Add the puréed beans, season with **salt** and **pepper,** stir, and heat through gently.

4. Beat the **egg yolk** and **cream** together in a small bowl. Blend in a little of the hot soup and add the mixture to the saucepan, stirring briskly. Reheat but do not let the soup boil. Serve with the crisp croutons.

SALADS AND DRESSINGS

SALADS AND DRESSINGS

The ancient Romans ate green leafy vegetables seasoned only with salt, and it is from their word for salt that we get the word salad. Today, salads can be anything from a side dish of lettuce tossed with oil and vinegar to a main course of meat or fish or a dessert of fresh fruits. This section contains a representative selection from virtually the whole range of salads. Here you will find not only instructions on how to make and dress crisp green salads but also the recipes for some tasty and unusual salad dressings. You will find old-fashioned Macaroni Salad as well as Oriental Noodle Salad. There are three recipes for perking up everyday tuna, and a sumptuous Curried Chicken Salad. You will also discover new ways to use carrots, peppers, tomatoes and even turnips in quick, tasty, salads.

Ham and Cheese Salad with Walnut Dressing ½

Preparation: **18 min**   Serves **6**   Cals per portion: **480**

1 x 15 oz (425g) can artichoke hearts

12 oz (350g) diced cooked ham

10 oz (275g) Swiss or strong Cheddar cheese

4 oz (115g) mushrooms, sliced

3 tablespoons finely chopped parsley

3 oz (75g) chopped walnuts

2 tablespoons water

2 tablespoons white or red wine vinegar

1 clove garlic, peeled

¼ teaspoon salt

Pinch cayenne pepper

4 tablespoons olive oil or vegetable oil

Lettuce leaves and whole radishes for garnish

1. Drain the **artichoke hearts,** rinse with cold water, drain again, and pat them dry with absorbent paper. Cut each heart in half and put the pieces into a large serving bowl. Add the **ham, cheese, mushrooms** and **parsley.**

2. Put the **walnuts** into a blender or a food processor fitted with the metal chopping blade. Add the **water, vinegar, garlic, salt, cayenne pepper** and **oil,** and blend until the nuts are pulverised – 5 to 10 seconds nonstop. If you are not using a blender or food processor, chop the nuts and the garlic very finely, and shake them with the other ingredients in a fastened, screw-topped jar.

3. Toss the salad with the dressing. The salad tastes best if left to stand at room temperature for an hour. If you refrigerate it, bring it back to room temperature before serving. Serve on a bed of shredded **lettuce leaves** and garnish with thinly sliced **radishes.**

> *Tips: 1.* You can omit the artichoke hearts and cheese, and substitute 8oz (225g) of cooked green beans and 6oz (175g) canned asparagus tips, chopped. *2.* For people who do not like nuts, use a standard oil and vinegar dressing (page 52).

Summer Meat and Cabbage Salad ⓧ ½

Preparation: **10 min**   Serves **4**   Cals per portion: **595**

3 tablespoons vegetable oil

1½ tablespoons red wine vinegar

½ teaspoon French or German mustard

Salt and black pepper

1 lb (450g) piece of mild salami

1 small onion, peeled and thinly sliced

½ small head young cabbage, trimmed and finely shredded

1 medium-sized crisp eating apple, cored and diced

Lettuce leaves for garnish

On a hot summer day, this salad can be a meal in itself.

1. In a serving bowl, combine the **oil, vinegar, mustard, salt** and **pepper.**

2. Remove the skin from the **salami** and cut it into ¼in (5mm) slices, then stack the slices and cut them into ¼in (5mm) strips.

3. Put the strips into the serving bowl with the **onion, cabbage** and the **apple.** Toss thoroughly to mix. If you have time, chill the salad for 45 minutes to 1 hour – it will have a better flavour. Spoon the salad onto the **lettuce leaves.** Serve with pumpernickel bread and butter.

> ***Tips: 1.*** *If you are preparing the salad in advance, toss the apple in a little lemon juice.* **2.** *You can use ham instead of salami.*

Spicy Beef Salad ⓧ

Preparation: **15 min**   Serves **4**   Cals per portion: **350**

1 tablespoon red wine vinegar

1 teaspoon French or German mustard

Salt and black pepper

4 tablespoons olive oil or vegetable oil

1 tablespoon finely chopped parsley

1 teaspoon ground cumin

1 clove garlic, peeled and finely chopped

12 oz (350g) diced cooked beef

2 stems celery, chopped

1 small onion, peeled and finely chopped

2 medium-sized green or red peppers, halved, seeded and chopped

Lettuce leaves for garnish

Here is a way to turn leftover beef into another main course. Serve with corn on the cob or crusty bread.

1. In a small serving bowl, combine the **vinegar, mustard, salt, pepper, oil, parsley, cumin** and **garlic.**

2. Add the **beef, celery, onion** and **peppers.** Toss well. Serve on the **lettuce leaves.**

> ***Tips: 1.*** *You can substitute cooked pork, ham or chicken for the beef.* **2.** *For a more elaborate salad, add one or more of the following: 3oz (75g) diced Cheddar or Swiss cheese, 4oz (115g) cooked sweetcorn kernels, 1 chopped ripe tomato.*

Curried Chicken Salad with Green Grapes

Preparation: **20 min**   Cooking: **4 min**   Serves **6**   Cals per portion: **240**

Serve this as a main course, with a cucumber salad, or as part of a cold buffet. If you make this salad with yoghurt instead of mayonnaise, you will reduce the calories per portion.

3 tablespoons vegetable oil

1 small onion, peeled and finely chopped

¾ teaspoon curry powder

½ teaspoon salt; pinch black pepper

6 tablespoons mayonnaise or natural yoghurt

Juice ½ lemon

½ teaspoon French mustard

1¼ lb (575g) diced cooked chicken

3 stems celery, chopped

8 oz (225g) green seedless grapes (halved if large)

1. In a small saucepan, heat 2 tablespoons of the **oil,** add the **onion,** and cook over low heat for 3 minutes. Stir in the **curry powder, salt** and **pepper,** and cook for another 30 seconds. Remove the mixture from the heat and let it cool. Stir in the **mayonnaise, lemon juice** and **mustard.**

2. Put the **chicken** into a serving bowl and add the curry-mayonnaise mixture, the remaining oil and the **celery.** Toss to mix. Add the **grapes** and toss again, gently. Chill the salad before serving if there is time.

Tips: 1. *Leftovers will keep well in the refrigerator for a day and, in fact, will taste even better after 24 hours.* **2.** *You can use diced cooked ham or lamb instead of the chicken.* **3.** *In place of the grapes, use 1 chopped apple, 2oz (50g) raisins or 4oz (115g) drained, canned pineapple chunks.* **4.** *Garnish with 2oz (50g) chopped walnuts or peanuts.*

Tuna and Basil Salad

Preparation: **10 min**   Serves **4**   Cals per portion: **300**

2 x 7 oz (198g) cans tuna, drained and flaked

1 medium-sized onion, peeled and finely chopped

3 stems celery, finely chopped

4 tablespoons olive oil or 2 tablespoons each olive oil and vegetable oil

1 tablespoon red wine vinegar

3 tablespoons chopped fresh basil or 2 teaspoons dried basil

1 teaspoon French mustard

¼ teaspoon salt

Pinch black pepper

1. Place the **tuna** in a large serving bowl. Mix in the **onion** and **celery,** and put aside.

2. In a small bowl, combine the **oil, vinegar, basil, mustard, salt** and **pepper.**

3. Pour the dressing over the tuna. Toss to mix well and serve on lettuce leaves or use as a filling for pitta bread.

Tip: *For another version of this salad, add ½ green or red pepper, chopped; 3 tablespoons chopped black olives; 2 chopped anchovy fillets; and 2 chopped medium-sized ripe tomatoes.*

Curried Tuna Salad

Preparation: **10 min**   Serves **4**   Cals per portion: **270**

2 x 7 oz (198g) cans tuna, drained and flaked

1 medium-sized onion, finely chopped

3 stems celery, finely chopped

6 tablespoons mayonnaise or natural yoghurt .

Juice ½ lemon

Salt and black pepper

2 teaspoons curry powder

1 medium-sized eating apple, cored and diced

1 oz (25g) raisins

If you use natural yoghurt instead of mayonnaise you will reduce the calories per portion.

1. Place the **tuna, onion** and **celery** in a serving bowl. Add the **mayonnaise, lemon juice, salt, pepper** and **curry powder, apple** and **raisins.** Toss to mix well.

2. Taste the salad for seasoning and add more curry powder if desired. Serve on lettuce leaves.

> **Tip:** *As a variation, substitute ½ to 1 teaspoon dried dill for the curry powder, and use 2oz (50g) walnuts instead of the apple and raisins.*

Tuna and Chickpea Salad

Preparation: **10 min**   Serves **4**   Cals per portion: **335**

1 x 15 oz (425g) can chickpeas (garbanzos), drained

1 large onion, peeled and finely chopped

1 stem celery, finely chopped

1 clove garlic, peeled and finely chopped

1 teaspoon dried dill

2 tablespoons finely chopped parsley

1½ tablespoons red wine vinegar

4 tablespoons olive oil or vegetable oil

Salt and black pepper

1 x 7 oz (198g) can tuna, drained

2 medium-sized tomatoes, chopped

Lettuce leaves for garnish

Served with French or good, crusty bread, this salad is a satisfying main course. Canned chickpeas are sometimes labelled 'garbanzos'.

1. In a large serving bowl, combine the **chickpeas, onion, celery, garlic, dill** and **parsley.** Add the **vinegar, oil, salt** and **pepper,** and toss to mix well.

2. Break the **tuna** into chunks and add it to the salad along with the **tomatoes.** Toss gently to mix. Serve on the **lettuce leaves** at room temperature or slightly chilled.

> **Tip:** *For a special occasion, substitute salmon for the tuna. Be sure to pick over the salmon and remove the dark skin and bones before adding it. You can also substitute cooked or canned haricot beans for the chickpeas.*

Macaroni Salad ½

Preparation: **10 min** Cooking: **9 min**   Serves **6** Cals per portion: **250**

Why not make a macaroni salad occasionally instead of the old standby potato salad. It's much easier and keeps well in the refrigerator. Save on preparation time by chopping the vegetables while the macaroni cooks.

10 oz (275g) elbow macaroni, farfalle (pasta bows) or shell pasta

2 stems celery, chopped

1 small green or red pepper, halved, seeded and chopped

1 small onion, peeled and finely chopped

5 tablespoons mayonnaise

Juice ½ lemon

1 teaspoon French mustard

½ teaspoon salt

Pinch black pepper

Lettuce leaves for garnish

1. Cook the **macaroni** according to packet directions, drain in a colander, and rinse under cold running water. Drain again thoroughly.

2. While the macaroni is cooking, combine the **celery, pepper, onion, mayonnaise, lemon juice, mustard, salt** and **black pepper** in a serving bowl. Add the macaroni to the bowl and toss well to mix. Serve on the **lettuce leaves.**

> **Tips: 1.** *Macaroni salad should not be kept at room temperature for long periods of time, because the mayonnaise will spoil. (For a picnic, make the salad without mayonnaise, substituting 3 tablespoons olive oil, increasing the amount of mustard to 1½ teaspoons, and adding 2 cloves of garlic, peeled and finely chopped.)* **2.** *For extra colour, add 2oz (50g) chopped black olives, 1 large, coarsely chopped tomato, or 2 or 3 chopped anchovy fillets.*

Oriental Noodle Salad

Preparation: **5 min** Cooking: **4 min**   Serves **4** Cals per portion: **510**

12 oz (350g) very thin egg noodles or thin spaghetti

3 tablespoons creamy peanut butter

3 tablespoons warm water

4 tablespoons vegetable oil

2 tablespoons soya sauce

Salt and black pepper

1 tablespoon sugar

1 tablespoon wine vinegar

2 cloves garlic, peeled and finely chopped

3 shallots, peeled and finely chopped

1. Cook the **noodles** according to packet directions, drain in a colander, and rinse under cold running water. Drain again thoroughly.

2. While the noodles are cooking, mix the **peanut butter** and **warm water** in a serving bowl to make a smooth paste. Stir in the **oil, soya sauce, salt, pepper, sugar, vinegar, garlic** and **shallots.** Add the noodles and toss thoroughly. Serve the salad at room temperature.

> **Tip:** *You can store leftovers in the refrigerator for 1 or 2 days, but be sure to let them return to room temperature before serving.*

Green Noodle and Pimento Salad ▷

Preparation: **7 min** Cooking: **7 min**   Serves **4** Cals per portion: **380**

9 oz (250g) green noodles

3 shallots, peeled and finely chopped

6 radishes, thinly sliced

2 stems celery, chopped

4 oz (115g) canned red pimentos, chopped

Juice ½ lemon

3 tablespoons olive oil

2 tablespoons soured cream

1 teaspoon dried basil

½ teaspoon salt

¼ teaspoon black pepper

Use the time while the noodles are cooking to chop the onions, celery and pimentos, and to slice the radishes.

1. Cook the **noodles** according to packet directions, drain then rinse under cold running water. Drain again thoroughly.

2. Transfer the noodles to a large serving bowl, add the **shallots, radishes, celery** and **pimentos.** Toss. Add the **lemon juice, oil, soured cream, basil, salt** and **pepper.** Toss again and serve at room temperature.

Tips: You can vary this salad in a number of ways:
1. Omit the salt and add 2 chopped anchovy fillets.
2. Add 2 tablespoons drained capers and 1 tablespoon finely chopped parsley, and decrease the amount of salt to ¼ teaspoon. 3. Add 1 x 7oz (198g) can tuna, drained and broken into small chunks.

Rice, Green Pea and Red Pepper Salad ½ 🐷

Preparation: **5 min** Cooking: **20 min**   Serves **4** Cals per portion: **300**

¾ pint (450ml) water

1 teaspoon salt

5 oz (150g) rice

2 stems celery, finely chopped

1 medium-sized red pepper, halved, seeded and chopped

2 shallots, peeled and finely chopped

3 tablespoons finely chopped parsley

8 oz (225g) frozen green peas

3 tablespoons olive oil or vegetable oil

1½ tablespoons red or white wine vinegar

½ teaspoon French mustard

Pinch black pepper

Prepare the celery, red pepper, shallots and parsley while the rice is cooking.

1. Pour the **water** into a large, heavy saucepan, add the **salt,** and bring to the boil over high heat. Stir in the **rice,** reduce the heat to moderate, and simmer, covered, for 15 minutes. All the liquid will be absorbed.

2. Put the **celery, red pepper, shallots** and **parsley** into a serving bowl. When the rice is done, put it into the bowl. Mix the **peas** into the rice. The hot rice will thaw the peas, and the peas will help cool the rice.

3. Let the mixture stand for 4 or 5 minutes while you prepare the dressing. In a small bowl, thoroughly combine the **oil, vinegar, mustard** and **black pepper.** Pour the dressing over the salad and toss gently to mix.

Tip: You can add either 4oz (115g) diced Cheddar or Swiss cheese, or 6oz (175g) drained, cooked chickpeas, kidney or lima beans.

Cracked Wheat Salad ½ 🐖

Preparation: **18 min**

Serves **6** Cals per portion: **175**

6 oz (175g) bulgur (cracked
wheat)

1 teaspoon salt

Juice 2 lemons

1 large clove garlic, peeled and
finely chopped

4 shallots, peeled and thinly
sliced

3 tablespoons chopped mint

4 tablespoons olive oil or
2 tablespoons each olive oil
and vegetable oil

Pinch black pepper

2 medium-sized tomatoes,
roughly chopped

3 tablespoons finely chopped
parsley

1 small cucumber, peeled and
roughly chopped

*Because there is no meat or mayonnaise to spoil, this is
an excellent salad for picnics or camping trips. Serve it
with fruit and cheese for a complete meal. A good time
to chop the garlic and parsley, slice the onions, cut up
the tomatoes and cucumber and chop the mint is while
the bulgur is soaking.*

1. Put the **bulgur** and **salt** into a bowl. Cover
with boiling water and leave to soak for
15 minutes, or until it is chewable.

2. When the bulgur is tender, drain well and
turn it into a serving bowl. Add the **lemon
juice, garlic, shallots, mint, oil** and **pepper.**
Toss to mix. Cover the salad and put it aside
until you are ready to serve. Just before
serving, add the **tomatoes, parsley** and
cucumber, and toss again.

*Tips: 1. The taste will improve if you prepare the salad
1 to 2 hours in advance to let the flavours blend, but
this is not essential. 2. Leftovers can be refrigerated.*

Beetroot and Apple Salad with Yoghurt Dressing

Preparation: **17 min**

Serves **4** Cals per portion: **120**

*Raw beetroot is used in this nutritious
salad, which tastes even better when
chilled.*

4 or 5 small young uncooked
beetroot

6 fl oz (175ml) natural yoghurt

¼ teaspoon salt

¼ teaspoon sugar

Juice ½ lemon

2 tablespoons mayonnaise

2 medium-sized eating apples,
cored and diced

Pinch black pepper

½ small onion, peeled and
chopped

1. Peel the uncooked **beetroot** and cut in half.
Cut each half into very thin slices.

2. In a serving bowl, combine the **yoghurt, salt,
sugar, lemon juice** and **mayonnaise.** Add the
beetroot, **apple** and **pepper** and toss until they
are well coated with the yoghurt mixture. Top
with the **onion** and serve.

*Tips: 1. Soured cream can be substituted for the
yoghurt, but it increases the calories per portion.
2. You can use 2 teaspoons of creamed horseradish
instead of the chopped onion.*

Bean Sprout and Bacon Salad ½

Preparation: **15 min**   Cooking: **5 min**   Serves **4**   Cals per portion: **180**

4 rashers bacon, cut into ¾ in (20mm) strips

2 tablespoons red wine vinegar

1 clove garlic, peeled and finely chopped

1 teaspoon Worcestershire sauce

¼ teaspoon dry mustard

¼ teaspoon salt

Pinch black pepper

1 lb (450g) fresh bean sprouts, or canned bean sprouts, drained

6 shallots, peeled and thinly sliced

1 small green or red pepper, halved, seeded and chopped

Lettuce leaves for garnish

1. Cook the **bacon** in a large frying pan over moderately high heat until crisp – about 5 minutes. Remove the bacon, drain on absorbent paper, and reserve.

2. Mix 2 tablespoons of the bacon fat with the **vinegar, garlic, Worcestershire sauce, mustard, salt** and **black pepper.** Put aside.

3. If using fresh **bean sprouts,** put them into a colander and run hot water over them for 2 to 3 minutes to wash and wilt them. Drain well, place in a serving bowl, and toss with the **shallots** and **pepper.** Crumble the reserved bacon and add to the salad.

4. Reheat the dressing and pour it while still hot over the salad. Toss and serve on **lettuce leaves.**

Tip: A quick way to cut the bacon is to stack the rashers and then snip them crosswise with kitchen scissors.

Coleslaw ½

Preparation: **8 min**   Serves **4**   Cals per portion: **210**

This basic coleslaw recipe lends itself to many variations, including the ones listed in the Tips below. Making this coleslaw with natural yoghurt instead of soured cream reduces the calories per portion.

1 small firm white cabbage (about 1 lb/450g)

2 medium carrots, peeled, grated

1 onion, peeled and thinly sliced

3 fl oz (90ml) mayonnaise

3 fl oz (90ml) soured cream or natural yoghurt

Juice ½ lemon

½ teaspoon salt

Pinch black pepper

1. Cut the stalk end from the **cabbage,** and remove any discoloured or limp outer leaves. Quarter the cabbage lengthwise, and trim off and discard the core at the point of each quarter.

2. Shred the cabbage finely. Place in a bowl and toss with the **carrots, onion, mayonnaise, soured cream, lemon juice, salt** and **pepper.**

*Tips: You can add any of the following combinations of ingredients to vary the coleslaw: **1.** 1 tablespoon creamed horseradish; **2.** ½ green or red pepper, halved, seeded and chopped; **3.** 2 tablespoons snipped fresh dill or 2 teaspoons dried dill; **4.** 1 teaspoon caraway or celery seeds; **5.** 1 or 2 canned pimentos, chopped; **6.** 1 eating apple, cored and chopped, but not peeled, with 2oz (50g) chopped nuts; **7.** 2oz (50g) raisins or seedless grapes, or 3oz (75g) diced peaches, pears, pineapple or orange.*

Grated Carrots with Herbs and Lemon ½ 🐷

Preparation: 20 min Cooking: **6 min**   Serves **6**   Cals per portion: **90**

1½ lb (700g) carrots

3 tablespoons olive oil or vegetable oil

1 large onion, peeled and finely chopped

1 or 2 cloves garlic, peeled and finely chopped

½ teaspoon dried marjoram or oregano

¼ teaspoon dried thyme

Juice 1 lemon

¼ teaspoon salt

Pinch black pepper

1. Peel the **carrots,** then grate them using the coarsest side of a grater or the shredder blade of a food processor.

2. Heat the **oil** in a large frying pan, and add the grated carrots, **onion** and **garlic.** Cook over moderately high heat, stirring continuously, for 5 minutes.

3. Sprinkle in the **marjoram** and **thyme,** and continue cooking and stirring for another 1 or 2 minutes. Add the **lemon juice** and toss lightly, then season with the **salt** and **pepper.** Toss again and chill until ready to serve.

Tips: 1. Substitute 2 tablespoons finely chopped parsley for the marjoram and thyme. 2. You can also serve this dish hot.

Cucumber Salad with Soya and Sesame Dressing

Preparation: 5 min   Serves **6**   Cals per portion: **35**

2 medium-sized cucumbers

½ teaspoon salt

Pinch black pepper

1 teaspoon sugar

1 tablespoon soya sauce

1 tablespoon cider vinegar

2 teaspoons sesame oil

1. Peel the **cucumbers** and cut them in half lengthwise. Scoop out the seeds with a teaspoon. Cut each half crosswise into ¼in (5mm) slices.

2. Combine the **salt, pepper, sugar, soya sauce, vinegar** and **oil.** Pour the dressing over the cucumbers and toss together. Serve chilled.

Tip: For a taste variation, substitute 2 teaspoons peanut butter blended with 2 teaspoons vegetable oil for the sesame oil.

Cucumber Salad with Walnuts ▷

Preparation: 7 min   Serves **6**   Cals per portion: **65**

2 medium-sized cucumbers

6 fl oz (175ml) natural yoghurt

2 oz (50g) chopped walnuts

1 small onion, peeled and finely chopped

¼ teaspoon salt

¼ teaspoon black pepper

1 tablespoon snipped dill

1. Peel the **cucumbers** and cut them in half lengthwise. Scoop out the seeds with a teaspoon. Cut each half crosswise into ¼in (5mm) slices.

2. Combine the **yoghurt, walnuts, onion, salt, pepper** and **dill.** Pour the dressing over the cucumbers and toss together. Serve chilled.

Roasted Pepper Salad

Preparation: **10 min**   Cooking: **15 min**   Serves **4**   Cals per portion: **130**

Serve these sweet and mellow roasted peppers as a salad or an appetiser.

8 medium-sized red or green peppers

1 clove garlic, peeled and finely chopped

4 tablespoons olive oil

1 tablespoon white wine vinegar

Salt and black pepper

1½ tablespoons mixed fresh herbs, finely chopped

4 lemon wedges

1. Preheat the grill. Put the **peppers** on their sides in the grill pan, 2in (50mm) from the heat, and turn frequently until the skins are blackened and charred – about 15 minutes. Dampen a clean tea towel with iced water, cover the peppers and allow to cool.

2. Meanwhile, in a small bowl, mix the **garlic, oil, vinegar, salt, pepper** and **fresh herbs.**

3. Peel, halve, core and seed the peppers (keep juices); cut them into large strips, or quarters, and arrange on a serving dish. Add any pepper juices to the oil and vinegar mixture, stir, and pour over the roasted peppers. Garnish with **lemon wedges** and serve at room temperature.

Basic Potato Salad with Variations ▷ 🐷

Preparation: **10 min**   Cooking: **5 min**   Serves **4**   Cals per portion: **285**

While the potatoes are cooking, chop the parsley, onion and celery.

1 lb (450g) potatoes, peeled and diced

1 tablespoon finely chopped parsley

1 small onion, peeled and finely chopped

1 stem celery, chopped

1 tablespoon vegetable oil

1 tablespoon cider vinegar

½ teaspoon salt

3 fl oz (90ml) mayonnaise

1 teaspoon prepared French mustard

Salad greens for garnish

1. Bring about ¾in (20mm) of lightly salted water to the boil in a medium-sized saucepan. Add the **potatoes,** place the lid askew on the pan and cook for about 5 minutes, or until just tender.

2. Meanwhile, mix the **parsley, onion, celery, oil, vinegar, salt, mayonnaise** and **mustard** in a serving bowl.

3. Drain the cooked potatoes thoroughly, add them to the bowl and toss gently to mix all the ingredients. Cover and refrigerate until cool. Serve on the **salad greens.**

> *Tips: Start with the basic recipe and add or substitute ingredients as shown to make the following variations:*
> *Caesar Potato Salad. Omit the onion and salt, and add 2 chopped anchovy fillets, 1 clove garlic (peeled and finely chopped), 2 teaspoons Worcestershire sauce and 1½oz (40g) grated Parmesan cheese.*
> *Potato and Bacon Salad. Double the vinegar, omit the celery and add 4 rashers of bacon, fried crisp and crumbled.*
> *Potato Salad with Egg. Add 1 chopped hard-boiled egg, 2 tablespoons chopped pickled cucumbers or finely chopped pepper and 2 tablespoons snipped fresh dill or ½ teaspoon dried dill.*

Potato Salad with Pepper and Olives ⊘

Preparation: **10 min**   Cooking: **5 min**   Serves **4**   Cals per portion: **220**

1 lb (450g) potatoes, peeled and diced

1 small onion, finely chopped

1 stem celery, chopped

1 clove garlic, peeled and finely chopped

1 small green or red pepper, halved, seeded and chopped

2 oz (50g) sliced stuffed olives

¼ teaspoon dried thyme

4 tablespoons olive oil or vegetable oil

Juice 1 lemon

½ teaspoon salt

¼ teaspoon black pepper

Put the potato cooking time to good use by chopping the onion, celery, pepper and garlic, and slicing the olives.

1. Bring about ¾in (20mm) of lightly salted water to the boil in a medium-sized saucepan. Add the **potatoes,** place the lid askew on the pan and cook for about 5 minutes, or until just tender.

2. While the potatoes are cooking, mix the **onion, celery, garlic, pepper, olives, thyme, oil, lemon juice, salt** and **black pepper** in a serving bowl.

3. Drain the cooked potatoes. Add them to the bowl and toss gently to mix all the ingredients. Cover and refrigerate until cool.

> **Tip:** *To vary the recipe, add 3 tablespoons finely chopped parsley and 3oz (75g) peeled prawns.*

Spinach-Bacon Salad with Warm Dressing ½

Preparation: **10 min**   Cooking: **6 min**   Serves **4**   Cals per portion: **240**

8 oz (225g) fresh spinach

4 oz (115g) mushrooms, thinly sliced

1 small onion, peeled and thinly sliced

6 rashers bacon, cut into ¾ in (20mm) strips

2 teaspoons prepared French mustard

2 teaspoons sugar

2 teaspoons white wine vinegar

1 teaspoon Worcestershire sauce

Juice ½ lemon

1. Trim the **spinach** of coarse stems and blemished leaves, and wash it. Pat the spinach dry with absorbent paper, tear into bite-sized pieces and put into a large serving bowl with the **mushrooms** and **onion.** Put aside.

2. Meanwhile, cook the **bacon** in a large frying pan over moderately high heat until crisp – about 5 minutes. Drain on absorbent paper and reserve. Pour off all but 3 tablespoons of the bacon fat.

3. Reduce the heat to low. Add the **mustard, sugar, vinegar, Worcestershire sauce** and **lemon juice** to the bacon fat. Stir to mix well, and heat through.

4. Pour the dressing over the salad, crumble the bacon over it, and toss thoroughly. Serve immediately.

> **Tip:** *To make in advance, prepare the salad and dressing, but do not combine. Cover the salad and refrigerate. Before serving, heat the dressing and toss with the salad.*

Tomato and Red Pepper Salad

Preparation: **15 min** Serves **4** Cals per portion: **95**

3 tablespoons olive oil or vegetable oil

1½ tablespoons cider vinegar

1 clove garlic, peeled and crushed

½ teaspoon salt

Pinch black pepper

1 teaspoon paprika

6 to 8 drops Tabasco sauce

2 tablespoons finely chopped parsley

4 medium-sized ripe tomatoes, cut into ¼ in (5mm) slices

2 medium-sized red peppers, halved, cored, seeded and cut into ¼ in (5mm) strips

1 medium-sized onion, peeled and thinly sliced

Lettuce leaves for garnish

The peppery dressing in this recipe is good with other raw vegetables as well as cold, cooked ones.

1. In a small bowl, combine the **oil, vinegar, garlic, salt, black pepper, paprika, Tabasco sauce** and **parsley.** Put aside.

2. Put the **tomatoes, peppers** and **onion** into a serving bowl. Pour the dressing over the vegetables and toss gently together. Serve on the **lettuce leaves.** The salad should be served cool, but not cold.

> **Tip:** *For a salad with more contrast, use 1 red pepper and 1 yellow pepper.*

Turnip and Pear Salad

Preparation: **18 min** Serves **4** Cals per portion: **150**

The combination of ingredients in this salad may be surprising, but the result is delicious.

3 tablespoons vegetable oil

1½ tablespoons cider vinegar

1 tablespoon sugar

½ teaspoon salt

¼ teaspoon dry mustard

Pinch ground nutmeg

Pinch paprika

Generous squeeze lemon juice

2 large, firm, ripe pears (with good skins)

3 or 4 medium-sized turnips

1 large head cos lettuce

1. In a serving bowl, combine the **oil, vinegar, sugar, salt, mustard, nutmeg, paprika** and **lemon juice.** Quarter, core and dice the **pears,** and add them to the dressing.

2. Peel the **turnips** and coarsely grate them, using the coarsest side of a grater or the shredder blade of a food processor. Add the turnips to the pears and dressing.

3. Wash the **lettuce,** pat it dry with absorbent paper and tear it into bite-sized pieces. Add it to the salad and toss together.

> **Tips: 1.** *You can substitute 12oz (350g) swede for the turnips.* **2.** *Instead of tearing the lettuce into bite-sized pieces and tossing it with the salad, toss the other ingredients without the lettuce and serve on whole lettuce leaves.* **3.** *Serve with cottage cheese on the side for a light lunch.*

Making a Green Salad

A simple green salad made from one or more varieties of raw green leafy vegetables, and tossed with a dressing, is one of the most popular side dishes. It should not, however, be dull and uninspiring. If you follow the suggestions below for choosing, preparing and mixing salad greens, and serving them with a suitable dressing, each salad will be an exciting part of the meal.

Choosing Salad Greens

For the best appearance, texture and flavour, use more than one variety of salad greens, however simple the salad: dark green with light green, and mild with tangy. Here are the most widely available salad greens.

Round (or cabbage) lettuce: A medium-green lettuce, with loosely clustered 'rumpled' leaves; rather resembling a spring cabbage in appearance, hence the name. Fairly limp leaves and very little characteristic flavour. Use a well-flavoured dressing just before serving – the leaves go limp very quickly.

Curly endive: Very frilly, loose lettuce, with widespread, feathery leaves – pale lemony-green in the centre, turning to darker green on the outer leaves. It has a slightly bitter taste which goes well with fairly robust dressings, such as blue cheese.

Escarole: A bulky, 'blown' lettuce, with snipped leaves that turn paler towards the centre of the lettuce. It has a good texture, a 'clean' flavour, and blends well with other salad greens, and with fruit. Escarole can take quite a highly flavoured dressing.

Iceberg lettuce: Crisp, pale green leaves, packed together in a tight head – a little of this lettuce goes a long way. It resembles a translucent white cabbage, is very crisp, and the one lettuce that's suitable for shredding. Bland and rather watery, Iceberg needs a really well-flavoured dressing.

Cos lettuce: Known also as Romaine, this is a broad, tapered lettuce, with dark green leaves on the outside and paler ones clustered in the centre. It has a wonderful crunch and a little more flavour than many of the salad greens.

Batavia: A moderately firm-headed lettuce, with widely spaced outer leaves that are crinkled and crimped at the edges. Good and crisp, it stands up well to strongly flavoured dressing.

Mâche: Also called lamb's lettuce, it has small, tongue-shaped green leaves, which grow on small clustered plants. The distinct peppery taste is very good for 'delicate' or smart salads. The leaves go limp very quickly.

Chicory: Flame-shaped bulbs of closely packed white to pale, yellow-green leaves – very crisp with a distinct bitter flavour. Can be divided into leaves, or shredded.

Spinach: Bland, dark green leaves which can only be used in a salad when very young and crinkly. They are very good served with a warm dressing and pieces of crispy bacon.

Watercress: Small, deep green leaves with a peppery, slightly bitter taste. Mixes well with other salad greens. Often used as a garnish.

How to Prepare Salad Greens

Separate the leaves of the salad greens and wash them in cold water; do not leave them to soak. Be sure to get rid of any grit that clings to them. Shake the leaves and then pat dry with absorbent paper. A salad spinner will do the job in seconds, but it does tend to bruise the leaves. Make sure the leaves are thoroughly dry, or the dressing will not cling to them.

Tear, do not cut, the greens into bite-sized pieces. The exception to this rule is Iceberg lettuce, which can be sliced or shredded.

Dressing and Serving Green Salads

Use only fresh, good-quality oil for making salad dressings. Mix and serve the salad in a glass, china or wooden salad bowl. A wooden bowl should have a perfect surface and be wiped very thoroughly after each use. Dressings can be prepared beforehand, but should only be added at the moment of serving.

Green Salad Extras

Add for contrast in taste, colour and texture:
- Fresh herbs (basil, mint, parsley, thyme, etc).
- Avocado, tomato and crumbled bacon.
- Bean sprouts, carrot, shallots and bamboo shoots.
- Cheese, ham, hard-boiled egg, tomato and onion.
- Onion, orange sections and rosemary.
- Radishes, shallots, cucumber, tomato and mushrooms.
- Tomato, crumbled bacon and hard-boiled egg.
- Courgettes, radishes, shallots and blue cheese.
- Cooked green beans, cooked potato, tuna, tomato and black olives.
- Cooked cauliflower, capers, anchovies and hard-boiled egg.
- Cooked peas, hard-boiled egg, Cheddar cheese and sweet and sour pickles.

Oil and Vinegar Dressing ⊙ ½

| Preparation: **2 min** | Makes about **10 fl oz (275ml)** | Cals per tablespoon: **90** |

8 fl oz (225ml) olive oil

2 fl oz (50ml) wine vinegar

1 teaspoon salt

¼ teaspoon black pepper

½ teaspoon prepared French mustard

Put all the ingredients into a jar, secure the lid and shake vigorously. Alternatively, whisk the dressing in a bowl until well blended. Store in the refrigerator. Shake again just before serving.

> **Tip:** *You can add any one or more of the following to the above basic dressing: 1 large clove garlic, peeled and crushed; ½ teaspoon curry powder or dried herbs, such as oregano, thyme, basil or dill; 2 tablespoons drained capers; 2 tablespoons chilli sauce or ½ teaspoon chilli powder; 2 tablespoons soured cream; 2 mashed anchovy fillets.*

Creamy Blue Cheese Dressing ⊙

| Preparation: **5 min** | Makes about **10 fl oz (275ml)** | Cals per tablespoon: **80** |

3 oz (75g) crumbled blue cheese

3 tablespoons single cream

4 fl oz (115ml) mayonnaise or soured cream

6 tablespoons olive oil

2 fl oz (50ml) white wine vinegar

1 teaspoon prepared English mustard

Salt and black pepper

If you like a salad dressing with bite, this one is for you.

1. In a small bowl, mash the **cheese** with the **cream** until smooth.

2. Add the **mayonnaise, oil, vinegar** and **mustard,** then **salt** and **pepper** to taste. Whisk the ingredients together until well mixed. Cover and store in the refrigerator. Serve over greens with a strong flavour, such as escarole, curly endive or watercress.

> **Tip:** *If you add chopped walnuts, the dressing will have an interesting crunch to it.*

Chilli Dressing

| Preparation: **5 min** | Makes about **9 fl oz (250ml)** | Cals per tablespoon: **50** |

4 fl oz (115ml) mayonnaise

2 tablespoons chilli sauce

1 small onion, peeled and finely chopped

½ small green pepper, halved, seeded and finely chopped

Juice ½ lemon

¼ teaspoon salt

This creamy dressing can be used in many ways: on wedges of lettuce or on cold seafood; as a dip for raw vegetables; as a spread for chicken sandwiches; or even spooned over hard-boiled eggs, boiled potatoes, carrots or beetroot.

Put all the ingredients into a small bowl and stir well to mix. Cover and store in the refrigerator.

> **Tip:** *Try equal quantities of this dressing and the Avocado Dressing for an interesting combination.*

Avocado Dressing

Preparation: **8 min**   Makes about **10 fl oz (275ml)**   Cals per tablespoon: **60**

1 medium-sized ripe avocado

4 fl oz (115ml) vegetable oil

Juice ½ lemon

1 small onion, peeled and finely chopped

¼ teaspoon salt

¼ teaspoon Tabasco sauce

Do not prepare this dressing more than 1 or 2 hours in advance as it will darken.

Cut the **avocado** in half, remove the stone and scoop the flesh into a bowl. Add the **oil, lemon juice, onion, salt** and **Tabasco sauce**, and blend until smooth. Chill. Serve over wedges of lettuce, tomato slices or cold, cooked seafood.

Tip: An electric blender does the work in seconds.

Yoghurt Dressing

Preparation: **4 min**   Makes about **5 fl oz (150ml)**   Cals per tablespoon: **20**

Generous squeeze lemon juice

1 tablespoon vegetable oil

4 fl oz (115ml) natural yoghurt

½ teaspoon paprika

Dash Tabasco sauce

½ teaspoon salt

½ small clove garlic, peeled and crushed

Put all the ingredients into a jar, secure the lid and shake vigorously. Alternatively, whisk the dressing in a bowl until well blended. Store in the refrigerator. Shake or stir again just before serving. Use to dress sliced cucumbers or tomatoes, cooked vegetables or cold poached fish.

Tip: To vary the dressing, add 1 teaspoon curry powder, or substitute 1 finely chopped shallot for the garlic and add 1 tablespoon chopped fresh mint or snipped dill.

Tomato Dressing

Preparation: **3 min**   Makes about **10 fl oz (275ml)**   Cals per tablespoon: **3**

8 fl oz (225ml) tomato juice

2 fl oz (50ml) wine vinegar

1 small onion, peeled and finely chopped

Pinch black pepper

¼ teaspoon salt

1 clove garlic, peeled and crushed

1 teaspoon Worcestershire sauce

Put all the ingredients into a jar, secure the lid and shake vigorously. Alternatively, whisk in a bowl until well blended. Store in the refrigerator. Shake or stir again just before serving.

Tips: 1. For extra flavour, add one of the following to the dressing: 1 tablespoon snipped dill (or 1 teaspoon dried dill); 1 teaspoon dried tarragon, 1 teaspoon crushed fennel seeds and ½ teaspoon dried thyme, or ½ teaspoon each dried basil and oregano. 2. You can simmer this dressing until thick and use it as a barbecue sauce.

Caesar Salad

Preparation: **12 min**   Cooking: **5 min**   Serves **4**   Cals per portion: **320**

Here is one of the best of all salads. Enjoy it as a first course or as a light lunch.

4 fl oz (115ml) olive oil

2 slices firm-textured white bread

1 egg

Salt and black pepper

1 clove garlic, peeled and crushed

Juice ½ lemon

3 tablespoons grated Parmesan cheese

3 or 4 anchovy fillets, rinsed and chopped

1 large head cos lettuce

1. Heat 4 tablespoons of the **oil** in a medium-sized frying pan over moderate heat. Cut the **bread** into ½in (15mm) cubes and cook in the oil over low heat for 5 minutes, or until golden-brown. Drain on absorbent paper and reserve.

2. While the croutons are browning, break the **egg** into a large serving bowl and beat it together with the **salt, pepper, garlic** and **lemon juice** until all the ingredients are well combined. Beat in the remaining oil, the **cheese** and the **anchovies.**

3. Wash the **lettuce**, shake it, pat dry with absorbent paper, tear it into bite-sized pieces and add to the bowl. Toss well and top with the croutons.

> **Tip:** *You can use a 3oz (75g) packet of croutons in place of the bread cubes, and omit Step 1.*

Cos Salad with Blue Cheese and Walnuts ⊙

Preparation: **10 min**   Serves **4**   Cals per portion: **265**

1 large head cos lettuce

2 fl oz (50ml) olive oil

1 tablespoon red wine vinegar

Salt and black pepper

2 oz (50g) crumbled blue cheese

3 oz (75g) coarsely chopped walnuts

8 cherry tomatoes or 1 medium-sized tomato cut into 8 wedges

1. Wash the **lettuce** and pat it dry with absorbent paper. Tear the lettuce into bite-sized pieces.

2. Put the **oil, vinegar, salt, pepper** and half the **cheese** into a large serving bowl. Mash the cheese with a fork, then blend it thoroughly with the oil and vinegar.

3. Add the lettuce, the remaining cheese, the **walnuts** and **tomatoes**, and toss thoroughly. Serve immediately.

> **Tip:** *For an extra tang, add 1 small red-skinned onion, peeled and thinly sliced.*

Tossed Watercress with Radishes and Pear

Preparation: **17 min**   Serves: **4**   Cals per portion: **105**

2 bunches watercress

1 small onion, peeled and thinly sliced

12 radishes, thinly sliced

1 medium-sized firm, ripe pear, peeled, cored and thinly sliced

3 tablespoons olive oil

Juice ½ lemon

¼ teaspoon salt

Pinch black pepper

½ teaspoon prepared French mustard

Spicy, peppery watercress is the basis of this tossed salad; it is far richer than lettuce in protein, calcium and Vitamin C, so makes a very nutritious salad.

1. Wash the **watercress** and dry it with absorbent paper. Cut off and discard the stem ends, tear the watercress into bite-sized pieces and place in a serving bowl. Add the **onion, radishes** and **pear** slices.

2. In a small bowl, mix the **oil, lemon juice, salt, pepper** and **mustard**. Pour this dressing over the salad, toss and serve.

Mediterranean Salad

Preparation: **10 min**   Serves **4**   Cals per portion: **340**

4 fl oz (115ml) olive oil

¼ teaspoon salt

1 tablespoon white wine vinegar

Pinch black pepper

2 oz (50g) stoned black olives

4 to 6 anchovy fillets, rinsed and chopped

1 medium-sized head cos lettuce

1 medium-sized onion, peeled and thinly sliced

2 medium-sized tomatoes, each cut into 8 wedges

1 medium-sized cucumber, peeled and thinly sliced

4 oz (115g) feta cheese cut into ½ in (15mm) cubes

To savour the true flavour of this salad, make an effort to find the feta cheese. Probably the best known of Greek cheeses, pure white feta is made from sheep's milk and preserved in brine.

1. Put the **oil, salt, vinegar, pepper, olives** and **anchovies** in a large serving bowl, and stir with a fork to mix well.

2. Wash the **lettuce**, pat it dry with absorbent paper, and tear it into bite-sized pieces. Add it to the bowl along with the **onion, tomatoes** and **cucumber**. Toss together with the dressing.

3. Add the **cheese** and toss gently to prevent the cheese from crumbling.

> **Tips: 1.** *To make this salad a main course for 4, increase the ingredients by half and serve with warmed pitta bread or with crusty French bread.* **2.** *If you cannot get feta, use another firm, white, crumbly cheese such as Caerphilly.*

Making a Fruit Salad

What is more refreshing than a salad made of fresh fruit served plain or with a simple dressing? Fruit salad can be served as an appetiser, side dish or dessert. And a good fruit salad is quick and simple to make. Create your own salad of fresh fruits by following the suggestions given below, or use one of the recipes that follow.

Choosing Fruits

Your choice of fruits will be limited by what is in season and what is available, but try to select those that complement one another. Consider colour, contrast and texture when combining fruits. For example, the crispness of a tart apple is a good foil for sweet ripe bananas. You can add nuts, soured cream, cottage cheese or even a raw vegetable. Here are a few combinations.
■ Sliced avocado with orange and grapefruit sections.
■ Honeydew melon with cubed watermelon and passion fruit.
■ Melon balls with grapes and whole or sliced strawberries.
■ Sliced apples and bananas with orange sections.
■ Orange sections, stoned prunes and nuts with ricotta or cottage cheese.
■ Sliced peaches and toasted almonds with cottage cheese.
■ Sliced peaches, plums and bananas with whole or sliced strawberries.
■ Pineapple chunks, orange sections, raisins and nuts with ricotta or cottage cheese.
■ Sliced apples and shredded cabbage with soured cream.

To brighten your fruit salad still further, add some desiccated coconut, chopped fresh mint or crystallised or preserved ginger.

Preparing Fruits

Prepare the fruits by removing any inedible parts, including tough skins, seeds or cores. If you are using oranges or other citrus fruits, divide the peeled fruit into sections and remove all the white membrane from each section. Slice or cube large fruits so that they are in bite-sized pieces. Count on about 8oz (225g) of prepared fruit per person.

Apples, avocados, bananas, peaches and pears darken when exposed to air and should be prepared last. When using fruits liable to discolour, dip them into a bowl of lemon water (the juice of 1 lemon mixed with 10fl oz (285ml) of water) as you cut the fruits to keep them bright and colourful.

Dressing and Serving Fruit Salads

Fruit salads can be served chilled or at room temperature, with or without a dressing. If you prefer to use a dressing, try one of the recipes below. Use a tangy dressing for appetiser salads and toss dessert salads with a sweet dressing or top with whipped cream.

Fruit salads are good side dishes for cold meats and poultry. If you want a change from sauces and chutneys, try serving chicken or pork with a fruit salad made of orange sections, sliced apples and cucumbers, moistened with a little orange juice, topped with a mustard vinaigrette and garnished with fresh herbs.

Oil and Vinegar Dressing for Fruit Salads

Preparation: **3 min**   Makes **6 fl oz (175ml)**   Cals per tablespoon: **90**

4 fl oz (115ml) vegetable oil

2 fl oz (50ml) white wine vinegar

1 tablespoon honey

Grated rind and juice 1 small lemon

½ teaspoon salt

Pinch black pepper

Put all the ingredients into a jar, secure the lid, and shake vigorously; or whisk in a bowl. Store in the refrigerator. Shake again just before serving.

Tip: Instead of the honey and lemon juice and rind, you can use 2 teaspoons sugar and 2 tablespoons finely chopped fresh mint.

Yoghurt and Honey Dressing

Preparation: **5 min**   Makes **6 fl oz (175ml)**   Cals per tablespoon: **30**

Finely grated rind ¼ lemon

Juice ½ lemon

1 tablespoon vegetable oil

4 fl oz (115ml) natural yoghurt

2 tablespoons honey

¼ teaspoon paprika

Dash Tabasco sauce

¼ teaspoon salt

Put all the ingredients into a jar, secure the lid and shake vigorously; or whisk in a bowl. Store in the refrigerator. Shake again just before serving on a fruit salad.

> **Tip:** *As a variation, you can omit the paprika and Tabasco sauce and add 1 or 2 teaspoons finely chopped fresh mint.*

Soured Cream and Orange Dressing

Preparation: **2 min**   Makes **9 fl oz (250ml)**   Cals per tablespoon: **40**

2 tablespoons raw or brown sugar

Juice ½ orange

8 fl oz (225ml) soured cream

Large pinch ground ginger

In a small bowl combine the **sugar** and **orange juice**, and stir until the sugar dissolves. Mix in the **soured cream** and **ginger**. Cover and store in the refrigerator. Serve with berries, peaches, nectarines, bananas or other fruit.

Sweet and Sour Fruit Dressing

Preparation: **2 min**   Makes **10 fl oz (275ml)**   Cals per tablespoon: **10**

8 fl oz (225ml) pineapple or orange juice

Juice 1½ lemons

1 tablespoon honey

1 clove garlic, peeled and finely chopped

½ teaspoon salt

¼ teaspoon paprika

Put all the ingredients into a jar, secure the lid and shake vigorously; or whisk in a bowl. Store in the refrigerator. Shake again just before serving.

> **Tips: 1.** *For variety, add 1 tablespoon of chopped fresh mint, dill or basil.* **2.** *This is a good dressing for apples, pears and bananas because the citrus juice keeps them from turning brown.* **3.** *You can use this dressing for a green salad too.*

Poppy Seed Dressing

Preparation: **8 min**   Makes **8 fl oz (225ml)**   Cals per tablespoon: **85**

1 oz (25g) sugar

¾ teaspoon dry mustard

¾ teaspoon salt

3 tablespoons cider vinegar

1 small onion, peeled and finely chopped

6 fl oz (175ml) vegetable oil

1 tablespoon poppy seeds

1. In a small saucepan, combine the **sugar, mustard, salt, vinegar** and **onion**. Stir over moderate heat for 3 minutes, or until the sugar dissolves. Remove from the heat.

2. Gradually whisk in the **oil** until the mixture thickens. Stir in the **poppy seeds**. Store in the refrigerator and whisk again just before serving.

Apple Salad with Soured Cream Dressing ½

Preparation: **10 min**   Serves **4**   Cals per portion: **240**

4 fl oz (115ml) soured cream or natural yoghurt

Juice ½ lemon

⅛ teaspoon ground cinnamon

4 medium-sized crisp eating apples

2 oz (50g) raisins

3 oz (75g) chopped walnuts or pine kernels

Lettuce leaves for garnish

1. In a serving bowl, combine the **soured cream** and **lemon juice**. Stir in the **cinnamon**.

2. Cut the **apples** into quarters lengthwise and cut out the cores. Dice the apple quarters, one by one, and stir the pieces into the soured cream mixture as you dice, to prevent the apples from turning brown.

3. Mix in the **raisins** and **walnuts**. Serve on the **lettuce leaves**. The salad tastes best slightly chilled.

Tip: If you toast the nuts and add them when still warm, the dressing will have a better flavour.

Pear, Celery and Pecan Salad

Preparation: **14 min**   Serves **4**   Cals per portion: **280**

3 fl oz (90ml) mayonnaise or natural yoghurt

1 tablespoon vegetable oil

Generous squeeze lemon juice

¼ teaspoon salt

Pinch black pepper

3 stems celery, diced

3 large firm, ripe pears

Lettuce leaves for garnish

3 oz (75g) pecan halves

1. In a serving bowl, combine the **mayonnaise, oil, lemon juice, salt** and **pepper**. Add the diced **celery**.

2. Stem and peel the **pears,** quarter them lengthwise, and cut out the cores. Dice each quarter into ¾in (20mm) pieces. Add the pears to the bowl and toss. Mound on the **lettuce leaves** and top with the **pecans**. The salad tastes best slightly chilled.

Tip: For variety, add 2oz (50g) diced ham or Cheddar or blue cheese. You can also use apples instead of the pears, and walnuts instead of the pecans.

VEGETABLES

(See also Oven-Baked Dishes)

VEGETABLES

Vegetables add a variety of flavours, textures and colours to a meal. Most can be cooked simply by steaming, boiling or sautéing; and few people need to be reminded that the fresher the vegetable and the less it is cooked, the more wholesome and flavourful it is. Indeed, fresh vegetables are so good that you will often want to eat them raw, or lightly cooked and tossed with butter. But even natural goodness can be tedious if it is never varied. The recipes that follow show you new ways of cooking everyday carrots, cabbages and green beans; ingenious ways to shorten the cooking time of slow-cooking beetroot and turnip; and quick, simple ways to turn staple potatoes into delectable dishes. The vegetables presented here are inexpensive either all year round – for example, cabbages and carrots – or seasonally – for example, fresh peas, sweetcorn and courgettes.

Bean Sprouts with Peppers ½

Preparation: **5 min** Cooking: **6 min**   Serves **4** Cals per portion: **100**

1 lb (450g) bean sprouts

1 red or green pepper

2 tablespoons peanut oil

2 teaspoons soya sauce

Salt and black pepper

Tip: If you do not have peanut oil, use vegetable oil and 1 teaspoon of peanut butter.

1. Trim the **bean sprouts,** put them in a colander and rinse under the tap for about 1 minute. Leave to drain.

2. Wash and quarter the **pepper** lengthwise and remove the seeds. Cut the quarters into fine strips.

3. Heat the **oil** in a large frying pan or wok and cook the pepper for 2 or 3 minutes, add the bean sprouts and cook for a further 2 minutes, stirring continuously. Season to taste with **soya sauce, salt** and **pepper.** Reheat until piping hot and serve immediately.

Broad Beans with Onion and Bacon ½

Preparation: **10 min** Cooking: **15 min**   Serves **4** Cals per portion: **245**

1 oz (25g) butter or margarine

2 oz (50g) finely chopped bacon

1 small onion, peeled and finely chopped

1 lb (450g) shelled broad beans (about 2 lb/1kg in the shell)

6 fl oz (175ml) boiling water

Salt and black pepper

1. Heat the **butter** in a heavy, medium-sized saucepan over a moderate heat. Add the **bacon** and cook for 2 minutes, then add the **onion** and cook for 5 minutes.

2. Add the shelled **broad beans** and **boiling water.** Cover and cook gently for 10 to 15 minutes, or until they are just tender. Add **salt** and **pepper.**

Green Beans with Garlic and Cheese ½ 🐷

Preparation: **6 min**   Cooking: **10 min**   Serves **4**   Cals per portion: **175**

1 lb (450g) green beans

1 small lemon

4 tablespoons olive oil or vegetable oil

2 cloves garlic, peeled and finely chopped

½ teaspoon black pepper

2 tablespoons grated Parmesan cheese

Tip: Frozen peas are equally delicious prepared in the same way, but only cooked for a few minutes.

1. Wash the **beans** and cut off the ends. Bring about ¾in (20mm) of lightly salted water to the boil in a medium-sized saucepan. Add the beans, cover, and cook for 8 minutes, or until almost tender, but still crisp.

2. Meanwhile, remove the peel from the **lemon** in strips with a swivel-bladed potato peeler. Cut the peel into very narrow strips about 1½in (40mm) long. Squeeze the juice from the lemon. Put both aside.

3. When the beans are cooked, drain them in a colander. Put the **oil** into the same saucepan and sauté the **garlic** for 1 minute. Add the beans and toss to coat them with the oil and garlic.

4. Add the strips of lemon peel, lemon juice and **pepper,** and toss again over the heat. Spoon the beans into a heated serving dish and sprinkle with the **cheese.** Serve at once.

Green Beans Italian Style ½ 🐷

Preparation: **5 min**   Cooking: **25 min**   Serves **4**   Cals per portion: **100**

Serve this dish hot, or make it in advance and serve it cold.

1 lb (450g) green beans

2 tablespoons vegetable oil or olive oil

1 clove garlic, peeled and finely chopped

2 tablespoons chopped parsley

½ teaspoon sugar

½ teaspoon salt

Pinch black pepper

6 fl oz (175ml) beef stock

1 medium-sized tomato, peeled and thinly sliced.

1. Wash the **beans** and cut off the ends. Put the beans into a deep frying pan with the **oil, garlic, parsley, sugar, salt** and **pepper,** and cook, covered, over low heat for 5 minutes.

2. Raise the heat to moderate. Add the **stock** and cook, uncovered, for 15 minutes, or until the beans are almost tender. Add the **tomato** and cook, uncovered, for another 5 minutes.

Tip: To serve the leftovers warm, sprinkle grated Parmesan cheese and a little oil over the top, and bake in the oven at 200°C (400°F, gas mark 6) until the cheese melts.

Warm Green Beans Vinaigrette ½ 🐷

Preparation: **5 min**   Cooking: **8 min**   Serves **4**   Cals per portion: **165**

1 lb (450g) green beans
1½ tablespoons cider vinegar
½ teaspoon salt
¼ teaspoon black pepper
1 teaspoon French mustard
4 tablespoons vegetable oil
1 small onion, peeled and finely chopped

1. Wash the **beans** and cut off the ends. Bring about ¾in (20mm) of lightly salted water to the boil in a medium-sized saucepan and add the beans. Cook, covered, for 8 minutes or until almost tender, but still crisp.

2. Meanwhile, make the dressing by mixing together the **vinegar, salt, pepper, mustard, oil** and **onion.** Drain the beans when cooked and toss immediately with the dressing.

Green Beans in Egg Sauce ½ 🐷

Preparation: **5 min**   Cooking: **10 min**   Serves **4**   Cals per portion: **70**

1 lb (450g) green beans
2 eggs
1½ tablespoons cider vinegar
½ small onion, peeled and finely chopped
1 clove garlic, peeled and finely chopped
¼ teaspoon salt
Pinch black pepper

Tip: Use the egg sauce with broccoli or carrots.

1. Wash the **beans** and cut off the ends. Bring about ¾in (20mm) of lightly salted water to the boil in a medium-sized saucepan and add the beans. Cook, covered, for 8 minutes or until almost tender, but still crisp. Drain, reserving 1½ tablespoons of the cooking water. Return the beans to the pan and place over a low heat.

2. Mix the **eggs** and **vinegar** in a bowl, add the reserved water, and beat the ingredients together with a fork. Pour the mixture over the beans, and remove from the heat.

3. Add the **onion, garlic, salt** and **pepper,** and stir until the beans are coated with the sauce.

Broad Beans in Soured Cream ½

Preparation: **15 min**   Cooking: **8 min**   Serves **4**   Cals per portion: **255**

1 lb (450g) frozen broad beans
1 oz (25g) butter or margarine
1 small onion, peeled and finely chopped
4 fl oz (115ml) soured cream or natural yoghurt at room temperature
¼ teaspoon salt
1½ teaspoons paprika

1. Bring about ¾in (20mm) of lightly salted water to the boil in a medium-sized saucepan. Add the **broad beans** and cook, covered, for 6 minutes. Drain in a colander.

2. In the same saucepan, melt the **butter** and cook the **onion** over low heat for 1 minute.

3. Return the beans to the saucepan, add the **soured cream, salt** and **paprika,** and stir all the ingredients together. Heat the mixture, but do not let it boil or the cream will curdle.

Broad Beans with Herbs ½ 🐷

Preparation: **10 min**   Cooking: **28 min**   Serves **4**   Cals per portion: **200**

This hearty dish tastes even better reheated the next day, after the flavours have blended.

2 rashers bacon, cut into ¾ in (20mm) strips

1 medium-sized onion, peeled and sliced

2 medium-sized carrots, peeled and thinly sliced

Pinch ground nutmeg

¼ teaspoon dried thyme

Pinch fennel or anise seeds (optional)

1 lb (450g) frozen broad beans

1 teaspoon salt

¼ teaspoon black pepper

2 tablespoons finely chopped parsley

8 fl oz (225ml) water

1. Cook the **bacon** in a heavy, medium-sized saucepan over moderately high heat until crisp – about 5 minutes. Transfer the bacon to absorbent paper, drain and reserve.

2. Place the **onion, carrots, nutmeg, thyme** and the **fennel seeds,** if used, in the saucepan with the bacon fat. Cook over moderate heat until the onion starts to colour – about 8 to 10 minutes.

3. Add the **broad beans** (break up if frozen solid), **salt** and **pepper,** 1 tablespoon of the **parsley** and the **water.**

4. Simmer, covered, for 10 to 15 minutes. Uncover, and cook another 5 minutes. Before serving, sprinkle with the remaining parsley and crumble the reserved bacon over the top.

> *Tip: For a main course, omit the bacon and substitute 2 tablespoons of butter or vegetable oil for cooking. Brown 12oz (350g) mild salami or cooked sausage, cut it into chunks and simmer with the beans.*

Grated Beetroot Russian Style ½ 🐷

Preparation: **10 min**   Cooking: **20 min**   Serves **4**   Cals per portion: **95**

1½ oz (40g) butter or margarine

2 medium-sized beetroot, coarsely grated

Juice ½ lemon

1 teaspoon salt

Pinch black pepper

4 fl oz (115ml) water

Heat the **butter** in a medium-sized frying pan. Add the **beetroot, lemon juice, salt, pepper** and **water.** Cover and cook over moderately low heat for 20 minutes, stirring from time to time. Add more water if the beetroot appears too dry, but there should be no liquid left at the end of cooking time.

> *Tips: 1. If you halve this recipe, do not reduce the amount of butter. 2. To vary this recipe, add 1 teaspoon of creamed horseradish mixed with 4 tablespoons of soured cream or natural yoghurt.*

Sweet and Sour Broccoli ▢ ½

Preparation: **6 min**   Cooking: **8 min**   Serves **4**   Cals per portion: **210**

This richly flavoured broccoli makes a tangy accompaniment to a main course of roast chicken.

1½ lb (700g) broccoli

6 rashers bacon, cut into ¾ in (20mm) strips

4 shallots, peeled and finely chopped

1 tablespoon brown sugar

2 tablespoons cider vinegar

Pinch dry mustard

¼ teaspoon salt

Pinch black pepper

> **Tips: 1.** *This dish is best eaten right away, since the bacon fat congeals when cool.* **2.** *You can substitute cauliflower for the broccoli.* **3.** *If you want to omit the bacon, cook the shallots in vegetable oil, add the sugar, vinegar, mustard, salt and pepper, and heat the mixture. Toss it with the broccoli and about 2 tablespoons of chopped walnuts.*

1. Trim the leaves and coarse stem ends from the **broccoli,** and cut the stems and the florets into bite-sized pieces.

2. Bring about ¾in (20mm) of lightly salted water to the boil in a large saucepan. Add the broccoli and cook, covered, for 5 minutes or until almost tender, but still crisp.

3. Meanwhile, place the **bacon** in a small frying pan and cook over moderately high heat for 5 minutes, or until crisp and brown. Remove from the pan and drain on absorbent paper.

4. Pour out all but 2 tablespoons of the bacon fat. Add the **shallots** to the pan and cook over low heat for 1 to 2 minutes, or until they are golden. Add the **sugar, vinegar, mustard, salt** and **pepper** to the shallots, and heat the mixture for 1 to 2 minutes.

5. Just before serving, crumble the bacon over the drained broccoli. Add the dressing and toss.

Sautéed Broccoli ▢ ½

Preparation: **5 min**   Cooking: **5 min**   Serves **4**   Cals per portion: **140**

1½ lb (700g) broccoli

3 tablespoons peanut oil or vegetable oil

1 teaspoon salt

Pinch black pepper

> **Tips: 1.** *This recipe works well with tender young green beans.* **2.** *Turn this into an Italian dish by substituting olive oil and adding 4 large slivered cloves of garlic. Heat the oil for 1 minute, remove the garlic, and stir-fry the broccoli as directed. Before serving, squeeze the juice of a small lemon over the broccoli, add salt and pepper, and toss.*

Here is a simple way to cook broccoli that turns it a dazzling emerald green while retaining its natural goodness.

1. Trim the leaves and coarse stem ends from the **broccoli.** Wash the broccoli and pat it dry with absorbent paper. Cut the florets from the stems, then divide them into smaller florets, roughly ¾ to 1½in (20 to 40mm) long. Halve any unusually chunky stems vertically. Slice the stems diagonally, about ¼in (5mm) thick.

2. Heat the **oil** in a large frying pan until small ripples appear. Add the broccoli, lower the heat to moderately high, and cook, stirring continuously, for 4 to 5 minutes or until the broccoli is almost tender, but still crisp.

3. Add the **salt** and **pepper**, and toss well.

VEGETABLES

Broccoli with Red Pepper ½ 🐷

Preparation: **10 min**   Cooking: **5 min**   Serves **4**   Cals per portion: **135**

1½ lb (700g) broccoli

1½ oz (40g) butter or margarine

1 small onion, peeled and chopped

1 red pepper, seeded and chopped

Grated rind and juice 1 lemon

1 teaspoon salt

¼ teaspoon black pepper

Tip: *Cauliflower can be substituted for the broccoli; and a yellow pepper adds an extra dash of colour.*

1. Trim the leaves and coarse stem ends from the **broccoli.** Cut the stems and the florets into ¾in (20mm) pieces.

2. Bring about ¾in (20mm) of lightly salted water to the boil in a medium-sized saucepan. Add the broccoli and cook, covered, for 5 minutes or until it is almost tender, but still crisp.

3. Meanwhile, melt the **butter** in a frying pan. Add the **onion** and the **red pepper** and cook over moderately low heat for about 5 minutes, or until soft.

4. Remove the pan from the heat. Add the **lemon rind, lemon juice, salt** and **pepper**. Drain the broccoli in a colander, put it into a serving dish, and toss it with the onion and pepper mixture.

Brussels Sprouts with Walnuts ½ 🐷

Preparation: **5 min**   Cooking: **10 min**   Serves **4**   Cals per portion: **180**

Brussels sprouts with walnuts make a festive vegetable to serve at Christmas.

1 lb (450g) Brussels sprouts

1½ oz (40g) butter or margarine

2 oz (50g) walnut or pecan pieces

¼ teaspoon salt

Pinch black pepper

Tip: *Omit the walnuts and add 1 or 2 chopped anchovies and 1 clove garlic, peeled and chopped, to the butter.*

1. Remove the loose and faded leaves and trim the stalk ends from the **Brussels sprouts.**

2. Bring about ¾in (20mm) of lightly salted water to the boil in a medium-sized saucepan. Add the Brussels sprouts, and cook, covered, for 8 to 10 minutes or until they are tender but still bright green. Drain them in a colander and rinse them quickly with cold water to preserve their colour and to stop them cooking.

3. Melt the **butter** in a large frying pan, add the **walnuts,** and cook over low heat for 3 minutes or until the nuts brown lightly. Add the Brussels sprouts, the **salt** and **pepper,** and continue cooking for about 2 minutes – or just long enough to heat through.

Sautéed Cabbage ½ 🐷

Preparation: **8 min**   Cooking: **10 min**   Serves **4**   Cals per portion: **160**

Cabbage and bacon are a robust combination. To speed preparation of this dish, prepare the carrots, onion and celery while the bacon is cooking, and while they are cooking, peel and chop the tomatoes.

1 small head cabbage (about 1¼ lb/575g)

4 rashers bacon, cut into ¾ in (20mm) strips

2 medium-sized carrots, peeled and coarsely grated

1 medium-sized onion, peeled and thinly sliced

2 stems celery, thinly sliced

2 medium-sized tomatoes, peeled and chopped

2 teaspoons sugar

½ teaspoon salt

Pinch black pepper

1. Quarter the **cabbage,** trim off and discard the core at the point of each quarter, then cut the quarters into very thin slices. Put aside.

2. Cook the **bacon** in a large, heavy frying pan over moderately high heat for 5 minutes, or until crisp. Remove from the pan and drain on absorbent paper.

3. Add the cabbage, **carrots, onion** and **celery** to the bacon fat in the pan. Cook, stirring occasionally, over moderate heat for 5 to 7 minutes or until the vegetables are almost tender, but still crisp.

4. Mix in the **tomatoes,** remove the pan from the heat, and season with the **sugar, salt** and **pepper.** Crumble the reserved bacon over the top and serve.

> **Tips: 1.** *If you prefer to omit the bacon, cook the vegetables in 2 tablespoons of butter or vegetable oil.* **2.** *Leftovers can be refrigerated and reheated. When reheating, add 1 tablespoon of butter, vegetable oil or melted bacon fat.*

VEGETABLES

Shredded Cabbage with Garlic ½ 🐷

Preparation: **5 min**   Cooking: **16 min**   Serves **4**   Cals per portion: **140**

Serve this full-flavoured cabbage as a side dish. Or cook 9oz (250g) of egg noodles, toss them in butter, and mix them with the cabbage for a light meal.

1 small head cabbage (about 1¼ lb/575g)

2 oz (50g) butter or margarine

2 cloves garlic, peeled and finely chopped

½ teaspoon salt

¼ teaspoon black pepper

1. Quarter the **cabbage,** trim off and discard the core at the point of each quarter, then cut the quarters into very thin slices.

2. Melt the **butter** in a large frying pan, over moderately high heat. Add the cabbage and **garlic,** and stir to coat the cabbage with the butter. Sauté about 1 minute.

3. Cover the pan and cook the cabbage over low heat for about 15 minutes or until it is almost tender but still crisp, stirring occasionally. Season with the **salt** and **pepper.**

> **Tip:** *As a variation, sauté a diced green pepper with the cabbage and season with 2 to 3 tablespoons white wine vinegar.*

Cabbage with Lemon Sauce ⊘ ½ 🐷

Preparation: **5 min**   Cooking: **10 min**   Serves **4**   Cals per portion: **120**

Serve this dish with roast pork, baked ham or sausages.

1 small head cabbage (about 1¼ lb/575g)

1 oz (25g) butter or margarine

1 tablespoon plain flour

7 fl oz (200ml) chicken stock

Juice ½ lemon

¼ teaspoon salt

Pinch black pepper

2 tablespoons grated Parmesan cheese

1. Quarter the **cabbage,** trim off and discard the core at the point of each quarter, then cut the quarters into ¼in (5mm) slices.

2. Bring ¾in (20mm) of lightly salted water to the boil in a large saucepan, and add the cabbage. Cover and cook for 5 minutes or until tender, but still crisp. Drain, and return the cabbage to the saucepan.

3. Melt the **butter** in a small saucepan. Mix in the **flour** and cook over low heat for 1 minute, stirring continuously.

4. Gradually stir in the **chicken stock.** Cook over moderate heat, stirring continuously, for 3 minutes or until the sauce thickens and is smooth.

5. Stir in the **lemon juice, salt** and **pepper.** Pour the sauce over the cabbage and toss to mix. Top with the **Parmesan cheese** and serve immediately.

Red Cabbage with Apples ½

Preparation: **10 min**   Cooking: **13 min**   Serves **4**   Cals per portion: **110**

1 small head red cabbage (about 1¼ lb/575g)

1 medium-sized onion, peeled and coarsely chopped

1½ tablespoons vegetable oil

3 tablespoons cider or wine vinegar

1½ tablespoons brown sugar or honey

¼ teaspoon salt

Pinch black pepper

1 medium-sized apple, cored and thinly sliced

1. Quarter the **cabbage,** trim off the core at the point of each quarter, then cut each quarter into very thin slices and put aside.

2. In a large frying pan over moderate heat, sauté the **onion** in the **oil** until it is soft – about 5 minutes. Stir in the **vinegar, sugar, salt** and **pepper.** Add the **apple** and cabbage.

3. Bring the liquid to the boil, then reduce the heat to moderate. Cover the pan and cook the cabbage until it wilts, about 8 to 10 minutes, stirring occasionally.

Orange-Ginger Carrots ½ 🐷

Preparation: **8 min**   Cooking: **13 min**   Serves **4**   Cals per portion: **80**

**8 medium-sized carrots
(about 1 lb/450g)**

2 teaspoons sugar

1 teaspoon cornflour

¼ teaspoon salt

¼ teaspoon ground ginger

2 fl oz (50ml) orange juice

½ oz (15g) butter or margarine

Tip: You can make this dish in advance and refrigerate it for 1 or 2 days; add a little more orange juice to keep the dish moist.

1. Peel the **carrots,** then slice, cutting them at a slight angle, about ¾in (20mm) thick.

2. Bring about ¾in (20mm) of lightly salted water to the boil in a medium-sized saucepan. Add the carrots and cook, covered, for 10 to 15 minutes or until they are almost tender, but still crisp. Drain.

3. Meanwhile, in a small bowl combine the **sugar, cornflour, salt, ginger** and **orange juice.** Pour the mixture over the carrots and cook over low heat, stirring, for 3 minutes. Remove from the heat and add the **butter.** Toss gently to mix.

Creamed Diced Carrots with Green Pepper ½

Preparation: **10 min**   Cooking: **18 min**   Serves **4**   Cals per portion: **220**

These creamed carrots are particularly good with chicken, turkey or pork.

1½ oz (40g) butter or margarine

8 medium-sized carrots (about 1 lb/450g) peeled and diced

1 small onion, peeled and chopped

1 small green pepper, seeded and chopped

1 tablespoon plain flour

4 fl oz (115ml) chicken stock or water

6 fl oz (175ml) single cream or milk

1 pinch each dried rosemary and ground nutmeg

¼ teaspoon salt

Pinch black pepper

1. Melt the **butter** in a medium-sized saucepan over moderate heat. Add the **carrots** and **onion,** and stir. Cover, lower the heat, and cook for 10 minutes. Add the **pepper,** cover, and cook another 2 minutes.

2. Sprinkle in the **flour,** stir, then add the **stock, cream** and **seasonings.** Stir well.

3. Bring the mixture just to the boil, stirring continuously, then cover and simmer for 4 to 5 minutes or until the carrots are just tender and slightly crunchy.

Tips: 1. If you want to prepare this dish in advance, slightly undercook the carrots and reheat slowly. 2. For extra taste and richness, add 2oz (50g) grated Swiss cheese to the carrots at the end of the cooking.

Carrot and Potato Purée

Preparation: **10 min**   Cooking: **23 min**   Serves **4**   Cals per portion: **125**

1 medium-sized onion, peeled and chopped

1 oz (25g) butter or margarine

8 medium-sized carrots (about 1 lb/450g), peeled and cut into ½ in (15mm) slices

3 small potatoes, peeled and quartered

½ pint (285ml) water

2 teaspoons sugar

½ teaspoon salt

Pinch black pepper

2 tablespoons finely chopped parsley

Tip: For a more unusual flavour, substitute turnips for the potatoes.

1. In a medium-sized saucepan over moderately high heat, cook the **onion** in the **butter** until soft and golden – about 3 or 4 minutes. Add the **carrots, potatoes** and **water,** and bring to the boil. Cover, reduce the heat to moderate, and simmer for 20 to 25 minutes or until the vegetables are tender.

2. Remove the carrots and potatoes with a slotted spoon and mash them well. Return the vegetables to the saucepan, add the **sugar, salt** and **pepper,** and stir. Cook for about 3 minutes longer, or until the mixture thickens slightly. Serve sprinkled with the **parsley.**

Cauliflower Fritters

Preparation: **10 min**   Cooking: **15 min**   Serves **4**   Cals per portion: **135**

1 small head cauliflower (about 1¼ lb/575g)

2 tablespoons plain flour

½ teaspoon salt

Pinch black pepper

1½ tablespoons water

1 egg, lightly beaten

1 medium-sized onion, peeled and chopped

2 fl oz (50ml) vegetable oil

Tip: You can make these fritters with broccoli instead of cauliflower; add a little grated lemon rind to the mixture.

1. Separate the **cauliflower** into small florets. Bring about ¾in (20mm) of lightly salted water to the boil in a medium-sized saucepan. Add the cauliflower, bring to the boil again, cover, and cook for 5 minutes. Drain in a colander. Coarsely chop the cauliflower and put aside.

2. While the cauliflower is cooking, put the **flour, salt, pepper, water** and **egg** in a bowl and mix well, then stir in the **onion** and chopped cauliflower.

3. In a frying pan, heat the **oil** over moderate heat until hot but not smoking. Drop the cauliflower mixture, a tablespoon at a time, into the hot oil and sauté for about 3 minutes on each side until golden-brown. Drain the fritters on absorbent paper and keep them warm in a very low oven until ready to serve. Cook the remaining mixture in the same way.

Cauliflower with Tomatoes

Preparation: **10 min**   Cooking: **11 min**   Serves **4**   Cals per portion: **160**

This dish is ideal for warm weather and picnics.

1 medium-sized head cauliflower (about 1½ lb/700g)

2 tablespoons vegetable oil

2 tablespoons olive oil

1 large onion, peeled and chopped

2 tablespoons cider vinegar

2 large tomatoes, peeled and chopped

½ teaspoon dried oregano

½ teaspoon dried basil

½ teaspoon salt

Pinch black pepper

1. Separate the **cauliflower** into small florets. Bring about ¾in (20mm) of lightly salted water to the boil in a large saucepan. Add the cauliflower. When the water returns to the boil, remove the cauliflower and drain.

2. Put the **vegetable oil, olive oil** and cauliflower into a large frying pan and cook over moderate heat until the edges of the cauliflower begin to brown – 3 to 4 minutes.

3. Add the **onion** and continue cooking for about 3 minutes. Add the **vinegar** and cover the pan. Lower the heat and cook for another 3 minutes.

4. Add the **tomatoes, oregano, basil, salt** and **pepper.** Cover and simmer until the cauliflower is tender – about 2 minutes. Do not overcook.

Tip: *Serve leftovers lightly chilled as a salad.*

VEGETABLES

Sweetcorn in Parsley Cream ½

Preparation: **3 min**   Cooking: **7 min**   Serves **4**   Cals per portion: **290**

1 lb (450g) frozen sweetcorn kernels, thawed and drained

1 oz (25g) butter or margarine

½ teaspoon salt

¼ teaspoon black pepper

2 teaspoons finely chopped parsley

1 teaspoon paprika

4 fl oz (115ml) double cream

1. Cook the **sweetcorn** and drain thoroughly. Melt the **butter** in a large frying pan over moderately low heat. Add the sweetcorn and cook for 4 to 5 minutes, stirring continuously to prevent sticking.

2. Season with the **salt, pepper, parsley** and **paprika.** Stir in the **cream** and bring just to serving temperature, but do not boil.

Tip: *Leftovers can be refrigerated and gently reheated.*

Sautéed Sweetcorn with Chillies ½

Preparation: **10 min**   Cooking: **11 min**   Serves **4**   Cals per portion: **330**

This tasty dish makes a satisfying light lunch.

2 oz (50g) butter or margarine

1 large onion, finely chopped

1 lb (450g) frozen sweetcorn kernels, thawed and drained

2 preserved green chillies, finely chopped

4 tomatoes, peeled and chopped

1½ teaspoons dried oregano

1 teaspoon salt

4 oz (115g) grated strong Cheddar cheese

1. Melt the **butter** in a large frying pan, add the **onion** and cook, covered, over moderate heat for 5 minutes.

2. Add the **sweetcorn, chillies, tomatoes, oregano** and **salt.** Cover and cook over moderate heat for 10 minutes, stirring once or twice.

3. Top with the **cheese,** reduce the heat and cook for 1 minute or until the cheese melts.

> *Tip:* To make a milder version of this dish, use 1 medium-sized pepper, seeded and finely chopped, in place of the chillies.

Grilled Aubergines ½

Preparation: **5 min**   Cooking: **10 min**   Serves **4**   Cals per portion: **190**

2 medium-sized aubergines

2 tomatoes, peeled and coarsely chopped

1 large onion, peeled and chopped

3 cloves garlic, peeled and finely chopped

1 teaspoon salt

Pinch black pepper

1 teaspoon dried basil

4 tablespoons olive oil or vegetable oil

2 tablespoons grated Parmesan cheese

1. Preheat the grill. Slice the **aubergines** into ¾in (20mm) rounds and put them onto a large oiled baking sheet. Scatter the chopped **tomatoes** and **onion** over the aubergines.

2. In a small bowl, combine the **garlic, salt, pepper, basil** and **oil.** Drizzle the mixture over the aubergines.

3. Grill aubergines 4in (100mm) from the heat for 10 to 15 minutes, or until soft and beginning to brown at the edges. Sprinkle with the **cheese** and serve.

> *Tips: 1.* If this recipe is halved, use a medium-sized onion instead of half a large one. *2.* For an alternative topping, sprinkle the aubergines with 3 tablespoons of chopped pitted olives.

Scalloped Aubergines ½

Preparation: **12 min**   Cooking: **30 min**   Serves **4**   Cals per portion: **170**

Rich and hearty, yet low in fat, this is a good main-course vegetable dish.

2 medium-sized aubergines

1 tablespoon olive oil

1 medium-sized onion, peeled and chopped

2 cloves garlic, peeled and finely chopped

1 teaspoon dried rosemary

1 teaspoon dried oregano

½ teaspoon salt

¼ teaspoon black pepper

4 tomatoes, peeled and chopped

4 oz (115g) grated Swiss cheese

1. Preheat the oven to 190°C (375°F, gas mark 5). Cut **aubergines** into ¾in (20mm) cubes. Bring about ¾in (20mm) of lightly salted water to the boil in a medium-sized saucepan, and add the aubergines. Boil for 1 minute – do not overcook. Drain the aubergines and put aside.

2. Heat the **oil** in the saucepan, add the **onion** and **garlic** and cook over low heat for 5 minutes.

3. Place the aubergines in a greased ovenproof dish and top them with the onion, garlic, **rosemary, oregano, salt, pepper** and **tomatoes.**

4. Bake for 25 minutes. Sprinkle with the **cheese** and bake for an additional 5 minutes, or until the cheese melts.

Tips: 1. This dish can easily be made in advance – just refrigerate and reheat. 2. For a richer dish, omit the oregano, rosemary and tomatoes, and substitute 1 egg beaten with 4fl oz (115ml) double cream; pour the mixture over the aubergines just before baking.

Mushrooms à la Crème ½

Preparation: **5 min**   Cooking: **10 min**   Serves **4**   Cals per portion: **135**

1 lb (450g) small button mushrooms

Juice 1 lemon

½ oz (15g) butter or margarine

1 tablespoon olive oil

½ small onion, peeled and finely chopped

¼ teaspoon salt

½ teaspoon black pepper

1½ tablespoons finely chopped parsley

4 fl oz (115ml) soured cream

1. Wash the **mushrooms**, trim the stems level with the caps and pat them dry. Sprinkle with a little of the **lemon juice.**

2. In a large, heavy frying pan, melt the **butter** with the **olive oil** over a moderately low heat. Add the **onion** and cook for 1 minute, then add the mushrooms and shake the pan so that they do not stick. Sprinkle with the **salt, pepper** and **parsley.** Shake the pan. Add the **soured cream** and 1 tablespoon lemon juice, stir, taste the sauce and add more lemon juice as desired. Cook for a further 5 minutes. Serve as an accompaniment to grilled meat or poultry, or on toast for a light meal.

Stuffed Baked Onions

Preparation: **15 min**   Cooking: **35 min**   Serves **4**   Cals per portion: **105**

Make the most of your oven and cook this dish at the same time as a joint of meat.

4 even-sized, large onions

½ teaspoon salt

½ teaspoon black pepper

¾ oz (20g) butter or margarine

2 stems celery, finely chopped

4 oz (115g) mushrooms, finely chopped

3 oz (75g) fresh breadcrumbs

1½ tablespoons finely chopped parsley

½ teaspoon dried thyme

6 fl oz (175ml) chicken stock or water

Tip: *For extra flavour, add ½ teaspoon finely grated orange rind to the breadcrumb mixture and the juice of an orange to the stock before baking.*

1. Preheat the oven to 180°C (350°F, gas mark 4). Trim the roots from the **onions** to make a flat base; skin them and cut a slice from the top. With a sharp-edged metal teaspoon, scoop out the flesh leaving a shell ¼in (5mm) thick. Put the shells in a greased casserole dish that holds them snugly and sprinkle the insides with **salt** and **pepper.** Put to one side. Finely chop the scooped-out onion flesh.

2. Melt half the **butter** in a medium-sized frying pan over moderate heat, add the chopped onion and the **celery.** Cook gently for 2 minutes, until the onion is just soft; add the **mushrooms** and cook for another 2 minutes.

3. Mix the **breadcrumbs** with the **parsley** and the **thyme.** Fill each onion shell with the mushroom mixture, top with the herbed breadcrumbs and a knob of the remaining butter. Pour the **stock** into the dish, cover loosely with foil and bake for 35 minutes, basting 2 or 3 times. Transfer the cooked onions to a warmed serving dish and the juices to a small saucepan. Boil the juices over a high heat until reduced by half. Pour over the onions.

Onions and Apples

Preparation: **5 min**   Cooking: **15 min**   Serves **4**   Cals per portion: **135**

4 rashers bacon, cut into ¾ in (20mm) strips

2 medium-sized green apples, cored and cut into ½ in (15mm) slices

½ tablespoon brown sugar

1 large onion, peeled and thinly sliced

2 fl oz (50ml) water

1. Cook the **bacon** in a medium-sized frying pan over moderately high heat until crisp – about 5 minutes. Drain on absorbent paper. Reserve the bacon fat.

2. Put the **apple** slices into the pan with the bacon fat, sprinkle the slices with the **sugar,** and scatter the **onion** on top. Cook over moderate heat for 5 minutes.

3. Add the **water,** then cover and simmer for 10 to 15 minutes, or until the onions are soft. If necessary, add more water during cooking. Crumble the reserved bacon over the top.

Creamed Onions

Preparation: **5 min**   Cooking: **20 min**   Serves **4**   Cals per portion: **115**

2 large onions, peeled and
cut in half crosswise

2 fl oz (50ml) milk

½ oz (15g) butter or margarine

¼ teaspoon salt

Pinch black pepper

Pinch ground nutmeg

2 fl oz (50ml) double cream

1. Place the **onions** in a heavy, medium-sized saucepan. Add the **milk** and enough water to cover the onions. Simmer for 10 to 12 minutes.

2. Drain the onions in a colander, let them cool slightly, then chop coarsely. Return the onions to the pan. Add the **butter, salt, pepper, nutmeg** and **cream.** Simmer, stirring occasionally, for 10 minutes.

Peas with Orange and Mint ½ 🐷

Preparation: **15 min**   Cooking: **7 min**   Serves **4**   Cals per portion: **175**

2 oranges

2 oz (50g) butter or margarine

1 lb (450g) frozen peas, thawed

4 shallots, peeled and sliced

2 tablespoons finely chopped
fresh mint (or 2 teaspoons dried
mint)

¼ teaspoon salt

Pinch black pepper

1. Grate the rind from both **oranges** and squeeze the juice from one.

2. Melt the **butter** in a medium-sized saucepan, add the orange juice and **peas,** and cook, covered, over moderate heat for 3 minutes.

3. Add the orange rind, **shallots** and **mint**, and continue cooking until the peas are tender – 3 to 4 more minutes. Season with the **salt** and **pepper,** and serve.

French Green Peas ½ 🐷

Preparation: **15 min**   Cooking: **5 min**   Serves **4**   Cals per portion: **150**

½ medium-sized head round or
cabbage lettuce

1½ oz (40g) butter or margarine

2 fl oz (50ml) water

1 teaspoon sugar

¼ teaspoon salt

Pinch black pepper

1 small onion, peeled and
chopped

1 lb (450g) frozen peas, thawed

1 tablespoon chopped
fresh parsley

The addition of lettuce to peas reduces the amount of water needed to cook them and adds a touch of elegance.

1. Remove the core and outer leaves of the **lettuce.** Slice the head into thin shreds.

2. Place the **butter, water, sugar, salt** and **pepper** into a medium-sized saucepan. Top with the lettuce, then the **onion**, then the **peas.** Sprinkle with the **parsley** and cover.

3. Bring to the boil, then lower the heat and simmer for about 5 minutes, or until the peas are tender. Spoon them with the juices into individual dishes.

VEGETABLES

Sautéed Green Peppers

Preparation: **3 min**   Cooking: **15 min**   Serves **4**   Cals per portion: **90**

4 medium-sized green peppers

2 tablespoons olive oil or vegetable oil

1 clove garlic, peeled and finely chopped

½ teaspoon red wine vinegar

Pinch sugar

1½ tablespoons capers, drained

1 tablespoon pitted black olives, chopped

¼ teaspoon dried oregano

¼ teaspoon dried rosemary

Pinch salt

¼ teaspoon black pepper

In summer, serve the peppers cold as a vegetable or as an appetiser.

1. Halve and seed the **peppers,** and slice lengthwise into ¼in (5mm) wide strips. Heat the **oil** in a medium-sized frying pan, add the sliced peppers and the **garlic,** and cook over moderate heat for 10 minutes or until the peppers become slightly limp.

2. Add the **vinegar, sugar, capers, olives, oregano** and **rosemary,** and cook for 5 minutes longer. Season with the **salt** and **black pepper.**

Tips: 1. If you cook the peppers for 5 to 10 minutes longer, the flavour is further enhanced. 2. To add colour, use a combination of red and green peppers.

Glorious Mashed Potatoes

Preparation: **9 min**   Cooking: **15 min**   Serves **4**   Cals per portion: **340**

These potatoes always draw praise – do not spoil it by letting people know how quick they are to prepare!

3 large potatoes

2 fl oz (50ml) milk

1 oz (25g) butter or margarine, softened

2 fl oz (50ml) soured cream

3½ oz (90g) cream cheese at room temperature

½ teaspoon salt

Pinch black pepper

2 teaspoons finely chopped chives

1. Peel the **potatoes** and cut them into ¼in (5mm) slices. Place the slices in a medium-sized saucepan, add water to cover, put the lid askew on the pan, and boil for 15 minutes or until tender.

2. Drain the potatoes and mash them with a potato masher or fork, adding the **milk** to moisten them. Mix in the **butter, soured cream** and **cream cheese** until well blended. Season with the **salt** and **pepper,** and sprinkle with the **chives.**

Tips: 1. If you have any leftover potatoes, shape them into patties and fry them in vegetable oil for 5 minutes each side. 2. To keep the potatoes warm for up to half an hour, put them into a covered ovenproof dish and stand in a roasting tin, half filled with hot water, in a moderately hot oven.

New Potatoes with Spring Onions ½

Preparation: **3 min**   Cooking: **18 min**   Serves **4**   Cals per portion: **210**

1½ lb (700g) small new potatoes, scrubbed (but not peeled)

1 teaspoon salt

1 oz (25g) butter or margarine

Grated rind 1 lemon

Juice ½ lemon

3 spring onions, finely chopped

¼ teaspoon black pepper

1. Place the **potatoes** in a saucepan with water to cover. Add the **salt** and bring to the boil. Place the lid askew on the pan and cook the potatoes for 15 to 20 minutes, depending on their size, until tender. Drain.

2. Add the **butter, lemon rind** and **lemon juice,** and stir well over the heat until the potatoes are glazed. Sprinkle with the **spring onions** and **pepper,** and serve.

Baked Sliced Potatoes ½

Preparation: **10 min**   Cooking: **20 min**   Serves **4**   Cals per portion: **220**

Some of these potatoes are crisp, some are chewy – but all are good to eat.

4 medium-sized potatoes

3 tablespoons vegetable oil or melted butter or margarine

1 teaspoon salt

½ teaspoon black pepper

½ teaspoon dried thyme, oregano, sage or basil

1. Preheat the oven to 220°C (425°F, gas mark 7). Peel the **potatoes** and cut them into thin slices. Place the slices in a bowl with the **oil, salt** and **pepper,** and add the **thyme** or other herbs. Toss to mix well. Place the slices in a large greased ovenproof dish, spreading out the slices so that they overlap slightly.

2. Bake the potatoes for about 20 minutes – or longer if you prefer them crisper.

VEGETABLES

Curried New Potatoes ½

Preparation: **3 min**   Cooking: **25 min**   Serves **4**   Cals per portion: **265**

2 oz (50g) butter or margarine

1½ lb (700g) small new potatoes, scrubbed (but not peeled) and quartered

1 teaspoon curry powder

1 teaspoon dry mustard

3 shallots, peeled and chopped

½ teaspoon salt

Pinch black pepper

Tip: To give the potatoes an extra gloss, stir in 1 to 2 tablespoons mango chutney.

1. Melt the **butter** in a large frying pan, preferably non-stick. Add the **potatoes** and cook them over moderate heat for about 10 minutes, stirring occasionally.

2. Sprinkle the **curry powder** and **mustard** over the potatoes, and stir well. Reduce the heat to low, cover the pan, and cook the potatoes another 10 minutes or until tender.

3. Stir in the **shallots, salt** and **pepper.** Increase the heat and cook until the potatoes are crisp and lightly browned – about 5 minutes.

Potato Pancakes

Preparation: **10 min**   Cooking: **20 min**   Serves **4**   Cals per portion: **296**

Try these with roast beef or pork, or with apple sauce for a light meal. The recipe will give you about 16 pancakes, each measuring about 2in (50mm) in diameter and ½in (15mm) thick.

3 large potatoes, peeled and coarsely grated

1 small onion, peeled and finely chopped

1 egg

2 tablespoons plain flour

¼ teaspoon salt

¼ teaspoon black pepper

5 tablespoons vegetable oil

1. Combine the **potatoes** with the **onion,** and set aside. Beat together the **egg, flour, salt** and **pepper.** Heat 3 tablespoons of the **oil** in a large frying pan.

2. Quickly mix the potatoes and onion with the egg mixture to form a batter. Drop rounded tablespoons of the batter into the pan, spacing the pancakes about ¾in (20mm) apart. (You will be able to cook only 8 at a time.) Flatten each pancake slightly with an egg slice.

3. Cook the pancakes for 5 minutes, then flip them over with the slice and cook for a further 5 minutes. Drain the pancakes on absorbent paper, put them on a platter, and place them in a warm oven while you make more pancakes.

4. Add the remaining oil to the pan and cook the rest of the batter precisely as you did the first batch. Serve hot.

Sautéed Sweet Potatoes ½

Preparation: **10 min**   Cooking: **15 min**   Serves **4**   Cals per portion: **200**

4 medium-sized sweet potatoes

2 tablespoons olive oil or vegetable oil

1 medium-sized red or green pepper, seeded and chopped

1 medium-sized onion, peeled and chopped

½ teaspoon salt

½ teaspoon paprika

1 tablespoon finely chopped parsley

1. Peel the **sweet potatoes** and cut them into ½in (15mm) cubes. Bring about ¾in (20mm) of lightly salted water to the boil in a medium-sized saucepan. Add the potatoes and cook, covered, for 5 to 6 minutes or until they are tender but not too soft. Drain.

2. Heat the **oil** in a large frying pan, and add the potatoes, **peppers, onion, salt, paprika** and **parsley.** Sauté over moderate heat for about 10 minutes, or until the potatoes begin to brown. Drain and serve.

> **Tip:** *Alternatively, omit the peppers and paprika and substitute 4 rashers of bacon cut into ¾in (20mm) strips. Reduce the amount of oil to about 1 tablespoon, and sauté the bacon for 2 minutes before adding the potatoes and onion.*

Spinach Dressed with Oil and Vinegar ⊘ ½ 🐷

Preparation: **5 min**   Cooking: **5 min**   Serves **4**   Cals per portion: **125**

A simple way to dress up spinach.

1 lb (450g) fresh spinach

3 tablespoons olive oil

2 cloves garlic, peeled and finely chopped

2 tablespoons red wine vinegar

½ teaspoon salt

Pinch black pepper

1. Trim the **spinach** of coarse stems and blemished leaves, and wash it. Shake dry.

2. Heat the **olive oil** and **garlic** in a large heavy saucepan over moderate heat, and cook until the garlic releases its fragrance – about 1 minute. Add the spinach by handfuls, stirring occasionally with a wooden spoon.

3. When all the spinach has been added, stir in the **vinegar, salt** and **pepper,** and cook over a gentle heat until the spinach just starts to soften. Serve hot, or at room temperature.

> *Tip: This dish can also be refrigerated and served slightly chilled as a side dish or salad.*

Spinach with Two Cheeses

Preparation: **15 min**   Cooking: **10 min**   Serves **4**   Cals per portion: **240**

Even if spinach is not your favourite vegetable, you should like this dish.

1 lb (450g) fresh spinach

2 oz (50g) butter or margarine

4 oz (115g) ricotta cheese or sieved cottage cheese

1 egg

2 tablespoons plain flour

¼ teaspoon salt

Pinch black pepper

Pinch ground nutmeg

2 tablespoons grated Parmesan cheese

> *Tip: To turn this into a more substantial dish, add a 7oz (198g) can drained flaked tuna or salmon.*

1. Preheat the oven to 220°C (425°F, gas mark 7). Trim the fresh **spinach** of coarse stems and blemished leaves, and wash it. Shake dry.

2. Place the spinach in a large saucepan with just the water that clings to the leaves and cook, covered, for 5 minutes or until it is just limp. Drain the cooked spinach in a sieve or colander, pressing out most of the liquid with the back of a large spoon. Chop the spinach finely.

3. Melt two-thirds of the **butter** in the same saucepan. Remove from the heat. Add the chopped spinach, **ricotta cheese, egg, flour, salt, pepper** and **nutmeg.** Beat with a spoon until thoroughly mixed.

4. Place the mixture into a greased, shallow ovenproof dish. Dot with the remaining butter, and sprinkle the top with the **Parmesan cheese.** Bake for 10 minutes or until the cheese browns.

Sweet and Sour Spinach

Preparation: **5 min**   Cooking: **7 min**   Serves **4**   Cals per portion: **140**

1 lb (450g) fresh spinach

4 rashers bacon, cut into ¾ in (20mm) strips

1 tablespoon plain flour

4 fl oz (115ml) water

2 tablespoons cider vinegar

1 teaspoon sugar

¼ teaspoon salt

Pinch black pepper

Tip: *For extra texture, add 2 table-spoons raisins and 1 tablespoon pine kernels to the spinach.*

1. Trim the fresh **spinach** of coarse stems and blemished leaves, and wash it. Shake dry.

2. Place the spinach into a large saucepan with just the water that clings to the leaves, and cook, covered, for 5 minutes or until it is just limp. Drain the cooked spinach well and press out as much liquid as you can. Put the spinach into a serving bowl and place in a warm oven.

3. While the spinach is cooking, fry the **bacon** in a frying pan over moderately high heat until crisp – about 5 minutes. Drain on absorbent paper, put aside, and pour off all but 1 tablespoon of the bacon fat. Blend the **flour** into the remaining fat in the pan.

4. Mix together the **water, vinegar, sugar, salt** and **pepper.** Add this slowly to the flour mixture, blending until thickened and smooth. Pour the sauce over the spinach. Serve with the bacon crumbled on top.

Courgette Patties

Preparation: **8 min**   Cooking: **16 min**   Serves **4**   Cals per portion: **180**

In summer, when you're desperate for a new way to cook courgettes, try these patties.

1 oz (25g) butter or margarine

2 tablespoons vegetable oil

10 oz (275g) coarsely grated courgettes

1¼ oz (35g) plain flour

2 eggs, lightly beaten

½ teaspoon salt

Pinch black pepper

1. Heat the **butter** and **oil** together in a large frying pan over moderate heat. Meanwhile, quickly mix the **courgettes** with the **flour, eggs, salt** and **pepper** to form a batter.

2. Drop tablespoons of the batter into the hot butter and oil to form 6 patties about 2in (50mm) in diameter. Flatten each patty slightly with the back of a spoon. Reserve the remaining batter.

3. Cook the patties for about 4 minutes on each side, or until they are golden-brown and crusty. Transfer them to a plate covered with absorbent paper and place in a warm oven. Using the remaining batter, cook 6 more patties in the same manner, adding another tablespoon of oil to the pan if needed.

Courgette Casserole ½ 🐷

Preparation: **10 min**   Cooking: **12 min**   Serves **4**   Cals per portion: **275**

This courgette and cheese casserole with its breadcrumb topping is a perfect vegetable dish for dinner parties.

2 oz (50g) butter or margarine

1 large onion, peeled and finely chopped

1 lb (450g) courgettes

1 egg, lightly beaten

4 oz (115g) grated strong Cheddar cheese

Pinch ground nutmeg

Salt and black pepper

½ teaspoon dried marjoram

Pinch dried thyme

2 tablespoons fine dry breadcrumbs

1. Preheat the oven to 220°C (425°F, gas mark 7). Melt two-thirds of the **butter** in a large frying pan over moderate heat. Add the **onion** and cook, covered, for 5 minutes or until soft.

2. Meanwhile, cut the **courgettes** into ¼in (5mm) slices. If they are large, quarter them. Add the courgettes to the onion, cover, and cook for 3 minutes or until just tender.

3. In a bowl, blend the **egg, cheese, nutmeg, salt, pepper, marjoram** and **thyme.** Remove the courgettes from the heat, and blend in the egg and cheese mixture.

4. Pour into a greased, shallow ovenproof dish, top with the **breadcrumbs,** and dot with the remaining butter. Bake, uncovered, for 10 minutes or until bubbling, then grill for 2 minutes or until golden-brown.

> **Tips: 1.** *Because of the sharpness of the cheese, you will need very little salt.* **2.** *This dish may be prepared – but not baked – a few hours in advance, covered, and refrigerated.*

VEGETABLES

Stuffed Courgettes ½ 🐷

Preparation: **15 min**   Cooking: **15 min**   Serves **4**   Cals per portion: **155**

4 large courgettes

6 oz (175g) sweetcorn kernels

4 oz (115g) cottage cheese

Salt and black pepper

2 shallots, peeled and finely chopped

3 tablespoons grated Parmesan cheese

Serve as a vegetable main course. While the courgettes are baking, you'll have more than enough time to make a tomato salad to serve with it.

1. Preheat the oven to 200°C (400°F, gas mark 6). Cut the **courgettes** in half lengthwise and scoop the seeds out of each half with a teaspoon.

2. Mix together the **sweetcorn, cottage cheese, salt, pepper** and **shallots.** Spoon the mixture into the courgette halves, mounding it slightly. Top with the **Parmesan cheese.**

3. Place the courgettes into a greased, shallow ovenproof dish and bake for 15 minutes, or until they are tender and the cheese topping has melted.

Baked Courgettes with Tomatoes ½ 🐷

Preparation: **10 min**   Cooking: **25 min**   Serves **4**   Cals per portion: **115**

This colourful dish has a distinctly Mediterranean flavour. Serve it with something simple – roast chicken, for example, or pasta and cheese.

4 medium-sized courgettes

2 medium-sized tomatoes

1 medium-sized green pepper, seeded and chopped

1 medium-sized onion, peeled and finely chopped

½ teaspoon salt

Pinch black pepper

3 tablespoons olive oil or vegetable oil

1. Preheat the oven to 200°C (400°F, gas mark 6). Trim the ends off the **courgettes** and remove the stem ends from the **tomatoes.** Cut both vegetables into ½in (15mm) slices and arrange them in a greased, shallow ovenproof dish with their edges overlapping slightly, alternating the tomato with the courgettes.

2. Scatter the **green pepper, onion, salt** and **black pepper** over the slices. Drizzle the **oil** evenly over the vegetables.

3. Place the dish in the oven and bake for 25 minutes, or until the courgettes are just tender.

> **Tip:** *This dish may be prepared in advance and baked just before serving, or it may be cooked and reheated.*

Savoury Grilled Tomatoes ½

Preparation: **15 min**   Cooking: **3 min**   Serves **4**   Cals per portion: **335**

6 large, firm, ripe tomatoes

½ teaspoon salt

Pinch black pepper

4 oz (115g) grated Swiss cheese

2 tablespoons grated Parmesan cheese

1 tablespoon French mustard

½ teaspoon dried marjoram or oregano

½ teaspoon dried basil

2 fl oz (50ml) double cream

1 oz (25g) butter or margarine, melted

4 tablespoons fine dry breadcrumbs

Although this is an ideal recipe for good summer tomatoes, it is also an excellent way to add flavour to the less fruity winter ones. It's a fine dish for lunch.

1. Preheat the grill. Remove the stem ends from the **tomatoes,** and cut the tomatoes into ½in (15mm) slices. Place the slices in a large, greased, shallow casserole dish and sprinkle them with the **salt** and **pepper.**

2. In a bowl, combine the **cheeses, mustard, marjoram, basil** and **cream.** Spread this mixture evenly over the sliced tomatoes.

3. In another bowl, combine the **butter** and **breadcrumbs.** Spoon over the tomatoes and grill 5in (130mm) from the heat for 3 minutes, or until bubbling and golden-brown.

> **Tip:** *You can substitute Cheddar cheese for the Swiss cheese, if you wish, or you can use thin slices of mozzarella.*

Cherry Tomatoes in Brown-Butter Sauce ⟨◎⟩ ½

Preparation: **4 min**   Cooking: **5 min**   Serves **4**   Cals per portion: **130**

2 oz (50g) butter or margarine

Juice ½ lemon

3 tablespoons finely chopped parsley

1 teaspoon dried tarragon

¼ teaspoon salt

¼ teaspoon black pepper

1 lb (450g) cherry tomatoes

Redolent of herbs and rich with butter, this savoury way of cooking cherry tomatoes comes from France.

1. Melt the **butter** in a heavy, medium-sized frying pan and stir over low heat until the butter turns a deep golden-brown. Stir in the **lemon juice, parsley, tarragon, salt** and **pepper.**

2. Add the **tomatoes,** raise the heat, and cook, swirling the pan continuously, until the tomato skins begin to burst – about 3 minutes. Serve with French bread for soaking up the herb butter.

Baked Stuffed Tomatoes ½ 🐷

Preparation: **10 min**   Cooking: **10 min**   Serves **4**   Cals per portion: **165**

4 large, firm, ripe tomatoes

¼ teaspoon salt

¼ teaspoon black pepper

1 small clove garlic, peeled and crushed

1 shallot, peeled and grated

¼ teaspoon dried basil

¼ teaspoon dried thyme

3 tablespoons fine dry breadcrumbs

3 tablespoons finely chopped parsley

2 tablespoons olive oil or vegetable oil

3 tablespoons grated Parmesan cheese

Fill tomato halves with spicy breadcrumb stuffing and bake them in the oven for a special treat.

1. Preheat the oven to 200°C (400°F, gas mark 6).

2. Discard the stem ends from the **tomatoes** and cut the tomatoes in half crosswise. Remove the seeds with a teaspoon.

3. In a small bowl, combine the **salt, pepper, garlic, shallot, basil, thyme, breadcrumbs, parsley, oil** and **cheese.** Spoon the mixture into the hollowed tomato halves.

4. Place the tomatoes in a greased shallow casserole dish and bake for 10 to 12 minutes. The tomatoes should be tender but still hold their shape. If baked longer than 12 minutes, they will be too soft. Serve hot or cold.

Tip: You can use small peppers instead of the tomatoes if you double the filling recipe. Cut the tops off 4 peppers and remove the seeds. Cook them in boiling water for 10 minutes, then stuff and bake them as you would the tomatoes.

Fried Tomatoes

Preparation: **10 min**   Cooking: **6 min**   Serves **4**   Cals per portion: **175**

For best results use only firm tomatoes.

6 ripe or green tomatoes

1 egg

3 oz (75g) fine dry breadcrumbs

½ teaspoon salt

½ teaspoon black pepper

½ teaspoon dried oregano or thyme

4 tablespoons vegetable oil

> **Tip:** *Try this recipe cold, served with a garlic mayonnaise.*

1. Wash and dry the **tomatoes,** but do not peel them. Cut a thin slice off the top and bottom of each tomato and discard. Cut the tomatoes into slices about ½in (15mm) thick.

2. In one pie plate or shallow bowl, beat the **egg** lightly; in another, combine the **breadcrumbs, salt** and **pepper** and the **oregano.** Dip the tomato slices on both sides into the beaten egg, then press the slices on both sides into the breadcrumb mixture.

3. Heat the **oil** in a medium-sized frying pan over moderately high heat. Slip half the slices into the pan using an egg slice and fry until golden-brown, then flip them with the slice, and fry on the other side – about 1½ to 2 minutes on each side. Transfer to absorbent paper to drain. Cook the remaining slices in the same manner.

Glazed Turnips ½

Preparation: **8 min**   Cooking: **17 min**   Serves **4**   Cals per portion: **110**

The brown sugar and orange bring out the natural sweetness of the turnips.

1 lb (450g) turnips

½ oz (15g) butter or margarine

2 oz (50g) firmly packed brown sugar

Grated rind and juice ½ orange

¼ teaspoon salt

¼ teaspoon black pepper

1. Peel the **turnips** and cut them into ½in (15mm) cubes. Bring about ¾in (20mm) of lightly salted water to the boil in a medium-sized saucepan. Add the turnips, cover, and cook for 15 to 20 minutes. Drain.

2. Meanwhile, melt the **butter** in a smaller saucepan, and add the **sugar, orange rind** and **orange juice**. Simmer the mixture for 2 or 3 minutes, or until it has thickened slightly. Keep warm until the turnips are done.

3. Add the drained turnips to the orange mixture and toss briefly over moderate heat until they are just glazed. Season with the **salt** and **pepper**.

> **Tip:** *Try the turnips creamed. After boiling, drain the turnips. Melt 1½ tablespoons of butter in the saucepan, add the turnips, 4 tablespoons cream, and ½ teaspoon grated lemon rind. Bring to the boil and serve.*

POULTRY

POULTRY

Poultry can often be one of the least expensive meats to use for a main course. It is high in protein, low in cholesterol and most people like it.

Chicken, in particular, is exceptionally versatile because of its mild flavour. It goes well with all types of vegetables, herbs and spices, and even fruits. Here you'll find many new and interesting delicacies, including golden nuggets of chicken with herbs and cheese, chicken breasts with an elegant mustard cream sauce and intriguingly spiced dishes from around the world. In some recipes, chicken or turkey has been substituted for more costly beef and veal, as in Chicken Stroganoff, Sautéed Chicken with Marsala and Chicken Scaloppines.

Although roast chicken and roast turkey breast take longer to cook than most foods in this book, they deserve a special place here. You will find that many quick, appetising dishes can be made from the leftovers, such as Chicken with Parsley Dumplings and Chicken in Apple and Onion Sauce. Turkey can be used in these dishes, too, making them doubly useful especially at Christmas.

Basic Grilled Chicken

Preparation: **3 min**   Cooking: **12-15 mins**   Serves **4**   Cals per portion: **325**

Grilled chicken is one of the simplest of all meat dishes. It is also remarkably versatile. Whether you cook the basic grilled chicken described in the main recipe or one of the variations given in the Tips below, you will have a tasty, satisfying main course.

1 oven-ready chicken (3 lb/1.4kg), split lengthwise or quartered

½ teaspoon salt

¼ teaspoon black pepper

2 oz (50g) butter or margarine, melted, or 2 fl oz (50ml) vegetable oil

1. Preheat the grill. Sprinkle the **chicken** with the **salt** and **pepper,** and brush with the **butter.**

2. Place the chicken, skin side down, on the rack of the grill pan, and grill 6in (150mm) from the heat for 10 to 15 minutes, basting occasionally with the melted butter.

3. Turn the chicken, brush with the butter, and grill 10 to 15 minutes longer, basting occasionally with the butter. Pierce the thickest part of the thigh with a fine skewer; if the meat is no longer pink and the juices are colourless, the chicken is done. If the chicken browns too quickly, reduce the heat or move the chicken farther away from the heat.

> **Tips:** *Vary plain grilled chicken by adding a simple, flavoured baste. Melt 2oz (50g) butter or margarine in a small saucepan, heat for 3 to 5 minutes and add any of the variations suggested below.*
> *Brush the chicken with the baste and grill immediately, basting occasionally. To give the chicken even more flavour, let it stand for 15 minutes or longer after you have brushed it with the baste.*
> ***Garlic-Grilled Chicken.*** *Add to the butter the juice of 1 lemon, 1 teaspoon dried oregano or rosemary, and 2 to 4 cloves garlic, peeled and crushed.*
> ***Curry-Grilled Chicken.*** *Add to the butter 2 teaspoons curry powder, 1 tablespoon chutney and ½ clove garlic, peeled and finely chopped.*

Grilled Citrus Chicken ½

Preparation: **15 min**   Cooking: **16 min**   Serves **4**   Cals per portion: **295**

4 small chicken leg joints

4 slices lime

¼ teaspoon salt

¼ teaspoon black pepper

Juice 1 lemon

2 cloves garlic, peeled and finely chopped

3 tablespoons olive oil

1 tablespoon chopped fresh mint (or 1 teaspoon dried mint)

1. Make three small deep cuts in the thickest part of each **chicken leg;** cut each slice of **lime** into three, and press one piece into each cut.

2. Stand the chicken legs in a shallow dish; add **salt** and **pepper, lemon juice, garlic, oil** and **mint.** Cover and chill for 4 hours or overnight.

3. Lift the chicken joints out of their marinade and place on the rack of the grill pan, underside uppermost. Place under a preheated grill, 3in (75mm) away from the heat, and grill for 7 to 8 minutes.

4. Turn the chicken joints over, brush with lemon and mint marinade, and grill for a further 7 to 8 minutes until chicken is tender.

5. Serve piping hot with a crisp salad.

Tip: When fresh limes are unavailable, baste each chicken leg with a little melted lime marmalade mixed with a squeeze of lemon juice.

Grilled Chicken with Lemon and Celery ½

Preparation: **3 min**   Cooking: **30 min**   Serves **4**   Cals per portion: **290**

Grilled chicken is an ideal low-calorie dish if it is not drowned in butter. You may, however, find dry-grilled chicken dull and monotonous. If so, add extra succulence and flavour with this variation. The chicken is rubbed with lemon instead of butter and further flavoured with celery. If you are counting calories very strictly, remove the skin before eating the chicken.

1 oven-ready chicken (3 lb/1.4kg), split lengthwise or quartered

Juice 1 large lemon

½ teaspoon salt

½ to 1 teaspoon black pepper

4 stems celery, cut in half

1. Preheat the grill. Make several deep cuts in the chicken flesh. Rub the **chicken** all over with the **lemon juice,** and sprinkle with the **salt** and **pepper.** Place the chicken, skin side down, on the rack of the grill pan. Put 2 pieces of the **celery** into the cavity of each chicken half or 1 piece into each quarter.

2. Place the grill pan 6in (150mm) from the heat, and grill the chicken for 12 to 15 minutes. Turn the chicken skin side up, and place the remaining pieces of celery over the chicken. Grill until golden-brown and tender – about 15 minutes. Pierce the thickest part of the thigh with a fine skewer; if the juices run clear, the chicken is done. Discard the celery. Serve with Baked Stuffed Tomatoes, page 83.

Roast Chicken

Preparation: **5 min**   Cooking: **1½ hours**   Serves **4**   Cals per portion: **325**

1 oven-ready chicken (3 lb/1.4kg)

1 teaspoon salt

1 or 2 cloves garlic, peeled and finely chopped

1 teaspoon dried thyme, oregano, rosemary or sage

1 oz (25g) butter or margarine, softened, or 2 tablespoons vegetable oil

¼ teaspoon black pepper

> **Tip:** *Use the giblets to make stock; any extra stock can be frozen.*

1. Preheat the oven to 190°C (375°F, gas mark 5).

2. Rub the **chicken** inside and out with the **salt, garlic** and **thyme** (or other herb if used). Truss the chicken neatly or secure with skewers.

3. Rub the outside of the chicken with the **butter** and season with the **pepper.** Place the chicken, breast side up, on a rack in a large roasting pan. Cover with foil.

4. Roast the chicken for 1 hour. Remove the foil and continue cooking for a further 30 minutes. A 5 to 9lb (2.3 to 4.1kg) chicken should be roasted at 160°C (325°F, gas mark 3) and takes 2½ to 2¾ hours. The chicken is done when you can easily move the drumstick. To check further, pierce the thickest part of the drumstick with a fine skewer; if the juices run clear, the chicken is done. Let the chicken rest for 10 minutes to distribute the juices and set the meat before carving.

Watercress Stuffing

Preparation: **17 min**   Cooking: **15 min**   Serves **4**   Cals per portion: **150**

2½ oz (65g) butter or margarine

1 medium-sized onion, peeled and finely chopped

2 stems celery, finely chopped

1 bunch watercress, finely chopped

3 oz (75g) diced dry bread

½ teaspoon salt

¼ teaspoon black pepper

Make the stuffing while the chicken is roasting and bake it on a shelf above the bird.

1. Preheat the oven to 190°C (375°F, gas mark 5). Melt the **butter** in a medium-sized pan over moderate heat. Add the **onion** and **celery,** and cook for 10 minutes, or until the vegetables are soft.

2. Stir in the **watercress** and cook, stirring, for 3 minutes. Add the **bread, salt** and **pepper,** and toss to mix. Spoon the mixture into a buttered, shallow casserole dish and bake for 15 minutes.

Chicken Florentine ½

Preparation: **5 min**   Cooking: **30 min**   Serves **4**   Cals per portion: **370**

4 good-sized chicken thighs or drumsticks

About ½ pint (285ml) chicken stock

1 lb (450g) fresh spinach

2½ oz (65g) butter or margarine

3 cloves garlic, peeled and finely chopped

½ teaspoon salt

¼ teaspoon black pepper

3 tablespoons fine dry breadcrumbs

3 tablespoons grated Parmesan cheese

1. Skin the **chicken.** Poach with sufficient **stock** to half cover for 20 minutes, until tender.

2. Preheat the grill. Trim the **spinach** of coarse stems and blemished leaves, wash it and shake dry. Melt half the **butter** in a large saucepan, add the **garlic, salt** and **pepper,** and cook over moderately low heat for 1 or 2 minutes, until golden but not brown. Add the spinach and cook, stirring, until it is just limp – 4 to 5 minutes. Transfer the spinach to a large, buttered, flameproof casserole dish.

3. Drain the chicken and place it on top of the spinach. Melt the remaining butter, combine with the **breadcrumbs** and **cheese,** and sprinkle the mixture over the chicken. Grill 4in (100mm) from the heat until the chicken is golden-brown – about 3 or 4 minutes.

Stir-Fried Chicken with Avocado and Cashews

Preparation: **10 min**   Cooking: **10 min**   Serves **4**   Cals per portion: **370**

3 chicken breasts, skinned and boned

4 tablespoons olive oil

1 small onion, peeled and finely chopped

1 clove garlic, peeled and finely chopped

1 medium-sized leek, split, cleaned and cut into matchstick strips

1 green pepper, cored, seeded and cut into matchstick strips

1 large ripe avocado (not too ripe), peeled, halved, stoned and cut into thin slivers

2 tablespoons cashew nuts

¼ teaspoon salt

¼ teaspoon black pepper

2 teaspoons soya sauce

Pinch ground ginger

1. Cut the **chicken breasts** into thin strips.

2. Heat the **olive oil** in a large deep frying pan, or in a wok; add the **onion** and **garlic** and stir-fry briskly for 3 minutes.

3. Add the chicken strips and stir-fry over moderate heat until they start to change colour. Add the **leek** and **pepper** strips and stir-fry for a further 2 minutes.

4. Add the **avocado, cashew nuts, salt, pepper, soya sauce** and **ground ginger;** stir-fry for a further 1 to 2 minutes. Serve piping hot.

> *Tip:* Cashew nuts are not always easy to buy; you can use shelled unsalted peanuts or halved blanched almonds instead.

Chicken and Vegetable Sauté ½

Preparation: **15 min**   Cooking: **15 min**   Serves **4**   Cals per portion: **430**

3 medium-sized potatoes, peeled and diced

6 rashers bacon, cut into ¾ in (20mm) strips

1 small onion, peeled and finely chopped

4 shallots, peeled and chopped

4 stems celery, diced

12 oz (350g) diced cooked chicken

¼ pint (150ml) double cream

½ teaspoon salt

¼ teaspoon black pepper

> *Tip:* You can omit the bacon and use 3 tablespoons vegetable oil instead of the bacon fat.

1. Bring ¾in (20mm) of lightly salted water to the boil in a large saucepan. Add the **potatoes,** put the lid askew on the pan, and cook for 5 minutes.

2. Meanwhile, cook the **bacon** in a heavy, medium-sized frying pan over moderately high heat until crisp – about 5 minutes. Drain the bacon on absorbent paper and reserve. Pour off half the bacon fat. Drain the potatoes.

3. Raise the heat and add the potatoes, **onion, shallots, celery** and **chicken** to the fat in the pan. Cook, stirring, to brown all the ingredients slightly – about 3 minutes.

4. Lower the heat. Add half the **cream,** pressing down on the mixture. Let the liquid cook off completely, then scrape up any crust that forms, and add to the mixture. Repeat with the rest of the cream. This will take about 12 minutes altogether.

5. Add the **salt** and **pepper,** and crumble the bacon over the top. Serve with peas or broccoli.

Chicken with Parsley Dumplings

Preparation: **12 min**   Cooking: **15 min**   Serves **4**   Cals per portion: **390**

2⅓ pints (1.3 litres) chicken stock

12 oz (350g) diced cooked chicken

1 clove garlic, peeled and finely chopped

¼ teaspoon black pepper

6 oz (175g) cooked peas or carrots (optional)

5 oz (150g) plain flour

2 teaspoons baking powder

½ teaspoon salt

2 tablespoons finely chopped parsley

2 oz (50g) butter or margarine

About 4 fl oz (115ml) iced water

1. In a large saucepan, combine the **chicken stock, chicken, garlic, pepper,** and the **peas** if used. Bring the mixture to the boil, lower the heat, and simmer for 1 minute.

2. In a mixing bowl, combine the **flour, baking powder, salt** and **parsley.** Rub in the **butter** until the mixture is the texture of coarse breadcrumbs. Stir in just enough **iced water** to make a light dough.

3. Bring the chicken mixture back to the boil, lower the heat, and simmer for 1 minute. Drop rounded tablespoons of the dumpling dough into the gently bubbling stock, spacing them as evenly as possible.

4. Cover and simmer for 15 minutes without lifting the lid. Ladle into soup plates. Serve with a green salad.

Chicken in Apple and Onion Sauce

Preparation: **10 min**   Cooking: **20 min**   Serves **4**   Cals per portion: **500**

3 oz (75g) butter or margarine

1 medium-sized green apple, peeled and diced

1 medium-sized onion, peeled and chopped

2 stems celery, chopped

4 fl oz (115ml) apple juice

½ teaspoon salt

¼ teaspoon black pepper

Pinch ground nutmeg

1 tablespoon plain flour

¼ pint (150ml) double cream

12 oz (350g) diced cooked chicken

1. Melt three-quarters of the **butter** in a large saucepan over moderate heat. Add the **apple, onion** and **celery,** and cook for 5 minutes.

2. Add the **apple juice, salt, pepper** and **nutmeg,** and simmer, covered, for 5 minutes, or until the vegetables are soft. Remove the lid and cook 5 minutes longer, or until most of the liquid has evaporated.

3. Meanwhile, melt the remaining butter in a small saucepan over low heat. Blend in the **flour** and cook, stirring, for 1 minute. Gradually add the **cream,** stirring continuously to make a thick sauce.

4. Add the sauce and the **chicken** to the vegetables. Cover and heat through.

> **Tip:** For a more unusual flavour, use cranberry juice instead of apple juice.

Curried Chicken with Tomatoes ½

Preparation: **18 min**   Cooking: **10 min**   Serves **4**   Cals per portion: **280**

3 tablespoons vegetable oil

1 medium-sized onion, peeled and coarsely chopped

2 medium-sized peppers, seeded and chopped

1 clove garlic, peeled and finely chopped

½ teaspoon ground cumin

Pinch cayenne pepper

¼ teaspoon paprika

1½ teaspoons curry powder

¼ teaspoon ground ginger

½ teaspoon salt

12 oz (350g) diced cooked chicken

5 medium-sized tomatoes, peeled and sliced

Juice ½ lemon

Save time by cutting up the cooked chicken while the spices are simmering.

1. Heat the **oil** in a large, heavy saucepan over moderate heat. Add the **onion** and **peppers,** and cook, covered, for 5 minutes, or until the onion is soft.

2. Add the **garlic, cumin, cayenne pepper, paprika, curry powder, ginger** and **salt.** Reduce the heat to low and simmer, covered, for 8 minutes longer, stirring occasionally.

3. Put the **chicken** and the **tomatoes** with their juice into the pan. Simmer for 10 minutes, or until the chicken has heated through and the liquid has thickened slightly.

4. Stir in the **lemon juice.** Serve with rice, noodles or potatoes.

> **Tips: 1.** You can make this dish in advance and refrigerate it for 1 or 2 days. **2.** Substitute beef or lamb for the chicken if you like.

Creamy Chicken Curry ½

Preparation: **5 min**   Cooking: **30 min**   Serves **4**   Cals per portion: **490**

2 oz (50g) butter or margarine

1 small onion, peeled and finely chopped

1 small apple, peeled, cored and finely chopped

2 tablespoons plain flour

12 fl oz (340ml) chicken stock

4 fl oz (115ml) double cream

½ teaspoon salt

4 teaspoons curry powder

Pinch cayenne pepper

¼ teaspoon ground ginger

1¼ lb (575g) diced cooked chicken

1. Melt the **butter** in a large, heavy frying pan over moderately high heat. Add the **onion** and **apple**, and cook for 5 minutes, or until tender.

2. Blend in the **flour,** add the **chicken stock** and **cream,** and cook, stirring continuously, until the sauce has thickened – about 10 minutes.

3. Stir in the **salt, curry powder, cayenne pepper** and **ginger.** Add the **chicken** and simmer, covered, over very low heat for 10 minutes. Serve with rice and Shredded Cabbage with Garlic, page 67.

Tips: 1. You can substitute turkey for the chicken. 2. Serve something refreshing with the curry such as a side dish of chopped cucumbers, shallots and radishes, moistened with a little white vinegar.

Chicken Ratatouille

Preparation: **5 min**   Cooking: **35 min**   Serves **4**   Cals per portion: **280**

1 x 15 oz (425g) can tomatoes in their own juice

1 clove garlic, peeled and crushed

1 small onion, peeled and thinly sliced

1 red pepper, seeded and sliced

1 small aubergine, cut into small cubes

¼ teaspoon salt

¼ teaspoon black pepper

1 tablespoon chopped fresh basil (or 1 teaspoon dried basil)

4 chicken portions (either small leg joints or chicken breasts)

1. Put the canned **tomatoes** into a shallow pan with the **garlic, onion, peppers, aubergine, salt, pepper** and **basil.** Simmer gently for 5 minutes.

2. Add the **chicken portions** and baste with the sauce; cover and simmer gently until tender. Serve piping hot.

Tip: When fresh tomatoes are plentiful, and reasonably priced, use 1¼lb (575g) skinned and roughly chopped, in place of the canned ones.

POULTRY

93

Chicken and Herb Patties

Preparation: **30 min**   Cooking: **6 min**   Serves **4**   Cals per portion: **370**

3 oz (75g) butter or margarine

1 small onion, peeled and finely chopped

½ teaspoon dried thyme

½ teaspoon dried marjoram

12 oz (350g) cooked chicken, finely chopped

2 tablespoons plain flour

2 tablespoons finely chopped parsley

1 tablespoon French mustard

1 teaspoon salt

Pinch black pepper

2 tablespoons milk

1 egg, lightly beaten

2 oz (50g) grated Parmesan or Pecorino cheese

1. Melt a third of the **butter** in a large, heavy frying pan. Add the **onion,** and cook over moderate heat until soft – about 5 minutes. Blend in the **thyme** and **marjoram,** and cook for 1 minute. Stir in the **chicken, flour, parsley, mustard, salt, pepper** and **milk,** and cook for 3 minutes. Remove the pan from the heat and stir in the **egg** and **cheese.**

2. Pour the mixture into a greased, shallow dish, spreading it evenly. Chill in the freezer for 15 minutes, or until stiff enough to shape.

3. Shape the mixture into 4 oval patties.

4. Melt the remaining butter in the pan over moderately high heat and brown the patties for 3 to 4 minutes on each side.

> *Tips: **1.** You can substitute leftover ham for the chicken, if you wish. **2.** These patties reheat well – a good dish to make in advance; they can also be frozen.*

Sautéed Chicken with Marsala ◎ ½

Preparation: **7 min**   Cooking: **8 min**   Serves **4**   Cals per portion: **465**

This dinner-party dish has a delicate and sophisticated flavour, yet it is fast and easy to prepare.

4 chicken breasts, skinned and boned

3 tablespoons vegetable oil

2 oz (50g) plain flour

½ teaspoon salt

Pinch black pepper

¼ pint (150ml) Marsala, sweet vermouth or sweet sherry

1½ oz (40g) butter or margarine

> *Tip: You can use veal fillet instead of the chicken breasts.*

1. Lay each **chicken breast** on the work surface and slice in two lengthwise.

2. Heat the **oil** in a heavy, medium-sized frying pan over moderately high heat. Place the **flour** in a shallow dish. Coat the chicken breasts with the flour and shake off any excess. Place half the pieces in the pan and brown them for 1 minute on each side. Continue cooking until the chicken is tender. Transfer to a warm plate, and season with the **salt** and **pepper.** Cook the remaining pieces.

3. Tip the pan and skim off most of the fat. Add the **Marsala** and boil briskly for 1 minute, scraping up any brown bits stuck to the pan. Add the **butter** and any juices that have accumulated from the chicken on the plate. When the sauce thickens, reduce the heat, add the chicken breasts, turning and basting them with the sauce once or twice. Serve immediately.

Tarragon Chicken Breasts ▷ ½

Preparation: **1 min**   Cooking: **25 min**   Serves **4**   Cals per portion: **410**

1 oz (25g) butter or margarine

4 chicken breasts, skinned and boned

2 teaspoons plain flour

½ teaspoon salt

¼ teaspoon black pepper

½ teaspoon dried tarragon

1 teaspoon French mustard

4 fl oz (115ml) dry white wine or chicken stock

4 fl oz (115ml) double cream

> **Tip:** *Use a coarse-grain mustard for a more interesting texture.*

1. Melt the **butter** in a heavy, medium-sized frying pan over moderately high heat. Add the **chicken breasts** and brown about 3 minutes on each side. Continue cooking until the chicken is tender. Do not overcook. Transfer the chicken to a warm plate.

2. Add the **flour, salt, pepper, tarragon** and **mustard.** Gradually stir in the **wine.** Cook, stirring and scraping up any brown bits stuck to the pan. Continue to cook until the liquid has reduced by half. Add the **cream** and cook until the mixture thickens slightly. Return the chicken and any accumulated juices to the pan to reheat. Spoon the sauce over the chicken. Serve with green beans or buttered new potatoes.

Chicken Breasts Geneva

Preparation: **15 min**   Cooking: **25 min**   Serves **4**   Cals per portion: **480**

2 oz (50g) butter or margarine

2 tablespoons vegetable oil

1 stem celery, cut into thin, 2 in (50mm) strips

2 small carrots, peeled and cut into thin, 2 in (50mm) strips

1 medium-sized onion, peeled and finely chopped

4 slices cooked ham, cut into thin strips

½ teaspoon salt

¼ teaspoon black pepper

1 oz (25g) plain flour

4 chicken breasts, skinned and boned

4 thin slices Swiss cheese

1. Preheat the grill. Melt half of the **butter** with 1 tablespoon of the **oil** in a heavy, medium-sized frying pan over moderate heat. Add the **celery, carrots, onion** and **ham.** Lower the heat, cover, and cook for 10 minutes, stirring occasionally. (The vegetables should not brown.) Meanwhile, blend the **salt, pepper** and **flour** in a small bowl.

2. Remove the contents of the pan to a plate, and set aside. Heat the remaining butter and oil in the same pan, over moderately high heat. Coat the **chicken breasts** with the flour mixture and shake off any excess. Place the chicken in the pan and brown for 3 minutes on each side. Continue cooking until the chicken is tender, lowering the heat to moderate, if necessary, to prevent burning.

3. Arrange the chicken pieces in a foil-lined, shallow flameproof dish. Top each piece with some of the vegetable-ham mixture, then with a slice of **cheese.** Grill until the cheese melts. Watch carefully to prevent the cheese from burning.

POULTRY

Chicken Escalopes with Mint

Preparation: **25 min**   Cooking: **8 min**   Serves **4**   Cals per portion: **690**

4 chicken breasts, skinned and boned

2 tablespoons seasoned flour

1 egg, beaten

3 tablespoons fine dry breadcrumbs

2 oz (50g) butter

2 tablespoons vegetable oil

7 fl oz (200ml) mayonnaise

7 fl oz (200ml) soured cream

¼ teaspoon salt

¼ teaspoon black pepper

Finely grated rind 1 orange

2 spring onions, chopped

1 tablespoon chopped fresh mint

Peeled segments of large orange

Sprigs fresh mint

1. Put the **chicken breasts** between two sheets of waxed paper; batten out with a rolling pin until quite thin.

2. Dust with **seasoned flour,** then dip into **beaten egg** and **breadcrumbs** to give an even coating.

3. Heat the **butter** and **oil** in a large shallow pan; add the chicken breasts and cook for about 4 minutes on each side.

4. For the sauce: Mix the **mayonnaise** with the **soured cream, salt, pepper, orange rind, spring onions** and **chopped mint.**

5. Drain the cooked chicken escalopes on absorbent paper, and arrange on a serving dish. Spoon sauce along the centre, and garnish with orange segments and mint.

> **Tip:** *For a less rich sauce, substitute thick natural yoghurt for the soured cream.*

Golden Chicken Nuggets ⊙

Preparation: **10 min**   Cooking: **10 min**   Serves **4**   Cals per portion: **420**

Serve these tasty nuggets as a main course (about 8 pieces per portion), or as a starter.

4 chicken breasts, skinned and boned

4 tablespoons fine dry breadcrumbs

2 tablespoons grated Parmesan cheese

1 teaspoon salt

¼ teaspoon black pepper

1 teaspoon dried thyme

1 teaspoon dried basil

3½ oz (90g) butter or margarine, melted

Lemon wedges

1. Preheat the oven to 200°C (400°F, gas mark 6). Cut each **chicken breast** into 1½in (40mm) cubes.

2. Combine the **breadcrumbs, cheese, salt, pepper, thyme** and **basil,** and spread the mixture on a plate. Dip the chicken cubes into the melted **butter,** then coat with the crumb mixture.

3. Arrange the cubes in a single layer on a foil-lined baking sheet. Bake for 10 minutes, or until tender. Serve with **lemon wedges.**

> **Tip:** *You can prepare these nuggets in advance. Cover and refrigerate, and bake just before serving.*

Chicken Scaloppines ⊘

Preparation: **10 min** Cooking: **7 min**　　　Serves **4** Cals per portion: **420**

Scaloppines should be made at the last minute – so have all ingredients ready and vegetables prepared before starting the chicken.

4 chicken breasts, skinned and boned

3 tablespoons vegetable oil

3 tablespoons plain flour

½ teaspoon salt

Pinch black pepper

1½ oz (40g) butter or margarine

Grated rind 1 lemon

2 cloves garlic, peeled and finely chopped

3 tablespoons parsley, finely chopped

4 fl oz (115ml) chicken stock

> **Tip:** *You can use turkey instead of chicken. Add a little chopped sage and a tablespoon or two of sherry.*

1. Lay each **chicken breast** on the work surface, place your hand flat over it, and halve the chicken horizontally.

2. Heat the **oil** in a heavy, medium-sized frying pan over moderately high heat. In a shallow dish, combine the **flour, salt** and **pepper.** Press the chicken into the flour mixture, coating the pieces on both sides. Shake off any excess flour. Place half the pieces in the pan and brown them for 1 minute on each side. Continue cooking until the chicken is tender. Transfer to a warm plate. Cook the remaining chicken breasts in the same way.

3. Add the **butter** to the pan, along with the **lemon rind, garlic** and **parsley.** Add the **chicken stock,** scraping up any brown bits stuck to the pan. Bring the liquid to the boil and let it cook until it thickens slightly.

4. Return the chicken breasts to the pan, along with any accumulated juices, and coat with the sauce. Serve with green beans and potatoes or rice.

Chicken Stroganoff

Preparation: **8 min** Cooking: **8 min**　　　Serves **4** Cals per portion: **460**

4 chicken breasts, skinned and boned

2 oz (50g) butter or margarine

1 teaspoon salt

1 medium-sized onion, peeled and finely chopped

6 oz (175g) mushrooms, sliced

1½ teaspoons paprika

¼ cup water

1 tablespoon plain flour

3 tablespoons dry sherry, dry vermouth or water

8 fl oz (225ml) soured cream or natural yoghurt

1. Cut each **chicken breast** crosswise (against the grain) into 10 or 12 strips. Melt the **butter** in a large, heavy frying pan over moderately high heat. Add the chicken and sprinkle with the **salt.** Cook for 2 minutes, stirring continuously. Add the **onion, mushrooms,** and **paprika,** and cook 2 minutes longer, continuing to stir. Add the **water.** Reduce the heat to moderate, cover, and cook for an additional 2 minutes.

2. Meanwhile, combine the **flour** and **sherry** in a small bowl. Add the mixture to the pan and cook, stirring rapidly, until the mixture thickens – about 1 minute.

3. Add the **soured cream** and stir until heated through. Do not let the mixture come to the boil. Serve with rice.

Chicken with Mustard Cream ½

Preparation: **10 min**   Cooking: **12 min**   Serves **4**   Cals per portion: **490**

This tasty dish is excellent for parties.

4 chicken breasts, skinned and boned

½ teaspoon garlic salt

¼ teaspoon black pepper

3 tablespoons French mustard

1½ oz (40g) plain flour

1¾ oz (45g) butter or margarine

¼ pint (150ml) double cream

> **Tip:** *Leftovers can be refrigerated for 1 or 2 days. When reheating, do so over a low heat; high heat may curdle the sauce and dry out the meat.*

1. Pound the **chicken breasts** between 2 sheets of waxed paper to a thickness of about ¼in (5mm). Season with the **salt** and **pepper.**

2. Spread both sides of the chicken breasts with 2 tablespoons of the **mustard.** Put the **flour** in a shallow dish, or on a sheet of waxed paper, and coat the chicken on both sides. Shake off any excess flour.

3. Melt the **butter** in a heavy, medium-sized frying pan over moderately high heat. Brown the chicken breasts in the butter for about 4 minutes on each side. (If the chicken has not started to brown after the first 2 minutes, turn up the heat.) Transfer the chicken breasts to a warm plate.

4. Pour the **cream** into the pan and boil rapidly for about 2 minutes, scraping up any brown bits stuck to the pan. Remove the pan from the heat and stir in the remaining tablespoon of mustard. Taste, and add more salt or mustard to the sauce, if you like.

5. Return the chicken to the pan and reheat briefly, basting with sauce. Serve with buttered green peas.

Chicken with Sherry and Raisins

Preparation: **15 min**   Cooking: **18 min**   Serves **4**   Cals per portion: **365**

1 oz (25g) butter or margarine

1½ tablespoons vegetable oil

8 small chicken thighs

1 medium-sized onion, peeled and chopped

¼ pint (150ml) dry sherry

8 fl oz (225ml) chicken stock

½ teaspoon salt

¼ teaspoon black pepper

1½ oz (40g) raisins

2 fl oz (50ml) tropical fruit juice, unsweetened

1. Heat the **butter** and **oil** in a large, heavy frying pan over moderately high heat. Add the **chicken thighs** and cook for 15 minutes, turning them frequently.

2. Add the **onion, sherry, chicken stock, salt,** and **pepper.** Cover, reduce the heat, and simmer for 15 minutes or until tender.

3. Transfer the chicken to a plate and put in a low oven to keep warm. Tilt the pan and skim the fat from the juices. Add the **raisins** and **fruit juice** to the pan. Boil, stirring, until the sauce has thickened – about 3 to 5 minutes. Pour the sauce over the chicken, and serve with new potatoes and a green salad.

Orange and Almond Chicken

Preparation: **12 min**   Cooking: **40 min**   Serves **4**   Cals per portion: **395**

2 tablespoons vegetable oil

1½ oz (40g) butter or margarine

8 small chicken thighs

1 lemon

2 small oranges

4 fl oz (115ml) water

¼ teaspoon ground ginger

½ teaspoon salt

¼ teaspoon black pepper

1½ oz (40g) slivered almonds

1. Heat the **oil** and three-quarters of the **butter** in a large, heavy frying pan over moderately high heat. Add the **chicken thighs** and cook for 15 minutes, turning them occasionally. Meanwhile, grate the rind from the **lemon** and from 1 **orange,** then squeeze the juice.

2. Pour all but 2 tablespoons of the fat from the pan. Add the lemon and orange rind and juice, **water, ginger, salt** and **pepper.** Cover, reduce the heat, and simmer for 15 minutes.

3. Meanwhile, peel the remaining orange, removing all the pith, and divide it into segments. Put the **almonds** and remaining butter into a small saucepan over moderately low heat, and cook until golden-brown – 3 to 5 minutes. Put aside.

4. When the chicken has cooked, skim the fat from the pan juices. Add the reserved orange segments, and simmer for 5 to 10 minutes longer, or until the sauce has thickened slightly. Sprinkle the almonds over the chicken.

Savoury Chicken ½

Preparation: **5 min**   Cooking: **35 min**   Serves **4**   Cals per portion: **340**

3 tablespoons olive oil or vegetable oil

8 small chicken thighs

1 medium-sized onion, peeled and chopped

2 cloves garlic, peeled and finely chopped

3 or 4 anchovy fillets, rinsed and finely chopped

2½ fl oz (75ml) dry white wine

2 tablespoons white wine vinegar

1 tablespoon tomato purée

2 tablespoons capers, drained

½ teaspoon salt

¼ teaspoon black pepper

1. Heat the **oil** in a large, heavy frying pan over moderately high heat. Add the **chicken thighs** and cook for 15 minutes, turning them occasionally. Pour all but 2 tablespoons of the fat from the pan.

2. Add the **onion, garlic, anchovies, wine, vinegar, tomato purée, capers, salt** and **pepper.** Cover, reduce the heat, and simmer for 20 minutes, turning the chicken once or twice. Tilt the pan and skim the fat from the sauce. Serve the chicken with pasta or rice.

> **Tip:** *For a richer, Provençale-style sauce, add 2 tablespoons brandy and 4 tomatoes, seeded and chopped.*

Chicken with Red Wine ½

Preparation: **8 min**   Cooking: **40 min**   Serves **4**   Cals per portion: **435**

1 oz (25g) plain flour

1 chicken (3 lb/1.4kg), cut into 8 small joints

1 oz (25g) butter or margarine

1½ tablespoons vegetable oil

6 fl oz (175ml) dry red wine

6 fl oz (175ml) chicken stock

1 small onion, peeled and finely chopped

2 cloves garlic, peeled and finely chopped

½ teaspoon dried thyme

1 bay leaf

½ teaspoon salt

Pinch black pepper

2 tomatoes, peeled and chopped

4 oz (115g) mushrooms, sliced

Prepare the onion and garlic while the chicken browns, and the tomatoes and mushrooms while the chicken simmers for the first 15 minutes.

1. Put the **flour** on a plate or piece of waxed paper and coat the **chicken** with it. Shake off any excess flour and put the chicken aside. Heat the **butter** and **oil** in a large, heavy frying pan over moderately high heat. Add the chicken and cook, turning the pieces once or twice, until browned – about 5 minutes.

2. Add the **wine, stock, onion, garlic, thyme, bay leaf, salt** and **pepper.** Cover, reduce the heat, and simmer for 15 minutes.

3. Add the **tomatoes** and **mushrooms.** Cover and simmer for 15 minutes longer.

4. Remove the cover, tilt the pan, and skim the fat from the juices. Cook an additional 5 minutes, or until the sauce thickens slightly. Serve with rice or noodles.

Tip: *You can make this dish in advance and refrigerate it for 1 or 2 days.*

Chicken and Sausage with Sage

Preparation: **2 min**   Cooking: **40 min**   Serves **4**   Cals per portion: **620**

8 oz (225g) coarse Continental sausage

¾ oz (20g) butter or margarine

1 tablespoon olive oil or vegetable oil

1 chicken (3 lb/1.4kg), cut into 8 small joints

½ teaspoon salt

¼ teaspoon black pepper

8 fl oz (225ml) dry white wine or chicken stock

1 teaspoon dried sage

Tip: *It is important to use a chunky 'high meat content' sausage.*

1. In a large, heavy frying pan, brown the **sausage** over high heat – about 5 minutes. Remove with a slotted spoon and put aside. Discard the fat.

2. Reduce the heat. In the same pan, melt the **butter,** then add the **oil** and **chicken.** Sprinkle the chicken with the **salt** and **pepper,** and cook, turning the pieces once or twice, until well browned – about 10 minutes.

3. Pour the **wine** over the chicken, and add the sausage and **sage.** Reduce the heat to low, cover, and cook until the chicken is done – about 25 minutes. Tilt the pan, skim off the fat, and serve the chicken immediately with its reduced cooking juices.

Chicken Paprika ½

Preparation: **3 min**   Cooking: **32 min**   Serves **4**   Cals per portion: **450**

3 tablespoons vegetable oil

1 oz (25g) plain flour

1 teaspoon salt

½ teaspoon black pepper

1 chicken (3 lb/1.4kg) cut into
8 small joints

1 small onion, peeled and
finely chopped

7 fl oz (200 ml) chicken stock

1 tablespoon paprika

4 fl oz (115ml) soured cream, at
room temperature

1. Heat the **oil** in a large, heavy frying pan over moderately high heat. In a shallow bowl, combine the **flour, salt** and **pepper,** and coat the **chicken** with it. Shake off any excess flour.

2. Place the chicken in the pan and cook, turning the pieces once or twice until well browned – about 10 minutes.

3. Add the **onion, stock** and **paprika,** cover, reduce the heat, and simmer for 20 minutes.

4. Place the chicken on a warm serving dish, and remove the pan from the heat. Tilt the pan and skim the fat from the juices. Stir in the **soured cream.** Pour the sauce over the chicken.

> **Tip:** *You can substitute natural yoghurt for the soured cream, reducing the number of calories per portion.*

Chicken with Vinegar Cream Sauce ½

Preparation: **5 min**   Cooking: **40 min**   Serves **4**   Cals per portion: **510**

¾ oz (20g) butter or margarine

1 tablespoon vegetable oil

1 chicken (3 lb/1.4kg) cut into
8 small joints

4 cloves garlic, peeled and
finely chopped

4 large carrots, peeled and cut
into ½ in (15mm) slices

1 large onion, peeled and
coarsely chopped

4 fl oz (115ml) white wine vinegar

8 fl oz (225ml) chicken stock

¼ teaspoon salt

Pinch black pepper

½ teaspoon dried thyme

1 bay leaf

8 fl oz (225ml) soured cream

1. Heat the **butter** and **oil** in a large, heavy frying pan over moderately high heat. Add the **chicken** and cook, turning the pieces once or twice, until browned – about 10 minutes.

2. Add the **garlic, carrots** and **onion,** and reduce the heat to moderate. Cover and cook for 10 minutes, or until the onion is soft.

3. Pour off and discard the fat from the pan. Add the **vinegar,** raise the heat to moderately high and cook until almost all of the vinegar has evaporated – 3 to 5 minutes.

4. Add the **chicken stock, salt, pepper, thyme** and **bay leaf.** Cook over moderate heat for 15 more minutes, stirring occasionally. Nearly all of the liquid will evaporate.

5. Remove the pan from the heat, stir in the **soured cream** and serve.

> **Tips: 1.** *This dish should not be reheated because the sauce will curdle.* **2.** *To freeze, complete the recipe to Step 5; add the soured cream just before serving.*

Mexican Chicken

Preparation: **5 min** Cooking: **45 min**   Serves **4** Cals per portion: **460**

3 tablespoons vegetable oil

1 chicken (3 lb/1.4kg), cut into 8 small joints

1 large onion, peeled and finely chopped

2 cloves garlic, peeled and finely chopped

1 tablespoon strong chilli powder

3 oz (75g) rice

12 fl oz (340ml) chicken stock

½ teaspoon salt

Pinch black pepper

3 medium-sized tomatoes, peeled and chopped

2 tablespoons sliced stuffed olives

1. Heat the **oil** in a large, heavy frying pan over moderately high heat. Add the **chicken** and cook, turning the pieces once or twice, until well browned – about 10 minutes.

2. Add the **onion, garlic** and **chilli powder**, and stir to mix. Reduce the heat to moderate and cook for 5 minutes.

3. Add the **rice, chicken stock, salt** and **pepper,** and cook, covered, for 25 minutes.

4. Add the **tomatoes** and **olives**, and stir. Cover and cook 5 minutes longer. Tilt the pan, skim the fat from the juices and serve.

Tip: *For a more 'robust' Mexican flavour, add 6oz (175g) canned sweetcorn kernels.*

Chicken Creole ½

Preparation: **5 min** Cooking: **40 min**   Serves **4** Cals per portion: **375**

1 oz (25g) butter or margarine

1 chicken (3 lb/1.4kg) cut into 8 small joints

1 medium-sized onion, peeled and thinly sliced

1 medium-sized pepper, seeded and cut into ½ in (15mm) strips

2 stems celery, chopped

3 medium-sized tomatoes, peeled and chopped

2 cloves garlic, peeled and finely chopped

½ teaspoon paprika

½ teaspoon dried thyme

½ bay leaf

½ teaspoon salt

Pinch black pepper

4 oz (115g) mushrooms, sliced

1. Melt the **butter** in a large, heavy frying pan over moderately high heat. Add the **chicken** and cook, turning the pieces once or twice, until well browned – about 10 minutes.

2. Add the **onion, pepper, celery, tomatoes, garlic, paprika, thyme, bay leaf, salt** and **black pepper.** Cover, reduce the heat, and simmer for 25 minutes, turning the chicken once or twice.

3. Remove the cover, tilt the pan, and skim the fat from the juices. Add the **mushrooms** and simmer, covered, 5 minutes longer. Serve with rice and a salad.

Tip: *You can make this dish in advance and refrigerate or freeze it.*

Chicken with Orange and Rosemary ½

Preparation: **5 min**   Cooking: **35 min**   Serves **4**   Cals per portion: **325**

2 tablespoons olive oil or vegetable oil

2½–3 lb (1.1–1.4kg) chicken, cut into 8 serving pieces, or 8 chicken drumsticks or thighs

¼ pint (150ml) chicken stock

Coarsely grated rind and juice 2 small oranges

2 cloves garlic, peeled and finely chopped

3 level teaspoons finely chopped fresh rosemary, or ½ teaspoon dried rosemary

1 teaspoon salt

½ teaspoon black pepper

1. Heat the **oil** in a large, heavy frying pan over moderately high heat. Add the **chicken** and cook, turning the pieces once or twice, until well browned – about 10 minutes.

2. Add the **chicken stock, orange rind** and **juice, garlic, rosemary, salt** and **pepper.** Cover, reduce the heat to low, and simmer for 30 minutes, turning the chicken pieces occasionally. Skim the fat from the pan juices and serve the chicken with its cooking juices. Serve with Carrot and Potato Purée, page 70, French Green Peas, page 75, or a salad.

> *Tips: 1. Lemons or limes make a delicious alternative to oranges. 2. Ask the butcher to cut the chicken into pieces, or buy four chicken pieces and cut them in half. 3. Four 1in (25mm) thick pork chops, well trimmed, can be substituted for the chicken.*

Chicken Oriental ½

Preparation: **10 min**   Cooking: **35 min**   Serves **4**   Cals per portion: **390**

2 tablespoons vegetable oil

2½–3 lb (1.1–1.4kg) chicken, cut into 8 small joints

3 tablespoons soya sauce

¼ teaspoon ground ginger

2 teaspoons sugar

¼ pint (150ml) chicken stock

1 medium-sized onion, peeled and chopped

½ medium red or green pepper, seeded and roughly chopped

2 cloves garlic, peeled and finely chopped

2 teaspoons cornflour

2 tablespoons cold water

2 teaspoons cider vinegar

1. Heat the **oil** in a large, heavy frying pan over moderately high heat. Add the **chicken** and cook, turning the pieces once or twice, until well browned – about 10 minutes.

2. Meanwhile, in a small bowl, mix the **soya sauce, ginger** and **sugar** until well blended. Stir in the **chicken stock** and pour the mixture over the chicken. Scatter the **onion, pepper** and **garlic** over the chicken.

3. Cover the pan, reduce the heat, and simmer for 25 minutes. Transfer the chicken to a deep serving dish and keep warm. Tilt the pan and skim the fat from the juices.

4. Combine the **cornflour, water** and **vinegar,** and add to the liquid in the pan. Bring to the boil and cook, stirring continuously, for 2 minutes. Pour the sauce over the chicken. Serve with rice.

POULTRY

Eastern Chicken

Preparation: **5 min**   Cooking: **44 min**   Serves **4**   Cals per portion: **320**

This intriguingly flavoured chicken tastes even better when served warm rather than piping hot.

1 teaspoon salt

2 cloves garlic, peeled and crushed

½ teaspoon ground cardamom or cinnamon

2 teaspoons chilli powder

½ teaspoon ground ginger

2 teaspoons plain flour

1 chicken (3 lb/1.4kg), cut into 8 small joints

4 fl oz (115ml) natural yoghurt

2 fl oz (50ml) water

1. Preheat the oven to 200°C (400°F, gas mark 6). In a small bowl, combine the **salt, garlic, cardamom, chilli powder, ginger** and **flour**. Rub the mixture onto the **chicken.**

2. Arrange the chicken, skin side up, in a single layer in a large buttered baking dish. Bake for 40 minutes.

3. Transfer the chicken to a warm serving dish. Pour all but 1 tablespoon of the fat from the baking dish. Let the dish cool for about 2 minutes.

4. Meanwhile, in a small bowl, beat the **yoghurt** and **water** with a fork until smooth, then add to the fat remaining in the baking dish, mixing thoroughly, and scraping up any brown bits stuck to the dish. Pour the yoghurt mixture over and around the chicken, and serve with rice.

Grilled Coriander Chicken

Preparation: **10 min**   Cooking: **22 min**   Serves **4**   Cals per portion: **395**

If you have time, grind your own spices for a fresher, more distinctive flavour.

2 teaspoons ground coriander

1 teaspoon ground cardamom

½ teaspoon ground ginger

½ teaspoon ground cloves

1 teaspoon black pepper

½ teaspoon salt

2 oz (50g) butter or margarine

4 small chicken legs

1 tablespoon olive oil or vegetable oil

This dish can be prepared up to 2 hours in advance; the spices will permeate the meat as in a marinade.

1. Put the **coriander, cardamom, ginger, cloves, pepper** and **salt** into a small bowl, add the **butter** and mix to a paste.

2. Preheat the grill. Wash and thoroughly dry the **chicken** pieces. Gently loosen the skin from the chicken by easing your fingers between the skin and the flesh. Be careful not to tear the skin. Push the spiced butter between the skin and the flesh; if the skin has been properly loosened, the butter can be squeezed into place by gentle pressure on the outside.

3. Brush each piece with **oil** and place in the grill pan with the non-skin side uppermost. Grill 6in (150mm) from the heat for 8 to 10 minutes, turn, brush with more oil and grill for a further 10 to 12 minutes, basting once or twice with the juices in the pan until the chicken is tender.

Chicken Kiev

Preparation: **20 min** Cooking: **6 min**

Serves **4** Cals per portion: **450**

3 oz (75g) butter or margarine

1½ tablespoons finely chopped parsley

Finely grated rind ¼ lemon

2 cloves garlic, peeled and crushed

3 tablespoons plain flour

½ teaspoon salt

1 teaspoon black pepper

1½ teaspoons dried tarragon

1 egg, lightly beaten

3 oz (75g) fresh breadcrumbs

4 chicken breasts, skinned and boned

Oil for deep-frying

Tip: As Chicken Kiev is quite fiddly to prepare, it is worth shaping several and freezing them.

1. In a small bowl mix two-thirds of the **butter**, ½ tablespoon of **parsley, lemon rind** and **garlic.** Shape into 4 finger-sized rolls and put them in the freezer.

2. Mix the **flour, salt, pepper, tarragon** and the remaining parsley. Put the **egg** in a wide bowl and the **breadcrumbs** on a plate. Melt the remaining butter.

3. Flatten each **chicken breast** between 2 pieces of waxed paper until they are about ¼in (5mm) thick. Place a finger of the cold butter on each piece and roll up the chicken, tucking in the ends, to make a parcel.

4. Heat the **oil** in a medium-sized saucepan, or deep fryer, over a moderate heat. Meanwhile, brush each chicken package with melted butter, roll in the flour, dip in the beaten egg and press into the breadcrumbs, making sure all sides are evenly coated. Lower into the hot oil and cook until golden-brown – about 6 to 8 minutes. Remove them with a slotted spoon and drain on absorbent paper.

Lemon Chicken ½

Preparation: **5 min** Cooking: **40 min**

Serves **4** Cals per portion: **420**

2 oz (50g) plain flour

1 teaspoon dried tarragon

1 teaspoon salt

1 chicken (3 lb/1.4kg, cut into 8 small joints

2 oz (50g) butter or margarine

Juice 2 lemons

1 small onion, peeled and finely chopped

1 clove garlic, peeled and finely chopped

Pinch black pepper

1. Preheat the oven to 200°C (400°F, gas mark 6). Combine the **flour, tarragon** and the **salt** in a bag. Add the **chicken** a few pieces at a time. Shake the bag to coat the chicken with the flour mixture. Remove the pieces from the bag and shake off any excess flour mixture.

2. Melt the **butter** in the oven in a large ovenproof dish. Coat the chicken on all sides with the butter, then turn the chicken skin side up.

3. In a small bowl, mix the **lemon juice, onion, garlic** and **pepper.** Drizzle this mixture evenly over the chicken, and bake for 40 minutes. Serve with Sautéed Broccoli, page 65, or French Green Peas, page 75.

Tip: You can substitute 4 good-sized, lean chump lamb chops for the chicken; trim the fat from the chops and baste frequently as they bake.

Chicken Braised in Apple Juice

Preparation: **10 min**   Cooking: **30 min**   Serves **4**   Cals per portion: **505**

3 oz (75g) butter or margarine

3 tablespoons maple syrup

1 teaspoon salt

Pinch ground cloves

¼ teaspoon dry mustard

1 teaspoon black pepper

1 chicken (3 lb/1.4kg), cut into 8 small joints

3 oz (75g) cornmeal or coarse oatmeal

4 fl oz (115ml) apple juice

Tip: *For a punchier flavour use dry cider instead of apple juice.*

1. Preheat the oven to 200°C (400°F, gas mark 6). Put the **butter, maple syrup, salt, cloves, mustard** and **pepper** into a large baking dish. Place the dish in the oven and heat until the butter melts.

2. Remove the dish from the oven, stir, then coat the **chicken** with the mixture. Put the **cornmeal** on a plate or a piece of waxed paper, and roll the chicken in the cornmeal to coat the pieces evenly. Shake off any excess.

3. Arrange the chicken, skin side up, in the baking dish. Pour the **apple juice** around the chicken, but not over it. Bake for 30 minutes, or until tender, basting occasionally with the juices. Add more apple juice if the liquid evaporates. Serve with Baked Sliced Potatoes, page 77.

Chicken and Asparagus with Tagliatelle ⊘

Preparation: **15 min**   Cooking: **4 min**   Serves **4**   Cals per portion: **485**

1 x 11 oz (300g) can asparagus tips

¼ pint (150ml) double cream

¼ teaspoon salt

¼ teaspoon black pepper

2 egg yolks

Finely grated rind ½ lemon

6 oz (175g) chopped cooked chicken

12 oz (350g) fresh green tagliatelle

1 tablespoon olive oil

1. Drain the **asparagus tips.** Put them into the liquidiser with the **cream, salt, pepper, egg yolks** and **lemon rind;** blend until smooth.

2. Add sufficient of the drained asparagus liquid to give a smooth coating consistency.

3. Put the sauce into a pan with the chopped **chicken** and heat through gently.

4. Meanwhile, cook the **tagliatelle** in a large pan of rapidly boiling, salted water for 3 minutes with the **olive oil;** drain thoroughly.

5. Toss the cooked pasta with the hot asparagus sauce and serve immediately.

Tip: *If you use dry tagliatelle, increase the cooking time by 4 to 5 minutes.*

Chicken and Mozzarella Kebabs

Preparation time: **20 min**   Cooking: **6 min**   Serves **4**   Cals per portion: **510**

3 chicken breasts, skinned and boned

Juice 1 lemon

4 tablespoons olive oil

1 clove garlic, peeled and crushed

1 tablespoon chopped fresh rosemary (or 1 teaspoon dried rosemary)

¼ teaspoon salt

¼ teaspoon black pepper

12 oz (350g) Mozzarella cheese

Seasoned flour

2 eggs, beaten

6 tablespoons fine breadcrumbs

Oil for deep-frying

Finely grated rind 1 lemon

Thin lemon wedges

Sprigs fresh rosemary

1. Cut the **chicken** into even-sized cubes, about 1in (25mm). Put into a shallow dish with the **lemon juice, olive oil, garlic, rosemary, salt** and **pepper.** Cover and chill for 3 to 4 hours.

2. Drain the chicken cubes from their marinade. Cut the **Mozzarella** into cubes slightly smaller than the chicken; thread alternately onto 4 kebab skewers; dust with **seasoned flour,** dip into **beaten egg,** and coat evenly with **breadcrumbs.** Chill briefly.

3. Lower the threaded skewers into a pan of hot **oil** and deep-fry for 5 to 6 minutes, until crisp and golden; drain thoroughly on absorbent paper, and sprinkle with **lemon rind.**

4. Serve immediately, garnished with **lemon wedges** and sprigs of **rosemary.**

> **Tip:** *For a more prominent lemon flavour, add the grated lemon rind to the breadcrumb coating.*

Marinated Chicken in Olive and Tomato Sauce

Preparation: **20 min**   Serves **4**   Cals per portion: **335**

10 oz (275g) cooked chicken, skinned and boned

1 lb (450g) tomatoes, skinned, seeded and chopped

6 tablespoons olive oil

2 tablespoons tomato purée

1 large clove garlic, peeled and crushed

¼ teaspoon salt

¼ teaspoon black pepper

1 teaspoon chopped fresh thyme (or a pinch of dried)

1 tablespoon medium sherry

12 pitted black olives, sliced

1. Cut or pull the **chicken** into strips; place in a shallow serving dish.

2. Put the chopped **tomatoes** into a liquidiser or food processor with the **olive oil, tomato purée, garlic, salt** and **pepper;** blend until smooth.

3. Stir the chopped **thyme, sherry** and **black olives** into the sauce.

4. Spoon the sauce evenly over the chicken. Cover and chill for 3 to 4 hours. Serve with a salad and/or cooked rice.

> **Tip:** *Remember that it is much easier to remove leftover cooked chicken from the carcass while it is still warm; if the chicken is added to the sauce while still warm the flavours blend more successfully.*

Chicken with Watercress Sauce

Preparation: **30 min**   Serves **4**   Cals per portion: **230**

4 skinned chicken breasts, poached

1 bunch watercress, trimmed and divided into sprigs

3 oz (75g) curd cheese

½ pint (285ml) chicken stock

¼ teaspoon salt

¼ teaspoon black pepper

1 clove garlic, peeled and crushed

1 tablespoon chopped chives

12 oz (350g) courgettes

Juice 1 lemon

1. Place the **chicken breasts** in a shallow serving dish.

2. Put the **watercress, curd cheese, stock, salt, pepper** and **garlic** into a liquidiser or food processor; blend until smooth.

3. Stir in the **chives** and spoon the sauce evenly over the chicken.

4. Top and tail the **courgettes.** Put through the shredder blade of the food processor, or grate them coarsely.

5. Mix the shredded courgettes with the **lemon juice** and arrange around the chicken. Sprinkle with extra chopped chives if liked.

> **Tip:** *To poach the chicken breasts: Put them into a deep frying pan with sufficient liquid (white wine, chicken stock, water, or a mixture) to half cover; add seasoning, cover, and simmer gently for about 18 minutes until just tender.*

Roast Turkey Breast with Herbs

Preparation: **10 min**   Cooking: **1¼ hours**   Serves **10**   Cals per portion: **375**

Cooking turkey does take time, but most of the cooking is unattended – and you will probably have leftovers for making Turkey Croquettes, page 109, or any of your own favourite recipes. You can substitute turkey in any cooked chicken recipe.

1 turkey breast (about 5½ lb/2.5kg), thawed if frozen

1 teaspoon dried thyme

1 teaspoon dried sage

2 tablespoons parsley, finely chopped

¼ teaspoon salt

Pinch black pepper

3½ oz (90g) butter or margarine, melted

1. Preheat the oven to 200°C (400°F, gas mark 6). Rinse the **turkey breast** and pat it dry with absorbent paper.

2. Place the turkey, skin side up, on a rack in a large roasting tin. Sprinkle the **thyme, sage, parsley, salt** and **pepper** over the turkey. Brush all over with the **butter.** Roast for 1 hour, basting occasionally with the pan juices.

3. Check to see if the turkey is browning too much. If it is, cover it loosely with foil. Roast for 15 minutes longer, or until the turkey is tender.

4. Remove from the oven and stand at room temperature for 10 minutes before carving.

> **Tip:** *The cooking time given above is for a 5½lb (2.5kg) turkey breast. If you use a larger one, you will have to increase the roasting time, allowing about 15 minutes per 1lb (450g).*

Turkey Croquettes

Preparation: **30 min**   Cooking: **12 min**   Serves **4**   Cals per portion: **450**

2 oz (50g) butter or margarine

1 oz (25g) unsifted plain flour

1 teaspoon salt

4 fl oz (115ml) milk

12 oz (350g) finely chopped cooked turkey

½ small onion, peeled and finely chopped

1 tablespoon lemon juice

1 teaspoon dried tarragon or parsley

1 egg

3 oz (75g) fine dry breadcrumbs

2½ fl oz (75ml) vegetable oil

Tips: 1. You can use chicken instead of turkey. 2. The croquettes can be made and cooked 1 or 2 days in advance and reheated in a 180°C (350°F, gas mark 4) oven.

1. Melt the **butter** in a saucepan over moderate heat, and blend in the **flour** and **salt**, stirring continuously.

2. Gradually stir in the **milk** and cook, continuing to stir, until the mixture thickens – about 3 minutes. Remove the saucepan from the heat, and stir in the **turkey, onion, lemon juice** and **tarragon.**

3. Pour the mixture into a buttered, shallow dish, spreading it evenly. Chill in the freezer for 15 minutes, or until firm enough to shape.

4. Take the dish from the freezer and shape the mixture into 4 oval patties.

5. Put the **egg** and **breadcrumbs** into separate small bowls. Beat the egg lightly. Heat the **oil** in a heavy frying pan over moderately high heat. Take each croquette and dip it first into the egg and next into the breadcrumbs, then place it in the pan. Fry the croquettes until they are nicely browned – about 6 minutes on each side.

Turkey Jambalaya

Preparation: **15 min**   Cooking: **30 min**   Serves **4**   Cals per portion: **460**

2 oz (50g) butter or margarine

6 oz (175g) rice

1 stem celery, finely chopped

½ medium-sized pepper, seeded and chopped

1 small onion, peeled and finely chopped

12 oz (350g) diced cooked turkey

3 medium-sized tomatoes, peeled and chopped

½ pint (285ml) chicken stock

¾ pint (450ml) dry white wine

Dash cayenne pepper

¼ teaspoon dried thyme or sage

This dish, when served with a salad or green vegetable, makes a complete meal.

1. Melt the **butter** in a heavy, medium-sized frying pan over moderate heat. Add the **rice, celery, pepper** and **onion.** Cook, stirring occasionally, until the vegetables are just tender – about 10 minutes.

2. Stir in the **turkey, tomatoes, chicken stock, wine, cayenne pepper** and **thyme.** Cover the pan and simmer, stirring occasionally, for 30 to 35 minutes, or until the rice is tender and the liquid has been absorbed. If the rice becomes too dry, add extra liquid.

POULTRY

Stir-fried Duck with Pineapple Sauce

Preparation: **10 min**   Cooking: **10 min**   Serves **4**   Cals per portion: **505**

Frozen duck portions, either on the bone or filleted, are now available from specialist poultry shops and large supermarkets. Allow them to thaw overnight in the refrigerator.

1¼ lb (575g) fillet or boned breast of duck, skinned and cut into ½ in (15mm) cubes

1 tablespoon plus 1½ teaspoons cornflour

2 tablespoons soya sauce

6 oz (175g) canned crushed pineapple in natural juice

1 tablespoon water

2 tablespoons olive oil or vegetable oil

3 slices fresh root ginger, crushed

1 tablespoon dry sherry

½ teaspoon salt

2 shallots, thinly sliced

1. Put the **duck** in a bowl with the tablespoon of **cornflour** and the **soya sauce** and toss. Leave to stand for 20 minutes, turning the duck occasionally.

2. Place the **crushed pineapple** and juice in a small saucepan and heat slowly. In a small bowl mix the remaining cornflour and **water** to a paste, and stir into the pineapple. Bring to the boil and keep warm.

3. Heat the **oil** in a wok or a medium-sized frying pan over a moderate heat. Add the **ginger,** brown it and then discard. Add the duck, stir-fry for 4 or 5 minutes. Add the **sherry** and **salt** and cook for a further 2 minutes. Transfer to a serving dish and pour the pineapple sauce over the duck. Garnish with the **shallots** and serve with steamed rice.

Chicken Livers with Sage ◌ ½

Preparation: **3 min**   Cooking: **10 min**   Serves **4**   Cals per portion: **325**

2 oz (50g) butter or margarine

1¼ lb (575g) chicken livers (sinews removed), chopped

1 small onion, peeled and finely chopped

1 teaspoon dried sage

4 fl oz (115ml) dry white wine

4 fl oz (115ml) chicken stock

½ teaspoon salt

¼ teaspoon black pepper

> **Tip:** *You can use strips of calves liver in place of the chicken livers.*

1. Heat the **butter** in a medium-sized, heavy frying pan over moderately high heat until bubbling. Add the **chicken livers, onion** and **sage,** and cook, stirring, until the livers are browned but still pink inside – about 5 minutes. Transfer to a plate and put aside.

2. Raise the heat and add the **wine** and **chicken stock** to the pan. Cook, stirring, and scraping up any brown bits stuck to the pan, until only about half the liquid remains – about 3 minutes.

3. Lower the heat. Return the livers and any accumulated juices to the pan, heat the livers for 1 minute, and season with the **salt** and **pepper.** Spoon the sauce over the livers, and serve with buttered noodles and French Green Peas, page 75, or Stuffed Courgettes, page 81.

Chicken Livers in Sherry ▣ ½

Preparation: **5 min**   Cooking: **10 min**   Serves **4**   Cals per portion: **360**

3 tablespoons plain flour

1 teaspoon salt

¼ teaspoon black pepper

1¼ lb (575g) chicken livers
(sinews removed), chopped

1¾ oz (45g) butter or margarine

1 clove garlic, peeled and
finely chopped

8 fl oz (225ml) dry sherry

> **Tips: 1.** *You can substitute 4fl oz
> (115ml) Marsala and 4fl oz (115ml)
> chicken stock for the sherry.*
> **2.** *Leftovers can be refrigerated
> overnight or frozen. Warm through
> over low heat.*

1. Mix the **flour** with the **salt** and **pepper** on a plate or a sheet of waxed paper. Press the **chicken livers** into the mixture, coating them on all sides. Shake off any excess flour.

2. Heat half the **butter** in a medium-sized, heavy frying pan over moderately high heat until bubbling. Add the livers and the **garlic,** and cook, stirring, until the livers are browned but still pink inside – about 5 minutes. Transfer the livers to a plate and put aside.

3. Raise the heat to high and add the **sherry** to the pan. Cook, stirring, and scraping up any brown bits until only about half the sherry remains – about 3 minutes. Remove from the heat and swirl in the remaining butter. Return the livers and any accumulated juices to the pan, baste with the sauce and heat for 1 minute. Serve with rice and accompany with Peas with Orange and Mint, page 75.

Madras-Style Chicken Livers ▣

Preparation: **7 min**   Cooking: **5 min**   Serves **4**   Cals per portion: **220**

1 medium-sized onion, peeled
and finely chopped

1 clove garlic, peeled and
finely chopped

2 tablespoons olive oil

1 oz (25g) butter

1 lb (450g) chicken livers,
trimmed and roughly chopped

2 teaspoons curry powder

1 tablespoon tomato purée

Small piece fresh root ginger,
peeled and crushed

½ pint (285ml) chicken stock

3 tablespoons mango chutney

1 tablespoon chopped fresh
coriander

2 tablespoons salted cashew
nuts, roughly chopped

1. Fry the **onion** and **garlic** in the **oil** and **butter,** in a large, shallow pan, for 3 minutes.

2. Add the **chicken livers** and fry until sealed on the outside; add the **curry powder** and cook for a further minute.

3. Mix the **tomato purée** with the crushed **ginger, stock, chutney, coriander** and **cashew nuts;** add to the chicken livers and simmer for 5 minutes.

4. Season to taste and serve piping hot with plain boiled rice, or fried rice, and a cucumber and yoghurt salad.

> **Tip:** *The rich juices which come out of the chicken livers are sufficient to thicken the sauce lightly; if you prefer a thicker sauce, add 1½ teaspoons cornflour blended with 1 tablespoon water.*

Devilled Chicken Livers  ½

Preparation: **5 min**   Cooking: **7 min**   Serves **4**   Cals per portion: **340**

1 oz (25g) plain flour

2 teaspoons paprika

1¼ lb (575g) chicken livers
(sinews removed), chopped

2 oz (50g) butter or margarine

1 small onion, peeled and
chopped

¼ teaspoon salt

Pinch black pepper

Pinch cayenne pepper

½ teaspoon dry English mustard

1 teaspoon Worcestershire sauce

4 fl oz (115ml) tomato sauce or
chilli sauce

4 fl oz (115ml) water

1. Mix the **flour** and **paprika** on a plate or a
sheet of waxed paper. Press the **chicken livers**
into the mixture, coating them on all sides.
Shake off any excess flour.

2. Heat the **butter** in a medium-sized, heavy
frying pan over moderately high heat until
bubbling. Add the livers and **onion,** and cook,
stirring, until the livers are browned but still
pink inside – about 5 minutes.

3. Lower the heat to moderate and stir in the
**salt, black pepper, cayenne pepper, mustard,
Worcestershire sauce, tomato sauce** and
water. Simmer for 2 minutes. Serve with
steamed rice and a green salad.

> *Tip: You can substitute calves liver, cut into strips, for the
> chicken livers.*

Chicken Livers in Vinegar Sauce ½

Preparation: **2 min**   Cooking: **12 min**   Serves **4**   Cals per portion: **370**

2 tablespoons vegetable oil

¾ oz (20g) butter or margarine,
softened

1¼ lb (575g) chicken livers
(sinews removed), chopped

1 teaspoon salt

½ teaspoon black pepper

1 medium-sized onion, peeled
and finely chopped

2 fl oz (50ml) red wine vinegar

1 small tomato, peeled
and chopped

4 fl oz (115ml) chicken stock

1 teaspoon plain flour

2 tablespoons finely chopped
parsley

1. Heat the **oil** and three-quarters of the **butter**
in a medium-sized, heavy frying pan over
moderately high heat for about 1 minute. Add
the **chicken livers, salt** and **pepper,** and cook,
stirring, until the livers are browned but still
pink inside – about 5 minutes. Transfer the
livers to a plate and put aside.

2. Lower the heat to moderate, add the **onion**
to the pan, and cook for 2 minutes or until
slightly browned. Add the **vinegar** and cook
until only 1 tablespoon of vinegar
remains – about 3 minutes. Add the **tomato**
and **chicken stock,** and bring to the boil.

3. Combine the **flour** and the remaining butter
with a fork, then add to the pan. Stir, and boil
gently, for 1 minute.

4. Reduce the heat to low, return the livers to
the pan along with any accumulated juices,
and simmer for 1 minute or until the livers are
heated through. Sprinkle with the **parsley,**
and serve with potatoes and a green salad.

BEEF

(See also recipes for Lamb, Pork and
Oven-Baked Dishes; some of which
work well with Beef)

BEEF

In this section you will find delicious, imaginative recipes for an assortment of inexpensive steaks, stews, meat loaves, hamburgers and one-pot meals. And as for speed – more than half the recipes require less than 30 minutes' cooking time.

Roast Beef

Preparation: **10 min**　Cooking: **50 min**　　　　Serves **6**　Cals per portion: **300**

Cooking beef this way is both fast and efficient. Serve one piece immediately; 2¾ lb (1.25kg) will give you 6 ample servings. Dice or slice the rest, freeze it, and use it to make recipes calling for cooked beef.

5½ lb (2.5kg) boneless blade or fresh silverside

1½ tablespoons soya sauce

1½ tablespoons vegetable oil

½ teaspoon black pepper

1. Preheat the oven to 220°C (425°F, gas mark 7). Cut the **meat** in half horizontally, and with cotton twine, tie each half across in two places and once lengthwise. Rub with the **soya sauce** and **oil,** and sprinkle with the **pepper.**

2. Place the pieces on a rack in a large roasting tin and roast for 10 minutes in the hot oven. Turn the heat down to 180°C (350°F, gas mark 4) and roast for 20 minutes per 1lb (450g) for rare and 30 minutes per 1lb (450g) for medium. For well-done beef turn the heat down to 160°C (325°F, gas mark 3) and cook for a further 20 minutes. Let the meat rest for 10 minutes on a warm dish before slicing.

Beef with Scrambled Eggs

Preparation: **7 min**　Cooking: **9 min**　　　　Serves **4**　Cals per portion: **320**

1½ tablespoons vegetable oil

12 oz (350g) finely chopped cooked beef

1 medium onion, peeled and finely chopped

2 medium-sized tomatoes, peeled and chopped

3 green chillies, seeded and finely chopped

1 teaspoon salt

¼ teaspoon ground cumin

¼ teaspoon dried oregano

6 eggs

1. Heat the **oil** in a large, heavy frying pan over moderate heat for about 1 minute. Add the **beef** and **onion,** and cook for 5 minutes.

2. Add the **tomatoes, green chillies, salt, cumin** and **oregano** to the pan, and cook for another 5 minutes, or until the mixture has thickened.

3. Beat the **eggs** lightly, add them to the mixture in the pan, and scramble until the eggs are just set – about 4 minutes. Serve with hot toast.

> **Tip:** *You can substitute cooked lamb, ham, tongue or poultry for the beef.*

Sliced Beef and Onions ½

Preparation: **20 min**   Cooking: **30 min**   Serves **4**   Cals per portion: **360**

2 oz (50g) butter or margarine

2 large onions, peeled and thinly sliced

1 tablespoon plain flour

1½ tablespoons red wine vinegar

½ pint (285ml) thin beef gravy or beef stock

8 slices cooked beef about ⅛ in (3mm) thick

¼ teaspoon salt

¼ teaspoon black pepper

2 oz (50g) fresh breadcrumbs

1 tablespoon finely chopped fresh parsley

1. Preheat the oven to 220°C (425°F, gas mark 7). Meanwhile, melt three-quarters of the **butter** in a large frying pan over a low heat. Add the **onions** and cook, covered, for 10 minutes. Mix in the **flour** and continue stirring for 2 minutes. Add the **vinegar**, then gradually stir in the **gravy** and cook until the sauce has slightly thickened – 5 to 6 minutes.

2. Spoon half the sauce over the bottom of a shallow baking dish and then add overlapping slices of the **beef;** season with the **salt** and **pepper.** Cover with the rest of the sauce and top with the **breadcrumbs.** Melt the remaining butter and spoon over the crumbs.

3. Cook in the oven for 30 minutes, or until a golden crust forms. Garnish with the chopped **parsley** and serve hot.

> **Tip:** This dish can be prepared a day in advance. Vary the recipe by adding 1 clove peeled and chopped garlic and 4oz (115g) chopped mushrooms to the onion sauce.

Devilled Beef Slices ½

Preparation: **10 min**   Cooking: **9 min**   Serves **4**   Cals per portion: **440**

8 drops Tabasco sauce

3 tablespoons French mustard

1 teaspoon salt

8 slices cooked beef about ¼ in (5mm) thick

3 oz (75g) fine dry breadcrumbs

3 tablespoons vegetable oil

1¾ oz (45g) butter or margarine

1 clove garlic, peeled and finely chopped

4 fl oz (115ml) beef stock

4 fl oz (115ml) dry white wine

1 teaspoon dried tarragon

1. In a small bowl, combine the **Tabasco sauce,** 2 tablespoons of the **mustard** and the **salt.** Spread the mixture on both sides of the **beef** slices. Put the **breadcrumbs** on a plate, and press the slices into them.

2. Heat the **oil** in a medium-sized, heavy frying pan over high heat for about 1 minute. Add half the beef slices and cook for 1 minute on each side. Remove the cooked slices, drain on absorbent paper, transfer to a plate and keep warm. Cook the remaining beef the same way.

3. To make the sauce, melt 1 tablespoon of the **butter** in the pan over low heat. Add the **garlic** and brown lightly – about 1 minute. Add the **stock, wine, tarragon** and the remaining mustard, bring to the boil and cook for 2 minutes. Remove from the heat, stir in the remaining butter and pour the sauce over the beef.

Beef and Potato Skillet  ½

Preparation: **7 min**   Cooking: **14 min**   Serves **4**   Cals per portion: **450**

3 tablespoons vegetable oil

1 medium-sized onion, peeled and finely chopped

12 oz (350g) diced cooked potatoes

12 oz (350g) diced cooked beef

¾ teaspoon salt

¼ teaspoon black pepper

¾ teaspoon dried thyme

4 fl oz (115ml) double cream

1. Heat the **oil** in a large, heavy frying pan over moderate heat. Add the **onion** and cook until soft – about 5 minutes. Add the **potatoes, beef, salt, pepper** and **thyme,** and cook until the potatoes begin to brown – about 6 minutes.

2. Add the **cream,** pressing down on the mixture with an egg slice. Cook for 3 to 4 minutes, or until the cream has almost evaporated. Serve with poached eggs and a tossed green salad with Tomato Dressing, page 53.

Beef Croquettes ½

Preparation: **29 min**   Cooking: **6 min**   Serves **4**   Cals per portion: **410**

6 tablespoons vegetable oil

1 medium-sized onion, peeled and finely chopped

3 tablespoons plain flour

8 fl oz (225ml) beef stock

12 oz (350g) very finely chopped cooked beef

½ teaspoon salt

¼ teaspoon black pepper

½ teaspoon dried thyme

1 tablespoon Worcestershire sauce

1 egg, lightly beaten

3 oz (75g) fine dry breadcrumbs

1. Heat half the **oil** in a medium-sized, heavy frying pan over moderate heat. Add the **onion** and cook, covered, until soft – about 5 minutes. Stir in the **flour,** cook for 1 minute, then gradually stir in the **beef stock.** Cook, stirring, for 1 minute, or until smooth and thickened.

2. Mix in the **beef, salt, pepper, thyme** and **Worcestershire sauce.** Spread the mixture evenly in a buttered, shallow baking dish or tray.

3. Chill in the freezer for 15 minutes, or until stiff enough to shape. Form the mixture into 4 oval patties about ¾in (20mm) thick. Dip them into the **egg,** then coat them with the **breadcrumbs.**

4. Rinse and dry the pan. Heat the remaining oil in it over moderately high heat for 1 minute. Add the croquettes, and cook until brown – about 3 minutes on each side. Drain on absorbent paper.

> **Tip:** Add any of the following: 1 tablespoon prepared mustard or horseradish; 3oz (75g) chopped, sautéed mushrooms; 2 tablespoons chopped capers, dill pickle or green pepper; 1 peeled and crushed clove garlic.

Minute Steaks Monaco ⊘

Preparation: **5 min**   Cooking: **13 min**   Serves **4**   Cals per portion: **410**

1 teaspoon salt

4 minute steaks (about 6 oz/175g each)

4 tablespoons vegetable oil

1 small aubergine (about 9 oz/250g), peeled and cut into ½ in (15mm) slices

4 oz (115g) mushrooms, quartered

8 fl oz (225ml) chicken stock

4 oz (115g) tomato purée

½ teaspoon dried oregano

1 tablespoon plain flour

2 tablespoons water

¼ teaspoon black pepper

> **Tip:** *For a sauce with a tangier flavour, add 1 clove garlic, peeled and crushed, and 1 tablespoon Worcestershire sauce.*

1. Heat a large, heavy frying pan over moderately high heat until very hot. Sprinkle the bottom of the pan with the **salt,** add the **steaks,** and cook for 1 minute on each side for rare; cook an additional minute per side for well done. Transfer the steaks to a plate and put in a low oven to keep warm.

2. Reduce the heat to moderate. Add the **oil** to the pan, and brown the **aubergine** slices on both sides along with the **mushrooms** – about 5 minutes. Stir in the **chicken stock, tomato purée** and **oregano,** and simmer, covered, for 5 minutes or until the aubergine is tender.

3. In a small bowl, blend the **flour** and **water** to a smooth paste. Stir into the liquid in the pan. Bring to the boil and cook, stirring continuously, until the mixture thickens – about 1 minute. Season with the **black pepper.**

4. Arrange the aubergine slices under the steaks on the serving plate, and top with the sauce and mushrooms. Serve with noodles and a green salad.

Peppered Steaks with Cream Sauce ⊘ ½

Preparation: **2 min**   Cooking: **10 min**   Serves **6**   Cals per portion: **315**

6 minute steaks (about 6 oz/175g each)

2 tablespoons black peppercorns, crushed

2 tablespoons vegetable oil

4 fl oz (115ml) beef stock

3 tablespoons double cream

1 tablespoon brandy

> **Tip:** *For a different, spicy flavour, use a mixture of white and black peppercorns with a few allspice berries. Crush them in a mortar with a pestle, or in a small but strong plastic bag with a rolling pin. Green, unripened peppercorns can also be used, but do not crush them.*

1. Dry the **steaks** with absorbent paper. Press the **crushed peppercorns** evenly onto both sides of the steaks. Heat the **oil** in a large, heavy frying pan over moderately high heat for about 1 minute. Add the steaks and cook for 1 minute on each side for rare; cook an additional minute per side for well done. Transfer the steaks to a serving dish and put in a low oven to keep warm.

2. Pour off and discard the oil from the pan. Add the **beef stock** and boil over high heat until only half the stock remains – about 5 minutes. Add the **cream,** and heat briefly.

3. Remove the pan from the heat. Stir in the **brandy,** together with any accumulated juices from the serving dish. Pour the sauce over the steaks and serve.

Skirt Steak with Mushrooms

Preparation: **6 min**   Cooking: **13 min**   Serves **4**   Cals per portion: **435**

The cooking time given is for rare steak. If you prefer beef well done, cook the steak a bit longer.

1½ lb (700g) skirt steak, trimmed of fat

½ teaspoon salt

¼ teaspoon black pepper

1 tablespoon vegetable oil

1 oz (25g) butter or margarine

1 clove garlic, peeled and finely chopped

4 oz (115g) mushrooms, thickly sliced

2 fl oz (50ml) beef stock or water

1 tablespoon finely chopped parsley

1. Cut the **steak** into 4 pieces, pat the pieces dry with absorbent paper and sprinkle them with the **salt** and **pepper.** Batten with a rolling pin to tenderise.

2. Heat the **oil** in a large, heavy frying pan over high heat for about 1 minute. Add the steak and cook for 3 minutes on each side. Transfer the steak to a plate and keep warm.

3. Melt the **butter** in the pan, then add the **garlic,** and cook, stirring, for 1 minute. Add the **mushrooms,** toss, and cook for 4 minutes, tossing occasionally.

4. Add the **beef stock** and stir, scraping up any brown bits stuck to the pan. Return the steak and any accumulated juices to the pan, and heat through. Sprinkle with the **parsley,** and serve with boiled potatoes and green beans or Baked Stuffed Tomatoes, page 83.

Steak and Curried Onions

Preparation: **5 min**   Cooking: **18 min**   Serves **4**   Cals per portion: **470**

This steak is mildly flavoured with curried onion. The time given is for rare steak. If you prefer beef well done, cook the steak a bit longer.

1 oz (25g) butter or margarine

2 tablespoons vegetable oil

1 large onion, peeled and thinly sliced

1 teaspoon curry powder

1½ lb (700g) skirt steak

½ teaspoon salt

¼ teaspoon black pepper

Tip: Add 1 tablespoon of currants or raisins to the onion during the last 3 minutes of cooking and sprinkle with 1 tablespoon of chopped toasted almonds.

1. Heat the **butter** and the **oil** in a large, heavy frying pan over moderate heat. Add the **onion** and **curry powder,** and cook until the onion is dark brown and crisp – about 12 minutes. (Be careful not to let the onion burn; turn down the heat if it is browning too quickly.) Transfer the onion to a warm plate, cover with foil, and set aside.

2. Meanwhile, trim the **steak** of fat and cut it into 4 pieces. Pat the pieces dry with absorbent paper and sprinkle them with the **salt** and **pepper.** Batten with a rolling pin to tenderise. Put the steak into the pan and cook over moderate heat for 3 minutes on each side.

3. Transfer the steak to a warm serving dish. Scatter the onion over the steak, and serve with rice, and Green Beans with Garlic and Cheese, page 62, or Orange-Ginger Carrots, page 69.

BEEF

Seasoned Grilled Steak

Preparation: **35 min**   Cooking: **6 min**   Serves **4**   Cals per portion: **375**

Juice 1 lemon

1 tablespoon vegetable oil

2 cloves garlic, peeled and finely chopped

1 tablespoon soya sauce

1 teaspoon salt

¼ teaspoon black pepper

¼ teaspoon aniseed, crushed, or ground allspice

1½ lb (700g) rump steak in one piece, and battened to tenderise

> **Tip:** *The steak will have a better flavour and texture if you marinate it for 4 hours.*

1. Preheat the grill. In a large saucepan, combine the **lemon juice, oil, garlic, soya sauce, salt, pepper** and **aniseed.** Bring to the boil over high heat and stir for about 30 seconds.

2. Put the **steak** into a glass or earthenware casserole dish and pierce all over with a fork. Pour the hot marinade over the steak, turn the steak over in the marinade to coat it well and marinate at room temperature for 30 minutes, turning once.

3. Place the steak on the rack of the grill pan about 3in (80mm) from the heat. Grill for 3 minutes on each side for rare; an additional 2 minutes per side for medium. Cut the steak on the diagonal into ½in (15mm) slices. Serve with baked potatoes or rice.

Steak with Herb Butter

Preparation: **15 min**   Cooking: **4 min**   Serves **4**   Cals per portion: **485**

1½ lb (700g) skirt steak about 2 in (50mm) thick

½ teaspoon salt

¼ teaspoon black pepper

2 oz (50g) butter or margarine, softened

1 clove garlic, peeled and finely chopped

1 tablespoon finely chopped parsley

½ teaspoon dried basil

¼ teaspoon dried thyme

1 tablespoon vegetable oil

> **Tip:** *When fresh herbs are available, they will give a much better flavour; batten some of the herbs into the steaks when you pound them flat.*

1. Put the **steak** on a chopping board, place your hand flat over it and, cutting parallel to your hand, slice the meat horizontally into 4 pieces.

2. Pound the slices with a wooden mallet until they are ¼in (5mm) thick. Trim off any excess fat.

3. Notch the edges of the steaks all around to prevent curling. Pat them dry with absorbent paper, and sprinkle them with the **salt** and half the **pepper.** Put aside.

4. In a small bowl, combine the **butter, garlic, parsley, basil, thyme** and the remaining pepper. Put aside.

5. Heat the **oil** in a large frying pan over moderately high heat for about 1 minute. Add the steaks and cook for 2 minutes on each side. Serve with a portion of herb butter on each steak.

Chinese Beef with Peppers ½

Preparation: **20 min**   Cooking: **12 min**   Serves **4**   Cals per portion: **355**

3 tablespoons cornflour

1 lb (450g) topside of beef, cut into thin strips about 2 in (50mm) long

4 tablespoons vegetable oil

3 medium-sized red or green peppers, seeded and cut into thin strips

3 medium-sized onions, peeled and thinly sliced

3 cloves garlic, peeled and finely chopped

3 tablespoons soya sauce

8 fl oz (225ml) water

1. Put the **cornflour** into a shallow bowl and toss the **beef** strips to coat evenly. Put aside.

2. Heat half the **oil** in a large, heavy frying pan over a brisk heat for about 1 minute. Add half the beef strips and cook, stirring once or twice, until no pink remains – about 1 or 2 minutes. Transfer the cooked strips to a plate. Cook the remaining steak in the same way and add to the plate.

3. Reduce the heat to moderate, and add the remaining oil, the **peppers, onions** and **garlic,** and cook for 5 minutes, or until the onions are soft. Return the steak and any accumulated juices to the pan.

4. Stir in the **soya sauce** and **water.** Continue cooking and stirring until the sauce has thickened – about 4 minutes. Serve with rice.

Beef Stroganoff ½

Preparation: **15 min**   Cooking: **10 min**   Serves **4**   Cals per portion: **420**

3 tablespoons plain flour

1 teaspoon salt

¼ teaspoon black pepper

1¼ lb (575g) topside of beef, cut into thin strips

2 oz (50g) butter or margarine

1 medium-sized onion, peeled and chopped

2 cloves garlic, peeled and finely chopped

9 oz (250g) mushrooms, sliced

8 fl oz (225ml) beef stock

2 tablespoons tomato purée

4 fl oz (115ml) soured cream

> **Tip:** *You can substitute natural yoghurt for the soured cream.*

1. In a large bowl, combine the **flour, salt** and **pepper.** Toss the **beef** strips in the mixture until they are evenly coated. Shake off any excess flour. Put the beef aside.

2. Heat the **butter** in a large, heavy frying pan over moderately high heat until bubbling. Add half the beef strips and cook, stirring once or twice, for 1 or 2 minutes, or until no pink remains. Transfer the cooked meat to a plate. Cook the remaining beef in the same way and add to the plate.

3. Reduce the heat. Add the **onion** and **garlic,** and cook for 5 minutes, or until the onion is soft. Add the **mushrooms, beef stock** and **tomato purée;** raise the heat, and cook for 2 minutes, scraping up any brown bits stuck to the pan.

4. Return the beef and any accumulated juices to the pan, and heat through – about 1 minute. Remove the pan from the heat and stir in the **soured cream.** Serve with buttered noodles and a lettuce and tomato salad.

BEEF

Beef with Curry Sauce ½

Preparation: **35 min**   Cooking: **10 min**   Serves **4**   Cals per portion: **400**

You can omit the 25 minute marinating time if you wish, but the dish will have a better flavour if it has a chance to absorb the seasonings

1½ teaspoons sugar

2 tablespoons soya sauce

2 cloves garlic, peeled and finely chopped

¾ teaspoon ground ginger

5 tablespoons vegetable oil

1¼ lb (575g) topside of beef, cut into thin strips 2 in (50mm) long

1 large onion, peeled and thinly sliced

2 teaspoons cornflour

1½ tablespoons curry powder

4 fl oz (115ml) cold water

¼ teaspoon salt

¼ teaspoon black pepper

1. In a large bowl, combine the **sugar, soya sauce, garlic, ginger** and 2 tablespoons of the **oil.** Add the **beef** strips, toss to coat them evenly with the mixture, and marinate for 25 minutes at room temperature.

2. Heat the remaining 3 tablespoons of oil in a large, heavy frying pan over moderately high heat for about 1 minute. Using a slotted spoon, transfer the steak from the marinade to the pan. Cook for 3 minutes, turning once. Transfer the slices to a plate. Add the **onion** to the pan, reduce the heat to moderate, and cook for 2 minutes.

3. Meanwhile, add the **cornflour, curry powder** and **water** to the marinade. When the onion has cooked, stir the marinade, pour it into the pan, and cook, stirring, for 1 minute, or until the sauce has thickened. Return the beef and any accumulated juices to the pan. Add **salt** and **pepper** to taste. Simmer until heated through – about 3 minutes. Serve with rice.

Spicy Oriental Beef ◎ ½ 🐷

Preparation: **16 min**   Cooking: **10 min**   Serves **4**   Cals per portion: **565**

1½ lb (700g) skirt steak, trimmed of fat and cut crosswise into very thin slices

5 tablespoons soya sauce

6 tablespoons vegetable oil

2 large carrots, peeled and cut into thin slices

4 large stems celery, cut into thin slices

1 teaspoon ground ginger

¼ to ½ teaspoon paprika

¼ teaspoon salt

1. In a large bowl, combine the **steak** slices and **soya sauce.** Heat half the **oil** in a large, heavy frying pan over moderately high heat for about 1 minute. Add the steak and cook, stirring, for 5 minutes, or until no pink remains.

2. Return the steak and pan juices to the bowl, and put aside. Heat the remaining oil in the same pan and add the **carrots.** Cook for 1 minute, then add the **celery, ginger, paprika** and **salt.** Cook, stirring, for 2 minutes longer, or until the vegetables are almost tender but still crisp. Do not overcook.

3. Reduce the heat, and return the steak and any accumulated juices to the pan. Simmer until heated through – about 2 minutes. Serve with rice or noodles and a cucumber salad.

Paprika Beef ½

Preparation: **10 min**   Cooking: **19 min**   Serves **4**   Cals per portion: **580**

1½ oz (40g) butter or margarine

1½ lb (700g) topside of beef, cut crosswise into thin strips 2 in (50mm) long

8 fl oz (225ml) double cream

1 tablespoon paprika

½ teaspoon salt

Tips: 1. *You can make this dish in advance and refrigerate it for up to 3 days, or freeze it.* **2.** *You can use natural yoghurt instead of the cream.*

1. Heat the **butter** in a large, heavy frying pan over moderately high heat until bubbling. Add half the **beef** strips and cook for 3 to 4 minutes on each side until brown. Using a slotted spoon, transfer the strips to a plate. Cook the remaining beef the same way and add to the plate.

2. Raise the heat. Add the **cream, paprika** and **salt** to the pan, and boil, stirring, for 4 minutes, or until the sauce has thickened slightly. Return the beef and any accumulated juices to the pan. Reduce the heat, and simmer, until heated through – about 3 minutes. Serve with noodles or rice.

Beef and Vegetables with Soya Sauce ½

Preparation: **8 min**   Cooking: **10 min**   Serves **4**   Cals per portion: **420**

2 oz (50g) butter or margarine

1 medium-sized onion, peeled and thinly sliced

1¼ lb (575g) rump steak, cut crosswise into thin slices

¼ teaspoon salt

4 oz (115g) mushrooms, sliced

1 large stem celery, thinly sliced

2 medium-sized carrots, peeled and thinly sliced

8 oz (225g) fresh bean sprouts

8 oz (225g) canned water chestnuts, drained and thinly sliced

2 tablespoons soya sauce

8 fl oz (225ml) beef stock

3 shallots, peeled and finely chopped

The estimated preparation time above assumes that you first trim and slice the steak – about 3 minutes. Use the 5 minutes while the onion is cooking to slice the mushrooms and celery and the 5 minutes while the steak browns to peel and slice the carrots, slice the water chestnuts and chop the shallots.

1. Melt the **butter** in a large, heavy frying pan over moderate heat. Add the **onion** and cook, stirring occasionally, for 5 minutes. Transfer the onion to a plate and put aside.

2. Raise the heat. Add the **steak** slices and cook, turning once or twice, until browned – about 5 minutes. Return the onion to the pan. Add the **salt, mushrooms, celery, carrots, bean sprouts, water chestnuts, soya sauce** and **beef stock.**

3. Reduce the heat and simmer for 5 minutes, or until the celery and carrots are tender, but still crisp. Do not overcook. Serve with rice and sprinkle with the **shallots.** Serve with additional soya sauce if you like.

BEEF

Beef Kebabs ½

Preparation: **30 min**   Cooking: **6 min**   Serves **4**   Cals per portion: **395**

3 tablespoons olive oil

Juice 1 lemon

½ teaspoon dried oregano

¼ teaspoon salt

Pinch black pepper

1 clove garlic, peeled and finely chopped

1½ lb (700g) rump steak, cut into ¾ in (20mm) cubes.

1. In a large bowl, combine the **oil, lemon juice, oregano, salt, pepper** and **garlic.** Add the **steak** cubes to the mixture and marinate for 20 to 25 minutes at room temperature. About 5 minutes before you are ready to cook the kebabs, preheat the grill.

2. Remove the steak from the marinade and thread it onto 4 skewers. Grill 4in (100mm) from the heat for 3 minutes on each side, basting occasionally with the marinade.

> *Tip: To make more elaborate kebabs, skewer cherry tomatoes, pepper chunks, onion wedges and mushrooms between the meat cubes.*

Hamburgers

Preparation: **5 min**   Cooking: **6 min**   Serves **4**   Cals per portion: **250**

Here are directions for making not only plain hamburgers but also 8 variations and 6 toppings.

1¼ lb (575g) very lean minced beef

1 small onion, peeled and finely chopped

½ teaspoon salt

¼ teaspoon black pepper

> **Variations:** *Add any of the following to the beef before shaping it into burgers.*
> *1. 3 tablespoons barbecue sauce;*
> *2. 6oz (175g) chopped ham, 1 tablespoon sweet pickle and 1 teaspoon French mustard;* *3. 3oz (75g) strong grated Cheddar cheese;* *4. 3 tablespoons chopped walnuts;* *5. 3 tablespoons soured cream, 1 tablespoon minced parsley and a pinch each dried thyme and oregano;* *6. 2oz (50g) chopped mushrooms;* *7. 2oz (50g) chopped stuffed green olives;*
> *8. Push a nugget of soft blue cheese, such as Roquefort, into the centre of the hamburger, making sure it is sealed by the meat.*

1. In a large bowl, combine the **beef, onion, salt** and **pepper.** Shape the mixture into hamburgers, each about 1in (25mm) thick.

2. *To pan-fry:* Heat a lightly oiled, large, heavy frying pan over moderate heat until hot. Cook the hamburgers 3 minutes on each side for rare, 4 for medium, 6 for well done. Do not press on them or you will force out the juices. *To grill:* Place the hamburgers 3in (75mm) from the heat, and cook 2 minutes on each side for rare, 3 to 4 for medium, 5 to 6 for well done. Serve on toasted hamburger buns.

> **Toppings:** *1. 3 tablespoons chilli sauce and ¼ teaspoon chilli powder heated until just bubbling with 1 tablespoon butter or margarine;* *2. 3½oz (90g) cream cheese with chives blended with 3 tablespoons soured cream;* *3. 1 tablespoon melted butter or margarine and 1 tablespoon garlic-flavoured oil and vinegar dressing mixed with 1 teaspoon chopped parsley and ½ teaspoon chopped chives;* *4. 1 tablespoon plain flour blended with 1 tablespoon butter or margarine, ¼ teaspoon curry powder, ¼ teaspoon salt, 2 or 3 sliced mushrooms and 4fl oz (115ml) water cooked until the sauce thickens – about 1 minute;* *5. 4oz (115g) finely shredded cabbage mixed with mayonnaise, 4 sliced stuffed olives and 2 slices cooked bacon, crumbled;*
> *6. Pour off excess fat from the pan, add about 4 tablespoons of wine and stir briskly to dissolve the juices. Pour the sauce over the hamburgers.*

Barbecued Hamburgers ◎ ½

Preparation: **7 min**   Cooking: **9 min**   Serves **6**   Cals per portion: **280**

2 oz (50g) fresh breadcrumbs

3 fl oz (90ml) milk

½ teaspoon salt

¼ teaspoon black pepper

1½ lb (700g) lean minced beef

2 small onions, peeled and finely chopped

1 tablespoon vegetable oil

4 fl oz (115ml) cider vinegar

1½ teaspoons chilli powder

Pinch dried oregano

4 teaspoons Worcestershire sauce

4 medium-sized tomatoes, peeled and chopped

1. In a large bowl, combine the **breadcrumbs, milk, salt** and **pepper.** Add the **beef** and half the chopped **onions.** Mix well and shape the mixture into 6 burgers, each about ¾in (20mm) thick.

2. Heat the **oil** in a large, heavy frying pan over moderate heat for about 1 minute. Add the burgers and cook for 2 minutes on each side. Meanwhile, in a small bowl, combine the remaining onions, the **vinegar, chilli powder, oregano, Worcestershire sauce** and **tomatoes.** Pour the mixture over the burgers and cook for 5 to 8 minutes, or until the sauce has thickened. Serve.

> *Tips: 1.* These burgers have a better flavour if they are made a day in advance, chilled, and then reheated the next day. *2.* The burgers are also very good served cold with mayonnaise.

Herbed Hamburgers ◎ ½

Preparation: **6 min**   Cooking: **7 min**   Serves **4**   Cals per portion: **365**

1¼ lb (575g) lean minced beef

½ teaspoon salt

¼ teaspoon black pepper

½ teaspoon dried thyme

¼ teaspoon dried rosemary

1 oz (25g) butter or margarine

1 tablespoon vegetable oil

1 tablespoon French mustard

1 tablespoon lemon juice

1½ teaspoons Worcestershire sauce

2 tablespoons chopped parsley

> *Tip:* This recipe can be made with minced lean lamb, and with mint used in place of the thyme and rosemary.

The flavours of the herbs, accompanied by the spiced lemon butter sauce, make this a special summer lunch dish.

1. In a large bowl, combine the **beef, salt, pepper, thyme** and **rosemary.** Shape the mixture into 4 burgers, each about ¾in (20mm) thick.

2. Heat half the **butter** with the **oil** and **mustard** in a large, heavy frying pan over moderate heat for about 1 minute. Add the burgers and cook 3 minutes on each side for rare, 4 for medium, and 6 for well done. Transfer them to a warm plate.

3. Add the **lemon juice** and **Worcestershire sauce** to the pan, and stir for 30 seconds. Remove the pan from the heat, and stir in the **parsley** and the remaining butter. Pour the sauce over the burgers.

BEEF

Hamburger Pancakes

Preparation: **6 min**   Cooking: **10 min**   Serves **4**   Cals per portion: **225**

9 oz (250g) lean minced beef

1 small onion, peeled and finely chopped

½ teaspoon salt

¼ teaspoon black pepper

¼ teaspoon baking powder

3 eggs, separated

3 tablespoons vegetable oil

This recipe shows how to make 9oz (250g) of minced beef go a long way.

1. In a large bowl, combine the **beef, onion, salt, pepper, baking powder** and **egg yolks.** In a separate bowl, beat the **egg whites** until just stiff, then fold them into the beef mixture.

2. Heat the **oil** in a very large, heavy frying pan over moderate heat for about 1 minute. Using a large spoon, drop the beef mixture into the pan, making 4 pancakes. Cook for 5 minutes, turn the pancakes with an egg slice, and cook 5 minutes longer.

Minced Steak with Onion Sauce

Preparation: **10 min**   Cooking: **15 min**   Serves **6**   Cals per portion: **310**

Getting this dish on the table in 25 minutes takes some organisation: prepare the ingredients and shape the patties while the onion is cooking. Then, while the patties are on the cooker, finish the sauce.

2 oz (50g) butter or margarine

1 tablespoon water

1 large onion, peeled and finely chopped

1½ lb (700g) lean minced beef

2 cloves garlic, peeled and finely chopped

1 tablespoon chopped chives

1 tablespoon finely chopped parsley

¼ teaspoon dried thyme

1 teaspoon salt

¼ teaspoon black pepper

2 tablespoons plain flour

8 fl oz (225ml) beef stock

1. Place half of the **butter,** the **water,** and all but 2 tablespoons of the **onion** in a medium-sized, heavy frying pan over moderately low heat. Cover and cook for 10 minutes, stirring occasionally to prevent browning.

2. Meanwhile, in a large bowl, combine the **beef, garlic, chives, parsley, thyme, salt, pepper** and the reserved 2 tablespoons of onion. Shape the mixture into 6 patties about ¾in (20mm) thick.

3. Heat the remaining butter in another heavy pan over moderate heat until bubbling. Add the patties and cook about 4 minutes on each side for medium. Transfer them to a warm plate and put aside.

4. To make the sauce, stir the **flour** into the onion and cook for 1 minute over moderately high heat. Add the **beef stock** and boil for 4 minutes, stirring, until the sauce has thickened. Return the patties to their pan to reheat briefly, and spoon the sauce over them. Serve with Glorious Mashed Potatoes, page 76, or new potatoes boiled in their jackets.

> **Tip:** *For a smoother sauce, purée it in a blender, reheat if necessary, and pour over the patties.*

Sweet and Sour Beef and Cabbage ½ 🐷

Preparation: **21 min** Cooking: **20 min**   Serves **6** Cals per portion: **250**

1 lb (450g) lean minced beef

3 tablespoons cooked rice

1 small onion, finely chopped

1 egg, lightly beaten

2 tablespoons water

½ teaspoon dried dill

1 teaspoon salt

½ teaspoon black pepper

2 tablespoons vegetable oil

1 medium-sized onion, sliced

4 medium-sized tomatoes, peeled and chopped

Juice 1 lemon

1 tablespoon honey

1 small cabbage (about 1 lb/450g), cut into 6 wedges

2 carrots, peeled and sliced

Here's a one-dish meal with all the flavour of stuffed cabbage but with only half the work. To save time, prepare the chopped onion, tomatoes, carrots and cabbage while the beef patties are browning.

1. In a large bowl, combine the **beef, rice, chopped onion, egg, water, dill,** ½ teaspoon of the **salt** and ¼ teaspoon of the **pepper.** Shape the mixture into 6 oval patties.

2. Heat the **oil** in a large, heavy frying pan over moderately high heat for about 1 minute. Add the patties and cook for 4 minutes on each side, or until browned. Transfer the patties to a plate.

3. Pour all but 2 tablespoons of the fat from the pan. Add the **sliced onion, tomatoes, lemon juice, honey,** the remaining salt and pepper and bring to the boil. Reduce the heat and add the **cabbage** wedges. Top with the patties and **carrots,** cover, and simmer for 20 minutes.

> **Tip:** *You can substitute lamb, pork or veal for the beef.*

Creamy Meatballs

Preparation: **13 min** Cooking: **27 min**   Serves **6** Cals per portion: **410**

3 oz (75g) fine dry breadcrumbs

1 small onion, peeled and finely chopped

1 teaspoon salt

Pinch ground nutmeg

4 fl oz (115ml) milk

9 oz (250g) lean minced beef

9 oz (250g) minced pork

9 oz (250g) minced veal

1½ oz (40g) butter

1 tablespoon plain flour

8 fl oz (225ml) beef stock

4 fl oz (115ml) double cream

1. In a large bowl, combine the **breadcrumbs, onion, salt, nutmeg** and **milk.** Add the **minced beef, pork** and **veal,** and mix thoroughly. Shape the mixture into meatballs, the size of a small plum.

2. Heat the **butter** in a large, heavy frying pan over moderate heat until bubbling. Cook the meatballs, turning frequently, for 20 minutes. Transfer them to a plate.

3. Add the **flour** to the dripping in the pan, stir until bubbling, then blend in the **beef stock** and **cream.** Boil for 4 to 5 minutes, stirring until the sauce thickens.

4. Return the meatballs and any accumulated juices to the pan. Spoon the sauce over the meatballs and heat through – about 2 minutes.

BEEF

Rice and Beef Porcupines

Preparation: **13 min**   Cooking: **30 min**   Serves **4**   Cals per portion: **370**

1 lb (450g) lean minced beef

1 medium onion, peeled and finely chopped

½ teaspoon dried oregano

¼ teaspoon dried rosemary

3 oz (75g) cooked rice

1 egg, beaten

¼ teaspoon salt

¼ teaspoon black pepper

2 tablespoons vegetable oil

6 oz (175g) tomato purée

8 fl oz (225ml) water

1. In a large bowl, combine the **beef, onion, oregano, rosemary, rice, egg, salt** and **pepper.** Shape the mixture into small balls about the size of a plum.

2. Heat the **oil** in a large, heavy frying pan over moderately low heat for about 1 minute. Cook the meatballs, turning frequently, until browned on all sides – about 5 minutes.

3. Add the **tomato purée** and **water,** cover and simmer for 30 minutes. Serve with a green salad and crusty bread.

Mediterranean Meatballs ½

Preparation: **20 min**   Cooking: **30 min**   Serves **4**   Cals per portion: **470**

1 lb (450g) lean minced beef

3 oz (75g) soft fresh breadcrumbs

1 small onion, peeled and finely chopped

1 clove garlic, peeled and finely chopped

1 egg, lightly beaten

½ teaspoon salt

½ teaspoon black pepper

2 tablespoons flour

2 tablespoons vegetable oil

4 fl oz (115ml) beef stock

4 medium-sized tomatoes, peeled and chopped

1 teaspoon dried tarragon

3 medium-sized courgettes, sliced

1 x 15 oz (425g) can chickpeas, drained

1. In a large bowl, combine the **beef, breadcrumbs, onion, garlic, egg,** and half the **salt** and **pepper.** Shape the mixture into small balls about the size of a plum. Dust the meatballs lightly with the **flour.**

2. Heat the **oil** in a large, heavy frying pan over moderate heat for about 1 minute. Cook the meatballs, turning frequently, until browned on all sides – about 5 minutes.

3. Pour off and discard the fat from the pan. Add the **beef stock** to the meatballs, bring to the boil, and cook for 30 seconds, scraping up any brown bits stuck to the pan. Add the **tomatoes,** the remaining salt and pepper and the **tarragon.** Cover, reduce the heat, and simmer for 25 minutes.

4. Add the **courgettes** and **chickpeas,** and cook, covered, for 4 to 5 minutes, or until the courgettes are tender but still crisp.

> **Tip:** *If you dampen your hands before shaping the meatballs they will be less likely to stick.*

Miniature Meat Loaves

Preparation: **13 min**   Cooking: **35 min**   Serves **6**   Cals per portion: **365**

Individual meat loaves cook in approximately half the time it takes to bake one large loaf.

1 oz (25g) butter or margarine

1 medium-sized onion, peeled and finely chopped

1½ lb (700g) minced beef

3 oz (75g) fresh breadcrumbs

4 oz (115g) canned pimentos, drained and chopped

1 egg, lightly beaten

2 fl oz (50ml) milk

½ teaspoon dried thyme

1 teaspoon salt

¼ teaspoon black pepper

3 rashers bacon, cut in half

1. Preheat the oven to 200°C (400°F, gas mark 6). Melt the **butter** in a small frying pan over moderate heat. Add the **onion** and cook for 5 minutes, or until soft.

2. In a large bowl, combine the cooked onion, the **beef, breadcrumbs, pimentos, egg, milk, thyme, salt** and **pepper.** Shape the mixture into 6 loaves, each about 4 x 1½ x 1½in (100 x 40 x 40mm). Put the loaves into a greased baking dish. Place a piece of the **bacon** on top of each loaf.

3. Bake for 35 minutes. Serve with a tomato sauce, if desired, and mashed or boiled potatoes.

> *Tips: 1. You can substitute 1 tablespoon of finely chopped, skinned and seeded tomato for the pimentos. 2. This recipe is a very good one for freezing.*

Sweet and Sour Meat Loaf

Preparation: **8 min**   Cooking: **30-40 min**   Serves **4**   Cals per portion: **320**

1¼ lb (575g) lean minced beef

1 medium-sized onion, peeled and finely chopped

1 stem celery, finely chopped

1 clove garlic, peeled and finely chopped

1 teaspoon salt

¼ teaspoon black pepper

1 teaspoon dry mustard

1 egg, lightly beaten

½ small green pepper, seeded and finely chopped

3 tablespoons tomato purée

1 tablespoon soft dark brown sugar

2 tablespoons cider vinegar

1. Preheat the oven to 200°C (400°F, gas mark 6). In a large bowl, combine the **beef, onion, celery, garlic, salt, pepper, mustard, egg** and **green pepper.** Pat the mixture into a 9in (230mm) pie plate, leaving ½in (15mm) of space around the edge to catch the juices. Separate the loaf into 4 equal wedges by cutting through the meat to the bottom of the pie plate.

2. In a small bowl, combine the **tomato purée, brown sugar** and **vinegar,** and pour over the meat mixture. Bake for 30 to 40 minutes, basting occasionally with the juices, until the meat is tender. Tip the pie plate and pour off the juices. Serve the meat loaf with buttered new potatoes and Broccoli with Red Pepper, page 66.

> *Tips: 1. You can substitute minced lamb, veal or pork for the beef. 2. Use a dampened knife to cut the meat mixture into wedges; it is much easier.*

BEEF

Beef and Potato Stew ½

Preparation: **13 min** Cooking: **15 min**   Serves **4** Cals per portion: **290**

16 fl oz (475ml) beef stock

13 oz (375g) lean minced beef

2 medium-sized potatoes (about 13 oz/375g), peeled and cut into ½ in (15mm) cubes

1 small onion, peeled and finely chopped

1 clove garlic, peeled and finely chopped

Pinch cayenne pepper

¼ teaspoon salt

¼ teaspoon dried thyme

¼ teaspoon dried marjoram

2 tablespoons tomato purée

1. Bring the **beef stock** to the boil in a large saucepan. Add the **beef,** cover, and boil for 3 minutes, or until the meat is no longer pink, stirring frequently to break up any large clumps.

2. Add the **potatoes, onion, garlic, cayenne pepper, salt, thyme, marjoram** and **tomato purée.** Reduce the heat, cover, and simmer for 15 minutes, or until the potatoes and meat are tender. Serve with green vegetables or a salad.

Tips: 1. The prepared recipe can be thinned down with stock and used as a sauce for pasta. *2.* Try a cheese topping: Put into an ovenproof dish, sprinkle with a good layer of grated cheese and brown under the grill.

Beef and Tomato Stew ½

Preparation: **12 min** Cooking: **15 min**   Serves **4** Cals per portion: **430**

2 tablespoons vegetable oil

1¼ lb (575g) lean minced beef

1 medium-sized onion, peeled and finely chopped

1 green chilli, seeded and finely chopped

12 oz (350g) frozen sweetcorn kernels, thawed

2 medium-sized courgettes, cut into ½ in (15mm) slices

4 medium-sized tomatoes, peeled and cut into ¾ in (20mm) pieces

½ teaspoon ground cumin

½ teaspoon dried oregano

1 teaspoon salt

¼ teaspoon black pepper

Here's how to streamline the preparation time of this dish. Peel and chop the onion and the chilli while the beef browns; prepare the tomatoes and courgettes while the onion and chilli cook.

1. Heat the **oil** in a large, heavy frying pan over moderately high heat for about 1 minute. Cook the **beef,** stirring frequently, for 5 minutes, or until browned. Add the **onion** and **chilli,** and cook for 5 more minutes, or until the onion is soft.

2. Add the **sweetcorn** to the pan and then the **courgettes, tomatoes, cumin, oregano, salt** and **pepper.** Simmer for 15 minutes, stirring occasionally, until the meat is tender. Serve with thick slices of crusty brown bread, or hot pitta bread.

Tips: 1. To make the dish more substantial, add 1 x 15oz (425g) can red kidney beans, drained. *2.* If you like an extra spicy stew, add 1 teaspoon chilli sauce.

Spicy Beef Hash ½

Preparation: **11 min**   Cooking: **20 min**   Serves **4**   Cals per portion: **390**

2 tablespoons vegetable oil

1¼ lb (575g) lean minced beef

1 medium-sized onion, peeled and finely chopped

1 clove garlic, peeled and finely chopped

6 medium-sized tomatoes, peeled and chopped

¼ pint (150ml) beef stock

1 teaspoon sugar

1 teaspoon ground cinnamon

Pinch ground cloves

¼ teaspoon ground cumin

1 teaspoon salt

2 oz (50g) raisins

This stew has an unusual flavour, both sweet and spicy. Save time by peeling and chopping the tomatoes while the beef is browning.

1. Heat the **oil** in a large, heavy saucepan over moderate heat for about 1 minute. Add the **beef, onion** and **garlic,** and cook, stirring frequently, about 7 minutes, or until the onion is soft and the beef has browned.

2. Add the **tomatoes, stock, sugar, cinnamon, cloves, cumin, salt** and **raisins.** Cover, reduce the heat, and simmer for 20 minutes, stirring occasionally. Serve with rice and a green vegetable.

Tip: *For extra colour, add 1oz (25g) pitted black olives and 1oz (25g) pitted green olives.*

Chilli Frittata

Preparation: **11 min**   Cooking: **22 min**   Serves **4**   Cals per portion: **380**

3 tablespoons vegetable oil

1 medium-sized onion, peeled and chopped

1 medium-sized pepper, seeded and chopped

9 oz (250g) lean minced beef

½ teaspoon dried oregano

¼ teaspoon dried basil

2 tablespoons chilli powder

1 teaspoon salt

2 medium-sized tomatoes, peeled and chopped

4 eggs

2 fl oz (50ml) milk

3 tablespoons grated Parmesan cheese

1. Heat 2 tablespoons of the **oil** in a large, heavy frying pan over moderate heat for about 1 minute. Add the **onion** and **pepper.** Cook for 3 minutes. Add the **beef** and cook, stirring, until browned – about 4 minutes.

2. Add the **oregano, basil, chilli powder,** ½ teaspoon of the **salt** and the **tomatoes.** Reduce the heat to low, cover, and cook for 15 minutes. Transfer the mixture to a bowl.

3. In the same pan, heat the remaining oil. Beat the **eggs, milk,** and remaining salt in a bowl, and pour into the pan. Cook over moderate heat, without stirring, until the eggs begin to set around the edges – 2 to 3 minutes.

4. Preheat the grill. Spoon the beef mixture evenly over the eggs and cook for 3 to 4 minutes. Sprinkle the **cheese** over the mixture, place the pan (but not the handle) under the grill about 4½in (115mm) from the heat for 2 minutes. Cut the frittata into wedges and serve.

Quick Chilli Con Carne

Preparation: **11 min**   Cooking: **17 min**   Serves **6**   Cals per portion: **350**

1½ tablespoons vegetable oil

1 medium-sized onion, peeled and chopped

1 medium-sized pepper, seeded and chopped

1¼ lb (575g) lean minced beef

2 cloves garlic, peeled and finely chopped

6 oz (175g) tomato purée

7 fl oz (200ml) chicken stock

¼ teaspoon ground cumin

¼ teaspoon cayenne pepper

2 teaspoons chilli powder

½ teaspoon dried oregano

1 teaspoon salt

2 x 15 oz (425g) cans red kidney beans, drained

1. Heat the **oil** in a large, heavy saucepan over moderate heat for about 1 minute. Add the **onion, pepper, beef** and **garlic,** and cook, stirring frequently, for 5 minutes, or until the onion is soft and the beef has browned.

2. Add the **tomato purée, stock, cumin, cayenne pepper, chilli powder, oregano** and **salt.** Cover, reduce the heat, and simmer for 15 minutes, stirring occasionally.

3. Stir in the **beans,** cover, and simmer for 2 or 3 minutes, until the beans are heated through. Serve with a green salad.

Tip: For a more special presentation, serve the chilli in bowls or taco shells and top with soured cream, chopped onions and diced cucumber.

Pan-Fried Macaroni and Beef

Preparation: **10 min**   Cooking: **13 min**   Serves **4**   Cals per portion: **355**

13 oz (375g) minced beef

2 courgettes, coarsely chopped

1 small onion, peeled and finely chopped

6 oz (175g) elbow macaroni

4 oz (115g) tomato purée

1 teaspoon salt

2 teaspoons Worcestershire sauce

¾ teaspoon dried basil

¾ teaspoon dried oregano

¾ pint (450ml) beef stock

Tip: You can substitute 1 medium-sized, chopped pepper for the courgettes.

This satisfying one-pot meal gives you more dinner for the pound than you are likely to find anywhere!
To save time, chop the onion and courgettes while the beef browns.

1. In a large, heavy frying pan over moderately high heat, cook the **beef,** stirring occasionally, for 5 minutes, or until browned. Using a slotted spoon, transfer the beef to a bowl and put aside. Add the **courgettes** and **onion** to the pan, and cook for 3 minutes.

2. Return the beef to the pan, and add the **macaroni, tomato purée, salt, Worcestershire sauce, basil, oregano** and the **stock.** Cover and reduce the heat, and simmer for 13 to 15 minutes, or until the macaroni is tender. Stir occasionally.

Easy Taco Dinner ◯ ½

Preparation: **14 min**   Cooking: **10 min**   Serves **4**   Cals per portion: **725**

2 tablespoons vegetable oil

1 medium-sized onion, peeled and chopped

1 large pepper, seeded and chopped

1¼ lb (575g) lean minced beef

¾ teaspoon ground cumin

1 teaspoon dried oregano

1 teaspoon chilli powder

½ teaspoon salt

2 to 4 green chillies, rinsed, seeded and chopped

1 x 15 oz (425g) can red kidney beans, drained

2 medium-sized tomatoes, diced

8 taco shells

6 oz (175g) grated strong Cheddar cheese

6 fl oz (175ml) soured cream

1 medium-sized cucumber, diced

1 small lettuce, or lettuce heart, shredded

1. Heat the **oil** in a large, heavy frying pan over moderate heat. Add the **onion** and **pepper,** and cook for 5 minutes, or until the onion is soft.

2. Add the **beef** and cook; stirring frequently, for 5 minutes, or until browned. Tilt the pan and skim off all but 2 tablespoons of the fat.

3. Stir in the **cumin, oregano, chilli powder, salt, chillies, beans** and **tomatoes.** Cover and simmer for 10 minutes, stirring once or twice.

4. Meanwhile, heat the **taco shells** according to packet directions. When the taco filling is cooked, transfer to a serving bowl. Serve with small bowls of the **cheese, soured cream, cucumber** and **lettuce.** Let everyone fill their own taco shells, allowing about 4 tablespoons of beef filling per taco, and garnish as desired.

Savoury Mince ½

Preparation: **5 min**   Cooking: **30 min**   Serves **4**   Cals per portion: **325**

1 tablespoon vegetable oil

2 onions, peeled and chopped

1¼ lb (575g) minced beef

1 tablespoon plain flour

8 fl oz (225ml) beef stock

1½ tablespoons Worcestershire sauce

½ teaspoon salt

½ teaspoon black pepper

1. Heat the **oil** in a medium-sized frying pan over moderate heat and fry the **onions** until soft. Add the **minced beef** and press down with a fork; fry until brown all over and separated. Sprinkle with **flour** and toss well.

2. Put the **stock** into a small saucepan and heat it to a gentle simmer. Gradually add the heated stock, **Worcestershire sauce, salt** and **pepper** to the meat and onions, stir well, cover and simmer gently for 30 minutes. Serve with mashed potatoes, buttered noodles, or on hot buttered toast.

Liver and Bacon Rolls ◎ ½

Preparation: **10 min**   Cooking: **15 min**   Serves **4**   Cals per portion: **440**

14 oz (400g) calf's liver in 1 piece

8 rashers lean bacon, trimmed of rind

Juice 1 lemon

1 teaspoon black pepper

1½ oz (40g) butter or margarine

4 tablespoons port

2 medium-sized cooking apples peeled, cored and sliced

3 shallots, peeled and finely sliced

4 fl oz (115ml) chicken stock

Look for the pale, tender and mild calf's liver. It may be more expensive than other varieties, but it is well worth it.

1. Peel and discard the thin membrane from the outside of the **liver.** With a sharp knife, slice the liver into 8 long, very thin slices. Lay a slice of liver on each rasher of **bacon,** making sure the bacon is just wider and longer than the liver slice. Sprinkle with the **lemon juice** and then the **pepper.** Roll up, with the bacon on the outside, and secure with a wooden cocktail stick or a little metal skewer.

2. Heat the **butter** in a medium-sized frying pan, add the bacon rolls and cook until lightly browned. Add the **port** and, when it starts to bubble, add the **apples, shallots** and the **stock.** Put the lid askew on the pan and cook over a low heat for 10 minutes. Serve with creamed potatoes and a green salad.

Sliced Liver in a Wine Sauce ◎ ½

Preparation: **10 min**   Cooking: **8 min**   Serves **4**   Cals per portion: **470**

1 lb (450g) calf's liver

2 tablespoons plain flour

1 teaspoon salt

1 teaspoon black pepper

2 tablespoons olive oil or vegetable oil

1½ oz (40g) butter or margarine

1 clove garlic, finely chopped

6 fl oz (175ml) white wine

2 tablespoons finely chopped parsley

1 teaspoon grated orange peel

6 fl oz (175ml) soured cream

1. Peel and discard the thin membrane from the outside of the **liver.** Slice the liver very thinly and cut into strips about ½in (15mm) wide. Mix the **flour, salt** and **pepper** on a plate and dredge the liver strips with the seasoned flour.

2. Heat the **oil** and **butter** in a large frying pan over moderately high heat, add the **garlic** and cook until just golden. Add the liver and cook quickly, turning with a spatula or fork, until sealed – about 3 minutes. With a slotted spoon, transfer the liver to a shallow dish and keep warm.

3. Pour in the **white wine,** add the **parsley** and **orange peel** and stir thoroughly. Allow the wine to bubble and reduce to half its volume. Reduce the heat and add the **soured cream;** stir and heat through. Taste and add more salt and pepper if necessary. Pour the hot sauce over the liver, and serve immediately with buttered noodles or boiled rice.

PORK, HAM AND SAUSAGES

PORK, HAM AND SAUSAGES

Pork is both nutritious and good to eat – especially when prepared in the appetising ways you will find here. Try the versatile gammon steak, for example. Simply cooked, it needs only a touch of spice or a glistening lemon-raisin sauce to make it exciting. In a really big rush? Stir-fry strips of pork with cucumbers in just 17 minutes. Or cook pork chops or sausages in new and unusual ways. Note that names of cuts of meat vary.

Casserole Roasted Pork with Vegetable Sauce

Preparation: **20 min**   Cooking: **1¾ hours**   Serves **6**   Cals per portion: **535**

Although this pork takes a while to cook, it needs little attention during that time and will serve 6 from an economical cut of meat. Leftovers can be used for sandwiches or in a recipe that calls for cooked pork. If you are feeding 6 and want leftovers for later use, roast a larger cut of pork, allowing about 30 minutes roasting time per 1lb (450g). An even simpler way to cook this cut of meat is to sprinkle it with about ½ teaspoon of salt and ¼ teaspoon of black pepper, place the pork on a rack in a roasting tin, and roast it, uncovered, for 35 minutes per 1lb (450g).

2 tablespoons vegetable oil

Piece of boned and rolled loin of pork (about 3lb/1.4kg)

1 large onion, peeled and chopped

1 large carrot, peeled and chopped

3 cloves garlic, peeled

1 teaspoon salt

½ teaspoon black pepper

¾ teaspoon dried rosemary

4 fl oz (115ml) dry white wine or chicken stock

4 fl oz (115ml) single cream

1. Preheat the oven to 160°C (325°F, gas mark 3). In a large roasting tin with a lid, heat the **oil** over moderately high heat for about 1 minute. Add the **pork** and brown it on all sides, turning it frequently – about 10 minutes. Transfer the roast to a plate.

2. Lower the heat to moderate. Put the **onion, carrot** and the whole cloves of **garlic** into the roasting tin, and cook, covered, for 5 minutes. Remove the tin from the heat, and add the **salt, pepper** and **rosemary.**

3. Return the roast to the tin, cover it and place it in the oven. Cook the meat, basting it several times with the pan juices, for about 90 minutes. Transfer the meat to a plate, and keep it warm.

4. Tilt the roasting tin and skim off all but about 1 tablespoon of the fat from the juices. Mash the vegetables with a fork and put the tin on the stove over a moderate heat. Add the **wine,** scraping up any brown bits stuck to the tin, and boil for 1 minute; then simmer for a further 2 minutes. Strain through a sieve.

5. Return the sauce to the roasting tin and add the **cream.** Heat the sauce gently for about 1 minute.

6. Carve the meat and serve with the sauce and with French Green Peas, page 75.

Spicy Pork Tacos ⊘

Preparation: **10 min**   Cooking: **6 min**   Serves **4**   Cals per portion: **570**

1 tablespoon vegetable oil

2 medium-sized onions, peeled and chopped

1 large stem celery, chopped

1 clove garlic, peeled and finely chopped

4 oz (115g) tomato purée

2 whole green chillies, rinsed, seeded and chopped

½ teaspoon dried oregano

¼ teaspoon salt

12 oz (350g) chopped cooked pork

8 taco shells

1 medium-sized avocado, peeled, stoned and thinly sliced

Juice 1 lemon

Shredded lettuce

4 fl oz (115ml) soured cream

Give the family a treat with these tasty, fun-to-eat tacos using leftover pork.

1. Heat the **oil** in a medium-sized frying pan over moderate heat. Add the **onions, celery** and **garlic.** Cook for 5 minutes, or until the onions are soft. Stir in the **tomato purée, chillies, oregano** and **salt.** Cover and simmer for 5 minutes, then add the **pork** and heat through – about 1 minute.

2. Meanwhile, heat the **taco shells** according to packet directions.

3. Toss the **avocado** slices with the **lemon juice.** Fill the taco shells with some of the meat mixture and some avocado slices and shredded **lettuce,** and top each with a spoonful of **soured cream.**

Tips: 1. You can substitute sliced cooked chicken or beef for the pork. 2. For extra 'bite', add a little chopped raw onion to each taco before serving. 3. Remember that taco shells should be warmed upside down – curved side uppermost.

Continental Pork and Peppers ⊘ ½

Preparation: **20 min**   Cooking: **7 min**   Serves **4**   Cals per portion: **240**

2 tablespoons vegetable oil

1 medium-sized onion, peeled and thinly sliced

3 medium-sized peppers, seeded and cut into ¼ in (5mm) strips

1 clove garlic, peeled and finely chopped

1 tablespoon paprika

½ teaspoon salt

½ teaspoon sugar

1 lb (450g) lean pork, cut into ¼ in (5mm) strips

1. Heat 1 tablespoon of the **oil** in a medium-sized frying pan over moderately high heat. Add the **onion, peppers** and **garlic,** and cook, covered, for 3 minutes.

2. Reduce the heat to moderate, and add the **paprika, salt** and **sugar** and cook, partially covered, for 10 minutes. Transfer the mixture to a warm bowl and put aside.

3. Heat the remaining oil in the pan over high heat for about 1 minute. Add the **pork** and cook, stirring frequently, until browned and cooked through – about 5 minutes. Return the onion and pepper mixture to the pan, and toss until heated through – about 2 minutes. Serve with buttered noodles.

Tip: If you use three different colours of peppers, the dish looks much more appetising.

Pork Stir-Fry with Vegetables and Peanuts ½

Preparation: 10 min   Cooking: **16 min**   Serves **4**   Cals per portion: **440**

2 tablespoons cornflour

1 lb (450g) lean pork, cut into
½ in (15mm) cubes

4 tablespoons vegetable oil

6 shallots, peeled and chopped

2 stems celery, cut diagonally
into ½ in (15mm) slices

8 oz (225g) mushrooms, sliced

2 tablespoons sugar

2 tablespoons white wine
vinegar

2 tablespoons soya sauce

4 fl oz (115ml) water

Pinch crushed dried chilli
flakes, or pinch chilli powder

1½ oz (40g) roasted, unsalted
peanuts

1. Put the **cornflour** into a large bowl and toss the **pork** cubes in it until coated. Heat 2 tablespoons of the **oil** in a large, heavy frying pan over moderately high heat for about 1 minute. Add half the pork and cook, stirring, for 5 minutes. Using a slotted spoon, transfer the cooked pork to a plate. Heat the remaining oil in the pan and cook the rest of the pork.

2. Add the **shallots, celery** and **mushrooms** to the pan and cook, stirring, for 1 minute.

3. In a small bowl, combine the **sugar, vinegar, soya sauce, water** and **chilli.** Pour the mixture into the pan and cook, scraping up any brown bits stuck to the pan, for 1 minute, or until the liquid thickens slightly.

4. Return the pork to the pan, add the **peanuts,** and toss until heated through.

Cucumber Pork

Preparation: **10 min**   Cooking: **7 min**   Serves **4**   Cals per portion: **230**

2 tablespoons vegetable oil

1 clove garlic, peeled and
finely chopped

¼ teaspoon dried chilli flakes, or
pinch chilli powder

1 teaspoon salt

4 shallots, peeled and thinly
sliced

12 oz (350g) lean pork, cut into
¼ in (5mm) strips

16 fresh mange tout

1 tablespoon sugar

1 tablespoon cider vinegar

2 tablespoons beef stock

1 large cucumber, seeded and
cut into thin, 2 in (50mm) strips

You can prepare the ingredients for this dish a short while beforehand, and cook them at the last minute.

1. Heat the **oil** in a medium-sized frying pan over moderately high heat. Add the **garlic, chilli** and **salt,** and cook, stirring, for 30 seconds.

2. Add the **shallots, pork** and **mange tout.** Cook, stirring, for 5 minutes or until the pork is no longer pink.

3. Combine the **sugar, vinegar** and **stock,** and add the mixture to the pan together with the **cucumber.** Cook, tossing the ingredients, until heated through and the pork is tender. Do not overcook or the pork will toughen. Serve with rice and Sautéed Broccoli, page 65.

> **Tip:** *Instead of using cucumber you can use courgettes cut into thin slivers.*

Sweet and Sour Pork ◁ ½

Preparation: **10 min**   Cooking: **7 min**   Serves **4**   Cals per portion: **320**

2 teaspoons vegetable oil

12 oz (350g) lean pork cut into ¼ in (5mm) strips

1 x 16 oz (450g) can pineapple pieces, undrained

2 tablespoons cornflour

3 tablespoons cider vinegar

Juice 1 lemon

3 tablespoons soya sauce

¼ teaspoon salt

2 tablespoons dark, moist brown sugar

1 large pepper, seeded and chopped

1 small onion, peeled and thinly sliced

Tip: *Use 2 slices of fresh pineapple, peeled and chopped, and ¼ pint (150ml) fruit juice.*

1. Heat the **oil** in a large, heavy frying pan over moderately high heat for about 1 minute. Add the **pork** strips and cook, stirring frequently, for 5 minutes or until browned.

2. Meanwhile, drain the juice from the **pineapple** pieces into a small bowl. Blend in the **cornflour, vinegar, lemon juice, soya sauce, salt** and **sugar**, and put aside.

3. Add the **pepper** and **onion** to the pan, and cook until the onion begins to soften – about 3 minutes.

4. Add the pineapple juice mixture to the pan, reduce the heat to moderate, and cook, stirring, for 3 minutes or until the liquid thickens slightly.

5. Add the pineapple pieces and heat through – about 1 minute. Serve with rice or crisp Chinese noodles and accompany with Cucumber Salad with Soya and Sesame Dressing, page 47.

Pork with Oranges and Wine ½

Preparation: **25 min**   Cooking: **15 min**   Serves **6**   Cals per portion: **275**

3 tablespoons olive oil or vegetable oil

1½ lb (700g) lean pork cut into ½ in (15mm) cubes

1 large onion, peeled and chopped

3 cloves garlic, peeled and finely chopped

¼ pint (150ml) dry white wine

⅓ pint (190ml) orange juice

½ teaspoon ground cumin

¼ teaspoon cayenne pepper

½ teaspoon salt

2 oranges, peeled and divided into segments

1. Heat the **oil** in a large, heavy frying pan over moderately high heat for about 1 minute. Add the **pork** and cook, stirring frequently, for 5 minutes or until browned.

2. Push the meat to one side of the pan, add the **onion** and **garlic** to the fat, and cook for 5 minutes or until the onion is soft.

3. Add the **wine** and boil for 2 minutes. Reduce the heat, and add the **orange juice, cumin, cayenne pepper** and **salt.** Cover and simmer for 15 minutes, until the pork is tender and cooked through. Add the **oranges** during the last 5 minutes of cooking. Serve with buttered rice or noodles.

Pork and Courgette Skillet ½

Preparation: **10 min**   Cooking: **20 min**   Serves **4**   Cals per portion: **265**

2 tablespoons olive oil or vegetable oil

1 lb (450g) lean pork, cut into ½ in (15mm) cubes

1 large onion, peeled and chopped

2 cloves garlic, peeled and finely chopped

⅔ pint (380ml) tomato juice

½ teaspoon salt

Pinch black pepper

½ teaspoon dried rosemary

1 teaspoon dried oregano

4 medium-sized courgettes cut into ½ in (15mm) slices

Practically a meal in itself, this dish need only be accompanied by buttered noodles, bread and a salad or fruit.

1. Heat the **oil** in a large, heavy frying pan over moderately high heat for about 1 minute. Add the **pork** and cook, tossing frequently, for 5 minutes, or until browned.

2. Lower the heat to moderate, add the **onion** and **garlic** and cook for 5 more minutes, or until the onion is soft.

3. Add the **tomato juice, salt, pepper, rosemary** and **oregano.** Simmer for 5 minutes, stirring once or twice.

4. Add the **courgettes** and cook for 5 minutes, or until the courgettes are tender but still crisp, the juice has thickened, and the pork is cooked through.

Tip: When tomatoes are plentiful, use 1lb (450g) skinned and chopped, with a little stock, in place of the tomato juice.

Pork Chops with Orange Sauce ½

Preparation: **9 min**   Cooking: **40 min**   Serves **4**   Cals per portion: **450**

1 tablespoon vegetable oil

4 lean pork chops, about ¾ in (20mm) thick

½ teaspoon salt

Pinch black pepper

¼ pint (150ml) chicken stock

1¼ teaspoons cornflour

¼ teaspoon ground cinnamon

8 fl oz (225ml) orange juice

1 orange

4 whole cloves

Tip: Leftovers can be refrigerated for 1 or 2 days, or frozen.

1. Heat the **oil** in a large, heavy frying pan over moderately high heat for about 1 minute. Add the **pork chops** and cook for 4 minutes on each side. Add the **salt, pepper** and **chicken stock;** cover, reduce the heat, and simmer for 35 minutes.

2. Meanwhile, in a small bowl combine the **cornflour, cinnamon** and half the **orange juice.** Grate the rind of half the **orange** and add it to the bowl. Peel the orange, cut it into ½in (15mm) slices, and add it to the mixture.

3. Transfer the chops to a warm plate. Add the remaining orange juice and the **cloves** to the pan and boil, stirring, for 4 or 5 minutes or until only about 4fl oz (115ml) of juice remains. Remove the cloves with a slotted spoon.

4. Add the cornflour mixture to the pan and boil for 1 or 2 minutes, stirring until thickened. Pour the sauce over the chops and serve.

Breaded Pork Chops with Herbs ½

Preparation: **15 min**   Cooking: **40 min**   Serves **4**   Cals per portion: **550**

While these pork chops bake, prepare a side dish, such as Cos Salad with Blue Cheese and Walnuts, page 54, or Potato Pancakes, page 78.

3 oz (75g) fine dry breadcrumbs

½ teaspoon salt

Pinch black pepper

¾ teaspoon dried rosemary, or 1 tablespoon chopped parsley

2 tablespoons plain flour

1 egg

4 pork chops, about ¾ in (20mm) thick

3 tablespoons vegetable oil

½ oz (15g) butter

1. Preheat the oven to 180°C (350°F, gas mark 4). In a shallow bowl, combine the **breadcrumbs, salt, pepper** and **rosemary.** Put the **flour** onto a plate, and lightly beat the **egg** in a shallow bowl. Coat the **pork chops** with the flour, dip them into the beaten egg, and then coat them with the breadcrumb mixture.

2. In a large, heavy frying pan with an ovenproof handle, heat the **oil** and **butter** over moderate heat for about 1 minute. Add the chops, and cook for 3 minutes on each side.

3. Spoon off all but 2 tablespoons of the fat. Cover tightly, and bake in the oven for 40 minutes or until the chops are tender and cooked through, turning once.

> **Tip:** *Instead of using a mixture of breadcrumbs and herbs, try using any stuffing mix.*

Pork Chops in Spicy Tomato Sauce ½

Preparation: **14 min**   Cooking: **30 min**   Serves **4**   Cals per portion: **490**

½ oz (15g) butter or margarine

1 tablespoon olive oil or vegetable oil

4 pork chops, about ¾ in (20mm) thick

¼ pint (150ml) dry red or white wine

4 oz (115g) tomato purée

3 fl oz (90ml) water

3 tablespoons chopped parsley

2 cloves garlic, peeled and finely chopped

½ teaspoon dried rosemary

½ teaspoon dried basil

½ teaspoon salt

Pinch black pepper

Try these pork chops with pasta. Spoon the sauce over cooked noodles and sprinkle with grated Parmesan cheese. Serve with a green salad.

1. Heat the **butter** and **oil** in a large, heavy frying pan over moderately high heat for about 1 minute. Add the **pork chops.** Cook for 4 minutes on each side, or until browned. Pour off all but 1 tablespoon of the fat.

2. Add the **wine** and boil for 1 minute or until reduced by half.

3. Stir in the **tomato purée, water, parsley, garlic, rosemary, basil, salt** and **pepper.** Reduce the heat, cover, and simmer for 30 minutes or until the chops are tender and cooked through; check occasionally and add a little extra water if the sauce seems too thick.

> **Tip:** *Instead of using dried herbs, look for the jars of Pesto sauce that can be found in supermarkets or delicatessens – add 2 teaspoons.*

Braised Pork Chops with Pears and Onions ½

Preparation: **10 min** Cooking: **50 min**   Serves **4** Cals per portion: **485**

½ oz (15g) butter or margarine

1 tablespoon vegetable oil

4 pork chops, about ¾ in (20mm) thick

2 medium-sized onions, peeled and sliced

4 fl oz (115ml) dry white wine

4 fl oz (115ml) chicken stock

¼ teaspoon salt

Pinch black pepper

2 medium-sized firm, ripe pears, peeled, cored, and cut into ¼ in (5mm) slices

> **Tip:** Cider also goes well with the pork and pears, and can be used as a cheaper substitute for the wine.

1. Preheat the oven to 180°C (350°F, gas mark 4). In a large, heavy frying pan with an ovenproof handle and a cover, heat the **butter** and **oil** over moderately high heat for about 1 minute. Add the **pork chops** and cook for 4 minutes on each side or until browned. Transfer the chops to a plate and put aside.

2. Reduce the heat to moderate, add the **onions** to the pan, and cook for 5 minutes or until soft. Spoon the onions over the chops. Add the **wine** to the pan and boil for 1 minute, scraping up any brown bits stuck to the bottom. Stir in the **chicken stock, salt** and **pepper.**

3. Return the chops and onions to the pan, and arrange the sliced **pears** on top. Bake, covered, for 40 minutes or until the chops are tender and cooked through. Check occasionally and add a little extra stock if the liquid is evaporating. Serve with boiled potatoes and Courgette Patties, page 80.

Pork and Vegetable Platter ½

Preparation: **10 min** Cooking: **45 min**   Serves **4**   Cals per portion: **500**

1 tablespoon vegetable oil

4 pork chops, about ¾ in (20mm) thick

8 fl oz (225ml) beef stock

4 fl oz (115ml) water

½ teaspoon salt

Pinch black pepper

4 medium-sized potatoes, scrubbed (but not peeled) and cut into ½ in (15mm) slices

1 lb (450g) carrots, peeled and coarsely chopped

½ teaspoon dried thyme

1 tablespoon chopped parsley

This no-fuss, one-dish dinner has everything – meat, potatoes and vegetables – but you may want to serve it with a salad such as Apple Salad with Soured Cream Dressing, page 58.

1. Heat the **oil** in a large, heavy frying pan over moderately high heat for about 1 minute. Add the **pork chops** and cook for 4 minutes on each side or until browned.

2. Tilt the pan and spoon off all but 2 tablespoons of the fat. Add the **beef stock, water, salt, pepper, potatoes, carrots, thyme** and **parsley.** Cover and cook over moderately low heat for 35 minutes or until the chops are tender and cooked through.

> **Tip:** For a sweeter-flavoured dish, try substituting apple juice for the stock.

Minced Pork Pie

Preparation: **5 min**   Cooking: **25 min**   Serves **4**   Cals per portion: **395**

1 lb 2 oz (500g) minced pork

1 large onion, peeled and finely chopped

½ teaspoon salt

¼ teaspoon black pepper

¼ teaspoon dried savory or marjoram

¼ teaspoon dried thyme or sage

Pinch ground cloves

¼ pint (150ml) beef stock

2 tablespoons plain flour

3 oz (75g) fine dry breadcrumbs

1 oz (25g) butter, cut into small pieces

1. Preheat the oven to 200°C (400°F, gas mark 6). In a medium-sized frying pan, combine the **pork, onion, salt, pepper, savory, thyme** and **cloves.** Add the **stock** and simmer for 10 minutes, stirring occasionally. Tilt the pan and skim off the fat from the liquid, then blend in the **flour.**

2. Transfer the mixture to an 8in (200mm) pie dish and cover with the **breadcrumbs** and knobs of **butter.** Bake for about 15 minutes, or until lightly browned. Serve with baked beans or red kidney beans.

Tip: If you have time, use your favourite pie pastry instead of the breadcrumbs. Use 2 pieces: line the pie dish with one, add the filling, and cover the pie with the other. Seal the edges together, cut several small slits in the top crust, and bake until the pie is slightly browned – about 30 minutes.

Pork Curry with Apples and Cream ½

Preparation: **8 min**   Cooking: **15 min**   Serves **4**   Cals per portion: **510**

2 tablespoons vegetable oil

2 medium-sized onions, peeled and chopped

2 cloves garlic, peeled and finely chopped

2 stems celery, diced

1¼ lb (575g) lean minced pork

8 fl oz (225ml) apple juice

2 teaspoons curry powder

1 teaspoon salt

¼ teaspoon ground ginger

1 teaspoon ground cumin

1 medium-sized cooking apple, cored and diced

1½ oz (40g) raisins

8 fl oz (225ml) soured cream

1. Heat the **oil** in a large, heavy frying pan over moderate heat. Add the **onions, garlic** and **celery** and cook for 5 minutes. Raise the heat, add the **pork,** and cook, stirring, for 5 minutes or until no pink remains.

2. Add the **apple juice, curry powder, salt, ginger, cumin, apple** and **raisins.** Stir, then reduce the heat and simmer for 5 to 8 minutes, or until most of the apple juice has evaporated but the mixture is not dry.

3. Remove the pan from the heat and stir in the **soured cream.** Return to the heat just long enough to heat through. Do not let the mixture boil or the soured cream will curdle. Serve with rice and a cucumber salad.

Tips: 1. You can substitute natural yoghurt for the soured cream. 2. Try coconut milk instead of the soured cream: steep 3oz (75g) desiccated coconut in 8fl oz (225ml) boiling water for 30 minutes. Strain through a sieve, pressing on the coconut.

Pork Balls with Mushrooms ½

Preparation: **17 min**   Cooking: **22 min**   Serves **4**   Cals per portion: **400**

1 lb (450g) lean minced pork

1 egg, lightly beaten

½ teaspoon dried thyme

½ teaspoon dried oregano

½ teaspoon salt

¼ teaspoon black pepper

2 oz (50g) fine fresh breadcrumbs

1 teaspoon French mustard

1 oz (25g) butter or margarine

1 tablespoon vegetable oil

8 oz (225g) mushrooms, sliced

2 fl oz (50ml) dry white wine

4 fl oz (115ml) chicken stock

4 fl oz (115ml) soured cream

1. In a mixing bowl, combine the **pork, egg, thyme, oregano, salt, pepper, breadcrumbs** and **mustard.** Shape the mixture into 1in (25mm) balls.

2. Heat the **butter** and **oil** in a large, heavy frying pan over moderately high heat for about 1 minute. Cook the meatballs, turning frequently, until browned on all sides – about 5 minutes.

3. Reduce the heat to low, add the **mushrooms**, and cook gently for about 2 minutes.

4. Add the **wine** and **chicken stock** and simmer for 10 minutes. Blend in the **soured cream** and simmer 5 minutes longer, until the sauce has thickened and the pork balls are cooked through. Serve hot with rice or noodles and Grated Carrots with Herbs and Lemon, page 47, or steamed broccoli with butter and lemon.

Tips: 1. You can substitute minced lamb or veal for the pork. 2. Press a whole blanched almond and half a tenderised, pitted prune into the centre of each meatball when shaping.

Spicy Gammon Steak ⊘

Preparation: **3 min**   Cooking: **16 min**   Serves **4**   Cals per portion: **370**

1 tablespoon vegetable oil

4 lean gammon steaks about ½ in (15mm) thick

2½ fl oz (75ml) pineapple or orange juice

2½ fl oz (75ml) tomato ketchup

2 tablespoons brown or white sugar

2 fl oz (50ml) cider vinegar

1 tablespoon French mustard

1 tablespoon Worcestershire sauce

¼ teaspoon black pepper

1. Heat the **oil** in a large, heavy frying pan over moderately high heat for about 1 minute. Add the **gammon steaks** and cook for 3 minutes on each side or until browned.

2. In a small bowl, combine the **fruit juice, tomato ketchup, sugar, vinegar, mustard, Worcestershire sauce** and **pepper.** Add the mixture to the pan and simmer for 10 minutes. Serve with Glorious Mashed Potatoes, page 76.

Tip: Chop any leftovers, add to baked beans, and heat them; this makes a tasty light meal for children.

Gammon Steak with Lemon-Raisin Sauce ▣ ½

Preparation: **5 min**   Cooking: **15 min**   Serves **4**   Cals per portion: **470**

The tangy sauce for this dish is easy to make and is a perfect foil for the richness of the gammon steaks.

2 oz (50g) butter or margarine

4 lean gammon steaks about ½ in (15mm) thick

8 fl oz (225ml) beef stock

4 fl oz (115ml) dry white wine

2 tablespoons cider vinegar or white wine vinegar

1 tablespoon firmly packed brown sugar

Grated rind and juice 1 lemon

3 oz (75g) raisins

¼ teaspoon black pepper

1. Heat ¾oz (20g) of the **butter** in a large, heavy frying pan over moderately high heat until bubbling. Add the **gammon steaks** and cook for 3 minutes on each side or until browned. Transfer the gammon to a warm plate, cover with foil, and put aside.

2. Add the **beef stock, wine, vinegar, sugar, lemon rind, lemon juice, raisins** and **pepper** to the pan, and cook, stirring, over moderately high heat for 4 to 5 minutes or until about 6fl oz (175ml) of liquid remains.

3. Add the gammon steaks and simmer until tender. Stir in the remaining butter. Serve with mashed potatoes or Shredded Cabbage with Garlic, page 67.

> **Tip:** *Use apple juice instead of white wine.*

Gammon Steak with Glazed Apple Rings ▣ ½

Preparation: **5 min**   Cooking: **15 min**   Serves **4**   Cals per portion: **365**

1¾ oz (45g) butter or margarine

4 gammon steaks about ½ in (15mm) thick

1 teaspoon brown sugar

¼ teaspoon ground cinnamon

1 medium-sized apple, cored and cut into 6 rings

2½ fl oz (75ml) cider or apple juice

¼ teaspoon black pepper

> **Tip:** *As a variation, use sliced firm pears instead of the apple rings.*

1. Heat a third of the **butter** in a large, heavy frying pan over moderately high heat until bubbling. Add the **gammon steaks** and cook for 3 minutes on each side or until browned. Transfer the gammon to a plate and put aside.

2. Pour off and discard the fat from the pan, then add the remaining butter and the **sugar** and **cinnamon.** Heat until the butter is bubbling, then add the **apple** rings and cook for 1 minute on each side or until they just begin to soften. Remove the apple rings and keep warm.

3. Add the **cider** to the pan and boil for 1 minute, scraping up any brown bits stuck to the surface. Return the gammon to the pan and simmer until tender. Add the apple rings and **pepper** and heat through. Serve with Brussels Sprouts with Walnuts, page 66.

Baked Gammon Steak ½

Preparation: **22 min**   Cooking: **20 min**   Serves **4**   Cals per portion: **365**

If you are short of time, bake the gammon as soon as you pour the marinade over it. Or you can use the marinating time to prepare the rest of the meal.

4 lean gammon steaks about ½ in (15mm) thick

Juice 1 lemon

1 tablespoon firmly packed brown sugar

¼ teaspoon curry powder

½ teaspoon French mustard

¼ teaspoon black pepper

1 oz (25g) butter or margarine, softened

1. Preheat the oven to 190°C (375°F, gas mark 5). Place the **gammon steaks** in a greased, ovenproof dish and put aside. In a small saucepan, combine the **lemon juice, sugar, curry powder, mustard** and **pepper.** Bring the mixture to the boil and pour over the gammon. Let the gammon marinate for 20 minutes at room temperature.

2. Bake the gammon for 20 minutes or until bubbling and tender. Transfer to a warm serving dish. Add the **butter** to the juices in the baking dish and stir until blended. Pour the sauce over the gammon, and serve with pumpkin.

Gammon Steak Florentine ⊘

Preparation: **17 min**   Cooking: **12 min**   Serves **4**   Cals per portion: **450**

1 lb (450g) fresh spinach

1 oz (25g) butter or margarine

4 lean gammon steaks about ½ in (15mm) thick

4 fl oz (115ml) chicken stock

4 fl oz (115ml) soured cream or natural yoghurt

Pinch ground nutmeg

¼ teaspoon salt

Pinch black pepper

1½ oz (40g) grated Parmesan cheese

> *Tip: You can use this spinach mixture with poached fish, chicken or eggs – all very good combinations.*

1. Preheat the grill. Trim the **spinach** of coarse stems and blemished leaves, wash it, and shake dry. Place the spinach in a large saucepan with just the water that clings to the leaves, and cook, covered, for 5 minutes or until just limp. Drain spinach thoroughly and put aside.

2. Heat the **butter** in a heavy frying pan over moderately high heat until bubbling. Add the **gammon steaks.** Cook for 4 to 5 minutes on each side, or until browned and tender. Transfer to a flameproof baking dish.

3. Add the **chicken stock** to the pan, and cook, stirring, for 3 minutes or until 2 tablespoons of stock remain. Reduce the heat to moderate, add the **soured cream** and heat through, but do not boil – about 2 minutes. Add the spinach, **nutmeg, salt** and **pepper.** Heat, stirring, for 1 minute.

4. Spread the spinach mixture over the gammon steaks and sprinkle with the **cheese.** Grill for 2 or 3 minutes or until the cheese is browned and bubbling. Serve with rice or Carrot and Potato Purée, page 70.

Ham with Mushrooms and Cream Sauce ½

Preparation: **15 min**   Cooking: **3 min**   Serves **4**   Cals per portion: **295**

Here is an elegant way to use leftover ham. You can serve it over toasted French bread for lunch or have it for dinner with buttered noodles or rice.

1 oz (25g) butter or margarine

1 small onion, peeled and chopped

½ teaspoon cornflour

¼ pint (150ml) double cream

1 tablespoon dry sherry

6 oz (175g) button mushrooms, sliced

8 oz (225g) diced cooked ham

Pinch black pepper

1. Melt the **butter** in a large frying pan over moderate heat. Add the **onion** and cook for 5 minutes or until soft.

2. Meanwhile, in a bowl, blend the **cornflour** with 1 tablespoon of the **cream** until smooth. Add the remaining cream and the **sherry.** Put aside.

3. Add the **mushrooms** to the pan and cook, stirring frequently, for 3 minutes.

4. Add the **ham, pepper** and the cream mixture to the pan. Cook, stirring frequently, over moderately high heat for 3 minutes or until the sauce thickens and the mixture is hot.

> **Tip:** *This makes a delicious filling for pancakes.*

Smothered Ham and Pork Patties

Preparation: **15 min**   Cooking: **20 min**   Serves **4**   Cals per portion: **400**

You can make this recipe with all ham or all pork.

8 oz (225g) finely chopped cooked ham

8 oz (225g) finely chopped cooked pork

1 medium-sized onion, peeled and finely chopped

1 egg, lightly beaten

3 oz (75g) fine dry breadcrumbs

¼ teaspoon dried marjoram or rosemary

¼ teaspoon salt

Pinch black pepper

4 tablespoons vegetable oil

1 medium-sized onion, peeled and thinly sliced

2 tablespoons plain flour

8 fl oz (225ml) beef or chicken stock

1 tablespoon French mustard

1. In a large bowl, combine the **ham, pork, chopped onion, egg,** two-thirds of the **breadcrumbs,** the **marjoram, salt, pepper** and 1 tablespoon of the **oil.** If the mixture is too sticky to shape easily, add more breadcrumbs. Divide the mixture into 4 balls. Put the remaining breadcrumbs in a shallow dish or pie plate. Roll the balls into the crumbs, flattening them into oval patties ¾in (20mm) thick.

2. Heat the remaining oil in a large, heavy, medium-sized frying pan over moderate heat for 1 minute. Add the patties, and cook for 5 to 6 minutes on each side. Using a slotted spoon, transfer them to a plate and put aside.

3. Reduce the heat. Add the **sliced onion** and cook for 5 minutes or until soft. Blend in the **flour,** stirring continuously, then slowly add the **stock.** Cook, stirring, until thickened – about 3 minutes. Blend in the **mustard.** Return the patties, along with any accumulated juices, to the sauce in the pan and reheat briefly. Spoon the sauce over the patties and serve.

Ham Loaves with Sweet and Sour Sauce

Preparation: **10 min**   Cooking: **35 min**   Serves **4**   Cals per portion: **305**

For a different way to use leftover ham, try these mildly spiced individual loaves baked in dariole moulds.

8 oz (225g) finely chopped cooked ham

8 oz (225g) minced pork

2 oz (50g) fine dry breadcrumbs

1 small onion, peeled and chopped

1 egg, lightly beaten

4 fl oz (115ml) milk

¼ teaspoon salt

Pinch black pepper

3 tablespoons firmly packed brown sugar

3 tablespoons cider vinegar

2 teaspoons prepared English mustard

1. Preheat the oven to 190°C (375°F, gas mark 5). In a large bowl, combine the **ham, pork, breadcrumbs, onion, egg, milk, salt** and **pepper.**

2. Butter eight small dariole moulds and pack the mixture into them, mounding it slightly in the centres but not letting it touch the top edges of the moulds. Bake for 20 minutes.

3. Meanwhile, in a small saucepan, combine the **sugar, vinegar** and **mustard.** Bring to the boil over moderately high heat, then cook, stirring, for 1 minute or until the sugar dissolves. Taste for seasoning, adding another tablespoon of vinegar and teaspoon of mustard if desired.

4. Pour the sauce evenly onto the ham loaves and bake an additional 15 minutes. Remove the loaves carefully from their moulds and serve hot with prepared horseradish or mustard on the side.

Ham and Cheese Strata ½

Preparation: **10 min**   Cooking: **20 min**   Serves **4**   Cals per portion: **445**

Turn a simple ham and cheese sandwich into a main-course meal by following this recipe.

8 slices firm-textured whole wheat or white bread

4 oz (115g) grated strong Cheddar cheese

5 oz (150g) finely chopped cooked ham

4 eggs, lightly beaten

8 fl oz (225ml) milk

¼ teaspoon salt

Pinch cayenne pepper

½ teaspoon prepared English mustard

½ oz (15g) butter or margarine

1. Preheat the oven to 200°C (400°F, gas mark 6). Butter a shallow casserole dish and arrange 4 slices of the **bread** on the bottom. If the bread will not fit neatly, trim off the crusts. Sprinkle the slices with half the **cheese** and all the **ham.** Top with the remaining 4 slices of bread.

2. Beat the **eggs, milk, salt, cayenne pepper** and **mustard** together, and pour the mixture evenly over the bread to the edges of the pan. Top with the remaining cheese and dot with the **butter.** Bake for 20 to 25 minutes, or until the egg mixture is set. Serve hot with Red Cabbage with Apples, page 68, or Spinach Dressed with Oil and Vinegar, page 79.

> **Tip:** *Try rye bread and Swiss cheese instead of whole wheat, or white bread and Cheddar cheese, and sprinkle the top with poppy seeds.*

Oriental Ham and Beef Balls ⊘

Preparation: **15 min** Cooking: **10 min**   Serves **6** Cals per portion: **340**

12 oz (350g) cooked ham, finely chopped

12 oz (350g) lean minced beef

4 shallots, peeled and finely chopped

4 oz (115g) fresh fine breadcrumbs

1 egg, lightly beaten

5 tablespoons milk

3 tablespoons vegetable oil

4 tablespoons firmly packed brown sugar

6 tablespoons water

6 tablespoons cider vinegar

1 teaspoon dry mustard

1 tablespoon soya sauce

2 tablespoons dry sherry

1. In a large bowl, combine the **ham, beef, shallots, breadcrumbs, egg** and **milk.** Shape the mixture into 1in (25mm) balls.

2. Heat the **oil** in a large, heavy frying pan over moderately high heat for about 1 minute. Cook the meatballs, turning frequently, until browned on all sides – about 5 minutes.

3. Meanwhile, in a small bowl, combine the **brown sugar, water, vinegar, mustard, soya sauce** and **sherry.** Pour this mixture over the meatballs, reduce the heat, cover, and simmer for 10 minutes, stirring occasionally until the meatballs are tender. Serve with rice and a green vegetable.

Tips: 1. You can substitute pork for the beef, but simmer the meatballs 5 minutes longer. 2. Make the balls smaller and serve them hot with cocktail sticks as hors d'oeuvres.

Ham Jambalaya ½

Preparation: **15 min** Cooking: **20 min**   Serves **4** Cals per portion: **285**

3 tablespoons vegetable oil

2 large onions, peeled and chopped

1 large pepper, seeded and chopped

2 or 3 cloves garlic, peeled and finely chopped

8 oz (225g) diced cooked ham

4 oz (115g) rice

½ teaspoon dried thyme

½ teaspoon salt

4 drops Tabasco sauce

4 medium-sized tomatoes, chopped

¾ pint (450ml) chicken stock

1. Heat the **oil** in a large, heavy frying pan over moderate heat. Add the **onions, pepper** and **garlic**, and cook for 5 minutes or until the onions are soft.

2. Add the **ham** and **rice,** and stir until the rice is well coated with oil – about 1 minute.

3. Add the **thyme, salt, Tabasco sauce, tomatoes** and **stock.** Cover and simmer for 20 to 25 minutes, or until the rice is tender and all the liquid has been absorbed. Serve jambalaya with a green salad and crusty bread.

Tips: 1. For a different texture and flavour, use half standard rice and half wild rice. 2. For a special occasion add about 2oz (50g) peeled prawns.

Sausage and Pepper Open Omelette ½

Preparation: **22 min**   Cooking: **10 min**   Serves **4**   Cals per portion: **630**

2 oz (50g) butter or margarine

2 tablespoons olive oil or vegetable oil

2 medium-sized new potatoes, scrubbed (but not peeled) and thinly sliced

8-10 oz (225-275g) continental sausage such as kabanos or chorizo, thickly sliced

1 medium-sized onion, peeled and chopped

1 medium-sized green pepper, seeded and chopped

6 eggs

¼ teaspoon salt

¼ teaspoon black pepper

1 level teaspoon dried oregano or marjoram

1. Heat the **butter** and **oil** in a large, heavy frying pan over high heat. Add the **potatoes.** Cook for 8-10 minutes, tossing frequently, until the potatoes are cooked through. Push the potatoes to one side and lower the heat to moderate. Add the **sausage, onion** and **green pepper** and fry for 5 minutes, until the onion and pepper are soft.

2. Beat the **eggs** with the **salt** and **pepper** and **oregano.** Toss the contents of the pan together then pour in the eggs. Reduce the heat to low, cover the pan, and cook until the eggs are almost set – about 5 to 6 minutes. Preheat the grill to high.

3. Place the pan (but not the handle) under the grill for 2 to 3 minutes, or until the omelette is lightly browned. Cut into wedges and serve with a salad.

> **Tips: 1.** *You can replace the sausage with grilled chipolata sausages or diced cooked ham.* **2.** *The omelette can be served cold.*

Toad in the Hole ½

Preparation: **15 min**   Cooking: **35 min**   Serves **4**   Cals per portion: **645**

This traditional dish is economical and easy to prepare.

4 oz (115g) plain flour

½ teaspoon salt

2 eggs

½ pint (285ml) milk

6 large spicy sausages

3 tablespoons pork or beef dripping, or vegetable oil

4 rashers streaky bacon, cut into 1½ in (40mm) strips

1. Preheat the oven to 200°C (400°F, gas mark 6). Prepare a batter by putting the **flour** and **salt** into a mixing bowl; make a well in the centre, add the **eggs** and break each yolk. Mix in the **milk,** gradually stirring in the flour, and whisking until the batter is smooth with no lumps. Put in the refrigerator for 30 minutes.

2. Grill the **sausages** until lightly browned on all sides; cut each sausage in half lengthways. Put the **dripping** and the **bacon** into an ovenproof casserole (about 10 x 12in/250 x 300mm), and bake for 5 minutes. Add the sausages and pour the batter over them. (The dish and the dripping must be sizzling hot when the batter is added.) Bake until the batter has risen and is golden-brown – about 35 minutes. Serve immediately with Creole Sauce, page 303, and green beans.

Sausages and Apples

Preparation: **1 min**   Cooking: **20 min**   Serves **4**   Cals per portion: **525**

The combination of pork and apples is traditional in the cooking of many countries.

1 lb (450g) pork sausages

2 large apples

4 fl oz (115ml) milk

2 oz (50g) plain flour

¼ teaspoon ground cinnamon

2 tablespoons brown sugar

4 fl oz (115ml) cider or apple juice

¼ teaspoon salt

¼ teaspoon black pepper

Tip: As a variation, use sliced firm pears instead of the apples.

1. Cook the **sausages** in a large, heavy frying pan over moderate heat for 10 minutes. Transfer the sausages to a plate and keep warm. Do not discard the fat in the pan.

2. Meanwhile, core the **apples,** but do not peel, and cut them into ½in (15mm) rings.

3. Place the **milk** and **flour** in separate small shallow bowls or saucers. Dip the apple rings into the milk, coat them with the flour, then place them in the pan. Reduce the heat. Sprinkle the rings with the **cinnamon** and **brown sugar,** and cook for 3 minutes on each side. Transfer the apples to the plate.

4. Add the **cider, salt** and **pepper.** Raise the heat and bring to the boil, scraping up any brown bits stuck to the pan. Cook until reduced by half – about 4 minutes. Return the apples and sausages to the pan to reheat briefly.

Sausage Pilaf ½

Preparation: **12 min**   Cooking: **22 min**   Serves **6**   Cals per portion: **430**

Try this sausage, rice and aubergine dish with a side dish of chilled natural yoghurt to spoon over the top, if desired.

1 small aubergine (about 8 oz/225g)

4 tablespoons vegetable oil

8 oz (225g) mushrooms, sliced

4 oz (115g) rice

¾ pint (450ml) chicken stock

½ teaspoon ground cumin

2 teaspoons salt

½ teaspoon black pepper

1 lb (450g) pork sausages

Tip: You can omit the aubergine and use more mushrooms, or substitute diced cooked chicken, ham or lamb for the sausage.

1. Cut the **aubergine** into ¼in (5mm) slices, then cut the slices into ¼in (5mm) strips.

2. Heat the **oil** in a large, heavy saucepan over moderate heat. Add the aubergine strips and **mushrooms.** Cook for 5 minutes or until the vegetables are soft.

3. Add the **rice** and stir until it is well coated with oil – about 1 minute. Add the **stock, cumin, salt** and **pepper.** Reduce the heat, cover, and simmer for 20 minutes, or until the rice is tender and all the liquid has been absorbed.

4. Meanwhile, cook the **sausages** in a heavy frying pan over moderate heat for 10 minutes, or until browned. Drain the sausages on absorbent paper and cut into ¾in (20mm) pieces and stir them into the rice mixture when the rice is cooked. Cover and heat through – about 2 or 3 minutes.

LAMB

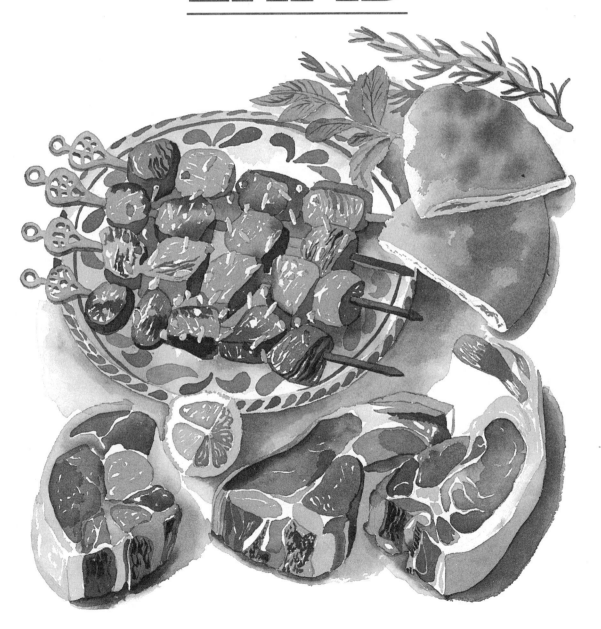

Joint of Lamb

Leftover Lamb

Lamb Fillet

Chops

Minced Lamb

(See also recipes for Beef and Pork;
some of which work well with Lamb
and Oven-Baked Dishes)

LAMB

Years ago, lamb was almost always cooked well done but, as it is a tender and succulent meat, it can suffer if left in the oven for too long. When overcooked, lamb can be tough, dry and greyish, but when taken from the heat slightly underdone, it is moist, tender, pinkish and full of flavour. Recipes in this chapter – such as Lamb Chops with Mushrooms and Wine, Honey-Orange Lamb Chops and Parsley Lamb Patties – give you a choice of how the meat should be cooked.

If you have always eaten your lamb well done, try removing it from the heat when it is medium rare. You will discover why lamb prepared this way has become so popular.

Roast Leg of Lamb

Preparation: **12 min**   Cooking: **1¼ hours**   Serves **6**   Cals per portion: **480**

1 small leg of lamb (about 3½ lb/1.6kg)

1 large clove garlic, peeled and cut into 6 slivers

½ teaspoon dried rosemary

½ teaspoon dried thyme

1 teaspoon salt

½ teaspoon black pepper

1 tablespoon olive oil or vegetable oil

Tip: Instead of using a leg joint, you can use a shoulder, remembering that you will get less meat for the same weight, and that the cooking time will be less – about 1 hour total.

1. Preheat the oven to 190°C (375°F, gas mark 5). With a sharp knife, trim any excess fat from the **lamb.**

2. With the point of a small knife, make 6 evenly spaced incisions about ¼in (5mm) wide and 1in (25mm) deep in the lamb. Insert a **garlic** sliver and a pinch of the **rosemary** and **thyme** into each slit. Sprinkle the lamb with the **salt** and **pepper,** and rub it all over with the **oil.**

3. Place the lamb in a roasting tin.

4. Roast for 1¼ hours for medium-rare (pink), 1½ hours for medium, and 1¾ hours for well done.

5. When the lamb is done, transfer it to a serving plate, cover with foil, and let it rest in a warm place for 10 minutes before carving.

Shepherd's Stew ½

Preparation: **16 min**   Cooking: **20 min**   Serves **4**   Cals per portion: **465**

3 tablespoons vegetable oil

1 large onion, peeled and coarsely chopped

3 medium potatoes, peeled and cut into ¾ in (20mm) cubes

4 medium-sized carrots, peeled and cut into ½ in (15mm) cubes

1 tablespoon plain flour

8 fl oz (225ml) beef stock

½ teaspoon dried rosemary

12 oz (350g) diced cooked lamb

4 oz (115g) frozen green peas, thawed

½ teaspoon salt

¼ teaspoon black pepper

1. Heat the **oil** in a large saucepan over moderate heat. Add the **onion, potatoes** and **carrots,** and cook for 5 minutes, or until the onion is soft. Sprinkle the vegetables with the **flour,** and cook, stirring, for 1 minute.

2. Gradually add the **beef stock,** stirring continuously, then the **rosemary.** Bring to the boil, partially cover the saucepan, lower the heat, and simmer, stirring occasionally, for 15 minutes, or until the carrots and potatoes are almost tender.

3. Add the **lamb, peas, salt** and **pepper** and mix well. Simmer for 5 more minutes. Serve with a fresh green salad and some crusty bread.

> *Tip:* Add ¾ pint (450ml) more beef stock and serve as a soup.

Lamb Pilaf ½

Preparation: **10 min**   Cooking: **25 min**   Serves **6**   Cals per portion: **375**

2 tablespoons vegetable oil

1 small onion, peeled and thinly sliced

12 oz (350g) diced cooked lamb

8 oz (225g) rice

2 oz (50g) raisins

2¼ pints (1.25 litres) beef stock

2 teaspoons finely chopped mint

½ teaspoon salt

¼ teaspoon black pepper

1½ oz (40g) slivered almonds

Not only does this recipe offer a flavoursome way to use leftover lamb, but it makes a little meat go a long way.

1. In a large flameproof casserole or a saucepan with a lid, heat the **oil** over moderate heat. Add the **onion,** and cook, stirring, until golden – about 5 minutes.

2. Stir in the **lamb, rice, raisins, beef stock, mint, salt** and **pepper.** Bring to the boil, lower the heat, cover and simmer for 25 minutes. Sprinkle with the **almonds.** Serve with Orange-Ginger Carrots, page 69.

> *Tips: 1.* As a variation, add ½ pint (285ml) tomato juice in place of the same quantity of stock. *2.* You can substitute cooked beef for the lamb.

Lamb with Shallots ⊘ ½

Preparation: **15 min**   Cooking: **5 min**   Serves **4**   Cals per portion: **435**

2 tablespoons cold water

4 teaspoons cornflour

1 teaspoon sugar

3 tablespoons soya sauce

1¼ lb (575g) boneless lamb shoulder, cut into thin slices

2 tablespoons dry sherry

2 teaspoons cider vinegar

3 tablespoons vegetable oil

1 clove garlic, peeled and finely chopped

6 shallots, peeled and sliced

1. In a mixing bowl, combine the **water, cornflour, sugar** and 2 tablespoons of the **soya sauce.** Add the **lamb,** and toss to coat. Marinate for 10 to 15 minutes at room temperature.

2. In a small bowl, combine the remaining tablespoon of soya sauce, the **sherry, vinegar** and 1 tablespoon of the **oil.** Place this sauce near the oven along with the **garlic** and **shallots.**

3. Heat the remaining oil in a large, heavy frying pan. When the oil is very hot, add the garlic and cook, stirring, for 30 seconds. Add the lamb and any marinade remaining in the bowl, and continue to cook, stirring, until no pink remains – about 3 to 5 minutes.

4. Add the shallots and stir for a few seconds. Add the sauce and continue to stir until smooth – about 1 minute. Serve with rice.

Lamb in Tomato and Wine Sauce

Preparation: **10 min**   Cooking: **45 min**   Serves **4**   Cals per portion: **600**

8 small noisettes of lamb (boned and rolled loin, tied at regular intervals, and cut into 1 in/25mm thick steaks)

2 tablespoons plain flour

¼ teaspoon salt

¼ teaspoon black pepper

1 oz (25g) butter

1 tablespoon olive oil or vegetable oil

½ pint (285ml) dry white wine

2 cloves garlic, peeled and finely chopped

1 lb (450g) tomatoes, skinned, seeded and chopped

2 tablespoons chopped parsley

2 tablespoons fried breadcrumbs

1. Dust the noisettes of **lamb** in **flour** and season with **salt** and **pepper.**

2. Heat the **butter** and **oil** in a large, deep frying pan; add the noisettes and fry until sealed on all sides.

3. Add the **wine, garlic** and **tomatoes** and bring to the boil; cover and simmer until the lamb is quite tender.

4. Spoon onto a serving dish and sprinkle with the chopped **parsley** and the **breadcrumbs.**

5. Serve with cooked noodles.

> *Tip: Instead of using fried breadcrumbs, which take time to prepare, you can use a good dry stuffing mix.*

Lamb with Ham and Pesto Sauce

Preparation: **15 min**   Cooking: **12 min**   Serves **4**   Cals per portion: **650**

1½ lb (700g) lamb fillet

2 tablespoons flour

¼ teaspoon salt

¼ teaspoon black pepper

3 tablespoons olive oil

1 oz (25g) butter

1 large clove garlic, peeled and crushed

4 oz (115g) button mushrooms, sliced

3 oz (75g) Parma ham, cut into thin strips

2 teaspoons Pesto sauce

3 tablespoons grated Parmesan cheese

1. Cut the **lamb fillet** into medallions about ¼in (5mm) thick; flatten slightly with a meat mallet.

2. Dust the pieces of lamb in **flour** and season with **salt** and **pepper.**

3. Heat half the **oil** and **butter** in a frying pan; add the pieces of lamb and fry for 5 minutes, turning them once. Remove the lamb to a plate.

4. Add the remaining butter and oil to the pan and heat until bubbling; add the **garlic** and **mushrooms** and fry for 3 minutes.

5. Add the **Parma ham** and **Pesto** and cook for a further minute; return the lamb to the pan and cook together, stirring, for about 2 minutes.

6. Sprinkle with **Parmesan cheese** and serve piping hot with cooked spaghetti.

> **Tip:** *Parma ham gives the best flavour, but other varieties of ham can be used instead – choose one with a good depth of flavour, avoiding prepacked tenderloin ham.*

Cheese-Glazed Lamb Chops ½

Preparation: **5 min**   Cooking: **27 min**   Serves **4**   Cals per portion: **490**

4 chump lamb chops, about ¾ in (20mm) thick, trimmed of excess fat

¼ teaspoon salt

Pinch black pepper

¼ pint (150ml) dry white wine

2 oz (50g) grated Gruyère or Swiss cheese

1 tablespoon French mustard

1½ tablespoons milk

1. Heat a large, heavy frying pan over high heat for about 1 minute, add the **lamb chops,** and brown for 1 minute on each side. (You will not need oil.) Sprinkle with the **salt** and **pepper.** Add the **wine,** cover, reduce the heat, and simmer for 25 minutes, or until the lamb chops are tender. A few minutes before the chops are done, preheat the grill.

2. Meanwhile, cream the **cheese, mustard** and **milk** together until smooth. Transfer the chops to the rack of the grill pan. Spread the cheese mixture evenly over the chops, and grill for 2 to 3 minutes until the glaze is speckled and brown.

Honey-Orange Lamb Chops ½

Preparation: **3 min**   Cooking: **12 min**   Serves **4**   Cals per portion: **460**

| |
1 tablespoon vegetable oil

4 chump lamb chops, about
¾ in (20mm) thick, trimmed of
excess fat

4 fl oz (115ml) orange juice

Juice ½ lemon

½ teaspoon dried tarragon

1 tablespoon honey

½ teaspoon salt

¼ teaspoon black pepper

1 teaspoon French mustard

½ oz (15g) butter or margarine

1. Heat the **oil** in a large, heavy frying pan over a moderate heat for 1 minute. Add the **lamb chops** and cook 3 minutes each side for medium rare, 5 minutes for medium and 6 minutes for well done. Transfer the chops to a plate.

2. Add the **orange juice, lemon juice** and **tarragon** to the pan and scrape up any brown bits stuck to the bottom. Bring to the boil and cook until only half the liquid remains. Reduce the heat and add the **honey, salt, pepper** and **mustard.** Mix thoroughly then swirl in the **butter.** Return the chops with any juices to the pan and heat through – about 1 minute. Serve with buttered noodles.

Parsley Lamb Patties   ½

Preparation: **5 min**   Cooking: **10 min**   Serves **4**   Cals per portion: **260**

1 lb (450g) lean minced lamb

½ teaspoon salt

¼ teaspoon black pepper

4 tablespoons chopped parsley

1 teaspoon grated lemon rind

1. Preheat the grill. Combine the **lamb, salt, pepper, parsley** and **lemon rind,** and shape the mixture into 4 patties.

2. Grill for 5 minutes on each side for rare, 7 minutes for medium and 8 to 9 minutes for well done. Serve with a green salad.

Devilled Lamb ½ 🐷

Preparation: **5 min**   Cooking: **5 min**   Serves **4**   Cals per portion: **445**

4 tablespoons chutney,
finely chopped

1 teaspoon French mustard

¼ teaspoon salt

¼ teaspoon black pepper

1 teaspoon lemon juice

8 thick slices cold cooked lamb
(about 1 lb/450g)

2 oz (50g) butter, melted

3 oz (75g) fresh breadcrumbs

1. In a small bowl combine the **chutney, mustard, salt, pepper** and **lemon juice.** Place a sheet of foil on the grill rack and preheat the grill.

2. Brush both sides of the **lamb** slices with **melted butter** and place on the foil. Spread with the chutney mixture and top with the **breadcrumbs** and the remaining butter. Grill until the breadcrumbs are browned. Serve with steamed rice and grilled tomatoes.

Curried Lamb and Vegetables ½

Preparation: **17 min**   Cooking: **8 min**   Serves **4**   Cals per portion: **460**

2 oz (50g) butter or margarine

2 tablespoons curry powder

¼ teaspoon ground ginger

2 cloves garlic, peeled and finely chopped

1 medium-sized onion, peeled and chopped

½ lb (225g) mushrooms, sliced

½ medium-sized pepper, seeded and chopped

1 stem celery, diced

1 lb (450g) minced lamb

1 teaspoon salt

¼ teaspoon cayenne pepper

2½ fl oz (75ml) double cream

1. Melt the **butter** in a large, heavy frying pan over moderate heat. Add the **curry powder, ginger, garlic, onion, mushrooms, pepper** and **celery.** Cook, stirring, for 1 minute, then cover and cook for 5 more minutes, or until the onion is soft.

2. Turn the heat to high, add the **lamb, salt** and **cayenne pepper,** and cook, tossing the lamb and vegetables continuously for 3 minutes. Reduce the heat, add the **cream** and simmer for 5 minutes. Serve with Shredded Cabbage with Garlic, page 67.

Herbed Lamb Patties ⊘ ½

Preparation: **8 min**   Cooking: **10 min**   Serves **6**   Cals per portion: **280**

1 tablespoon olive oil or vegetable oil

8 shallots, peeled and sliced

1½ lb (700g) minced lamb

¼ teaspoon black pepper

½ teaspoon salt

½ teaspoon dried thyme or basil

1 teaspoon dried rosemary

1 tablespoon finely chopped parsley

Juice ½ lemon

1. Heat the **oil** in a large, heavy frying pan over moderate heat, add the **shallots** and cook for 1½ minutes.

2. Preheat the grill. In a small bowl, combine the cooked shallots, the **lamb, pepper, salt, thyme, rosemary, parsley** and **lemon juice.** Shape the mixture into 6 patties, and grill for 5 minutes on each side for rare, 6 for medium, and 7 for well done. Serve with Broad Beans in Soured Cream, page 63, and a tomato salad.

> **Tips: 1.** For a change in taste, grill the patties for 5 minutes, then turn and grill for 3 more minutes. Top each patty with a thin slice of strong Cheddar cheese, and grill for 2 minutes, or until the cheese has melted. **2.** To pan grill, sprinkle ¼ teaspoon of salt in a heavy frying pan, heat over moderately high heat, and cook the patties for 5 minutes on each side for rare, 6 for medium, and 7 for well done.

Lamb Satay ⊘

Preparation: **5 min** Cooking: **10 min**   Serves **4** Cals per portion: **380**

1¼ lb (575g) boneless lean lamb, cut into ¾ in (20mm) cubes

2 teaspoons vinegar

1 medium-sized onion, peeled and finely chopped

2 cloves garlic, peeled and crushed

½ teaspoon anchovy paste

1 tablespoon dark soya sauce

2 tablespoons desiccated coconut

2 tablespoons hot water

The cubes of lamb should be marinated for 2 hours before cooking, so prepare well in advance. While the lamb is marinating, soak the bamboo skewers in water.

1. Place the **lamb** in a bowl. In a small bowl, combine the **vinegar, onion, garlic, anchovy paste, soya sauce, coconut** and **water,** and pour over the lamb. Mix well, cover and leave at room temperature for 2 hours.

2. Preheat the grill. Thread the cubes of lamb onto bamboo skewers and lay each filled skewer on the rack of the grill pan. Grill for 10 minutes, turning and basting the meat frequently with leftover marinade. Serve with steamed rice and bottled satay sauce.

Mushroom Crumbed Cutlets ½

Preparation: **10 min** Cooking: **15 min**   Serves **4** Cals per portion: **505**

8 lamb cutlets

1 oz (25g) butter

2 shallots, peeled and finely chopped

2 oz (50g) mushrooms, very finely chopped

1 teaspoon fresh oregano, chopped

1 tablespoon chopped parsley

3 oz (75g) fresh breadcrumbs

½ teaspoon salt

½ teaspoon black pepper

1 egg, lightly beaten

1 tablespoon water

3 tablespoons plain flour

2 tablespoons olive oil or vegetable oil

1. Put each **lamb cutlet** between two pieces of waxed paper and flatten the 'eye' of the meat slightly with a mallet or rolling pin. Put aside.

2. Melt the **butter** in a medium-sized frying pan and gently fry the **shallots** for 2 minutes. Add the **mushrooms** and fry a further 2 minutes. Remove the pan from the heat and stir in the **oregano, parsley, breadcrumbs, salt** and **pepper.**

3. Dilute the **egg** with the **water** and beat it briefly. Put the **flour** on a plate and coat each cutlet, then dip in the beaten egg and coat with the mushroom mixture by pressing onto the meat with the blade of a knife.

4. Heat the **oil** in a large frying pan over a moderate heat and fry the cutlets for about 7 minutes on each side, or until they are crisp and golden. Drain on absorbent paper and serve immediately.

Lamb and Spinach Bake ½

Preparation: **20 min**   Cooking: **25 min**   Serves **4**   Cals per portion: **500**

1 lb (450g) fresh spinach

½ teaspoon salt

½ teaspoon black pepper

Pinch of nutmeg

1 oz (25g) butter or margarine

1 oz (25g) plain flour

½ pint (285ml) milk

3 oz (75g) grated, strong Cheddar cheese

12 oz (350g) cooked lamb, finely chopped

2 tablespoons fresh breadcrumbs

Tip: This dish is equally delicious made with chopped ham – use blue cheese instead of Cheddar.

1. Preheat the oven to 180°C (350°F, gas mark 4). Trim the **spinach** of coarse stems and blemished leaves, wash it and shake dry. Put the spinach in a large saucepan with just the water that clings to the leaves and cook, covered, for 5 minutes, or until just limp. Drain the spinach, pressing out most of the liquid with the back of a large spoon. Chop the spinach finely. Season with half the **salt** and **pepper** and with the **nutmeg.**

2. Melt the **butter** in a large saucepan, stir in the **flour** and cook over a gentle heat, stirring continuously, for 1 or 2 minutes. In another saucepan, heat the **milk** then add it to the flour mixture; stir well and bring to the boil. Beat in half the **grated cheese** and season with the remaining salt and pepper.

3. Put the spinach into a large, shallow ovenproof dish, cover with the **lamb,** then with the cheese sauce. Sprinkle with the remaining cheese and top with the **breadcrumbs.** Bake for 20 to 25 minutes or until brown and bubbling.

Peppered Lamb Fillet

Preparation: **10 min**   Cooking: **6-7 min**   Serves **4**   Cals per portion: **540**

1½ lb (700g) lamb fillet

2 tablespoons finely crushed black peppercorns

¼ teaspoon salt

2 oz (50g) butter

2 cloves garlic, peeled and finely chopped

4 tablespoons brandy

Tip: Rather than allowing the brandy to bubble away in the pan, warm it in a metal ladle, set light to it, and spoon it directly over the lamb.

1. Cut the **lamb fillet** into medallions about ¼in (5mm) thick; flatten slightly with a meat mallet.

2. Press the small pieces of lamb into the crushed **peppercorns** so as to coat them evenly on both sides; season with **salt.**

3. Heat the **butter** and **garlic** in a large, deep frying pan; add the peppercorned lamb and fry for 2 to 3 minutes on either side.

4. Add the **brandy,** heat briefly, and then carefully set light to the surface of the cooking liquid.

5. As soon as the flames die down, spoon onto warm serving plates; serve with crusty bread and a green salad.

Battered Lamb Chops ⊘ ½ 🐷

Preparation: **10 min**   Cooking: **4-5 min**   Serves **4**   Cals per portion: **505**

8 thin loin lamb chops or cutlets

2 eggs

½ teaspoon salt

½ teaspoon black pepper

1 teaspoon finely grated lemon rind

3 tablespoons finely grated Parmesan cheese

3 oz (75g) dry breadcrumbs

4 fl oz (115ml) vegetable oil

1. Flatten the meat on each **chop** with a mallet or meat pounder.

2. Lightly beat together the **eggs, salt, pepper,** and **lemon rind** in a deep dish. Put the **Parmesan cheese** and **breadcrumbs** on separate plates or pieces of waxed paper. Turn the chops in the cheese, then dip in the egg mixture, allowing excess egg to drip back into the dish, and press in the breadcrumbs to ensure a good coating on both sides. Put to one side.

3. Heat the **oil** in a large frying pan over moderately high heat until very hot. Slide the chops into the pan and, as soon as one side becomes crisp – about 2 minutes – turn them with a metal spatula or wooden tongs. When the chops are crisp and golden-brown on both sides, transfer to absorbent paper to drain. Serve while very hot with lemon wedges and Warm Green Beans Vinaigrette, page 63.

Lamb in Lemon and Basil Sauce

Preparation: **10 min**   Cooking: **45 min**   Serves **4**   Cals per portion: **650**

2 oz (50g) butter

2 tablespoons olive oil

4 chump lamb chops

1 medium-sized onion, peeled and thinly sliced

2 large carrots, peeled and roughly chopped

2 stems celery, chopped

2 tablespoons chopped fresh basil

Juice 2 lemons

¼ teaspoon salt

¼ teaspoon black pepper

¼ pint (150ml) chicken stock

Thin wedges of lemon

1. Heat the **butter** and **oil** in a large, deep frying pan; add the **lamb chops,** fry until golden on both sides and transfer to a plate.

2. Add the **onion, carrot** and **celery** to the fat remaining in the pan and fry gently for 5 minutes.

3. Return the chops to the pan; add the **basil, lemon juice, salt** and **pepper,** and simmer until all the lemon and lamb juices have evaporated.

4. Add the **chicken stock,** cover the pan, and simmer gently until the chops are tender.

5. Garnish with **lemon wedges** and serve with rice.

> **Tip:** This is based on a traditional Greek recipe; if it is too greasy for your liking, reduce the butter and oil by half.

Lamb, Pepper and Almond Meatballs

Preparation: **10 min**   Cooking: **13 min**   Serves **4**   Cals per portion: **540**

1½ lb (700g) minced lean lamb

Finely grated rind 1 orange

1 large clove garlic, peeled and crushed

1 teaspoon ground ginger

1 medium-sized red pepper, seeded and finely chopped

1½ oz (40g) chopped toasted almonds

¼ teaspoon salt

¼ teaspoon black pepper

2 egg yolks

3 tablespoons apricot jam

Juice ½ orange

3 tablespoons oil

1. Mix the **minced lamb** with the **orange rind, garlic, ginger, red pepper, almonds, salt, pepper** and **egg yolks;** using lightly floured or dampened hands, shape the mixture into small balls about 1in (25mm) in diameter.

2. Chill the shaped meatballs for 1 hour.

3. Thread the meatballs onto 4 kebab skewers and place on the rack of the grill pan.

4. Heat the **apricot jam** and **orange juice** until melted; stir in the **oil.**

5. Brush the apricot baste evenly over the meatball kebabs and cook under a preheated grill for 5 minutes.

6. Turn the skewers carefully, brush with the apricot baste once again, and grill for a further 5 to 7 minutes until crisp on the outsides and tender in the centres.

7. Serve piping hot with a salad.

Lamb and Feta Kebabs

Preparation: **25 min**   Cooking: **10 min**   Serves **4**   Cals per portion: **600**

1½ lb (700g) lean lamb, cut into 1½ in (40mm) cubes

6 tablespoons olive oil

Juice 2 lemons

2 large cloves garlic, peeled and finely chopped

1 tablespoon chopped fresh oregano

1 tablespoon chopped fresh thyme

1 tablespoon chopped fresh marjoram

¼ teaspoon salt

¼ teaspoon black pepper

3 oz (75g) feta cheese, crumbled

1 tablespoon chopped, toasted pine kernels

Warm pitta bread

1. Put the cubed **lamb** into a shallow dish with the **olive oil, lemon juice, garlic, fresh herbs, salt** and **pepper;** stir the lamb into the marinade.

2. Cover and chill for 4 hours.

3. Drain the cubes of lamb from their marinade and thread onto 4 kebab skewers; place on the rack of the grill pan and brush with some of the marinade.

4. Cook under a preheated grill for 5 minutes; turn the kebabs, brush once again, and continue grilling for a further 5 minutes, until tender but still pink in the centre.

5. Sprinkle with the crumbled **feta** and the **pine kernels** and serve immediately with the warm **pitta bread,** and a tomato and onion salad.

> **Tip:** *It is the fresh herbs which give this lamb dish its characteristic flavour, but you can use one-third the quantity of dried herbs if necessary.*

FISH
AND
SHELLFISH

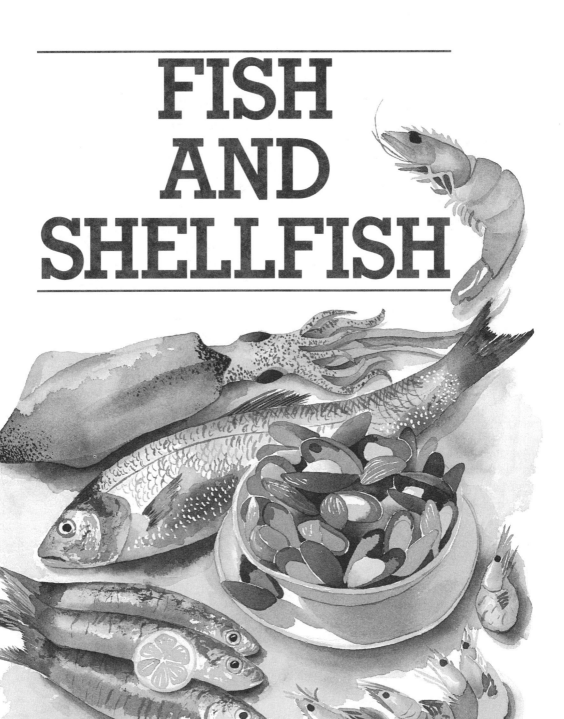

FISH AND SHELLFISH

In this section you will find recipes for both fish fillets and whole fish, including tasty new ways to dress up canned tuna and salmon; a fish stew; garlic-flavoured mussels; an oyster pie; and squid. Because fish varies in price and availability, a choice is given in most recipes so that you can opt for the one that is in season or more reasonably priced.

Grilled Sole

Preparation: **5 min**   Cooking: **8 min**   Serves **4**   Cals per portion: **300**

3 oz (75g) butter or margarine

1 teaspoon Worcestershire sauce

¼ teaspoon celery salt

4 bay leaves

Pinch black pepper

4 tablespoons grated Parmesan cheese

4 whole sole or plaice, cleaned

1. Preheat the grill. Melt the **butter** in a small saucepan over low heat. Add the **Worcestershire sauce, celery salt, bay leaves, pepper** and **cheese.** Stir to mix. Pour half the mixture into the bottom of the grill pan while the mixture is hot. Place the **sole** in the pan. Pour the remaining mixture over the fish.

2. Grill, without turning, for 8 minutes or longer, depending on the thickness of the fish. If the fish flakes easily when tested with a fork, it is done. Serve with Coleslaw, page 46, and French fried potatoes.

Baked Sole Knots ½

Preparation: **20 min**   Cooking: **25 min**   Serves **6**   Cals per portion: **330**

2 lb (900g) sole fillets, skinned

2 oz (50g) butter

1 medium-sized onion, peeled and finely chopped

6 tomatoes, skinned, seeded and chopped

6 anchovy fillets, chopped

6 oz (175g) button mushrooms, sliced

¼ teaspoon salt

¼ teaspoon black pepper

Small croutons

Tip: The sole looks attractive when served, if it is prepared as above. To reduce the preparation time, cut the fish fillets into random pieces.

1. Cut the **sole fillets** into strips, about 6 × ½in (150 × 15mm); tie each one into a knot.

2. Place the sole knots into an ovenproof dish.

3. Put the **butter** in a large frying pan and fry the **onion** until pale golden; add the chopped **tomatoes** and cook together for 2 to 3 minutes.

4. Add the **anchovy fillets, mushrooms, salt** and **pepper** to taste; cook together for a further 2 to 3 minutes.

5. Spoon the mushroom mixture evenly over the fish; cover with foil or a lid.

6. Cook at 190°C (375°F, gas mark 5) for 25 minutes.

7. Serve garnished with **croutons,** and accompanied by a green vegetable such as broccoli, and new potatoes.

Grilled Devilled Fish ⊘ ½

Preparation: **5 min** Cooking: **5 min**   Serves **4** Cals per portion: **180**

1½ lb (700g) thick fish fillets
(whiting, sea bream, hake, etc),
skinned

2 fl oz (50ml) tomato juice

4-6 drops Tabasco sauce

1 tablespoon vegetable oil

1 tablespoon French mustard

1 tablespoon creamed
horseradish

¼ teaspoon salt

1 tablespoon Worcestershire
sauce

1. Preheat the grill. Grease the rack of the grill pan and place the **fish fillets** on it. Combine the **tomato juice, Tabasco sauce, oil, mustard, horseradish, salt** and **Worcestershire sauce.** Spread the mixture evenly over the fish.

2. Grill, without turning, for 5 minutes or longer, depending on the thickness of the fish. If the fish flakes easily when tested with a fork, it is done.

> **Tip:** *For a milder version, substitute 2fl oz (50ml) of sweet chilli sauce for the tomato juice and Tabasco sauce.*

Grilled Fish with Peppery Almond Butter ⊘ ½

Preparation: **5 min** Cooking: **5 min**   Serves **4** Cals per portion: **320**

1½ lb (700g) plaice or sole fillets,
skinned

1 oz (25g) plain flour

½ teaspoon salt

½ teaspoon paprika

2 oz (50g) butter or margarine

1 tablespoon vegetable oil

2 tablespoons flaked, blanched
almonds

Juice ½ lemon

5 or more drops Tabasco sauce

1. Preheat the grill. Pat the **fish** dry with absorbent paper. Combine the **flour, salt** and **paprika** in a shallow dish or plate. Coat the fish fillets with the flour mixture. Shake off any excess flour.

2. In a small frying pan, melt a third of the **butter,** stir in the **oil,** and brush the rack of the grill pan with some of the mixture. Place the fish on the rack, and brush the fish with the remaining butter and oil mixture. Grill without turning, for 5 minutes or longer, depending on the thickness of the fish. If the fish flakes easily when tested with a fork, it is done. Transfer to a warm plate.

3. While the fish is grilling, melt the remaining butter in the pan over moderate heat. Add the **almonds** and cook, stirring continuously, until lightly browned. Using a slotted spoon, remove the almonds from the pan and scatter them over the fish.

4. Add the **lemon juice** and **Tabasco sauce** to the pan, heat, and pour over the fish. Serve with boiled new potatoes or French Green Peas, page 75.

Baked Fish with Shallots and Ginger

Preparation: **5 min**   Cooking: **20 min**

Serves **4**   Cals per portion: **240**

1 whole sea bream or sea bass (about 2¾ lb/1.25kg), cleaned

2 tablespoons soya sauce

3 tablespoons dry sherry

3 shallots, peeled and thinly sliced

1 teaspoon grated fresh root ginger or ¼ teaspoon ground ginger

1 clove garlic, peeled and finely chopped

¼ teaspoon sugar

¼ teaspoon salt

1. Preheat the oven to 180°C (350°F, gas mark 4). Make cuts in the **fish,** about ¾in (20mm) apart, through the flesh and down to the bone, from the gills to the tail. Do this on both sides of the fish.

2. In a small bowl, combine the **soya sauce, sherry, shallots, ginger, garlic, sugar** and **salt.** Place the fish in a greased, large, shallow casserole, and sprinkle the mixture evenly over the fish. Bake for 20 minutes or longer, depending on the thickness of the fish. If the fish flakes easily when tested with a fork, it is done. Serve with Brussels Sprouts with Walnuts, page 66.

Italian Sweet and Sour Fish ½

Preparation: **10 min**   Cooking: **2 min**

Serves **4**   Cals per portion: **515**

2 large onions, peeled and thinly sliced

2 cloves garlic, peeled and finely chopped

¼ pint (150ml) olive oil

Juice 1 lemon

3 tablespoons dry white wine

2 teaspoons sugar

¼ teaspoon salt

¼ teaspoon black pepper

2 oz (50g) raisins

2 oz (50g) pine kernels

1½ lb (700g) small plaice fillets, skinned

2 tablespoons plain flour

1. Fry the **onions** and **garlic** gently in 6 tablespoons of the **olive oil** in a large frying pan for 5 minutes.

2. Add the **lemon juice, white wine, sugar, salt** and **pepper;** bring to the boil and simmer for 3 minutes. Add the **raisins** and **pine kernels.**

3. Dust the **plaice fillets** with **flour.** Heat the remaining olive oil in a large frying pan; add the fillets and fry for just 1 minute on each side.

4. Drain the fish on absorbent paper and arrange, slightly overlapping, on a flat serving platter.

5. Spoon the onion mixture over the top; cover, and chill for 3 to 4 hours.

6. Serve with a green salad.

> **Tip:** Add grated orange rind to the onion mixture and garnish with fresh orange segments.

169

Baked Stuffed Bream

Preparation: **5 min**   Cooking: **20 min**   Serves **4**   Cals per portion: **380**

3 oz (75g) soft fresh breadcrumbs

2 oz (50g) butter or margarine, melted

¼ teaspoon black pepper

1 small onion, peeled and chopped

1 small pepper, seeded and chopped

Pinch dried thyme

1 teaspoon salt

3 oz (75g) chopped mushrooms

1 whole sea bream or sea bass (about 2¾ lb/1.25kg), cleaned

1. Preheat the oven to 190°C (375°F, gas mark 5). In a mixing bowl, combine the **breadcrumbs,** two-thirds of the melted **butter,** the **black pepper, onion, pepper, thyme,** ¼ teaspoon of the **salt** and the **mushrooms.** Put aside.

2. Sprinkle the **fish** inside and out with the remaining salt. Stuff the fish loosely with the breadcrumb mixture, and close the opening with skewers, or sew with kitchen string.

3. Place the fish in a greased, large casserole. Brush the fish with the remaining melted butter. Bake for 20 minutes or longer, depending on the thickness of the fish. If the fish flakes easily when tested with a fork, it is done. Serve with New Potatoes with Spring Onions, page 77.

Baked Whiting with Cucumbers, Dill and Cream ½

Preparation: **20 min**   Cooking: **20 min**   Serves **4**   Cals per portion: **340**

Crisp but tender cucumber, a touch of dill and some cream are ideal accompaniments for delicate whiting (also known as sand whiting).

4 whole whiting (about 12 oz/350g each), cleaned

¾ teaspoon salt

¼ teaspoon black pepper

1 small onion, peeled and finely chopped

1 large cucumber, peeled

2 tablespoons snipped fresh dill or ½ teaspoon dried dill

1 oz (25g) butter or margarine

4 fl oz (115ml) single cream

Tip: *This is a delicious addition to a barbecued meal.*

1. Preheat the oven to 190°C (375°F, gas mark 5). Wash the **whiting,** dry them with absorbent paper, and sprinkle with the **salt** and **pepper.** Place them in a greased shallow casserole dish and cover with the **onion.**

2. Slice the **cucumber** in half lengthwise, scoop out the seeds with a spoon, then cut the halves into ½in (15mm) slices. Scatter the cucumber around the fish. Sprinkle the fish and cucumber with the **dill,** and dot with the **butter.**

3. Bake for 10 minutes. Pour the **cream** around the fish, and bake for 10 more minutes, or until done. To check, insert a knife along the backbone at the thickest part of the fish; when the flesh separates easily from the bone, it is done. Transfer the fish to a warm serving dish, surround with the cucumber, and pour the sauce over the fish. Serve with rice.

Curried Fillets

Preparation: **10 min**   Cooking: **10 min**   Serves **4**   Cals per portion: **460**

3 oz (75g) butter or margarine

1 teaspoon finely chopped fresh root ginger or ¼ teaspoon ground ginger

1 medium-sized onion, peeled and chopped

4 shallots, peeled and chopped

1 clove garlic, peeled and finely chopped

2 teaspoons curry powder

1½ lb (700g) mullet, sea bream or sea bass fillets, skinned

2 fl oz (50ml) water

2 fl oz (50ml) dry sherry or dry white wine (optional)

½ teaspoon salt

1. Preheat the oven to 180°C (350°F, gas mark 4). In a medium-sized frying pan melt three-quarters of the **butter** over moderate heat. Add the **ginger, onion, shallots, garlic** and **curry powder,** and cook for 5 minutes. Remove the pan from the heat.

2. With the remaining butter, grease a shallow casserole dish. If the **fillets** are very thin, fold them in half. They should be about ¾in (20mm) thick when folded. Place the fillets in the dish in one layer and spread the onion mixture evenly over them. Pour the **water,** and the **sherry** if used, evenly over the fillets, and sprinkle with the **salt.** Bake for 10 minutes or longer, depending on the thickness of the fish. If the fish flakes easily when tested with a fork, it is done. Serve with Shredded Cabbage with Garlic, page 67.

Chilled Fish Curry ⊘ ½

Preparation: **20 min**   Serves **4**   Cals per portion: **270**

12 oz (350g) cooked haddock fillet

6 oz (175g) peeled prawns

1 yellow pepper, seeded, and cut into long thin strips

1 avocado pear, halved, stoned, peeled and cut into thin slivers

2 bananas, peeled and cut into thin slices

Juice 1 lemon

5 tablespoons natural yoghurt

4 tablespoons mayonnaise

2 teaspoons curry powder

1 clove garlic, peeled and crushed

¼ teaspoon salt

¼ teaspoon black pepper

Fresh coriander or parsley

1. Flake the **haddock** coarsely and mix with the **prawns** and **pepper** strips.

2. Toss the **avocado** and **banana** in **lemon juice** and add them to the fish mixture. Reserve the lemon juice.

3. Spoon onto a serving dish and chill, covered.

4. Mix the **yoghurt** with the **mayonnaise, curry powder, garlic,** and **salt** and **pepper,** and thin with a little of the reserved lemon juice.

5. Spoon the prepared sauce evenly over the chilled fish and garnish with the **herbs.**

6. Serve with a wild rice salad – stir a little oil and vinegar dressing into cooked wild rice.

Baked Cutlets with Olives and Tomatoes ½

Preparation: **10 min**   Cooking: **38 min**   Serves **4**   Cals per portion: **230**

2 tablespoons olive oil or vegetable oil

1 small onion, peeled and chopped

1½ oz (40g) chopped green olives

½ small pepper, seeded and chopped

4 medium-sized tomatoes, peeled and chopped

4 fl oz (115ml) dry white wine

2 fl oz (50ml) tomato purée

½ teaspoon salt

¼ teaspoon black pepper

1½ lb (700g) small fish cutlets (cod, salmon, etc)

1. Heat the **oil** in a large saucepan over moderate heat. Add the **onion, olives** and **pepper,** and cook for 3 minutes. Add the **tomatoes,** and cook 5 minutes longer. Add the **wine, tomato purée, salt** and **black pepper,** and simmer for 20 minutes.

2. About 10 minutes before the sauce is done, preheat the oven to 180°C (350°F, gas mark 4). Place the **fish cutlets** in a greased shallow casserole dish, and spoon the sauce over them. Bake for 10 minutes or longer, depending on the thickness of the fish. If the fish flakes easily when tested with a fork, it is done.

Tips: 1. If this recipe is halved, use half a small onion and 1 large or 2 small tomatoes. 2. When you have the time, prepare the sauce, let it cool, and marinate the cutlets in it for at least 2 hours.

Crumbed Oven-Fried Fish ½

Preparation: **5 min**   Cooking: **5 min**   Serves **4**   Cals per portion: **300**

4 fl oz (115ml) milk

½ teaspoon salt

3 oz (75g) fine dry breadcrumbs

1 teaspoon paprika

1½ lb (700g) plaice or sole fillets

2 oz (50g) butter or margarine, melted

1 lemon, cut into thin wedges

Tip: Choose plump fish fillets for this recipe – thin fillets tend to dry out at such a high temperature.

1. Adjust the oven rack to slightly above the middle of the oven, and preheat to 220°C (425°F, gas mark 7). Put the **milk** into a shallow bowl or pie plate, and stir in the **salt.** Mix the **breadcrumbs** with the **paprika** on a plate or a sheet of waxed paper. Dip the **fish fillets** into the milk, then coat with the breadcrumb mixture. Place the fillets in a single layer in a large, shallow, greased casserole.

2. Pour the melted **butter** over the fillets. Bake for 5 minutes. If the fish flakes easily when tested with a fork, it is done. Garnish with the **lemon wedges.** Serve with Coleslaw, page 46, or Spinach-Bacon Salad with Warm Dressing, page 49.

Pan-Fried Whiting with Lemon Butter Sauce ½

Preparation: **15 min**   Cooking: **11 min**   Serves **4**   Cals per portion: **395**

4 whole small whiting or trout (about 12 oz/350g each), cleaned

½ teaspoon dried rosemary

½ teaspoon salt

¼ teaspoon black pepper

1 oz (25g) plain flour

4 fl oz (115ml) vegetable oil

2 oz (50g) butter or margarine

Juice 1 lemon

2 tablespoons finely chopped parsley

1. Wash the **fish** and dry with absorbent paper. Sprinkle each fish inside with the **rosemary,** and outside with the **salt** and **pepper.** Place the **flour** on a plate or a sheet of waxed paper, and coat the fish with the flour. Shake off any excess flour.

2. Heat the **oil** in a large, heavy frying pan over moderately high heat for about 1 minute. Carefully place the fish in the oil, and cook for 5 minutes on each side, or until golden-brown. To test whether the fish is cooked, insert a knife to one side of the backbone at the thickest part of the fish; when the flesh separates easily from the bone, it is done. Transfer the fish to a warm plate.

3. Discard the oil in the pan. Reduce the heat to low, and add the **butter, lemon juice** and **parsley.** Cook for about 30 seconds, scraping up any brown bits stuck to the pan. Pour the sauce over the fish, and serve with Baked Courgettes with Tomatoes, page 82.

Creamed Cod and Potatoes

Preparation: **12 min**   Cooking: **7 min**   Serves **4**   Cals per portion: **430**

4 medium-sized potatoes (about 1¼ lb/575g), peeled and cut into small dice

6 fl oz (175ml) single cream

2 oz (50g) butter or margarine

1¼ lb (575g) cod or haddock fillets, skinned and roughly chopped

1 teaspoon salt

Pinch black pepper

1 tablespoon snipped fresh dill (or ¼ teaspoon dried dill)

Here is one of those simple dishes which is subtle in flavour and satisfying to eat.

1. Place the **potatoes** in a large saucepan, add water to cover, and boil for 5 minutes, or until they are just tender but not too soft. Drain and put aside.

2. Heat the **cream** and **butter** in a large, heavy frying pan over moderate heat until the butter melts. Add the **cod fillets,** and cook for 2 to 3 minutes, or until the fish turns opaque – do not allow the mixture to boil.

3. Add the potatoes, **salt** and **pepper,** and continue to cook, stirring, 3 to 4 minutes longer, until heated through; the mixture should not brown. Sprinkle with the **dill.**

Creamed Smoked Haddock ½

Preparation: **10 min** Cooking: **8 min**   Serves **6** Cals per portion: **315**

1½ lb (700g) smoked haddock
fillet

½ pint (285ml) milk

½ pint (285ml) water

¼ pint (150ml) olive oil

3 cloves garlic, peeled and
crushed

½ teaspoon black pepper

2 oz (50g) black olives

> **Tip:** *Salt is unnecessary, as the fish
> contains sufficient natural salt.*

1. Put the **haddock** into a deep frying
pan; add the **milk** and **water,** cover and
simmer until the fish is just tender (about
8 minutes).

2. Drain the fish thoroughly, discarding any
skin and bone; flake the flesh and pound until
smooth (this can be done in a food processor
or liquidiser).

3. Gradually beat in the **olive oil** and add
garlic and **pepper** to taste.

4. Heat through gently in a double saucepan,
or in a heat-proof bowl over a pan of
simmering water.

5. Put into a warm serving dish and stud with
olives. Serve with crusty bread or croutons,
and a salad.

Fish Stew with Carrots and Potatoes ½

Preparation: **10 min** Cooking: **26 min**   Serves **4** Cals per portion: **305**

2 oz (50g) butter or margarine

2 medium-sized onions, peeled
and chopped

2 medium-sized potatoes, peeled
and diced

2 medium-sized carrots, peeled
and cut into ½ in (15mm) slices

1 pint (570ml) chicken stock

4 fl oz (115ml) dry white wine or
dry vermouth

1 bay leaf

¼ teaspoon dried thyme

½ teaspoon salt

¼ teaspoon black pepper

1¼ lb (575g) firm white fish
(monkfish, cod or haddock),
skinned and cut into 2 in (50mm)
pieces

1 tablespoon finely
chopped parsley

*Serve this one-dish meal in soup bowls with plenty of
crusty bread to mop up the juices.*

1. Melt the **butter** in a large saucepan over
moderate heat. Add the **onions, potatoes** and
carrots, and cook, covered, for 10 minutes.

2. Add the **chicken stock, wine, bay leaf,
thyme, salt** and **pepper,** and bring to the
boil – about 3 minutes. Cover and simmer
for 10 minutes, or until the vegetables are
almost tender.

3. Add the **fish** and continue to simmer,
covered, for 3 to 5 minutes or until the fish
flakes easily when tested with a fork. Sprinkle
with the **parsley.**

> **Tip:** *For a richer fish stew, stir in 4fl oz (115ml) double
> cream or soured cream just before serving.*

Herrings with Mustard Cream ½

Preparation: **5 min**   Cooking: **12 min**   Serves **4**   Cals per portion: **360**

4 herrings, gutted and cleaned

1 tablespoon olive oil

¼ teaspoon salt

¼ teaspoon black pepper

2 teaspoons coarse-grain mustard

1 tablespoon white wine vinegar

3 fl oz (90ml) mayonnaise

3 fl oz (90ml) soured cream

3 spring onions, finely chopped

1. Place **herrings** on rack of grill pan; brush lightly with **oil** and season with half the **salt** and **pepper.**

2. Grill under preheated grill for 6 minutes; turn fish carefully, brush once again with oil and grill for a further 6 minutes.

3. While fish are cooking, make the sauce. Mix the **mustard** with the **wine vinegar,** then beat in the **mayonnaise** and **soured cream.** Mix in the **spring onions.**

4. Serve the fish with its sauce, plain boiled potatoes and a tomato salad.

> **Tip:** *If two or three cuts are made in the fleshiest part of each fish, they will cook more evenly.*

Fish and Potato Pancakes ½

Preparation: **12 min**   Cooking: **16 min**   Serves **4**   Cals per portion: **240**

12 oz (350g) cod or haddock fillets, finely chopped

2 eggs, lightly beaten

12 oz (350g) potatoes, peeled and finely grated

2 tablespoons plain flour

1 small onion, peeled and finely chopped

1 tablespoon chopped parsley

Pinch ground nutmeg

1 teaspoon salt

¼ teaspoon black pepper

1 oz (25g) butter or margarine

1. In a large bowl, combine the **chopped fish, eggs, potatoes, flour, onion, parsley, nutmeg, salt** and **pepper.**

2. Melt half of the **butter** in a medium-sized, heavy frying pan over moderate heat. Using a large spoon, drop enough of the mixture into the pan to make 4 pancakes; flatten each slightly with a fish slice, and cook for 4 minutes, or until the bottoms are brown. Turn carefully with the fish slice, and cook for 4 minutes on the other side. Drain on absorbent paper on a plate. Put in a low oven to keep warm. Melt the remaining butter, and cook the rest of the mixture to make 4 more pancakes. Serve with lemon wedges or apple sauce.

Baked Devilled Tuna ½ 🐷

Preparation: **15 min**   Cooking: **10 min**   Serves **4**   Cals per portion: **500**

2 oz (50g) butter or margarine

1 medium-sized onion, peeled and chopped

3 oz (75g) sliced mushrooms

2 teaspoons dry mustard

1 teaspoon chilli powder

½ teaspoon salt

2 tablespoons fresh toasted breadcrumbs

8 fl oz (225ml) double cream

2 x 7 oz (200g) cans tuna, drained and flaked

1 teaspoon Worcestershire sauce

Pinch cayenne pepper

2 eggs, lightly beaten

1. Preheat the oven to 200°C (400°F, gas mark 6). Heat half of the **butter** in a medium-sized, heavy frying pan over moderate heat. Add the **onion,** and cook for 3 minutes, then add the **mushrooms** and cook 3 minutes longer.

2. Stir in the **mustard, chilli powder, salt, breadcrumbs, cream, tuna, Worcestershire sauce** and the **cayenne pepper.** Simmer the mixture for 2 minutes. Remove the pan from the heat, allow to cool slightly, then stir in the **eggs.**

3. Spoon the mixture into 4 greased, individual ovenproof dishes. Melt the remaining butter and pour some over the top of each one. Place the dishes on a baking tray, and bake for 10 minutes.

> **Tip:** Serve this dish cold for a picnic or as a delicious hors d'oeuvre which can be spread on thin slices of crusty French bread.

Baked Sardines with Cucumber

Preparation: **15 min**   Cooking: **20 min**   Serves **4**   Cals per portion: **300**

1 small cucumber

1 oz (25g) butter

2 tablespoons olive oil

1 clove garlic, peeled and crushed

Finely grated rind ½ lemon

1 tablespoon snipped fresh dill, or 1 teaspoon dried dill

¼ teaspoon salt

¼ teaspoon black pepper

16 medium-sized fresh sardines

1. Halve the **cucumber** lengthways and remove seeds; cut into ½in (15mm) slices.

2. Heat the **butter** and **olive oil** in a large frying pan until bubbling; add cucumber and **garlic** and cook, stirring continuously, for 4 minutes. Add **lemon rind, dill, salt** and **pepper.**

3. Place half the cucumber mixture in a shallow ovenproof dish; lay **sardines** on top and cover with the remaining cucumber mixture.

4. Cover dish and cook at 190°C (375°F, gas mark 5) for 20 minutes.

5. Serve with small potatoes cooked in their skins and a green vegetable, such as French beans.

> **Tip:** This cooking method can be used for larger whole fish, such as sea bass, small salmon trout, etc.

Salmon Loaf with Cucumber-Dill Sauce

Preparation: **15 min**   Cooking: **30 min**   Serves **4**   Cals per portion: **475**

2 x 7 oz (200g) cans salmon

About 4 fl oz (115ml) milk

2 oz (50g) butter or margarine

**1 small onion, peeled
and chopped**

2 tablespoons plain flour

1 stem celery, finely chopped

4 oz (115g) fine dry breadcrumbs

2 eggs, lightly beaten

½ teaspoon salt

¼ teaspoon black pepper

**2 tablespoons snipped fresh dill
(or 1 teaspoon dried dill)**

8 fl oz (225ml) soured cream

1 tablespoon cider vinegar

¾ cucumber, seeded and diced

1. Preheat the oven to 180°C (350°F, gas mark 4). Drain the **salmon,** saving the liquid. Combine the salmon liquid with enough **milk** to make 8fl oz (225ml). Put aside.

2. Melt the **butter** in a large saucepan over moderate heat. Add the **onion,** and cook for 3 minutes. Blend in the **flour,** and cook for 1 minute, stirring continuously.

3. Gradually add the salmon liquid and milk mixture, and cook, stirring continuously, until very thick – about 3 minutes. Remove from the heat. Add the salmon, **celery, breadcrumbs, eggs, salt, black pepper** and half of the **dill,** and mix well.

4. Transfer the salmon mixture to a buttered, 8in (200mm) casserole dish, and form the mixture into a loaf. Bake for 30 minutes.

5. Meanwhile, in a small serving bowl, combine the **soured cream, vinegar, cucumber** and the remaining dill. Serve this sauce on the side with the salmon loaf.

Sautéed Scallops

Preparation: **5 min**   Cooking: **5 min**   Serves **4**   Cals per portion: **220**

**1¼ lb (575g) small shelled
scallops, rinsed**

3 tablespoons plain flour

½ teaspoon salt

½ teaspoon pepper

2 oz (50g) butter

**1 tablespoon olive oil or
vegetable oil**

1. Dry the **scallops** thoroughly with absorbent paper. On a plate mix together the **flour, salt** and **pepper,** and roll the scallops in the seasoned flour.

2. Heat the **butter** and the **oil** in a large frying pan over a moderate heat and, when it is bubbling, drop in the scallops one by one. Treat the scallops carefully – they should be gently shaken in the pan. Cook until golden, about 3 to 5 minutes. Serve on warm plates with Dill Mayonnaise, page 301, and lemon wedges.

Steamed Mussels with Garlic and Butter Sauce

Preparation: **25 min** Cooking: **10 min**   Serves **4** Cals per portion: **365**

Serve these mussels as a first course for 8 or a main course for 4. Have plenty of crusty bread on the table to dip into the delicious cooking juices.

4½ lb (2kg) mussels

4 oz (115g) butter at room temperature

2 shallots, peeled and chopped

6 cloves garlic, peeled and finely chopped

8 fl oz (225ml) dry white wine or dry vermouth

½ teaspoon salt

Pinch black pepper

6 tablespoons chopped parsley

1. Scrub the **mussels** thoroughly with a stiff brush under cold running water, discarding any with open or broken shells. With scissors or a small, sharp knife, remove the 'beard' that extends from the side of the mussel.

2. Melt 1½oz (40g) of the **butter** in a very large, non-aluminium pan over low heat. Add the **shallots** and 2 teaspoons of the **garlic,** and cook for 2 minutes. Add the mussels, **wine, salt** and **pepper.** Cover, bring to the boil, and cook, shaking the pot occasionally, for 3 minutes, or until the mussels open (discard any that do not open). Using a slotted spoon, place the mussels in individual serving bowls.

3. Mix together the remaining butter and garlic and the **parsley.** Stir the mixture into the cooking juices in the pan, heat through quickly, and pour over the mussels.

Lettuce, Egg and Prawn Cocottes ½ 🐷

Preparation: **10 min** Cooking: **15 min**   Serves **4** Cals per portion: **270**

1 medium-sized leek, split, cleaned and shredded

1 clove garlic, crushed

1 oz (25g) butter or margarine

1 oz (25g) wholemeal flour

½ pint (285ml) milk

½ teaspoon ground cumin

½ teaspoon ground nutmeg

¼ teaspoon salt

¼ teaspoon black pepper

2 tablespoons chopped parsley

3 oz (75g) finely shredded crisp lettuce

6 oz (175g) peeled prawns

4 eggs

2 tablespoons natural yoghurt

1 teaspoon Pesto sauce

1. Fry the **leek** and **garlic** gently in the **butter** for 4 minutes; stir in the **flour** and cook for 30 seconds.

2. Gradually stir in the **milk** and bring to the boil, stirring continuously, until the sauce is thickened and smooth.

3. Beat in the **cumin, nutmeg,** and **salt** and **pepper** to taste.

4. Add **parsley, lettuce** and **prawns;** divide among 4 greased, individual, shallow ovenproof dishes.

5. Make a hollow in the centre of each one and carefully crack in an **egg;** stand dishes in roasting tin and add sufficient hot water to come halfway up the sides of the dishes.

6. Cover tin completely with foil. Bake at 180°C (350°F, gas mark 4) for about 15 minutes, until eggs are just set.

7. Mix the **yoghurt** with the **Pesto;** spoon a little over each egg and serve immediately with hot crusty bread and a salad.

Oyster, Mussel and Mushroom Pie

Preparation: **15 min**   Cooking: **10 min**

Serves **4**   Cals per portion: **450**

2 x 3⅔ oz (105g) cans smoked oysters

1 x 8.8 oz (250g) can cooked mussels

About 8 fl oz (225ml) double cream

2 oz (50g) butter or margarine

4 oz (115g) mushrooms, thinly sliced

2 tablespoons plain flour

¼ teaspoon Worcestershire sauce

Generous squeeze lemon juice

Pinch cayenne pepper

¾ teaspoon salt

¼ teaspoon black pepper

2½ oz (65g) soft fresh breadcrumbs

1. Preheat the oven to 220°C (425°F, gas mark 7). Drain the **smoked oysters.** Drain the **mussels,** reserving their brine. Make the mussel brine up to 12fl oz (340ml) with **cream.** Put aside.

2. Melt half the **butter** in a medium-sized, heavy frying pan over moderate heat. Add the **mushrooms,** and cook for 3 minutes, or until lightly browned. Transfer the mushrooms to a plate and put aside.

3. Reduce the heat and melt ½oz (15g) of the remaining butter in the pan. Blend in the **flour,** and cook for 1 minute, stirring continuously. Gradually add the mussel juice and cream mixture and cook, stirring continuously, until the mixture thickens – about 3 minutes. Remove from the heat.

4. Add the mussels, smoked oysters, the cooked mushrooms and any accumulated juices, the **Worcestershire sauce, lemon juice, cayenne pepper, salt** and **black pepper.** Pour the mixture into a greased, shallow ovenproof dish.

5. Sprinkle with the **breadcrumbs,** and dot with the remaining butter. Bake until the crumbs are browned – about 10 minutes.

Grilled Prawns with Basil Butter ◎ ½

Preparation: **6 min**   Cooking: **4 min**

Serves **4**   Cals per portion: **250**

32 good-sized prawns, heads and tails left on

3 oz (75g) butter

2 tablespoons olive oil

3 cloves garlic, peeled and finely chopped

2 tablespoons chopped fresh basil

¼ teaspoon salt

¼ teaspoon black pepper

Shredded lettuce

1. Thread the **prawns** onto 4 kebab skewers; place on the rack of the grill pan.

2. Melt the **butter** with the **olive oil** and stir in the **garlic, basil, salt** and **pepper.**

3. Brush the prawns with some of the basil butter and grill under the preheated grill for 2 minutes. Turn the skewers, brush with the flavoured butter once more and grill for a further 2 minutes.

4. Serve the skewered prawns on a bed of **shredded lettuce** with the extra hot basil butter served separately, and some crusty bread.

Malayan Fried Squid ⏺ ½

Preparation: **10 min**   Cooking: **8 min**   Serves **4**   Cals per portion: **355**

1¼ lb (575g) squid, prepared, cleaned, and cut into ½ in (15mm) rings

4 fl oz (115ml) vegetable oil

1 large onion, peeled and thinly sliced

2 teaspoons concentrated anchovy sauce

1½ teaspoons chilli powder

1 tablespoon brown sugar

Juice 1 lemon

4 tablespoons plain flour

Tip: *Squid tends to jump and splutter during frying – cover the pan with a wire mesh pan guard or fine metal colander if necessary.*

1. Wash the **squid** thoroughly in cold water, drain and dry well with absorbent paper.

2. Heat the **oil** in a large, heavy frying pan over moderate heat. Add the **onion** and fry gently for 2 minutes. Add the **anchovy sauce** and **chilli powder** and cook for a further 2 minutes. Add the **sugar** and **lemon juice** and stir.

3. Put the **flour** on a plate or sheet of waxed paper. Dip the squid in the flour, shake off the excess and slip into the pan. Do not crowd the pan – if necessary cook in two batches. As soon as one side becomes golden, turn with a long-handled perforated spoon. Squid should not be cooked for longer than 3 or 4 minutes, or it will become tough. Serve with lemon wedges, rice and a green salad.

Sautéed Squid ½

Preparation: **15 min**   Cooking: **30 min**   Serves **4**   Cals per portion: **350**

1 lb (450g) squid, prepared, cleaned, and cut into ½ in (15mm) rings

4 tablespoons olive oil or vegetable oil

1 medium onion, finely chopped

2 cloves garlic, peeled and finely chopped

½ pint (285ml) dry white wine

4 medium-sized tomatoes, peeled and chopped

½ teaspoon salt

½ teaspoon dried thyme

12 oz (350g) potatoes

2 tablespoons finely chopped parsley

½ teaspoon black pepper

1. Wash the **squid** thoroughly in cold water, drain and dry with absorbent paper. Put aside.

2. Heat the **oil** in a heavy, medium-sized saucepan, add the **onion** and the **garlic** and cook over a moderate heat for 1 minute. Add the squid and turn it in the oil with a long-handled perforated spoon. When the squid turns opaque add the **wine** and let it bubble for 2 minutes. Add the **tomatoes, salt** and **thyme;** cover and simmer for 20 minutes.

3. Meanwhile, peel and chop the **potatoes** into ¾in (20mm) pieces. Add them, together with the **parsley** and **pepper,** to the pan; cover and cook until the potatoes are just tender – about 10 minutes. Serve with hot crusty bread and a green salad.

EGGS
AND
CHEESE

Eggs Fried or Sautéed Whole

Baked Eggs

Boiled Eggs

Omelettes

Cheese Dishes

Melted Cheese

(See also Oven-Baked Dishes)

EGGS AND CHEESE

Why not try one of these egg or cheese dishes in place of meat? They are inexpensive and suitable as main courses for lunch or dinner. Some, such as Mexican Eggs, and Swiss Cheese and Onion Gratin, are good for brunch, too. For something simple, turn to pages 189-190 for instructions on making large, economical omelettes which are browned under the grill before being cut into wedges for serving. Because eggs and cheese are staple items in most households, many of the recipes make excellent 'last minute' meals.

Mexican Eggs

Preparation: **15 min**   Cooking: **10 min**   Serves **4**   Cals per portion: **460**

Packets of tortillas are available in most supermarkets. If you like, fry them lightly on both sides in some oil and keep them warm while the eggs are cooking.

2 fl oz (50ml) vegetable oil

1 medium-sized onion, peeled and finely chopped

1 medium-sized pepper, seeded and finely chopped

5 medium-sized tomatoes, peeled and chopped

1 whole canned chilli pepper, rinsed, seeded and chopped, or ¼ teaspoon crushed dried red pepper

2 cloves garlic, peeled and finely chopped

½ teaspoon salt

½ teaspoon ground cumin

2 teaspoons chilli powder

¼ teaspoon dried oregano

4 corn tortillas

4 eggs

4 oz (115g) grated mild cheese

1. Preheat the grill. Heat half the **oil** in a large, heavy saucepan over moderate heat. Add the **onion** and **pepper,** and cook for 5 minutes, or until the onion is soft.

2. Raise the heat and add the **tomatoes, chilli pepper, garlic** and **salt;** cook for 5 minutes, or until slightly thickened. Stir in the **cumin, chilli powder** and **oregano,** and remove the sauce from the heat.

3. While the sauce is cooking, arrange the **tortillas** on an ungreased baking sheet.

4. About 2 minutes before the sauce is done, heat the remaining oil in a medium-sized, heavy frying pan over moderate heat. Break the **eggs** into the pan, spacing them so that they do not overlap. Lower the heat slightly and cook for 1 minute, or until the whites are just set. Using an egg slice, carefully remove the eggs from the pan, and place an egg on each tortilla.

5. Pour the sauce over the eggs, sprinkle with the **cheese,** and place under the grill for 1 minute, or until the cheese begins to melt. Serve with a green salad or a salad of sliced oranges and avocados.

> **Tip:** *If you want to get a head start on this dish, make the sauce in advance, then reheat it while the eggs are cooking.*

Potato Eggs with Lemon 🐷

Preparation: **25 min**   Cooking: **20 min**   Serves **4**   Cals per portion: **320**

In this elegant but hearty dish, the egg whites are whipped and spread over mashed potatoes; the yolks nestle in pockets made in the whites.

3 large potatoes (about 1½ lb/700g) peeled and cut into ¼ in (5mm) slices

2 fl oz (50ml) milk

1 oz (25g) butter or margarine, softened

½ teaspoon salt

¼ teaspoon black pepper

1 tablespoon snipped fresh dill or ½ teaspoon dried dill

1 small onion, peeled and finely chopped

2 tablespoons finely chopped parsley

4 eggs

Grated rind ½ lemon

1. Preheat the oven to 180°C (350°F, gas mark 4). Place the **potatoes** in a large saucepan, add water to cover, put the lid askew on the pan and boil for 15 minutes, or until tender.

2. Drain and mash the potatoes, adding the **milk** to moisten them. Stir in the **butter,** ¼ teaspoon of the **salt,** and the **pepper.**

3. Mix the **dill, onion** and **parsley** into the potatoes, transfer the mixture to a greased shallow ovenproof dish and put aside.

4. Separate the **eggs.** Beat the whites until stiff, beat in the remaining salt, then gradually beat in the **lemon rind.**

5. Spread the beaten egg whites lightly over the potatoes, shaping them into peaks as you would a meringue. With half an eggshell, make 4 depressions in the egg whites, then slide an egg yolk into each depression. Bake for 20 minutes, or until the eggs are set.

> **Tip:** *You can make the mashed potatoes in advance (steps 1 and 2).*

Savoury Baked Eggs ½

Preparation: **10 min**   Cooking: **17 min**   Serves **4**   Cals per portion: **390**

2½ fl oz (75ml) mayonnaise

¼ teaspoon salt

Pinch black pepper

¼ teaspoon paprika

¼ teaspoon Worcestershire sauce

1 tablespoon chopped chives

4 fl oz (115ml) milk

4 oz (115g) strong Cheddar cheese

8 eggs

> **Tip:** *For a milder-tasting sauce, substitute 2½fl oz (75ml) of soured cream for the mayonnaise.*

1. Preheat the oven to 180°C (350°F, gas mark 4). In a saucepan, combine the **mayonnaise, salt, pepper, paprika** and **Worcestershire sauce** and the **chives.**

2. Gradually add the **milk,** stirring continuously, until smooth. Add the **cheese,** and cook over low heat, stirring until the cheese has melted.

3. Grease 4 individual baking dishes and pour 2 tablespoons of sauce into each one. Break 2 **eggs** into each dish and top with the rest of the sauce. Place the dishes in a pan containing about ½in (15mm) of hot water and bake for 17 to 20 minutes, or until the eggs are cooked to the desired consistency.

Eggs with Chicken and Asparagus Cream

Preparation: **15 min**   Cooking: **20 min**   Serves **4**   Cals per portion: **515**

8 oz (225g) minced or finely chopped cooked chicken

2 egg yolks

3 tablespoons double cream

¼ teaspoon salt

¼ teaspoon black pepper

1 teaspoon mixed dried herbs

1 tablespoon Worcestershire sauce

2 oz (50g) butter

8 eggs

1 x 10 oz (275g) can asparagus tips

3 tablespoons mayonnaise

3 tablespoons single cream

1. Preheat the oven to 190°C (375°F, gas mark 5). Mix the minced **chicken** with the **egg yolks, double cream, salt** and **pepper, mixed herbs** and **Worcestershire sauce.**

2. Grease 4 good-sized cocotte dishes (about 4in/100mm in diameter) with **butter.**

3. Press the chicken mixture over the base and around the sides of each dish; carefully crack 2 **eggs** into the centre of each one and dot with butter.

4. Stand the dishes in a roasting tin and add sufficient hot water to come halfway up the sides of the dishes; cover completely with foil, and bake in the preheated oven for 20 minutes.

5. Meanwhile, make the sauce. Drain the canned **asparagus;** put the asparagus, **mayonnaise** and **single cream** into a liquidiser or food processor and blend until smooth. Add enough of the asparagus liquid to give a spooning consistency.

6. Spoon a pool of sauce onto each serving plate and carefully unmould the cooked chicken and egg moulds on top. Serve immediately with crusty bread.

Eggs with Black Butter Sauce ◎ ½ 🐷

Preparation: **3 min**   Cooking: **4 min**   Serves **4**   Cals per portion: **375**

3 tablespoons olive oil

4 large eggs

2 oz (50g) butter

Juice ½ lemon

1 tablespoon capers

2 tablespoons chopped parsley

¼ teaspoon salt

¼ teaspoon black pepper

4 crumpets, lightly toasted

Tip: *For a more substantial meal, serve 2 eggs per person, and use slightly more black butter.*

1. Heat the **olive oil** in a large, shallow frying pan; carefully crack in each **egg** and fry over a moderate heat until the whites are set and slightly crisp at the edges.

2. Heat the **butter** in a small pan; bubble fairly briskly until it starts to turn dark brown.

3. Add the **lemon juice, capers,** half the **parsley, salt** and **pepper** to the butter and heat through.

4. Place the **crumpets** on serving plates; top each one with a well-drained fried egg and spoon over the hot black butter.

5. Serve immediately, sprinkled with the remaining parsley.

Eggs with Chicken Livers ⊘

Preparation: **7 min**   Cooking: **13 min**   Serves **4**   Cals per portion: **385**

Speed up this dish by preparing the onion and peppers while the chicken livers are cooking. Then, while the onion mixture cooks, peel and chop the tomatoes and the parsley.

2 oz (50g) butter or margarine

1 lb (450g) chicken livers, drained and sinews removed

½ teaspoon salt

¼ teaspoon black pepper

1 medium-sized onion, peeled and thinly sliced

2 medium-sized peppers, seeded and cut into strips

2 medium-sized tomatoes, peeled and chopped

1 tablespoon chopped parsley

4 eggs

1. Melt half the **butter** in a medium-sized, heavy frying pan over moderately high heat until bubbling. Add the **livers, salt** and **pepper,** and cook, stirring, until the livers are browned on the outside but still pink inside – about 5 minutes. Transfer to a plate and put aside.

2. Reduce the heat to moderately low, and melt the remaining butter in the pan. Add the **onion** and **peppers,** and cook, stirring occasionally, for 5 minutes, or until the vegetables have softened.

3. Add the **tomatoes** and 2 teaspoons of the **parsley** and simmer for 5 minutes. Return the livers to the pan for 1 minute to heat through.

4. Break the **eggs** over the mixture, being careful not to break the yolks. Cover and simmer just until the whites of the eggs are set – about 3 minutes. Sprinkle with the remaining parsley, and serve with a green salad and crusty bread.

> **Tip:** *For a meatless version of this dish, omit the chicken livers, cook the eggs in the vegetable mixture, sprinkle 3oz (75g) of grated Parmesan cheese over the top and put under the grill until the cheese browns slightly.*

Creamed Curried Eggs ½

Preparation: **17 min**   Cooking: **10 min**   Serves **4**   Cals per portion: **335**

The preparation time includes 15 minutes for cooking the eggs.

1¾ oz (45g) butter or margarine

1 medium-sized onion, peeled and chopped

1½ tablespoons plain flour

1½ teaspoons curry powder

¾ teaspoon salt

12 fl oz (340ml) milk

8 hard-boiled eggs

1. Melt the **butter** in a saucepan over moderate heat. Add the **onion,** and cook for 5 minutes, or until soft.

2. Remove the pan from the heat and stir in the **flour, curry powder** and **salt,** and then the **milk.** Cook, stirring continuously, for 1 minute, or until the sauce thickens. Peel the **eggs,** quarter them lengthwise, and add them to the sauce. Serve with boiled rice and chutney.

> **Tip:** *If you are using refrigerated hard-boiled eggs, warm them in the sauce for about 1 minute before serving.*

Crisp Curried Eggs ⊘ ½

Preparation: **10 min**   Serves **4**   Cals per portion: **560**

8 hard-boiled eggs

2 oz (50g) melted butter

3 oz (75g) crisp golden
breadcrumbs

½ pint (285ml) mayonnaise

¼ teaspoon salt

¼ teaspoon black pepper

Juice ½ lemon

Curry powder to taste

1. Shell the **hard-boiled eggs;** dip the eggs
into melted **butter** and roll in the **breadcrumbs**
to give an even coating. Chill briefly.

2. Combine the **mayonnaise, salt** and **pepper,**
lemon juice and **curry powder.**

3. Serve the eggs on a pool of curried
mayonnaise, accompanied by crusty bread
or poppadoms, and a watercress salad.

> *Tip: To bring out the flavour of the curried
> mayonnaise, squeeze lime juice over each portion.*

Spinach Eggs ½

Preparation: **15 min**   Cooking: **12 min**   Serves **4**   Cals per portion: **485**

12 perfect spinach leaves

2 oz (50g) butter

8 tablespoons double cream

2 oz (50g) grated Parmesan
cheese

8 eggs

¼ teaspoon salt

¼ teaspoon black pepper

Black lumpfish roe

> *Tip: Check that the white has set,
> otherwise the eggs will collapse
> when turned out.*

1. Preheat the oven to 190°C (375°F, gas
mark 5).

2. Blanch the **spinach leaves** briefly in boiling
water.

3. Grease 4 good-sized cocotte dishes
(about 4in/100mm in diameter) with **butter,**
line the inside of each with well-drained
spinach leaves.

4. Pour a little **cream** into each one and
sprinkle with half the grated **cheese.**

5. Carefully crack 2 **eggs** into each dish; spoon
over the rest of the cream, sprinkle with the
remaining Parmesan and season with **salt**
and **pepper.** Dot with knobs of butter.

6. Place the dishes in a roasting tin and add
sufficient hot water to come halfway up the
sides of the dishes. Cover completely with foil
and bake in the preheated oven until the eggs
are just set – about 12 minutes.

7. Carefully unmould onto small, warm serving
plates and serve with hot garlic bread.
Garnish each portion with a small spoonful of
lumpfish roe.

Egg Croquettes with Chicken

Preparation: **35 min** Cooking: **5 min**   Serves **4** Cals per portion: **390**

Use the 15 minutes it takes to boil the eggs to chop the chicken, olives and parsley and to make the sauce.

1¾ oz (45g) butter or margarine

2 oz (50g) plus 2 tablespoons plain flour

¼ pint (150ml) milk

4 oz (115g) finely chopped cooked chicken

1 tablespoon finely chopped stuffed olives

1 tablespoon finely chopped parsley

4 hard-boiled eggs, finely chopped

½ teaspoon salt

¼ teaspoon black pepper

3 oz (75g) fine dry breadcrumbs

2 tablespoons vegetable oil

1 egg, lightly beaten

1. Melt two-thirds of the **butter** in a saucepan over moderate heat. Blend in the 2 tablespoons of **flour,** and cook for 1 minute. Add the **milk,** and cook, stirring continuously with a wire whisk, until the sauce is very thick – about 5 minutes. Remove from the heat.

2. Add the **chicken, olives, parsley, hard-boiled eggs, salt** and **pepper.** Mix well, then place in the freezer for 12 minutes, or until the mixture is stiff enough to shape.

3. Put the remaining flour onto a plate or a sheet of waxed paper, and the **breadcrumbs** on another. Shape the chilled egg and chicken mixture into 8 oval patties about ¾in (20mm) thick.

4. Heat the **oil** and the remaining butter in a medium-sized, heavy frying pan over moderately high heat. Coat each patty with the flour, then dip into the **beaten egg,** and finally coat with the breadcrumbs. Shake off any excess crumbs. Cook the patties for 2 to 3 minutes on each side. Serve immediately.

Baked Eggs with Onions and Cheese

Preparation: **17 min** Cooking: **14 min**   Serves **4** Cals per portion: **310**

The ingredients for this dish are almost always on hand, making it ideal for unexpected guests. To save time, make the sauce and grate the cheese while the eggs are cooking.

1 oz (25g) butter or margarine

2 medium-sized onions, peeled and sliced

1 tablespoon flour

½ pint (285ml) milk

½ teaspoon salt

¼ teaspoon black pepper

6 hard-boiled eggs, sliced

2 oz (50g) grated strong Cheddar cheese

1. Preheat the oven to 200°C (400°F, gas mark 6). Melt the **butter** in a saucepan over moderately high heat. Add the **onions,** and cook, stirring occasionally, for 3 minutes, or until they begin to soften.

2. Blend in the **flour,** and cook, stirring, for 30 seconds. Add the **milk, salt** and **pepper,** stirring continuously. Bring to the boil, lower the heat, and simmer for 1 minute, stirring frequently.

3. Arrange the **eggs** in a greased 9in (230mm) pie plate. Pour the sauce over the eggs and mix gently. Sprinkle the **cheese** over the top and bake for 10 minutes. Place under the grill, about 3in (80mm) from the heat. Grill for 4 to 5 minutes to brown.

Chinese Omelette

Preparation: **5 min**   Cooking: **17 min**   Serves **4**   Cals per portion: **310**

1 tablespoon soya sauce

1 tablespoon cider vinegar

1 teaspoon sugar

8 fl oz (225ml) chicken stock

2 teaspoons cornflour

2 tablespoons vegetable oil

1 clove garlic, peeled and
finely chopped

3 shallots, peeled and
finely chopped

6 oz (175g) canned bean sprouts,
drained

8 oz (225g) minced cooked pork
or chicken, or 8 oz (225g) peeled
prawns

4 eggs

½ teaspoon salt

1. Combine the **soya sauce, vinegar, sugar** and three-quarters of the **chicken stock** in a saucepan. Bring the mixture to the boil.

2. Mix the **cornflour** with the remaining stock. Add this mixture to the saucepan and continue to boil, stirring continuously, for 2 minutes. Keep the sauce warm over very low heat.

3. Heat the **oil** in a medium-sized, heavy frying pan over high heat. Add the **garlic** and **shallots,** and toss for 30 seconds. Add the **bean sprouts** and toss for 30 seconds. Add the **pork** and toss for 2 minutes.

4. Beat the **eggs** with the **salt,** and add to the pan. Reduce the heat to low. Cook for 2 minutes, then cover and cook for 2 more minutes, or until the eggs are set.

5. Loosen the bottom of the eggs from the pan with a spatula and invert the omelette onto a serving dish. Cut into 4 wedges. Reheat the reserved sauce and pour over the omelette wedges. Serve with Fried Rice, page 214.

Country Omelette

Preparation: **9 min**   Cooking: **14 min**   Serves **4**   Cals per portion: **295**

4 rashers bacon, cut into ¾ in
(20mm) strips

1 medium-sized onion, peeled
and chopped

2 small potatoes, peeled and cut
into small dice

1 medium-sized pepper, seeded
and chopped

½ teaspoon salt

¼ teaspoon black pepper

8 eggs, lightly beaten

1. Cook the **bacon** in a medium-sized, heavy frying pan, preferably non-stick, over moderate heat for 3 minutes. Leaving the bacon in the pan, pour off all but 2 tablespoons of the fat.

2. Add the **onion, potatoes** and the **pepper** to the pan. Cook, stirring occasionally, for 10 minutes, or until the vegetables are tender. Sprinkle with the **salt** and **black pepper.**

3. Pour the **eggs** over the vegetables and bacon, and as the eggs cook, push the edges towards the centre with an egg slice to allow any uncooked portion to run underneath. When the bottom is firm – in about 3 to 4 minutes – cover and cook for 1 minute, or until set but not dry. Cut into 4 wedges and serve.

EGGS AND CHEESE

Rolled Chicken Omelette

Preparation: **10 min** Cooking: **3-4 min**   Serves **4** Cals per portion: **470**

6 eggs

2 tablespoons milk

¼ teaspoon salt

¼ teaspoon black pepper

2 oz (50g) butter

6 oz (175g) chopped cooked chicken

7 tablespoons mayonnaise

3 spring onions, finely chopped

1 clove garlic, peeled and crushed

3 tablespoons single cream

2 tablespoons grated Parmesan cheese

1 tablespoon dry sherry

Poppy seeds

1. Beat the **eggs** with the **milk** and half the **salt** and **pepper;** melt the **butter** in a large, non-stick omelette pan, add the egg mixture and cook over a gentle heat, stirring from time to time, until the underside of the omelette is set.

2. Mix the **chicken** with 4 tablespoons of **mayonnaise, spring onions, garlic,** and the rest of the salt and pepper; spread over the omelette while it is still warm, and roll up. Turn onto a plate and allow to cool.

3. For the sauce, mix the remaining mayonnaise with the **cream, cheese** and **sherry,** and spoon over the omelette. Sprinkle with **poppy seeds.**

4. Cover with a loose 'cloche' of foil and keep chilled until ready to serve.

> **Tip:** *This is a great dish to take on a picnic, or for summer eating in the back garden; try adding prawns to the omelette instead of chicken.*

Pasta Omelette with Anchovies ½

Preparation: **8 min** Cooking: **6 min**   Serves **4** Cals per portion: **290**

3 tablespoons olive oil or vegetable oil

4 oz (115g) cooked pasta

4 eggs

1½ oz (40g) grated Parmesan cheese

6 anchovy fillets, rinsed and chopped

¼ teaspoon black pepper

2 tablespoons chopped fresh basil or parsley

1. Preheat the grill. Heat the **oil** over moderate heat in a medium-sized, heavy frying pan. Add the **pasta,** and cook for 8 minutes, or until golden and crisp on the bottom.

2. Meanwhile, in a small bowl, beat the **eggs** with the **cheese, anchovy fillets, pepper** and **basil.** Pour the mixture over the pasta, tilting the pan from side to side over the heat until the eggs are just set – about 3 minutes.

3. Place the pan (but not the handle) under the grill about 3in (80mm) from the heat. Grill until the top of the omelette has puffed and browned – about 3 minutes. Remove from the grill, cut into 4 wedges, and serve.

> **Tip:** *Canned tuna fish can be used instead of the anchovy fillets.*

Picnic Tortilla

Preparation: **5 min**   Cooking: **9 min**   Serves **4**   Cals per portion: **365**

5 eggs

3 egg yolks

2 tablespoons natural yoghurt

4 tablespoons milk

¼ teaspoon salt

¼ teaspoon black pepper

2 tablespoons olive oil

1 medium-sized onion, peeled and thinly sliced

1 clove garlic, crushed

4 oz (115g) new potatoes, thinly sliced

3 oz (75g) cooked peas (or frozen peas, thawed)

1 small green and 1 small yellow pepper, seeded and thinly sliced

2 oz (50g) stuffed olives, halved

2 oz (50g) grated cheese

1. Beat the **eggs** with the **egg yolks, yoghurt, milk, salt** and **pepper.**

2. Heat the **oil** in a large frying pan; add the **onion** and **garlic** and fry gently for 3 minutes. Add the **potatoes, peas, peppers** and **olives,** and stir-fry for a further 3 minutes.

3. Pour the egg mixture into the pan and cook until set on the underside; sprinkle with the grated **cheese** and place under a preheated grill until the tortilla is just set and golden-brown.

4. Serve immediately, cut into wedges. Alternatively, the cooled tortilla can be wrapped in clear plastic film and taken on a picnic to eat cold – take a jar of mayonnaise with you to serve as an accompaniment.

Tip: *For a really well-shaped tortilla use a non-stick pan.*

Soft Eggs with Watercress Sauce

Preparation: **10 min**   Cooking: **4 min**   Serves **4**   Cals per portion: **150**

4 eggs

8 oz (225g) frozen spinach, thawed and drained

1 oz (25g) butter

¼ teaspoon salt

¼ teaspoon black pepper

1 bunch watercress, chopped

4 tablespoons mayonnaise

2 tablespoons natural yoghurt

4 anchovy fillets, halved lengthwise

1. Soft-boil the **eggs** for approximately 3 minutes.

2. Meanwhile, heat the **spinach** through with the **butter** and half of the **salt** and **pepper,** over a gentle heat.

3. Mix the chopped **watercress** with the **mayonnaise, yoghurt,** and the remaining salt and pepper.

4. Carefully shell the eggs and arrange each one on a bed of hot spinach.

5. Spoon over the watercress dressing and garnish with the **anchovy fillets.** Serve immediately with warm, crusty bread.

Cheddar Egg Cups ½

Preparation: **10 min**   Cooking: **15 min**   Serves **4**   Cals per portion: **370**

1 oz (25g) butter or margarine

2 tablespoons plain flour

8 fl oz (225ml) milk

Few drops Tabasco sauce

2 oz (50g) grated strong Cheddar cheese

6 oz (175g) chopped cooked ham

4 eggs

1½ oz (40g) soft fresh breadcrumbs

> **Tip:** *As a variation, you can use Swiss cheese instead of the Cheddar, but add 1 small onion, peeled, chopped and cooked in ½oz (15g) butter until golden.*

1. Preheat the oven to 180°C (350°F, gas mark 4). Melt the **butter** in a saucepan over low heat. Blend in the **flour,** and cook, stirring continuously, until just bubbling – about 1 minute.

2. Stir in the **milk** and the **Tabasco sauce.** Raise the heat and cook, stirring, until the mixture thickens – about 3 minutes. Continue cooking and stirring for 1 minute, then remove from the heat.

3. Add all but 2 tablespoons of the **cheese,** and cook, stirring continuously, until the cheese melts.

4. Divide the **ham** evenly among 4 greased, individual baking dishes and top with the cheese sauce. Break the **eggs,** one into each dish. Sprinkle the **breadcrumbs** and the remaining cheese evenly over the eggs. Bake for 15 minutes, or until the eggs are set as you like them.

Swiss Cheese and Onion Gratin

Preparation: **12 min**   Cooking: **25 min**   Serves **4**   Cals per portion: **555**

3½ oz (90g) butter or margarine

2 medium-sized onions, peeled and sliced

2 eggs, lightly beaten

2 egg yolks

4 oz (115g) grated Swiss cheese

8 fl oz (225ml) single cream

4 fl oz (115ml) milk

Pinch ground nutmeg

1 teaspoon salt

¼ teaspoon black pepper

1½ oz (40g) fine dry breadcrumbs

1. Preheat oven to 180°C, (350°F, gas mark 4). Melt two-thirds of the **butter** in a saucepan over moderately low heat. Add the **onions,** and cook for 10 minutes, or until very soft.

2. Meanwhile, in a mixing bowl, combine the **eggs, egg yolks, cheese, cream, milk, nutmeg, salt** and **pepper.**

3. When the onions are cooked, spread them out in a greased, 9in (230mm) pie plate. Melt the remaining butter in the saucepan. Add the egg mixture to the pie plate, and sprinkle the **breadcrumbs** and melted butter over the top. Bake for 25 minutes, or until puffed and set.

> **Tips: 1.** *Leftovers can be refrigerated and reheated in a 160°C (325°F, gas mark 3) oven, but do not freeze the gratin or it will turn rubbery.* **2.** *You can substitute 6 shallots, peeled and chopped, for the onions, but cook them for only 5 minutes before adding them to the pie plate.*

Cheddar and Nut Loaf

Preparation: **10 min**   Cooking: **50 min**   Serves **6**   Cals per portion: **500**

6 oz (175g) Cheddar cheese

8 oz (225g) self-raising flour

¼ teaspoon salt

¼ teaspoon black pepper

3 oz (75g) butter

1 tablespoon poppy seeds

2 tablespoons chopped parsley

3 tablespoons chopped walnuts

2 eggs

¼ pint (150ml) natural yoghurt

Fresh tomato sauce

> **Tip:** *Try topping each portion with a generous spoonful of cream cheese.*

1. Preheat the oven to 180°C (350°F, gas mark 4).

2. Grease a loaf tin and line with greaseproof paper.

3. Grate two-thirds of the **cheese;** cut the remainder into small cubes.

4. Sieve the **flour** with **salt** and **pepper;** rub in the **butter** and add the grated cheese, **poppy seeds, parsley** and **walnuts.**

5. Beat the **eggs** with the **yoghurt,** add to the other ingredients and mix well; mix in the cubed cheese and put into the prepared tin.

6. Bake in the preheated oven for 50 minutes to an hour – test with a fine skewer.

7. Unmould carefully, cut into thick slices and serve in shallow soup bowls with a generous pool of hot **tomato sauce.**

Cheese Crêpes

Preparation: **30 min**   Cooking: **15 min**   Serves **4**   Cals per portion: **600**

4 oz (115g) flour

½ teaspoon salt

1 egg

¼ pint (150ml) water

¼ pint (150ml) natural yoghurt

8 oz (225g) cooked, well-drained spinach (or thawed frozen spinach)

Pinch ground nutmeg

8 oz (225g) garlic-flavoured cream cheese

Black pepper

3 oz (75g) grated Gruyère cheese

> **Tip:** *When making pancakes, it's well worth making more than you need and freezing them; interleave with waxed paper before wrapping and freezing.*

1. Preheat oven to 190°C (375°F, gas mark 5). Sieve the **flour** and **salt** into a bowl; add the **egg** and half the **water** and beat until smooth.

2. Gradually beat in the remaining water and the **yoghurt;** cover and leave to stand for 10 minutes.

3. Mix the **spinach** with the **nutmeg** and **cream cheese,** add **pepper** to taste.

4. Using a lightly oiled pan, cook 8 small pancakes with the prepared batter (keep them warm as you go).

5. Divide the filling among the pancakes and roll each one up; place in a greased, shallow ovenproof dish and sprinkle with the **grated cheese.**

6. Bake in the preheated oven for 15 minutes. Serve piping hot, with a side salad if liked.

Watercress and Walnut Tartlets

Preparation: **30 min**   Cooking: **25 min**   Serves **4**   Cals per portion: **545**

8 oz (225g) shortcrust pastry

Beaten egg to glaze

1 tablespoon grated Parmesan cheese

3 eggs

1 egg yolk

4 tablespoons milk

4 tablespoons thick natural yoghurt

4 oz (115g) chopped watercress

2 spring onions, finely chopped

¼ teaspoon salt

¼ teaspoon black pepper

3 oz (75g) Lancashire cheese, crumbled

1½ oz (40g) chopped walnuts

1. Preheat oven to 190°C (375°F, gas mark 5). Roll out the **pastry** on a floured surface and use to line 4 individual fluted flan tins (preferably with loose bottoms); press up the edges well.

2. Line with greaseproof paper and baking beans and bake 'blind' for 10 minutes.

3. Remove paper and beans; brush pastry rims with the **beaten egg,** sprinkle with the **Parmesan cheese** and return to the oven for 5 minutes.

4. Beat the **eggs** with the **egg yolk, milk** and **yoghurt;** add the **watercress, spring onions, salt** and **pepper.**

5. Scatter the **crumbled cheese** in the pastry cases and spoon the watercress and egg mixture over the top; sprinkle with the **walnuts.**

6. Bake in the preheated oven for about 25 minutes until just set. Serve warm with a salad.

Vegetable Frittata

Preparation: **13 min**   Cooking: **9 min**   Serves **4**   Cals per portion: **270**

1 oz (25g) butter or margarine

1 tablespoon olive oil

½ medium-sized onion, peeled and chopped

1 clove garlic, peeled and finely chopped

8 oz (225g) mushrooms, sliced

6 oz (175g) chopped cooked spinach

4 eggs, lightly beaten

2½ oz (65g) grated Parmesan cheese

¼ teaspoon dried marjoram

1 teaspoon dried basil

½ teaspoon salt

¼ teaspoon black pepper

You can use 8oz (225g) of frozen spinach, thawed, drained and squeezed dry.

1. Preheat the grill. Heat the **butter** and **oil** in a medium-sized, heavy frying pan over moderately high heat. Add the **onion** and **garlic,** and cook for 5 minutes, or until the onion is soft. Add the **mushrooms** and cook, tossing, for 1 minute, then add the **spinach** and cook, tossing for 1 more minute.

2. In a small bowl, combine the **eggs, cheese, marjoram, basil, salt** and **pepper.** Pour over the vegetables in the pan, reduce the heat to low and cook until the eggs are almost set – about 7 minutes.

3. Place the pan (but not the handle) under the grill about 3in (80mm) from the heat. Grill for 2 to 3 minutes, or until the frittata is lightly browned. Cut into 4 wedges and serve.

Cheese and Potato Soufflé

Preparation: **20 min**   Cooking: **20 min**   Serves **4**   Cals per portion: **560**

3 large potatoes (about 1½ lb/700g), peeled and cut into thin slices

1 teaspoon salt

1 oz (25g) butter or margarine

1 small onion, peeled and chopped

1 stem celery, finely chopped

4 fl oz (115ml) double cream

¼ teaspoon black pepper

3 eggs, separated

4 oz (115g) grated strong Cheddar cheese

1. Preheat the oven to 200°C (400°F, gas mark 6). Place the **potatoes** in a large saucepan, add the **salt** and enough water to cover. Set the lid askew on the pan and boil for 15 minutes, or until tender.

2. Meanwhile, melt the **butter** in a medium-sized, heavy frying pan over moderate heat. Add the **onion** and **celery,** and cook for 5 minutes, or until the onion is soft. Remove from the heat and put aside.

3. Drain the potatoes and mash, adding the **cream** to soften them. Beat in the **pepper,** the cooked onion and celery. Taste, and add more salt or pepper if needed.

4. Mix the yolks of the **eggs** and **cheese** together, add to the potatoes, and mix well. Beat the egg whites until soft peaks have formed, and fold the whites into the potatoes with a spatula.

5. Spoon the mixture into a greased casserole or soufflé dish. Bake until the top has puffed and browned – about 20 to 25 minutes. Serve immediately.

> *Tip:* Try using carrots or swedes instead of the potatoes.

Cheese Soufflé Pudding

Preparation: **5 min**   Cooking: **25 min**   Serves **4**   Cals per portion: **300**

This tasty cheese pudding is easy to make and is almost as light and airy as a true soufflé.

2 eggs

¼ pint (150ml) single cream

3 oz (75g) grated Cheddar cheese

3 oz (75g) grated Parmesan cheese

¼ teaspoon salt

Pinch black pepper

1. Preheat the oven to 220°C (425°F, gas mark 7). Break the **eggs** into a mixing bowl, add the **cream,** and beat lightly. Add the **Cheddar cheese, Parmesan cheese, salt** and **pepper,** and beat again until combined.

2. Pour the mixture into a deep, greased ovenproof or soufflé dish and bake for 25 minutes, or until golden-brown.

> *Tip:* You can use Swiss cheese instead of Cheddar.

Cheese Soufflé Baked in Tomatoes

Preparation: **15 min**   Cooking: **15 min**   Serves **4**   Cals per portion: **295**

Use these elegant-looking soufflé-stuffed tomatoes as a main course, allowing 2 tomatoes for each person. Serve with a green salad and crusty bread. Or, if you prefer, serve them as a side dish or starter for 8.

8 medium-sized firm, ripe tomatoes

¾ oz (20g) butter or margarine

1 tablespoon plain flour

2½ fl oz (75ml) single cream

½ teaspoon salt

¼ teaspoon black pepper

4 oz (115g) grated Swiss or strong Cheddar cheese

3 eggs, separated

1. Preheat the oven to 180°C (350°F, gas mark 4). Slice off the tops of the **tomatoes** and scoop out most of the pulp with a teaspoon. Discard the tops and save the pulp for another use. Put the tomato shells aside.

2. Melt the **butter** in a saucepan over low heat. Blend in the **flour,** and gradually stir in the **cream, salt** and **pepper.** Cook, stirring continuously, until smooth and thick – about 3 minutes.

3. Remove from the heat and beat in the **cheese** and the **egg yolks.** Beat the egg whites until soft peaks have formed, then fold into the egg and cheese mixture with a spatula.

4. Spoon the mixture into the tomatoes, filling each about three-quarters full. Place them in a greased, shallow ovenproof dish. Bake until the soufflés have puffed and browned – about 15 minutes. Serve immediately.

Lettuce and Chicory Soufflé

Preparation: **15 min**   Cooking: **35 min**   Serves **4**   Cals per portion: **425**

4 oz (115g) crisp lettuce, chopped

4 oz (115g) chicory, finely shredded

2 oz (50g) butter

Pinch ground nutmeg

¼ teaspoon salt

¼ teaspoon black pepper

¾ oz (20g) flour

¼ pint (150ml) milk

Finely grated rind ½ lemon

Few drops Tabasco sauce

4 oz (115g) grated Gruyère cheese

4 eggs, separated

¾ teaspoon cream of tartar

2 oz (50g) grated Parmesan cheese

1. Preheat the oven to 190°C (375°F, gas mark 5). Put the **lettuce** and **chicory** into a pan with ½oz (15g) of the **butter,** the **nutmeg, salt** and **pepper;** cover and cook for 3 minutes.

2. Melt the remaining butter in a pan; stir in the **flour** and cook for 1 minute. Gradually stir in the **milk** and bring to the boil, stirring until lightly thickened.

3. Beat in the **lemon rind, Tabasco sauce, Gruyère cheese, egg yolks** and lettuce.

4. Whisk the egg whites until foamy; add the **cream of tartar** and whisk until stiff.

5. Fold lightly but thoroughly into the sauce mixture; put into a greased soufflé dish which has been sprinkled inside with half the **Parmesan cheese.** Sprinkle the top with the remaining Parmesan.

6. Bake in the preheated oven for about 35 minutes until well risen, golden, and just set to the touch. Serve immediately.

Cottage Cheese Soufflé

Preparation: **12 min**   Cooking: **20 min**   Serves **4**   Cals per portion: **310**

2 oz (50g) butter or margarine

½ small onion, peeled and finely chopped

3 tablespoons plain flour

6 fl oz (175ml) milk

8 oz (225g) creamed cottage cheese

2 whole canned pimentos, coarsely chopped

4 eggs, separated

¼ teaspoon salt

Pinch black pepper

Tip: Leftovers can be served cold and are especially delicious with mayonnaise.

1. Preheat the oven to 220°C (425°F, gas mark 7). Melt the **butter** in a saucepan over moderate heat. Add the **onion**, and cook for 3 minutes, or until pale golden.

2. Blend in the **flour**. Add the **milk** gradually, and cook, stirring continuously, until the mixture is smooth and very thick – about 3 minutes.

3. Remove from the heat and add the **cottage cheese, pimentos,** the yolks of the **eggs** and the **salt** and **pepper.** Mix thoroughly.

4. Beat the egg whites until soft peaks have formed, then fold into the mixture with a spatula. Pour into a greased, straight-sided casserole. Bake for 20 minutes, or until the soufflé is puffed and brown and quivers gently when you nudge the dish.

Parmesan and Basil Roulade

Preparation: **15 min**   Cooking: **15 min**   Serves **6**   Cals per portion: **360**

1½ oz (40g) butter

1½ oz (40g) flour

¾ pint (450ml) milk

¼ teaspoon salt

¼ teaspoon black pepper

3 eggs, separated

2 tablespoons chopped fresh basil

2 tablespoons chopped fresh parsley

1½ oz (40g) grated Parmesan cheese

4 oz (115g) herb-flavoured cream cheese

Tip: Some cream cheeses are quite firm; to make spreading easier, beat a little milk or cream into the cheese.

1. Preheat the oven to 190°C (375°F, gas mark 5).

2. Melt the **butter;** stir in the **flour** and cook for 30 seconds. Gradually add the **milk,** and bring to the boil, stirring continuously, until the sauce has thickened. Add **salt** and **pepper** to taste.

3. Beat the **egg yolks, basil, parsley** and **Parmesan cheese** into the sauce; whisk the egg whites until stiff but not dry, and fold lightly but thoroughly into the cheese sauce.

4. Spread evenly in a large swiss-roll tin lined with greaseproof paper; bake in the preheated oven until golden and 'spongy' to the touch – about 15 minutes.

5. Beat the **cream cheese** until soft.

6. Turn the baked mixture carefully onto a sheet of greaseproof paper as soon as it comes out of the oven; remove the lining paper, spread with the softened cream cheese and roll up. Serve immediately, cut into slices, accompanied by a salad or green vegetable.

Peppers Stuffed with Ricotta Cheese

Preparation: **15 min**   Cooking: **20 min**   Serves **4**   Cals per portion: **345**

4 medium-sized peppers, halved lengthwise, cored and seeded

1 tablespoon vegetable oil

1 medium-sized onion, peeled and chopped

1 clove garlic, peeled and finely chopped

8 oz (225g) ricotta cheese

1½ oz (40g) grated Parmesan cheese

3 oz (75g) fresh breadcrumbs

3 eggs

3 tablespoons soured cream

¼ teaspoon dried thyme

¼ teaspoon dried rosemary

Pinch ground nutmeg

2 tablespoons finely chopped parsley

½ teaspoon salt

¼ teaspoon black pepper

1. Preheat the oven to 200°C (400°F, gas mark 6). Bring about 2in (50mm) of lightly salted water to the boil in a saucepan over moderately high heat. Add the **peppers,** and cook for 5 minutes. Drain.

2. Meanwhile, heat the **oil** in a medium-sized, heavy frying pan over moderate heat. Add the **onion** and **garlic,** and cook for 3 minutes. Remove from the heat and put aside.

3. In a mixing bowl, combine the **ricotta cheese, Parmesan cheese, breadcrumbs, eggs, soured cream, thyme, rosemary, nutmeg, parsley, salt** and **black pepper.** Mix in the onion and garlic.

4. Place the pepper halves close together in a greased, 10in (250mm) ovenproof dish, and spoon the filling into them. Add 2fl oz (50ml) of water to the baking dish and bake for 20 minutes.

> **Tips: 1.** As an alternative, use cottage cheese instead of the ricotta. Or substitute feta cheese for some of the ricotta cheese and use 2 tablespoons of snipped dill in place of the rosemary. **2.** Cover leftover stuffed pepper halves with tomato sauce and reheat in a 180°C (350°F, gas mark 4) oven.

Feta and Ricotta Cheese Fondue

Preparation: **5 min**   Cooking: **5 min**   Serves **4**   Cals per portion: **285**

Place this dish in the centre of the table and let everyone dip chunks of crusty bread into it. It is both tasty and fun.

1¾ oz (45g) butter or margarine

4 oz (115g) feta cheese, cut into ½ in (15mm) cubes

8 oz (225g) ricotta cheese

Pinch black pepper

Juice 1 lemon

1 tablespoon finely chopped parsley

1. Melt the **butter** in a medium-sized, heavy frying pan or a saucepan over low heat. Add the **feta cheese, ricotta cheese** and **pepper.** Cook, stirring continuously, and mashing the cheeses slightly, until they soften and begin to bubble – about 5 minutes.

2. Stir in the **lemon juice,** and garnish with the **parsley.** Serve at once; as the fondue cools, it loses its flavour and consistency.

> **Tip:** As an alternative, substitute grated Swiss cheese for the feta.

PASTA AND RICE

PASTA AND RICE

Pasta is the ideal base for a quick, economical meal. It is also extremely versatile, combining well with almost any meat, seafood or vegetable. Many of the dishes described here are substantial enough for a main course, requiring only green salad for a well-balanced meal. Pasta comes in many shapes and sizes, plain, wholemeal or flavoured, and most are interchangeable in recipes. Try flat, wide noodles (tagliatelle) instead of the more common 'round' spaghetti with delicate sauces, and one of the many short, tubular shapes with meat or chunky sauces.

The pasta in the following recipes is dry and should be cooked according to the packet directions, tossed with the sauce as described, and served immediately – so be sure to have the sauce ready for the cooked pasta. Remember that fresh pasta requires less cooking time than the dry variety.

Also included in this section are recipes for rice, bulgur wheat and cornmeal.

Spaghetti alla Carbonara

Preparation and cooking: **20 min**   Serves **4**   Cals per portion: **650**

1 lb (450g) spaghetti

½ oz (15g) butter or margarine

6 rashers bacon, cut into matchstick strips

3 eggs (at room temperature)

2 fl oz (50ml) single cream (at room temperature)

¼ teaspoon salt

½ teaspoon black pepper

2 tablespoons finely chopped parsley

4 tablespoons grated Parmesan cheese

This dish may be made with any size of macaroni, spaghetti or noodles. Once the spaghetti is cooked, work swiftly to combine the bacon, eggs and cream with the pasta so that the dish can be served really hot.

1. Cook the **spaghetti** according to packet directions.

2. Meanwhile, heat the **butter** in a medium-sized, heavy frying pan over moderate heat and fry the **bacon** until brown and crisp. Put the pan aside and keep hot. In a small bowl, beat the **eggs** with the **cream, salt, pepper,** half the **parsley** and half the **cheese.**

3. Immediately the spaghetti has been drained, return it to the warm saucepan placed over a low heat. Add the bacon, with its fat, and mix swiftly. Remove the pan from the heat, add the egg mixture and quickly turn the spaghetti over several times until well coated, and the sauce just begins to thicken.

4. Transfer the spaghetti to a heated serving dish, sprinkle with the rest of the parsley and the cheese, and serve immediately.

Spaghetti with Oil, Garlic and Cheese ½

Preparation and cooking: **20 min**   Serves **4**   Cals per portion: **685**

1 lb (450g) thin spaghetti

2 fl oz (50ml) olive oil

6 cloves garlic, peeled and finely chopped

2 oz (50g) butter or margarine

¼ teaspoon salt

¼ teaspoon black pepper

2 oz (50g) grated Parmesan cheese

Tip: If you like the flavour of garlic but prefer not to eat it, simply strain the oil over the spaghetti before tossing.

1. Cook the **spaghetti** according to packet directions.

2. About 5 minutes before the spaghetti is done, heat the **oil** in a medium-sized frying pan over low heat. Add the **garlic,** and cook for 3 minutes. Stir in the **butter** until melted. Remove from heat.

3. Drain the spaghetti thoroughly in a colander, place in a warm serving bowl, and toss with the sauce and the **salt** and **pepper.** Sprinkle with the **cheese,** and serve with Spinach-Bacon Salad, page 49, or a tomato salad seasoned with basil.

Spaghetti Florentine ½

Preparation and cooking: **25 min**   Serves **4**   Cals per portion: **640**

12 oz (350g) thin spaghetti

2 tablespoons vegetable oil

12 oz (350g) lean minced beef

1 medium-sized onion, peeled and chopped

2 cloves garlic, peeled and finely chopped

2 stems celery, chopped

5 medium-sized tomatoes, peeled and chopped, or 1 x 15 oz (425g) can tomatoes, drained and chopped

1 teaspoon salt

¼ teaspoon black pepper

¼ teaspoon each dried basil and oregano

1 lb (450g) fresh spinach, rinsed and with the stems removed, or 8 oz (225g) frozen spinach, thawed

2 oz (50g) grated Parmesan cheese

1. Cook the **spaghetti** according to packet directions.

2. Meanwhile, heat the **oil** in a large, heavy frying pan over moderately high heat for about 1 minute. Add the **beef,** and cook, stirring occasionally, for 5 minutes, or until browned.

3. Push the beef to one side of the pan and add the **onion, garlic** and **celery.** Reduce the heat to moderate, and cook for 5 minutes, or until the onion is soft. Add the **tomatoes, salt, pepper, basil, oregano** and **spinach.** Cover and simmer for 10 minutes.

4. Drain the spaghetti thoroughly in a colander, and toss with the sauce in the pan. Sprinkle with the **cheese,** and serve hot with a green salad.

Tip: If you have the time, baking will make this dish even better. Cook the beef, tomato and spinach mixture for 5 minutes, then stir in 2 lightly beaten eggs, and toss with the pasta. Spoon into a lightly greased, shallow casserole dish, sprinkle with the cheese, and bake in a preheated 200°C (400°F, gas mark 6) oven for 20 minutes, or until golden.

Spaghetti with Grated Courgettes and Cheese ◎ ½

Preparation and cooking: **20 min**   Serves **4**   Cals per portion: **650**

1 lb (450g) thin spaghetti

2 oz (50g) butter or margarine

3 cloves garlic, peeled and finely chopped

2 medium-sized courgettes, coarsely grated

2 large carrots, peeled and grated

½ teaspoon dried oregano or marjoram

½ teaspoon dried rosemary

4 fl oz (115ml) soured cream

4 fl oz (115ml) natural yoghurt

¼ teaspoon salt

Pinch black pepper

2 oz (50g) grated Parmesan cheese

1. Cook the **spaghetti** according to packet directions.

2. Meanwhile, melt the **butter** in a large, heavy frying pan over moderate heat. Add the **garlic,** and cook for 30 seconds. Add the **courgettes** and **carrots** and cook, stirring frequently, for 4 or 5 minutes, or until just tender but still crisp. Reduce the heat, stir in the **oregano** and **rosemary,** and remove from the heat.

3. Add the **soured cream** and **yoghurt** to the pan, and mix thoroughly. Return to heat for 1 minute to heat through, but do not boil or the soured cream and yoghurt will curdle. Season with the **salt** and **pepper.**

4. Drain the spaghetti thoroughly in a colander, place in a warm serving bowl, and pour the sauce over it. Serve the **cheese** separately.

> *Tips: 1. If you like, use 8fl oz (225ml) natural yoghurt and omit the soured cream. **2.** Add 6oz (175g) of diced cooked ham or chicken.*

Spaghetti with Tuna and Tomatoes ◎

Preparation and cooking: **20 min**   Serves **4**   Cals per portion: **575**

1 lb (450g) spaghetti

2 oz (50g) butter or margarine

2 cloves garlic, peeled and finely chopped

5 medium-sized tomatoes, peeled and chopped, or 1 x 15 oz (425g) can tomatoes, chopped, with their juice

1 x 7 oz (200g) can tuna in brine, drained

¼ teaspoon salt

¼ teaspoon black pepper

3 tablespoons finely chopped parsley

1. Cook the **spaghetti** according to packet directions.

2. Meanwhile, melt half of the **butter** in a large frying pan over low heat. Add the **garlic,** and cook for 3 minutes, or until golden. Add the **tomatoes,** and cook for 10 minutes, stirring occasionally.

3. Add the **tuna** to the pan, breaking up the chunks with the side of a spoon. Stir to mix, and cook for 5 minutes over moderate heat. Remove from the heat, and stir in the **salt, pepper, parsley** and remaining butter.

4. Drain the spaghetti thoroughly in a colander, and toss with the sauce in the pan.

Spaghetti Tetrazzini ◁ ½

Preparation and cooking: **20 min**

Serves **4**   Cals per portion: **615**

12 oz (350g) spaghetti

2 oz (50g) butter or margarine

1 small onion, peeled and chopped

1 small pepper, seeded and chopped

2 stems celery, chopped

8 oz (225g) mushrooms, chopped

8 fl oz (225ml) single cream

6 oz (175g) diced cooked chicken

¼ teaspoon salt

¼ teaspoon black pepper

1. Cook the **spaghetti** according to packet directions.

2. Meanwhile, melt the **butter** in a large, heavy frying pan over moderate heat. Add the **onion, pepper** and **celery,** and cook for 3 minutes. Add the **mushrooms,** and cook 2 or 3 minutes longer, or until they are just tender.

3. Add the **cream** to the pan, raise the heat to high, and boil for 6 to 8 minutes, or until the sauce thickens. Stir in the **chicken, salt** and **black pepper,** and cook for another minute, or until the chicken is heated through.

4. Drain the spaghetti thoroughly in a colander, and toss with the sauce in the pan.

Spaghetti with Meat Sauce

Preparation: **15 min**   Cooking: **20 min**

Serves **6**   Cals per portion: **595**

½ oz (15g) butter

1 tablespoon vegetable oil

3 cloves garlic, peeled and finely chopped

1 medium-sized onion, peeled and chopped

8 oz (225g) lean minced beef

8 oz (225g) minced pork

4 fl oz (115ml) dry red or white wine

5 medium-sized tomatoes, peeled and chopped, or 1 x 15 oz (425g) can tomatoes, chopped, with their juice

1 tablespoon chopped parsley

1 bay leaf

½ teaspoon each dried oregano and basil

1 teaspoon salt

¼ teaspoon black pepper

12 oz (350g) thin spaghetti

1. Heat the **butter** and **oil** in a large frying pan over moderately high heat for about 1 minute. Add the **garlic** and **onion** to one side of the pan and the **beef** and **pork** to the other. Cook for 6 minutes, or until the onion is soft and the meat has browned. Stir the meat occasionally, but try to keep it separate from the garlic and onion.

2. Add the **wine** to the pan and boil for 3 minutes. Add the **tomatoes, parsley, bay leaf, oregano, basil, salt** and **pepper.** Stir to mix, cover, reduce the heat, and simmer for 20 minutes, stirring occasionally.

3. While the sauce is simmering, cook the **spaghetti** according to packet directions.

4. Remove the sauce from the heat, skim off all but about 1 tablespoon of the surface fat, and keep warm until the spaghetti is done. Drain the spaghetti thoroughly in a colander, and toss with the sauce in the pan.

Tips: 1. *If you have time, make the sauce in advance and let it simmer gently for 1 hour.* **2.** *You can use 1lb (450g) beef instead of half beef, half pork.* **3.** *The dish can be topped with grated cheese.*

Spaghetti with Sausages and Peas ⊘ ½

Preparation and cooking: **20 min**

Serves **4**   Cals per portion: **870**

12 oz (350g) spaghetti

12 oz (350g) pork sausages

2 fl oz (50ml) olive oil or vegetable oil

½ teaspoon dried rosemary

4 shallots, peeled and finely chopped

10 oz (275g) frozen peas

4 fl oz (115ml) dry white wine

1 oz (25g) butter or margarine, cut into small pieces

1½ oz (40g) grated Parmesan cheese

1. Cook the **spaghetti** according to packet directions.

2. Meanwhile, bring about ¾in (20mm) of water to the boil in a large saucepan. Prick the **sausages** in several places with a fork, drop them into the boiling water, and cook for 5 minutes. Drain.

3. Heat the **oil** in a large frying pan over moderate heat. Cut the sausages into thin slices, add them to the pan, and cook, stirring frequently, for 5 minutes, or until browned.

4. Add the **rosemary, shallots** and **peas,** cover, and cook for 4 minutes. Raise the heat, add the **wine,** and boil for 3 minutes. Stir in the **butter** and **cheese** until melted. Drain the spaghetti thoroughly in a colander, and toss with the sauce in the pan.

Tip: You can substitute Italian sausages for the pork sausages. If you do, add ½ teaspoon of fennel seeds, for a complementary flavour.

Spaghetti with Chicken Livers ⊘ ½

Preparation and cooking: **20 min**

Serves **4**   Cals per portion: **580**

12 oz (350g) spaghetti

3 tablespoons olive oil or vegetable oil

4 shallots, peeled and finely chopped

6 fl oz (175ml) dry white wine

8 oz (225g) chicken livers, sinews removed, and chopped

1¾ oz (45g) butter or margarine

¼ teaspoon dried sage

½ teaspoon salt

Pinch black pepper

1½ oz (40g) grated Parmesan cheese

2 tablespoons finely chopped parsley

1. Cook the **spaghetti** according to packet directions.

2. Meanwhile, heat the **oil** in a medium-sized frying pan over moderate heat. Add the **shallots,** and cook for 5 minutes, or until soft.

3. Add the **wine** to the pan, and simmer for 2 minutes. Add the **chicken livers, butter, sage, salt** and **pepper,** and simmer for 10 more minutes.

4. Drain the spaghetti thoroughly in a colander, and place in a warm serving bowl. Toss the chicken liver mixture with the spaghetti, and sprinkle with the **cheese** and **parsley.** Serve with a green salad or with Baked Courgettes with Tomatoes, page 82.

Tip: You can use chicken stock instead of wine; if you do, omit the salt.

Fettucine in Vegetable Sauce 🐷

Preparation and cooking: **25 min**

Serves **4**   Cals per portion: **550**

12 oz (350g) fettucine

2 fl oz (50ml) olive oil or vegetable oil

1 medium-sized onion, peeled and chopped

3 cloves garlic, peeled and finely chopped

2 large carrots, peeled and cut into thin slices

8 medium-sized tomatoes, peeled and chopped

1 teaspoon dried oregano

1 teaspoon dried basil

2 tablespoons chopped parsley

1 teaspoon salt

¼ teaspoon black pepper

1¾ oz (45g) butter or margarine, cut into small pieces

This recipe makes a meatless main course for 4 or a side dish for 6. Before you put the fettucine water on to boil, prepare the onion, garlic and carrots; while they cook, peel and chop the tomatoes.

1. Cook the **fettucine** according to packet directions.

2. Meanwhile, heat the **oil** in a large frying pan over moderate heat. Add the **onion, garlic** and **carrots,** and cook for 5 minutes, or until the onion is soft. Add the **tomatoes, oregano, basil, parsley, salt** and **pepper,** and simmer, partially covered, for 12 minutes, or until the sauce thickens slightly. Remove from the heat and stir in the **butter** until it melts.

3. Drain the fettucine thoroughly in a colander, and toss with the sauce in the pan. Serve with Sautéed Peppers, page 76, or steamed broccoli tossed in butter.

Tips: 1. Stir in 8oz (225g) of sliced mushrooms during the last 5 minutes of cooking. 2. This sauce can be served over chicken, fish or steamed vegetables as well as pasta. If you need only half this recipe for your meal, refrigerate or freeze the remaining sauce for later use.

Fettucine with Mussel Sauce 🐷

Preparation and cooking: **20 min**

Serves **4**   Cals per portion: **670**

1 lb (450g) fettucine

4 fl oz (115ml) olive oil or 2 fl oz (50ml) each olive oil and vegetable oil

2 cloves garlic, peeled and finely chopped

1 x 8.8 oz (250g) can mussels

¾ teaspoon dried oregano

¼ teaspoon salt

¼ teaspoon black pepper

3 tablespoons chopped parsley

1. Cook the **fettucine** according to packet directions.

2. Meanwhile, heat the **oil** in a medium-sized frying pan over low heat. Add the **garlic** and cook for 3 minutes, or until golden. Add the **mussels** and their juices, the **oregano, salt** and **pepper.** Simmer for 5 minutes. Stir in the **parsley.**

3. Drain the fettucine thoroughly and divide among 4 soup bowls. Pour equal amounts of the sauce over each serving, making sure the mussels are distributed evenly. Serve with fresh crusty bread and a salad.

Fettucine with Green Sauce

Preparation and cooking: **20 min**   Serves **4**   Cals per portion: **570**

1 lb (450g) fettucine

1 lb (450g) fresh spinach or 8 oz (225g) frozen chopped spinach, thawed

2 tablespoons olive oil or vegetable oil

4 cloves garlic, peeled and finely chopped

3 oz (75g) grated Parmesan cheese

1 teaspoon dried basil

½ teaspoon salt

Pinch black pepper

Tip: Make an extra batch of sauce and freeze it.

1. Cook the **fettucine** according to packet directions.

2. Meanwhile, trim the fresh **spinach** of coarse stems and blemished leaves, wash it and shake dry. Place the spinach in a large frying pan with just the water that clings to the leaves, and cook, covered, for 3 to 5 minutes, or until it is just limp. (Thawed frozen spinach needs no cooking.) Drain the cooked spinach in a sieve or colander, pressing out most of the liquid with the back of a large spoon. Chop the spinach finely.

3. Wipe the pan dry. Heat the **oil** in the pan over low heat. Add the **garlic,** and cook for 3 minutes, or until golden. Remove from the heat, and add the spinach, **cheese, basil, salt** and **pepper.**

4. Drain the fettucine thoroughly in a colander, and toss with the sauce in the pan.

Noodles with Ricotta Cheese

Preparation and cooking: **20 min**   Serves **4**   Cals per portion: **490**

12 oz (350g) noodles

6 oz (175g) ricotta or cottage cheese

3 oz (75g) grated Parmesan cheese

½ teaspoon salt

¼ teaspoon grated nutmeg

Pinch of pepper

½ oz (15g) butter

3 tablespoons finely chopped fresh parsley or basil

1. Preheat the oven to 160°C (325°F, gas mark 3). Cook the **noodles** according to packet directions.

2. Meanwhile, cream the **ricotta cheese** until smooth, beat in the grated **Parmesan cheese** and season with the **salt, nutmeg** and **pepper.**

3. Drain the noodles in a colander and put them into an ovenproof serving dish. Stir in the cheese mixture, toss lightly, dot with the **butter** and place the dish in the oven for 5 minutes. Top with the finely chopped **parsley** and serve immediately.

Gazpacho Noodles ⊘ ½ 🐷

Preparation: **4 min** Cooking: **8 min**

Serves **4** Cals per portion: **485**

1 medium-sized red pepper, seeded and chopped

1 medium-sized green pepper, seeded and chopped

¼ cucumber, seeded and chopped

8 ripe tomatoes, halved, seeded and chopped

3 tablespoons roughly chopped parsley

4 spring onions, chopped

2 cloves garlic, peeled

¼ pint (150ml) tomato juice

4 tablespoons olive oil

½ teaspoon salt

¼ teaspoon black pepper

1 tablespoon chopped fresh basil

6 oz (175g) green noodles

6 oz (175g) yellow noodles

1. Put the **red pepper, green pepper, cucumber, tomatoes, parsley, spring onions, garlic, tomato juice, olive oil,** half the **salt,** all the **pepper,** into a liquidiser or food processor; blend until fairly smooth.

2. Stir in the chopped **basil** and keep to one side.

3. Cook the **noodles** in a large pan of boiling water, with the remaining salt, for 6 to 7 minutes, until just tender; drain thoroughly.

4. Return the cooked pasta to the pan with the prepared sauce and heat through gently for 2 minutes.

5. Serve piping hot, with or without a sprinkling of grated cheese.

> **Tip:** *This pasta dish is delicious served with blue cheese crumbled over it.*

Macaroni with Onions and Garlic ½ 🐷

Preparation and cooking: **22 min**

Serves **6** Cals per portion: **665**

12 oz (350g) long macaroni

1 oz (25g) butter or margarine

4 tablespoons olive oil or vegetable oil

6 medium-sized onions, peeled, halved and thinly sliced

3 cloves garlic, peeled and finely chopped

8 oz (225g) mozzarella cheese, diced

¼ teaspoon salt

Pinch black pepper

The ingredients are simple, but this is a special dish.

1. Cook the **macaroni** according to packet directions.

2. Meanwhile, heat the **butter** and **oil** in a large, heavy frying pan over moderately low heat. Add the **onions** and cook for 15 minutes, stirring frequently. Add the **garlic,** and cook 1 minute longer.

3. Drain the macaroni thoroughly in a colander, then toss with the onions in the pan. Add the **cheese,** and toss again. Season with the **salt** and **pepper.**

> **Tip:** *Add 2 teaspoons sugar when cooking the onions and they will take on a delicious caramel flavour.*

Macaroni with Bacon, Tomatoes and Chilli ½ 🐷

Preparation and cooking: **23 min**   Serves **4**   Cals per portion: **530**

12 oz (350g) long macaroni

6 rashers bacon, cut into ¾ in (20mm) strips

1 large onion, peeled and chopped

2 cloves garlic, peeled and finely chopped

5 medium-sized tomatoes, peeled and chopped, or 1 x 15 oz (425g) can tomatoes, chopped, with their juice

½ teaspoon ground chilli powder

½ teaspoon dried basil

¼ teaspoon salt

3 oz (75g) grated Parmesan cheese

1. Cook the **macaroni** according to packet directions.

2. Meanwhile, cook the **bacon** in a large, heavy frying pan over moderate heat for 5 minutes, or until crisp. Using a slotted spoon, transfer the bacon to absorbent paper to drain.

3. Pour off all but 3 tablespoons of the bacon fat. Add the **onion** to the pan, and cook for 5 minutes or until soft. Add the **garlic,** and cook 1 minute longer.

4. Add the **tomatoes, chilli powder, basil** and **salt.** Simmer until the sauce has thickened slightly – about 12 minutes.

5. Drain the macaroni thoroughly in a colander, and toss with the sauce in the pan. Sprinkle with the **cheese,** crumble the reserved bacon over the top, and serve hot.

Pasta Shells with Peppers ◎ ½

Preparation and cooking: **20 min**   Serves **4**   Cals per portion: **550**

12 oz (350g) small pasta shells

8 fl oz (225ml) chicken or beef stock

2 fl oz (50ml) olive oil

1 large green pepper, seeded and cut into ¼ in (5mm) strips

1 large red pepper, seeded and cut into ¼ in (5mm) strips

3 cloves garlic, peeled and finely chopped

1 oz (25g) butter or margarine

1 teaspoon dried marjoram or rosemary

1 teaspoon dried basil

¼ teaspoon salt

Pinch black pepper

2 oz (50g) grated Parmesan cheese

This light sauce is excellent with shell-shaped pasta because it clings easily to the shells. You can also use spirals. Serve as a main course for 4 or a side dish for 6.

1. Cook the **pasta shells** according to packet directions.

2. Meanwhile, boil the **stock** in a saucepan until reduced by half – about 5 minutes.

3. Heat the **oil** in a large frying pan over moderate heat. Add the **green pepper** and **red pepper,** and cook for 3 or 4 minutes, or until just tender. Add the **garlic,** and cook about 15 seconds. Stir in the **butter, marjoram, basil, salt, black pepper,** and the reduced stock.

4. Drain the pasta shells thoroughly in a colander, place in a warm serving bowl and pour the sauce over them. Sprinkle with the **cheese,** and serve with a green salad, or green beans with butter and lemon.

Pasta Shells with Chillies and Pimentos ⊘ ½ 🐷

Preparation and cooking: **20 min**   Serves **4**   Cals per portion: **515**

12 oz (350g) small pasta shells

2 canned whole green chillies, rinsed, seeded and chopped

3 oz (75g) canned pimentos, drained and chopped

8 fl oz (225ml) soured cream

¼ teaspoon salt

¼ teaspoon dried oregano

Pinch chilli powder

3½ oz (90g) grated strong Cheddar cheese

1. Cook the **pasta shells** according to packet directions.

2. Meanwhile, place the **chillies, pimentos, soured cream, salt, oregano** and **chilli powder** in a large frying pan, and stir.

3. About 1 minute before the pasta is done, heat the sauce mixture in the pan over moderate heat. Drain the pasta thoroughly in a colander; add to the chilli and pimento mixture with the **cheese,** and toss thoroughly. Serve with a green salad.

> **Tip:** To reduce calories, use yoghurt instead of the soured cream, but be sure to heat the sauce gently and to rinse the chillies, or the sauce may curdle.

Pasta with Avocado and Smoked Mackerel ⊘ 🐷

Preparation: **5 min**   Cooking: **7 min**   Serves **4**   Cals per portion: **595**

12 oz (350g) pasta shells

½ teaspoon salt

3 tablespoons olive oil

¼ teaspoon black pepper

4 tablespoons mayonnaise

Grated rind and juice ½ lemon

4 tablespoons natural yoghurt

2 tablespoons dry vermouth

1 clove garlic, peeled and crushed

4 oz (115g) smoked mackerel, flaked

1 ripe avocado, halved, stoned, peeled and chopped

1 tablespoon chopped fresh dill

1. Cook the **pasta shells** in a large pan of boiling water, with half the **salt,** for 6 to 7 minutes, until just tender; drain thoroughly, rinse under cold water and drain once again.

2. Toss the cooked pasta shells with the **oil** and remaining salt, and the **pepper.**

3. Mix the **mayonnaise** with the **lemon rind** and **juice, yoghurt, vermouth** and **garlic;** stir in the flaked **mackerel,** chopped **avocado** and the **dill.**

4. Stir the fish and avocado dressing into the cooked pasta.

5. Serve in shallow individual bowls, garnished with extra dill if liked.

> **Tip:** This is an excellent recipe for using up leftover cooked fish – make sure that it is completely free of skin and bone.

Macaroni and Cheese

Preparation: **20 min**   Cooking: **30 min**   Serves **4**   Cals per portion: **630**

12 oz (350g) small elbow
macaroni

8 oz (225g) cottage cheese

8 fl oz (225ml) soured cream

1 egg, lightly beaten

¾ teaspoon salt

Pinch black pepper

2 teaspoons French mustard

8 oz (225g) grated strong
Cheddar cheese

1. Preheat the oven to 200°C (400°F, gas mark 6). Cook the **macaroni** according to packet directions.

2. Meanwhile, in a large bowl, combine the **cottage cheese, soured cream, egg, salt, pepper, mustard** and half of the **cheese.**

3. Drain the macaroni thoroughly in a colander, and toss with the cheese mixture in the bowl. Spread the mixture evenly in a greased, shallow ovenproof dish. Top with the remaining cheese, and bake for 30 to 35 minutes, or until set. If the macaroni and cheese are browning too quickly, cover with foil after 20 minutes of baking.

Macaroni with Tomato and Mozzarella Sauce ½

Preparation and cooking: **25 min**   Serves **4**   Cals per portion: **750**

12 oz (350g) elbow macaroni

8 medium-sized tomatoes,
chopped

1 small onion, peeled and
chopped

2 cloves garlic, peeled and
finely chopped

½ teaspoon salt

1½ tablespoons red wine vinegar

4 tablespoons olive oil or
2 tablespoons each olive oil and
vegetable oil

¼ teaspoon black pepper

2 tablespoons finely chopped
fresh basil

4 oz (115g) pitted small olives

8 oz (225g) mozzarella cheese,
diced

3 oz (75g) grated Parmesan
cheese

Here is a pasta dish with an uncooked sauce that is perfect for warm weather and picnics. While the macaroni is cooking, you will be able to prepare the tomatoes, onion and garlic, and combine them with the other ingredients just before serving.

1. Cook the **macaroni** according to packet directions.

2. Meanwhile, in a mixing bowl, combine the **tomatoes, onion, garlic, salt, vinegar, oil, pepper, basil** and **olives.**

3. Drain the macaroni thoroughly in a colander, and return to the saucepan. Add the **mozzarella cheese** and **Parmesan cheese,** and toss until just combined. Then add the tomato mixture and toss well. Serve at room temperature, or cold.

> *Tip: To reduce the calories per serving, use only 3 tablespoons of oil and 1 tablespoon of vinegar.*

Macaroni with Peppers and Pimentos ½

Preparation: **15 min**   Cooking: **35 min**   Serves **4**   Cals per portion: **590**

12 oz (350g) medium elbow
macaroni

2 oz (50g) butter or margarine

1 large onion, peeled
and chopped

1 medium-sized pepper, seeded
and chopped

3 oz (75g) canned pimentos,
drained and chopped

2 tablespoons finely chopped
parsley

4 eggs, lightly beaten

8 fl oz (225ml) milk

3 tablespoons grated
Parmesan cheese

½ teaspoon salt

¼ teaspoon black pepper

3 tablespoons fine dry
breadcrumbs

*This recipe takes only 15 minutes of your time because
the 35 minutes' cooking time is unattended.*

1. Preheat the oven to 180°C (350°F, gas
mark 4). Cook the **macaroni** according to
packet directions.

2. Meanwhile, melt half the **butter** in a large
frying pan over moderate heat. Add the **onion,**
and cook for 5 minutes, or until soft. Add the
pepper, pimentos and **parsley,** and mix well.

3. Drain the macaroni thoroughly in a
colander, and toss with the vegetables in the
pan. Place the macaroni and vegetables in a
greased, deep ovenproof dish.

4. In a small bowl, beat together the **eggs,
milk, cheese, salt** and **black pepper.** Pour the
mixture over the pasta, sprinkle with the
breadcrumbs, dot with the remaining butter,
and bake for 35 minutes, or until set.

Brunch Pasta ½

Preparation: **12 min**   Cooking: **6 min**   Serves **4**   Cals per portion: **580**

3 oz (75g) green noodles

3 oz (75g) yellow noodles

½ teaspoon salt

¼ teaspoon black pepper

6 tablespoons single cream

4 oz (115g) salami, diced

2 tablespoons chopped parsley

4 large eggs

2 oz (50g) butter

4 tablespoons grated Parmesan
cheese

1. Preheat the oven to 190C (375F, gas
mark 5). Cook the **noodles** in a large pan of
boiling water, with half the **salt,** for 6 to
7 minutes, until just tender; drain thoroughly.

2. Mix the cooked noodles with the remaining
salt, the **pepper, cream,** diced **salami** and
parsley; divide among 4 shallow, greased,
individual ovenproof dishes, making a hollow
in the centre of each one.

3. Carefully crack an **egg** into each dish; dot
with knobs of **butter** and sprinkle with the
cheese.

4. Bake in the oven for 6 minutes. Serve
immediately with small side salads.

Farfalle with Spiced Olive Sauce ▣ ½ 🐷

Preparation: **4 min**   Cooking: **8 min**   Serves **4**   Cals per portion: **565**

12 oz (350g) farfalle (bow-shaped pasta)

½ teaspoon salt

6 tablespoons olive oil

½ teaspoon ground ginger

Generous pinch ground nutmeg

¼ teaspoon black pepper

1 clove garlic, peeled and finely chopped

3 tablespoons capers

1 oz (25g) pitted green olives, sliced

1 oz (25g) pitted black olives, sliced

2 tablespoons finely chopped parsley

1½ oz (40g) grated Parmesan cheese

1. Cook the **farfalle** in a large pan of boiling water, with half the **salt**, for 6 to 7 minutes, until just tender; drain thoroughly and return to the pan.

2. Put the **olive oil, ginger, nutmeg, pepper**, the remaining salt, the **garlic, capers, olives** and **parsley** into a pan; heat through for 3 minutes. Remove from heat and leave on one side.

3. Add the flavoured oil to the farfalle, and stir over the heat for 1 to 2 minutes.

4. Serve immediately, sprinkled with the grated **cheese.**

> *Tip: To make this pasta dish more substantial, stir in 6oz (175g) mozzarella cheese, cut into small cubes.*

PASTA AND RICE

Red Hot Rice ½

Preparation: **10 min**   Cooking: **20 min**   Serves **6**   Cals per portion: **435**

1¾ oz (45g) butter or margarine

1 medium-sized onion, peeled and chopped

12 oz (350g) long-grain rice

1 medium-sized red pepper, seeded and chopped

1 teaspoon chilli powder

1 teaspoon dried oregano

½ pint tomato juice

3 tablespoons tomato purée

1½ pints (850ml) chicken stock

1 teaspoon salt

1. Melt the **butter** in a large, heavy saucepan over moderate heat. Add the **onion,** and cook for 5 minutes, or until soft.

2. Stir in the **rice, pepper, chilli powder, oregano, tomato juice** and **tomato purée,** then add the **chicken stock** and **salt.** Stir once, cover, and bring to the boil. Reduce the heat and simmer for 20 minutes, or until the rice is tender and the liquid has been absorbed.

> *Tip: For a more substantial dish, stir 6oz (175g) warm, diced, leftover pork or ham into the cooked rice and sprinkle with grated Cheddar cheese.*

Kedgeree ◎ ½ 🐷

Preparation: **10 min**   Cooking: **15 min**   Serves **4**   Cals per portion: **540**

2 tablespoons olive oil or
vegetable oil

1 medium-sized onion, peeled
and chopped

1 teaspoon curry powder

8 oz (225g) long-grain rice

1⅓ pints (760ml) water

1 lb (450g) smoked haddock
or cod

6 fl oz (175ml) milk

1½ oz (40g) butter

3 hard-boiled eggs; 2 roughly
chopped, 1 sliced

¼ teaspoon salt

½ teaspoon black pepper

1 tablespoon chopped parsley

1. Heat the **oil** in a large saucepan over a moderate heat and gently fry the **onion** until soft. Stir in the **curry powder** and the **rice,** and mix well. Pour in the **water** and simmer for 15 minutes. If the rice gets too dry too fast, turn down the heat and add a little extra hot water.

2. Meanwhile, put the **smoked fish** and the **milk** into a large frying pan over a moderate heat. Bring to the boil and simmer for 2 minutes. Drain, peel off the skin and discard, along with any remaining bones. Break the fish into large flakes.

3. As soon as the rice has absorbed all the water and is tender, add the flaked fish, **butter, chopped egg, salt** and **pepper.** Stir well. Garnish with **parsley** and the **sliced egg.**

Fried Rice ½

Preparation: **12 min**   Cooking: **14 min**   Serves **6**   Cals per portion: **355**

4 tablespoons vegetable oil

3 eggs, lightly beaten

1 large onion, peeled
and chopped

6 oz (175g) canned bamboo
shoots, drained and thinly sliced

1 large pepper, seeded and
chopped

8 oz (225g) mushrooms, thinly
sliced

1 lb (450g) cold cooked rice

¼ teaspoon salt

¼ teaspoon black pepper

Soya sauce

1. Heat 1 tablespoon of the **oil** in a large, heavy frying pan (or a wok) over moderate heat. Add the **eggs,** and swirl the pan so that the eggs coat the bottom to form a thin omelette. Cook for 2 minutes, or until set. Transfer the omelette to a plate and let it cool.

2. Heat the remaining oil in the pan over moderate heat. Add the **onion, bamboo shoots** and **pepper,** and cook for 3 minutes, or until the onion just begins to soften. Add the **mushrooms,** and cook 3 minutes longer.

3. Reduce the heat to low, add the **rice, salt** and **pepper,** and cook, stirring frequently, until heated through – about 4 minutes. Cut the omelette into thin strips and toss into the rice mixture. Serve with the **soya sauce.**

> *Tips: 1. Leftovers can be refrigerated for 1 or 2 days.*
> *2. For a heartier main-course dish, add 8oz (225g)*
> *diced cooked chicken, ham or pork.*

Nasi Goreng ◎ ½

Preparation: **10 min** Cooking: **10 min**   Serves **4** Cals per portion: **440**

3 eggs

¼ teaspoon salt

¼ teaspoon black pepper

½ oz (15g) butter

1 tablespoon vegetable oil

4 rashers bacon, cut into
½ in (15mm) strips

2 red chilli peppers, cored,
seeded and cut into thin slices

2 cloves garlic, peeled and
finely chopped

2 large onions, peeled and
finely chopped

8 oz (225g) large peeled prawns

1½ tablespoons light soya sauce

14 oz (400g) boiled rice, cooled

2 tablespoons sultanas, washed

2 tablespoons chopped parsley

1 medium-sized cucumber,
seeded and diced

There are many variations of this popular dish throughout South-east Asia. It is a good way to use leftover rice for a light meal, and you can vary the garnishes to suit your taste.

1. Beat the **eggs** with the **salt** and **pepper** in a small bowl. Over a moderate heat, warm a large frying pan and add the **butter.** When hot, pour in the beaten egg, tilting the pan to spread the mixture evenly and thinly. Cook until the bottom of the pancake is lightly brown and the top firm. Transfer to a plate.

2. Add the **oil** to the pan, heat, then add the **bacon, chillies** and **garlic;** stir and cook for 2 minutes. Add the **onion** and **prawns** and cook, stirring, for 2 to 3 minutes; remove with a slotted spoon and put aside. Pour in the **soya sauce,** stir, add the **rice** and **sultanas** and toss until the mixture is heated through. Roll up the egg pancake and cut into thin strips; add this to the rice and quickly mix. Heap the rice onto a serving dish, sprinkle with the **parsley,** garnish the top with the prawns and surround with the diced **cucumber.**

Singapore Rice ½ 🐷

Preparation: **10 min** Cooking: **20 min**   Serves **4** Cals per portion: **400**

1¾ oz (45g) butter or margarine

1 small onion, peeled and
chopped

2 pints (1.1 litres) chicken stock

¼ teaspoon ground cardamom

¼ teaspoon ground nutmeg

¼ teaspoon ground ginger

½ teaspoon ground cinnamon

Grated rind ½ orange

½ teaspoon salt

Pinch black pepper

12 oz (350g) long-grain rice

1. Melt the **butter** in a large, heavy saucepan over moderate heat. Add the **onion,** and cook for 5 minutes, or until soft.

2. Add the **chicken stock, cardamom, nutmeg, ginger, cinnamon, orange rind, salt** and **pepper,** and bring to the boil. Add the **rice,** stir once, cover, and return to the boil. Reduce the heat and simmer for 20 minutes, or until the rice is tender and the liquid has been absorbed.

Tip: Add some chopped toasted almonds for the last few minutes of cooking time.

Curried Rice ½ 🐷

Preparation: **8 min**   Cooking: **20 min**   Serves **4**   Cals per portion: **395**

1¾ oz (45g) butter or margarine

1 small onion, peeled and chopped

8 oz (225g) long-grain rice

1⅓ pints (760ml) chicken or beef stock

2 oz (50g) raisins

1 teaspoon curry powder

2 fl oz (50ml) soured cream or natural yoghurt

3 tablespoons chutney

1. Melt the **butter** in a large, heavy saucepan over moderate heat. Add the **onion,** and cook for 5 minutes, or until soft. Add the **rice,** and stir to coat with the butter.

2. Add the **stock, raisins** and **curry powder.** Stir once, cover, and bring to the boil. Reduce the heat and simmer for 20 minutes, or until the rice is tender and the liquid has been absorbed. Serve hot or cold with the **soured cream** and **chutney.**

Tip: *For a light lunch or supper dish, stir in 8oz (225g) diced, cooked meat.*

Brown Rice with Chicken and Herbs

Preparation: **5 min**   Cooking: **40 min**   Serves **4**   Cals per portion: **440**

1⅓ pints (760ml) water

¾ teaspoon salt

8 oz (225g) brown rice

2 chicken breasts, skinned and boned

2 tablespoons finely chopped parsley

¼ teaspoon dried tarragon

¼ teaspoon dried basil

¼ teaspoon dried thyme

¼ teaspoon dried rosemary

2 tablespoons plain flour

1¾ oz (45g) butter or margarine

2 medium-sized onions, peeled and thinly sliced

1⅓ pints (760ml) chicken stock

3 tablespoons tomato purée

1. Bring the **water** to the boil with ½ teaspoon of the **salt** in a large saucepan. Add the **rice,** lower the heat, cover, and simmer for 40 minutes. The rice will be chewy.

2. While the rice is cooking, cut the **chicken breasts** crosswise into ½in (15mm) strips and put aside. In a small bowl, combine the **parsley, tarragon, basil, thyme, rosemary, flour** and the remaining salt. Put aside.

3. About 15 minutes before the rice is done, melt the **butter** in a large, heavy frying pan over moderate heat. Add the **onions,** and cook for 5 minutes, or until soft.

4. Push the onions to one side of the pan. Add the chicken and cook, stirring, for 3 minutes. The chicken will be pink. Add the herb mixture, stir thoroughly, and cook for 1 minute.

5. Add the **chicken stock** and **tomato purée.** Bring to the boil, and cook, stirring, for 3 minutes, or until the sauce has thickened. Pour the chicken and sauce over the rice, and serve.

Bulgur Pilaf 🐷

Preparation: **10 min**   Cooking: **15 min**   Serves **4**   Cals per portion: **295**

Serve this nutritious cracked-wheat dish with chicken or lamb in place of rice for a change. Bulgur is available in health food stores and in some supermarkets.

1½ oz (40g) butter or margarine

1 small onion, peeled and chopped

1 clove garlic, peeled and finely chopped

8 oz (225g) bulgur (cracked wheat)

¾ pint (450ml) chicken or beef stock

¼ teaspoon salt

Pinch black pepper

¼ teaspoon dried sage (optional)

1. Melt the **butter** in a large saucepan over moderate heat. Add the **onion** and **garlic,** and cook for 1 minute.

2. Add the **bulgur,** and cook, stirring, for 1 minute to coat the grains with the butter. Stir in most of the **stock,** the **salt** and **pepper,** and the **sage,** if used. Bring to the boil, lower the heat, cover, and simmer for 15 minutes. If it becomes too dry, add the remaining stock. The bulgur will be chewy.

> **Tip:** *Different qualities of bulgur vary as to the amount of liquid they absorb. It is better, therefore, not to add all the stock at once.*

Bulgur with Bacon

Preparation: **12 min**   Cooking: **15 min**   Serves **4**   Cals per portion: **280**

4 rashers bacon, cut into ¾ in (20mm) strips

6 shallots, peeled and thinly sliced

8 oz (225g) bulgur (cracked wheat)

1 pint (570ml) chicken stock

> **Tips:** *Try one of the following variations. **1.** Add 1 stem celery, chopped, or 4oz (115g) chopped mushrooms with the shallots. **2.** Stir in ¼ teaspoon Dijon mustard and 1 teaspoon Worcestershire sauce or 2oz (50g) raisins before serving. **3.** Top with 1½oz (40g) chopped almonds or walnuts sautéed in ¾oz (20g) butter or margarine.*

1. Cook the **bacon** in a medium-sized, heavy frying pan over moderately high heat for 5 minutes, or until crisp. Using a slotted spoon, transfer the bacon to absorbent paper to drain. Pour off all but 2 tablespoons of the bacon fat.

2. Reduce the heat. Add the **shallots** to the pan, and cook for 3 to 4 minutes, or until they just begin to soften.

3. Add the **bulgur** and most of the **chicken stock,** stir once, cover, reduce the heat, and simmer for 15 to 20 minutes, or until the bulgur is tender and the stock has been absorbed. Add the remaining stock if necessary. Crumble the reserved bacon over the top and serve.

Baked Cornmeal and Cheese ½ 🐷

Preparation: **13 min**   Cooking: **30 min**   Serves **4**   Cals per portion: **645**

1½ pints (850ml) milk

7 oz (200g) yellow cornmeal (fine semolina)

3 eggs, lightly beaten

Pinch cayenne pepper

½ teaspoon salt

Pinch black pepper

3 oz (75g) grated Parmesan cheese

3 oz (75g) butter or margarine

1. Preheat the oven to 200°C (400°F, gas mark 6). Heat the **milk** in a large, heavy saucepan over moderately high heat to just below the boiling point. Reduce the heat and gradually stir in the **cornmeal.** Cook, stirring continuously to prevent lumps forming, for 5 minutes, or until the mixture is thick. Remove from the heat.

2. Using a wire whisk, beat the **eggs** into the mixture, whisking vigorously. Add the **cayenne pepper, salt, black pepper** and half of the **cheese.** Pour the mixture into a greased, shallow dish. Dot with the **butter,** and sprinkle with the remaining cheese. Bake for 30 to 35 minutes, or until set. Cut into squares and serve with a tomato sauce.

Polenta with Walnut Sauce ½ 🐷

Preparation: **10 min**   Cooking: **30 min**   Serves **6**   Cals per portion: **430**

7 oz (200g) yellow cornmeal (fine semolina)

2 cloves garlic, peeled

Pinch salt

¼ teaspoon black pepper

7 oz (200g) walnut halves or pieces

6 tablespoons olive oil

1 tablespoon white wine vinegar

Juice ½ lemon

2 tablespoons finely chopped parsley

Tips: 1. Use an ice-cream scoop for shaping the polenta, or spread it in a layer ¾in (20mm) thick and cut into rounds with a small pastry cutter. 2. If the dish is made in advance, keep it tightly covered to preserve the flavours.

1. In a large saucepan, bring 1¾ pints (1 litre) of lightly salted water to the boil over a high heat. Gradually sprinkle in the **cornmeal** so that it does not form lumps and the water continues to boil. Then lower the heat and cook, stirring continuously, for 30 minutes until the polenta is elastic and comes away from the sides of the pan.

2. In a strong bowl or mortar, pound the **garlic** and the **salt** to a pulp, then add the **pepper** and **walnuts** and continue pounding until you have a paste. Mix in the **olive oil, vinegar** and **lemon juice** and adjust the seasoning to suit your taste. The sauce should resemble thin cream; if it is too thick, add a little water or more lemon juice. Add the **parsley** and stir.

3. With a tablespoon dipped in cold water, shape the polenta into 'eggs', and put on a serving dish to cool. Pour the sauce over the eggs and serve with cold meat and a salad.

BREADS
AND
CAKES

BREADS AND CAKES

With only a little extra time you can make your own pancakes, biscuits, and even muffins from scratch rather than using packet mixes. Follow the recipes on these pages, and you will find that home-made quick breads (breads that do not require a preliminary rising) are not only easy to make but far better tasting than breads made from instant bread mixes. Using the Magic Mix recipe, for example, you can get drop scones ready for the oven in less than 5 minutes; the use of cream speeds preparation time. The other breads take no more than 15 minutes to assemble, while the cooking period is unattended baking time.

Magic Mix

Preparation: **5 min**   Makes **1¾ lb (800g)**   Cals per 4oz (115g): **375**

Keep this mix on hand for making a quick batch of pancakes or very light drop scones. (Follow the recipes given below.)

1½ lb (700g) sifted plain flour

2 tablespoons baking powder

3 oz (75g) skimmed milk powder

2½ teaspoons salt

In a large mixing bowl, thoroughly combine the **flour, baking powder, milk powder** and **salt.** Spoon the mixture into a large glass screwtop jar or plastic container. Cover tightly and store in the refrigerator. Magic Mix will keep for about a month.

Baking Powder Drop Scones:
Preheat the oven to 220°C (425°F, gas mark 7). In a mixing bowl, stir 8oz (225g) Magic Mix and ½ pint (285ml) single cream with a fork just enough to moisten the mix. The dough will be slightly sticky; do not overmix or the scones will be tough. Drop heaped tablespoons of the dough onto a lightly greased baking tray, spacing the scones about 1¼in (32mm) apart. Bake for 8 to 10 minutes, or until lightly browned. To add a different accent to these scones, stir one of the following into the Magic Mix before pouring in the cream:
1. 1 teaspoon caraway seeds or dried oregano, thyme or sage.
2. 1½ oz (40g) grated strong Cheddar cheese or grated Parmesan cheese. 3. 3 rashers crisp bacon, crumbled.
4. 2 tablespoons chopped chives.
5. ½ teaspoon curry powder.

Pancakes: In a mixing bowl, beat 1 egg lightly with a fork, then add 4oz (115g) Magic Mix, and 2 tablespoons melted butter, margarine or vegetable oil. Stir just enough to moisten the mix – the batter should be lumpy. Lightly grease a griddle or large frying pan and heat it over moderate heat until a drop of water dances when sprinkled on it. Using about 2 tablespoons of batter for each pancake, pour the batter onto the griddle, allowing plenty of space between pancakes. Cook until bubbles form and then break on the tops of the pancakes, then turn and cook on the other side until golden. Serve with butter and golden syrup.
You may also want to try one of the following pancake variations: 1. Just before cooking, stir in 1 firm banana, chopped. 2. Stir ¼ teaspoon each ground cinnamon and ground nutmeg into the dry ingredients, then just before cooking, stir in 1 peeled, cored and finely chopped, tart eating apple. 3. Just before cooking, add 2oz (50g) grated strong Cheddar cheese. 4. Substitute unsifted wholemeal flour for 2oz (50g) of the Magic Mix. 5. Before turning the pancakes, dot them with 3oz (75g) crumbled cooked sausage meat or thin slices of cooked sausages.

Peanut Loaf

Preparation: **10 min**   Cooking: **50 min**   Makes **1 loaf**   Cals per ½in (15mm) slice: **180**

This loaf makes a good snack for children and it is very nutritious.

12 fl oz (340ml) water

4 oz (115g) creamy peanut butter

4 oz (115g) plain flour

5 teaspoons baking powder

1 teaspoon salt

2 oz (50g) skimmed milk powder

8 oz (225g) wholemeal flour

4 oz (115g) brown sugar (optional)

4 oz (115g) raisins, washed

3 oz (75g) peeled, unsalted peanuts, chopped

1. Preheat the oven to 180°C (350°F, gas mark 4). Generously grease a loaf tin, 9 x 5½ x 3in (230 x 140 x 80mm).

2. In a small saucepan warm a third of the **water,** add the **peanut butter** and stir until it has melted. Remove from the heat and add the remaining water.

3. Sift the **plain flour, baking powder, salt** and **milk powder** into a mixing bowl. Stir in the **wholemeal flour, sugar** if used, **raisins** and **peanuts,** then add the peanut butter mixture and stir just until all ingredients are combined. Turn into the loaf tin and smooth the top with a spatula. Bake until a metal skewer inserted into the centre of the loaf comes out clean – about 50 minutes. Cool on a wire rack before slicing.

Malt Loaf

Preparation: **10 min**   Cooking: **45 min**   Makes **1 loaf**   Cals per ½in (15mm) slice: **120**

Make the best of unused oven space and bake this loaf at the same time as a roast. Slicing will be easier if the loaf is kept in an airtight tin for about 2 days.

2 tablespoons black treacle

2 tablespoons malt extract

4 fl oz (115ml) cold milk

8 oz (225g) self-raising flour

1 teaspoon bicarbonate of soda

1 teaspoon salt

4 oz (115g) sultanas, washed

4 oz (115g) brown sugar

2 eggs, well beaten

1. Preheat the oven to 190°C (375°F, gas mark 5). Grease and flour a loaf tin, 8 x 4 x 3in (200 x 100 x 80mm).

2. In a small saucepan, melt the **treacle** and **malt extract** over a low heat. Take the pan from the heat, gradually add the cold **milk** and stir. Allow to cool.

3. Sift the **flour, bicarbonate of soda** and **salt** into a mixing bowl, stir in the **sultanas** and **sugar.** Make a well in the centre and pour in the treacle and malt mixture, then the **eggs** and mix until well combined. Pour into the loaf tin and bake until lightly browned and springy to the touch – about 45 minutes. Transfer to a wire rack to cool.

Date Bread

Preparation: **10 min**   Cooking: **45 min**   Makes **1 loaf**   Cals per ½in (15mm) slice: **170**

3¾ oz (100g) butter or margarine, cut into small pieces

5 oz (150g) brown sugar

6 fl oz (175ml) buttermilk

5 oz (150g) plain flour

1 teaspoon salt

1 teaspoon bicarbonate of soda

4 oz (115g) wholemeal flour

4 oz (115g) stoned and roughly chopped dates

1 egg, beaten

1. Preheat the oven to 180°C (350°F, gas mark 4). Line the bottom of an 8 x 4 x 3in (200 x 100 x 80mm) loaf tin with greaseproof paper and grease the lining and the sides.

2. Put the **butter** and **sugar** into a small saucepan and stir over a low heat until the butter has melted and the sugar dissolved. Add the **buttermilk** and put on one side to cool.

3. Meanwhile, sift the **plain flour, salt** and **bicarbonate of soda** into a mixing bowl, add the **wholemeal flour** and **dates** and mix well. Add the **egg** to the cool butter mixture and beat for about 1 minute. Pour the liquid into the dry ingredients and stir to a smooth batter. Turn into the loaf tin and bake until a metal skewer inserted into the centre of the loaf comes out clean – about 45 minutes.

> **Tip:** *If you like, add a pinch of cinnamon to the sifted flour and 3oz (75g) chopped walnuts with the dates.*

Banana Bread

Preparation: **15 min**   Cooking: **50 min**   Makes **1 loaf**   Cals per ½in (15mm) slice: **190**

4 oz (115g) butter or margarine

5 oz (150g) brown sugar

2 eggs, beaten

3 ripe bananas, well mashed

8 oz (225g) plain flour

½ teaspoon salt

1 tablespoon baking powder

½ teaspoon grated nutmeg

3 oz (75g) chopped walnuts

This bread will keep moist for over a week if it is put in an airtight container, or wrapped in plastic film.

1. Preheat the oven to 180°C (350°F, gas mark 4). Line the bottom of an 8 x 4 x 3in (200 x 100 x 80mm) loaf tin with greaseproof paper and grease the lining and the sides.

2. Cream the **butter** and **sugar** in a mixing bowl until light and fluffy. Add the **eggs** and continue beating for 1 minute; add the **banana** pulp and continue beating for another minute.

3. In another bowl, sift the **flour, salt, baking powder** and **nutmeg.** Gradually add the flour to the banana mixture and beat until thoroughly blended. Add the **walnuts** and mix well. Turn into the loaf tin and bake until a metal skewer inserted into the centre comes out clean – about 50 minutes. Serve warm or cold.

Gingerbread ½

Preparation: **10 min**   Cooking: **30 min**   Makes **1 loaf**   Cals per ½in (15mm) slice: **170**

4 oz (115g) butter or margarine

6 fl oz (175ml) dark treacle

4 oz (115g) firmly packed brown sugar

4 fl oz (115ml) milk

8 oz (225g) self-raising flour

1 teaspoon ground ginger

1 teaspoon ground mixed spice

Pinch salt

½ teaspoon bicarbonate of soda

2 eggs, well beaten

1. Preheat the oven to 180°C (350°F, gas mark 4). Line the bottom of a 9in (230mm) square or round cake tin with waxed paper.

2. Put the **butter, treacle** and **sugar** into a small saucepan and stir over a low heat until the butter has melted; add the **milk** and stir. Put the saucepan on one side to cool.

3. Meanwhile, sift the **flour, ginger, spice, salt** and **bicarbonate of soda** into a mixing bowl. Add the **eggs** and mix well, then add the cool butter mixture and stir until well combined. Pour the batter into the cake tin and bake until cooked and just firm to the touch – about 30 to 35 minutes. Allow the gingerbread to cool in the pan before turning out. Serve plain or buttered, or topped with a Lemon Icing, page 234.

Cheesy Potato Rolls ½

Preparation: **15 min**   Cooking: **15 min**   Makes **10**   Cals per roll: **145**

5 oz (150g) peeled potatoes, chopped into ¾ in (20mm) pieces

8 oz (225g) plain flour

4 teaspoons baking powder

1 teaspoon salt

4 oz (115g) finely grated strong Cheddar cheese

4 fl oz (115ml) milk

1 tablespoon caraway, poppy or sesame seeds

1. Put the **potatoes** into a medium-sized saucepan, cover with warm water and boil until tender – about 10 minutes. Drain and mash. Allow to cool slightly.

2. Meanwhile, preheat the oven to 220°C (425°F, gas mark 7). Grease and flour a large baking sheet.

3. Sift the **flour, baking powder** and **salt** into a mixing bowl. Add the **cheese** and the potatoes and quickly blend with your fingers. Add the **milk** and mix to make a soft but fairly dry dough. Break the dough into 10 pieces and swiftly shape into balls. Place them on the baking sheet – evenly spaced – and sprinkle with the **caraway seeds.** Bake for about 15 minutes until golden-brown. Eat while still hot.

Irish Soda Bread

Preparation: **5 min**   Cooking: **40 min**   Serves **8**   Cals per portion: **210**

Soda bread is at its best when eaten warm on the day it is made; leftovers can be toasted for next morning's breakfast. A heavy cast-iron casserole gives an even distribution of heat, but a deep cake tin or loaf tin will do as well.

12 oz (350g) plain flour

1 teaspoon salt

1 teaspoon bicarbonate of soda

4 oz (115g) wholemeal flour

About ½ pint (285ml) buttermilk or soured milk

> *Tips: 1. Natural yoghurt can be used if buttermilk or soured milk is not available. 2. This bread can be made with all plain flour. 3. Try adding 2 teaspoons caraway seeds to the dry mixture.*

1. Preheat the oven to 200°C (400°F, gas mark 6). Grease a heavy 9in (230mm) casserole, and put it in the oven to warm. Sift the **plain flour, salt** and **bicarbonate of soda** into a large mixing bowl. Add the **wholemeal flour** and blend together. Make a well in the centre of the flour and gradually add the **buttermilk,** stirring the mixture with a fork until a soft dough is formed. If the dough crumbles, add more buttermilk as required.

2. Flour your hands, put the dough onto a floured surface and lightly knead it for 2 or 3 minutes. Shape the dough into a round loaf, slightly smaller than the size of your casserole or cake tin, and about 2in (50mm) thick. Place it in the casserole and, with a knife, score a large cross, about ¾in (20mm) deep, on the top of the dough. Cover with a lid or foil and bake for 25 minutes; remove the lid and bake for a further 15 minutes until the bread becomes lightly browned. Place on a wire rack to cool. Break into wedges and slice.

Maritime Oatcakes

Preparation: **12 min**   Cooking: **15 min**   Makes **24**   Cals per oatcake: **85**

These crisp biscuits can be served in place of bread, with a salad, or as a snack

6 oz (175g) plain flour

½ teaspoon salt

½ teaspoon bicarbonate of soda

4 oz (115g) oatmeal

1 tablespoon sugar

4 oz (115g) butter or margarine, cut into small pieces

3 to 4 tablespoons water

1. Preheat the oven to 180°C (350°F, gas mark 4). In a mixing bowl, combine the **flour, salt** and **bicarbonate of soda,** then stir in the **oatmeal** and **sugar.** Cut in the **butter** with a knife or fork until the mixture resembles coarse crumbs. Mix in just enough **water** to make a firm but not dry dough.

2. Roll the dough into 1½in (40mm) balls. Place them on lightly greased baking sheets, pressing each one with the heel of your hand to a thickness of about ¼in (5mm). Bake for 15 to 20 minutes, or until lightly browned. Serve warm with butter.

> *Tip: The oatcakes can be frozen, and taken direct from the freezer to warm through in a moderately hot oven.*

High-Fibre Muffins ½

Preparation: **10 min**   Cooking: **15 min**   Makes **20**   Cals per muffin: **125**

8 oz (225g) plain flour

2½ oz (65g) granulated sugar

1 teaspoon salt

1 teaspoon bicarbonate of soda

4 oz (115g) oatmeal

3 oz (75g) bran or wheatgerm

3 oz (75g) raisins, chopped
dried prunes or apricots

2 eggs, lightly beaten

Generous ½ pint (300ml)
buttermilk

4 fl oz (115ml) golden syrup

These muffins are full of flavour, high in fibre, vitamin B, protein and minerals. Serve them as a snack with a crisp apple.

1. Preheat the oven to 180°C (350°F, gas mark 4). In a mixing bowl, combine the **flour, sugar, salt** and **bicarbonate of soda.** Stir in the **oatmeal, bran** and **raisins.**

2. Combine the **eggs, buttermilk** and **golden syrup.** Add them to the flour and oatmeal mixture and stir until the dry ingredients are just moistened.

3. Spoon the batter into greased, 2in (50mm) patty tins, filling each tin two-thirds full. Bake for 15 to 20 minutes, or until a metal skewer inserted into a muffin comes out clean.

Tip: *Leftover muffins can be frozen and reheated in a 180°C (350°F, gas mark 4) oven.*

Canadian Muffins ½

Preparation: **15 min**   Cooking: **15 min**   Makes **16**   Cals per muffin: **200**

7 oz (200g) plain flour

2½ teaspoons baking powder

½ teaspoon salt

5 oz (150g) butter or margarine,
softened

4 oz (115g) caster sugar

2 eggs, lightly beaten

½ pint (285ml) milk

2 oz (50g) wheatgerm

6 oz (175g) raisins, dried currants
or finely chopped dried apricots

1. Preheat the oven to 190°C (375°F, gas mark 5). In a mixing bowl, combine the **flour, baking powder** and **salt,** and put aside.

2. In a large bowl, beat the **butter** with a rotary or electric mixer until light and fluffy. Gradually blend in the **sugar,** then the **eggs.** Beat well.

3. Alternately mix in a little of the flour mixture and a little of the **milk** until all have been added. Stir in the **wheatgerm** and **raisins.**

4. Spoon the batter into greased, 2in (50mm) patty tins, filling each tin two-thirds full. Bake for 15 to 20 minutes, or until a metal skewer inserted into a muffin comes out clean.

Tip: *Add ½ teaspoon ground ginger and ½ teaspoon mixed spice to the muffin mixture.*

Apple-Nut Muffins

Preparation: **15 min**   Cooking: **20 min**   Makes **12**   Cals per muffin: **200**

Sweet and rich, these muffins make a good snack. Butter them and serve warm with coffee or tea.

8 oz (225g) plain flour

1½ teaspoons baking powder

1½ teaspoons salt

1 teaspoon ground cinnamon

4 oz (115g) caster sugar

1 medium-sized eating apple, peeled, cored and diced into ¼ in (5mm) pieces

3 oz (75g) chopped walnuts or pecans

8 fl oz (285ml) soured cream

1 egg, lightly beaten

4 fl oz (115ml) milk

1. Preheat the oven to 220°C (425°F, gas mark 7). Sift together the **flour, baking powder, salt, cinnamon** and 3oz (75g) of the **sugar** into a mixing bowl. Stir in the **apple** and **walnuts.**

2. In a small bowl, blend three-quarters of the **soured cream** with the **egg** and **milk.** Add the mixture to the dry ingredients and stir until the dry ingredients are just moistened.

3. Spoon the batter into greased, 2in (50mm) patty tins, filling each tin two-thirds full. Drop 1 teaspoon of the remaining soured cream into the centre of each muffin. Sprinkle the top of each muffin with 1 teaspoon of the remaining sugar. Bake for 20 to 25 minutes, or until a metal skewer inserted into a muffin comes out clean.

> **Tip:** *You can substitute 1 firm, ripe pear for the apple, or 6fl oz (175ml) buttermilk or natural yoghurt for 6fl oz (175ml) of the soured cream.*

Chocolate Cake Express

Preparation: **7 min**   Cooking: **40 min**   Serves **6**   Cals per portion: **420**

This dark, moist cake is almost as fast to make as a cake from a packet mix. It is best eaten the same day it is made.

6 oz (175g) plain flour

6 oz (175g) granulated sugar

2 oz (50g) cocoa powder

1 teaspoon bicarbonate of soda

½ teaspoon salt

1 teaspoon vanilla essence

1 tablespoon cider vinegar

4 fl oz (115ml) vegetable oil

8 fl oz (225ml) water

1 tablespoon icing sugar

1. Preheat the oven to 190°C (375°F, gas mark 5). Grease and line an 8in (200mm) cake tin. In a mixing bowl, combine the **flour, granulated sugar, cocoa, bicarbonate of soda** and **salt.** Make a well in the centre of the mixture, and add the **vanilla, vinegar** and **oil,** then gradually stir in the **water.** Continue stirring until thoroughly blended, but do not overmix.

2. Pour the batter into the cake tin and bake for 35 to 40 minutes, or until a metal skewer inserted into the centre of the cake comes out clean. Do not overbake; the secret of this cake is moistness. Cool in the tin on a wire rack for 10 minutes, then transfer the cake from the tin to the rack to cool completely. Sift the **icing sugar** over the top, and serve.

Morning-Coffee Cake 🐷

Preparation: **12 min**   Cooking: **30 min**   Serves **8**   Cals per portion: **235**

For a special treat, bake this rich, tasty cake to eat as a mid-morning snack. It smells as good as it tastes and is easy to make.

5 oz (150g) plain flour

6 oz (175g) moist dark brown sugar

¼ teaspoon salt

2 oz (50g) butter or margarine

½ teaspoon baking powder

¼ teaspoon bicarbonate of soda

½ teaspoon ground cinnamon

1 egg, lightly beaten

4 fl oz (115ml) buttermilk

2 oz (50g) raisins

1. Preheat the oven to 190°C (375°F, gas mark 5). In a mixing bowl, combine the **flour, sugar** and **salt.** Cut in the **butter** with a knife or fork until the mixture resembles coarse crumbs. Put aside 4 tablespoons of the mixture for the topping.

2. Stir in the **baking powder, bicarbonate of soda** and **cinnamon.** In a small bowl, beat the **egg** and **buttermilk** together and add to the mixture. Stir until the dry ingredients are just moistened. Mix in the **raisins.**

3. Pour the batter into a greased and lined, shallow 8in (200mm) cake tin and scatter the reserved topping over the batter. Bake for 30 to 35 minutes, or until a metal skewer inserted into the centre of the cake comes out clean.

> **Tip:** *For a crunchier topping, add 3 tablespoons chopped nuts.*

Soured Cream Spice Cake

Preparation: **6 min**   Cooking: **30 min**   Serves **6**   Cals per portion: **370**

8 fl oz (225ml) soured cream

6 oz (175g) caster sugar

2 eggs, lightly beaten

6 oz (175g) sifted plain flour

1 teaspoon bicarbonate of soda

1 teaspoon baking powder

½ teaspoon salt

1 teaspoon ground cinnamon

½ teaspoon ground cloves

½ teaspoon ground nutmeg

2 oz (50g) chopped nuts or dates

1. Preheat the oven to 180°C (350°F, gas mark 4). Grease and line an 8in (200mm) square cake tin. In a mixing bowl, combine the **soured cream, sugar** and **eggs.**

2. In a separate bowl, combine the **flour, bicarbonate of soda, baking powder, salt, cinnamon, cloves** and **nutmeg.** Stir into the soured cream mixture, then stir in the **nuts.**

3. Pour the batter into the tin and bake for 30 minutes, or until a metal skewer inserted into the centre of the cake comes out clean. Cool in the tin on a wire rack for 10 minutes, then transfer the cake from the tin to the rack to cool completely. If you wish, decorate the cake with Cream Cheese Icing, or Butter Cream Icing, page 234.

Carrot Cake

Preparation: **12 min**   Cooking: **35 min**   Serves **6**   Cals per portion: **465**

2½ oz (65g) moist dark brown sugar

2 eggs

6 fl oz (175ml) vegetable oil

¾ teaspoon salt

4 oz (115g) sifted plain flour

1 teaspoon bicarbonate of soda

1 teaspoon ground cinnamon

2 large carrots, peeled and coarsely grated

3 oz (75g) chopped walnuts or pecans

1 teaspoon grated orange rind

1 teaspoon grated lemon rind

1. Preheat the oven to 180°C (350°F, gas mark 4). Grease and line a 9in (230mm) round cake tin. Place the **sugar, eggs** and **oil** into a mixing bowl, and with an electric mixer at medium speed, beat the ingredients together for 2 minutes.

2. In a small bowl, combine the **salt, flour, bicarbonate of soda** and **cinnamon,** and add to the sugar mixture. Beat at slow speed for 1 minute, then fold in the **carrots, walnuts, orange rind** and **lemon rind.**

3. Pour the batter into the tin and spread evenly. Bake for 30 minutes, or until a metal skewer inserted into the centre of the cake comes out clean. Cool in the tin on a wire rack for 10 minutes, then transfer the cake from the tin to the rack and let it cool completely. If you wish, decorate with Cream Cheese Icing, or Butter Cream Icing, page 234.

> **Tip:** *Transform this recipe into an apple cake by substituting 2 large peeled, cored and grated apples for the carrots.*

Lazy Day Golden Cake

Preparation: **8 min**   Cooking: **35 min**   Serves **6**   Cals per portion: **340**

6 oz (175g) sifted plain flour

4 oz (115g) caster sugar

2 teaspoons baking powder

½ teaspoon salt

6 fl oz (175ml) milk

3½ oz (90g) butter or margarine, cut into small pieces

1 egg

½ teaspoon vanilla essence

1. Preheat the oven to 180°C (350°F, gas mark 4). Grease and line an 8in (200mm) square cake tin. Put the **flour, sugar, baking powder, salt, milk, butter, egg** and **vanilla** into a mixing bowl. With an electric mixer at medium speed, beat the ingredients together for 3 minutes, or until well blended.

2. Pour the mixture into the tin and bake for 35 minutes. Cool in the tin on a wire rack for 10 minutes, then transfer the cake from the tin to the rack and let it cool completely. If you wish, frost the cake with Cream Cheese Icing or Butter Cream Icing, page 234.

> **Tip:** *The cake can be flavoured with the finely grated rind ½ orange or lemon.*

Fruit Shortcake

Preparation: **15 min**   Cooking: **25 min**   Serves **6-8**   Cals per portion: **270**

8 oz (225g) self-raising flour

Generous pinch salt

2 oz (50g) cornflour

4 oz (115g) dark soft brown sugar

8 oz (225g) natural yoghurt or quark

1 egg, beaten

Few drops vanilla essence

4 tablespoons chopped blanched almonds

12 oz (350g) fresh strawberries

Whipped cream or crème fraiche

> **Tip:** Try adding finely grated orange rind to the shortcake mixture, and sprinkle the strawberries with an orange-based liqueur such as Cointreau.

1. Preheat the oven to 190°C (375°F, gas mark 5).

2. Put the **flour, salt, cornflour, sugar, yoghurt,** beaten **egg** and **vanilla essence** into a bowl; work quickly together to a smooth dough, adding half the **almonds.**

3. Press into a rectangular fluted flan tin, about 4 x 14in (100 x 355mm). Sprinkle with the remaining almonds.

4. Bake in the oven for 25 minutes, until risen and pale golden.

5. Cut into slices and serve warm with the **strawberries** and **cream.**

Lemon Tart

Preparation: **20 min**   Cooking: **30 min**   Serves **6**   Cals per portion: **250**

6 oz (175g) shortcrust pastry

Finely grated rind 2 lemons

Juice 1 lemon

1 oz (25g) butter

1 oz (25g) soft brown sugar

3 eggs

¼ pint (150ml) thick natural yoghurt

1. Preheat the oven to 190°C (375°F, gas mark 5).

2. Roll out the **pastry** quite thinly and use to line a 9in (230mm), loose-bottomed flan tin; press up the edges well.

3. Put the **lemon rind** and **juice, butter** and **sugar** into a small pan; stir over a gentle heat until dissolved.

4. Remove from the heat and beat in the **eggs** and **yoghurt;** pour into the pastry case.

5. Bake in the oven for 30 minutes, until just set.

6. Serve warm, cut into wedges.

> **Tip:** Try making this tart with limes rather than lemons; for a special occasion, spoon a little Tequila over each portion.

Prune and Nut Tart

Preparation: **15 min**   Cooking: **25 min**

Serves **6**   Cals per portion: **400**

6 oz (175g) shortcrust pastry

8 oz (225g) pitted prunes

6 tablespoons brandy

2 eggs

6 tablespoons double cream

1½ oz (40g) caster sugar

Finely grated rind ½ lemon

3 tablespoons ground almonds or walnuts

1½ oz (40g) melted butter

2 tablespoons icing sugar

Tip: For really luscious prunes, steep them in the brandy overnight – use half as much brandy again as suggested.

1. Preheat the oven to 200°C (400°F, gas mark 6). Roll out the **pastry** quite thinly and use to line an 8in (200mm), loose-bottomed flan tin; press up the edges well.

2. Put **prunes** into a bowl with the **brandy** and leave on one side.

3. Beat the **eggs** with the **cream, sugar, lemon rind, almonds** and **butter.**

4. Drain the prunes and put them into the pastry case; reserve the brandy.

5. Pour the egg mixture over the prunes. Bake in the oven for 25 minutes. Sprinkle with the **icing sugar.**

6. Spoon the reserved brandy over the top of the hot tart and serve immediately with cream.

Apricot Pie

Preparation: **20 min**   Cooking: **35 min**

Serves **8**   Cals per portion: **415**

1 lb (450g) puff pastry

6 oz (175g) curd cheese

2 oz (50g) caster sugar

3 egg yolks

2 tablespoons apricot jam

2 oz (50g) chopped walnuts

4 oz (115g) dried apricots, soaked and chopped

Finely grated rind ½ orange

1 egg white, beaten

2 tablespoons sugar crystals (white or brown)

1. Preheat the oven to 200°C (400°F, gas mark 6).

2. Roll out the **puff pastry** thinly; line a 9in (230mm) deep, fluted flan tin with half the pastry.

3. Beat the **curd cheese** with the **sugar, egg yolks** and **apricot jam;** add the **walnuts, apricots** and **orange rind,** and spoon into the pastry case.

4. Brush the pastry rim with a little of the **egg white;** lay the remaining pastry over the top and pinch edges to seal.

5. Glaze with the remaining beaten egg white and sprinkle with the **sugar crystals.**

6. Bake in the oven for 35 minutes. Serve straight from the oven, cut into generous-sized wedges.

Crunchy Health Cookies ½ 🐷

Preparation: **10 min**   Cooking: **12-15 min**   Makes **30 cookies**   Cals per cookie: **70**

1 tablespoon honey

1 tablespoon treacle

4 oz (115g) butter or margarine

1 tablespoon water

¼ teaspoon bicarbonate of soda

4 oz (115g) rolled oats

1½ oz (40g) desiccated coconut

3 oz (75g) molasses

1½ oz (40g) wheatgerm

1. Preheat the oven to 180°C (350°F, gas mark 4). Put the **honey,** the **treacle, butter** and the **water** into a small saucepan and bring to the boil slowly, stirring continuously. Add the **bicarbonate of soda** and mix well.

2. In a mixing bowl, combine the **rolled oats, desiccated coconut, molasses** and **wheatgerm.** Pour the honey mixture over the dry ingredients and mix thoroughly.

3. Grease two or three baking sheets and drop the batter onto them in rounded teaspoons, allowing room for spreading. Bake for 12 to 15 minutes. Allow the cookies to cool slightly before removing them from the trays. Store in an airtight tin as soon as they are cold.

Aniseed Biscuits

Preparation: **15 min**   Cooking: **20-25 min**   Makes **20 biscuits**   Cals per biscuit: **200**

1 lb (450g) plain flour

2 teaspoons ground cinnamon

1 tablespoon aniseed

1 tablespoon sesame seeds

2 oz (50g) caster sugar

5 tablespoons dry white wine

Finely grated rind ½ lemon

Finely grated rind ½ orange

8 fl oz (225ml) olive oil

1 egg white, beaten

2 tablespoons chopped, shelled hazelnuts

1. Preheat the oven to 180°C (350°F, gas mark 4).

2. Sift the **flour** and **cinnamon** into a bowl; add the **aniseed, sesame seeds** and **caster sugar.**

3. Make a well in the centre; add the **white wine, lemon rind** and **orange rind,** and gradually beat in the **olive oil.** Work to a smooth dough with your hands.

4. Divide into 20 even-sized pieces and shape each one into a flat biscuit; place on lightly greased baking sheets, allowing room for spreading.

5. Brush the biscuits with beaten **egg white** and sprinkle with the **hazelnuts.**

6. Bake in the oven for 20 to 25 minutes. Cool on a wire rack.

> ***Tip:*** *These biscuits are excellent served at the end of a meal – they are delicious dipped into your last half glass of wine.*

Orange and Chocolate Biscuits

Preparation: **25 min**   Cooking: **12 min**   Makes about **16 biscuits**   Cals per biscuit: **175**

8 oz (225g) plain flour

Pinch ground ginger

Pinch ground cardamom

3 oz (75g) caster sugar

5 oz (150g) butter, softened

2 egg yolks

Finely grated rind 1 orange

3 oz (75g) plain chocolate, melted

1. Preheat the oven to 190°C (375°F, gas mark 5). Sift the **flour, ginger** and **cardamom** into a bowl; add the **sugar, butter, egg yolks** and **orange rind,** and work to a smooth dough with the fingers.

2. Put into a piping bag fitted with a large star nozzle; pipe into 3in (80mm) lengths on greased baking sheets.

3. Bake for 10 to 12 minutes until pale golden.

4. Cool slightly and then dip each end of each biscuit into melted **chocolate.** Leave on waxed paper for a few minutes to set.

Walnut Dreams

Preparation: **12 min**   Cooking: **20 min**   Makes **18 biscuits**   Cals per biscuit: **100**

4 oz (115g) butter, softened

1 oz (25g) icing sugar

1 teaspoon vanilla essence

4 oz (115g) sifted plain flour

Pinch ground nutmeg

Pinch salt

3 oz (75g) finely chopped walnuts

1. Preheat the oven to 150°C (300°F, gas mark 2). In a mixing bowl, cream the **butter** and **icing sugar** with an electric mixer at medium speed until light and fluffy. Stir in the **vanilla, flour, nutmeg, salt** and **walnuts.**

2. Roll the dough into ¾in (20mm) balls. Place them about 1in (25mm) apart on a lightly greased baking sheet, pressing each one to a thickness of about ½in (15mm).

3. Bake for 20 minutes, or until the bottoms are golden-brown. Cool on a wire rack.

Date and Walnut Crackles

Preparation: **15 min**   Makes **24 pieces**   Cals per piece: **70**

6 oz (175g) cornflakes or branflakes

3 oz (75g) stoned dates

3 oz (75g) walnuts

2 tablespoons honey

¾ oz (20g) butter, softened

Juice ½ small lemon

3 tablespoons icing sugar

1. Blend the **cornflakes, dates** and **walnuts** in a blender or food processor until well chopped, but not too fine – or hand-crush the cereal and chop the dates and nuts.

2. In a bowl, combine the cereal mixture with the **honey, butter** and **lemon juice.** Knead until well mixed; roll into ¾in (20mm) balls.

3. Sprinkle the **icing sugar** on a sheet of waxed paper, and roll the balls in the sugar. Store in an airtight container.

BREADS AND CAKES

Cream Cheese Icing

Preparation: **4 min**   Makes about **12 oz (350g)**   Cals per tablespoon: **60**

4 oz (115g) cream cheese, softened

1½ oz (40g) butter or margarine, softened

½ teaspoon vanilla essence

6 oz (175g) icing sugar, sifted

Wonderfully rich and creamy, this icing never has any lumps. The recipe will cover an 8in (200mm) round or square cake or 12 small cakes. To fill and ice a two-layer cake, double the recipe.

In a mixing bowl, beat the **cream cheese, butter** and **vanilla** with a wooden spoon, or an electric mixer at medium speed, until smooth. Gradually beat in the **sugar** until well blended.

> **Tip:** *You can use the same variations for Cream Cheese Icing as given for Butter Cream Icing, see below.*

Butter Cream Icing

Preparation: **5 min**   Makes about **9 oz (250g)**   Cals per tablespoon: **70**

This recipe will cover an 8in (200mm) round or square cake or 12 small cakes. To fill and ice a two-layer cake, double the recipe and the amounts in the variations, if used.

2½ oz (65g) butter or margarine, softened

6 oz (175g) icing sugar, sifted

2 tablespoons milk

½ teaspoon vanilla essence

In a mixing bowl, cream the **butter** with a wooden spoon, or an electric mixer at medium speed, until light and fluffy. Gradually beat in about half the **sugar** until well blended. Beat in the **milk** and **vanilla.** Gradually beat in the remaining sugar. If necessary, add a few drops more milk to make the icing spread more easily.

> **Tips:** *Try one of these variations: **1. Chocolate Icing.** Blend 2oz (50g) melted plain chocolate into the butter or ¾oz (20g) sifted cocoa into the sugar. **2. Mocha Icing.** Stir 2 tablespoons sifted cocoa and 1½ teaspoons instant coffee granules into the icing sugar. **3. Cherry Cream Icing.** Mix in 2 tablespoons chopped glacé cherries. **4. Nut Icing.** Mix in 1oz (25g) chopped hazelnuts or walnuts. **5. Pineapple Icing.** Mix in 2 tablespoons well-drained crushed pineapple. **6. Almond Icing.** Mix in ¼ teaspoon almond essence. **7. Banana Icing.** Mix in 1 mashed banana. **8. Coconut Icing.** Mix in 1½oz (40g) desiccated coconut. **9. Orange Icing.** Omit the milk and vanilla, and add the grated rind and juice of ½ small orange. **10. Lemon Icing.** Omit the milk and vanilla, and add the grated rind and juice of ½ lemon.*

DESSERTS

Fruit Dishes

Cream, Custard and Chocolate Dishes

Puddings and Pies

Sauces and Toppings

DESSERTS

Many of these dessert recipes can be put together in 15 minutes or less, then cooked on top of the cooker or baked – and some need no cooking at all. Most of them can be made in advance – you don't have to rush to prepare them at the last moment. Choice fresh fruit, such as ripe peaches, juicy grapes or succulent pears, can provide a delicious finish to a meal – served as they are, or accompanied by some cheese. For more fresh fruit preparations, turn to *Making a Fruit Salad*, page 56.

Superb Cheesecake

Preparation: **25 min**   Cooking: **30 min**   Serves **8**   Cals per portion: **570**

You must allow at least 6 hours or overnight chilling for this cake, but you can make it as much as a week in advance and refrigerate it.

6 oz (175g) crushed digestive biscuits

3 oz (75g) butter or margarine, melted

1 lb (450g) cream cheese, softened

2 eggs

Squeeze lemon juice

6 oz (175g) caster sugar

8 fl oz (225ml) soured cream

1 teaspoon vanilla essence

Tip: If the cheesecake is for eating at one sitting, top with canned black cherries or serve them at the side.

1. Preheat the oven to 190°C (375°F, gas mark 5). In a mixing bowl, combine the **crushed biscuits** with the **butter.** Turn the mixture into a greased, 9in (230mm), cake tin and press the crumbs firmly over the bottom and two-thirds of the way up the sides.

2. Put the **cream cheese, eggs, lemon juice** and two-thirds of the **sugar** into a mixing bowl. Use an electric mixer or whisk set at medium speed to beat the ingredients together until smooth.

3. Pour the mixture into the crust, and bake for 20 minutes. Cool in the tin on a wire rack for 15 minutes.

4. While the cheesecake is cooling, raise the oven temperature to 220°C (425°F, gas mark 7). Blend the **soured cream,** the remaining sugar and the **vanilla essence,** and spread the mixture gently over the cheese filling. Return the cheesecake to the oven, and bake for a further 10 minutes.

5. Cool the cheesecake in the tin on a wire rack until it reaches room temperature, then cover with foil and chill for 6 hours or overnight. Cut into slim wedges and serve.

Bananas Flambé ◎ ½

Preparation: **4 min** Cooking: **6 min**   Serves **4** Cals per portion: **520**

Measure out all the ingredients before you start to cook.

2 oz (50g) butter, cut into small pieces

3 oz (75g) dark soft brown sugar

½ teaspoon ground cinnamon

4 firm, ripe bananas, peeled and cut in half lengthwise

Juice ½ small lemon

1 pint (570ml) hard vanilla ice cream

2 tablespoons orange liqueur such as Cointreau or curaçao

2 fl oz (50ml) dark rum

1. Melt the **butter** in a large frying pan over moderate heat, then stir in the **sugar** and **cinnamon.** When the mixture is bubbling, add the **bananas** and **lemon juice.** Cook for 3 or 4 minutes, spooning the syrup over the bananas. The bananas should not overcook and become mushy.

2. Spoon the **ice cream** into 4 dessert dishes.

3. Add the **liqueur** and **rum** to the pan, and heat for about 5 seconds. Carefully light the syrup with a match. When the flames die down, serve with the bananas over the ice cream.

> *Tips: 1. Make sure that the ice cream is **very hard** or it will melt too fast when you add the hot bananas and syrup. 2. The bananas may be served without the ice cream. 3. Substitute sliced fresh pineapple for the bananas.*

Bananas Romanoff ◎

Preparation: **15 min**   Serves **4** Cals per portion: **390**

4 ripe but firm bananas

Juice 1 lemon

2 oz (50g) small meringues

7 fl oz (200ml) double cream

½ teaspoon vanilla essence

2 egg whites

1 oz (25g) caster sugar

1. Peel the **bananas** and cut into diagonal slices; toss the banana slices in the **lemon juice.**

2. Crush the **meringues** coarsely.

3. Whip the **cream** with the **vanilla essence** until it holds its shape.

4. Whisk the **egg whites** until stiff but not dry and then whisk in the **sugar;** fold lightly into the whipped cream.

5. Drain the banana slices on absorbent paper; fold the banana and crushed meringues into the lightened cream.

6. Spoon into stemmed glasses and serve immediately.

> *Tip: This dessert is delicious made with strawberries, or other berry fruits.*

Peaches in Macaroon Meringue

Preparation: **5 min**　Cooking: **21 min**　　　　　Serves **4**　Cals per portion: **220**

1 oz (25g) butter or margarine, softened

4 ripe peaches, halved and stoned

2 egg whites, at room temperature

Pinch cream of tartar

1½ oz (40g) sugar

2 oz (50g) crumbled macaroons or ratafias

¼ teaspoon almond essence

1 tablespoon dry sherry

> **Tip:** You can substitute 2oz (50g) chopped toasted almonds for the macaroons.

1. Preheat the oven to 190°C (375°F, gas mark 5). Grease a shallow casserole with half of the **butter.** Place the **peaches** in the dish, stone side uppermost, and dot the centres with the remaining butter. Cover with foil and bake for 15 minutes.

2. Meanwhile, in a small bowl, use an electric mixer or whisk to beat the **egg whites** and **cream of tartar** to soft peaks. Gradually add the **sugar,** beating until stiff. Fold in the crumbled **macaroons, almond essence** and **sherry.**

3. Remove the baking dish from the oven and place a heaped tablespoon of meringue on each peach half. Return to the oven and bake for 6 to 8 minutes, or until the meringue is slightly browned. Serve at once.

Syllabub

Preparation: **15 min**　　　　　　　　　　Serves **4**　Cals per portion: **345**

Here is an ideal warm-weather dessert that has few ingredients, is easy to make and requires no cooking. The sharpness of the lemon peel prevents the syllabub from being too rich.

1 lemon

2 tablespoons caster sugar

2 fl oz (50ml) dry white wine

½ pint (285ml) double cream

1. Finely grate the **lemon** rind into a bowl and add the squeezed and strained juice. Add the **sugar** and the **wine** and stir once or twice. Cover and allow to stand overnight, or for about 8 hours.

2. Pour the **cream** into a bowl and whisk until it begins to thicken. If the cream and the bowl are chilled first, the cream will thicken faster.

3. Gradually add the lemon marinade to the cream and continue to whisk until it forms soft peaks. The texture should be very light. Do not over-whisk or the cream will separate. Spoon into small wine glasses and chill. Serve with brandy snaps or small macaroons.

> **Tips: 1.** After marinating, the syllabub can be made and served immediately, while the cream is still cold.
> **2.** Top each serving with a teaspoon of chopped, toasted nuts.

Cassis Peaches

Preparation: **10 min**   Serves **4**   Cals per portion: **80**

4 large fresh peaches

7 fl oz (200ml) apple juice

1 tablespoon Cassis

1 tablespoon chopped fresh mint

1. Make a nick in the stalk end of each **peach;** scald with boiling water for 45 seconds to loosen the skins. Peel off carefully.

2. Mix the **apple juice** with the **Cassis** and chopped **mint.**

3. Place the peaches in tall, stemmed glasses and pour over the Cassis-flavoured fruit juice.

Pears in Wine

Preparation: **7 min**   Cooking: **8 min**   Serves **4**   Cals per portion: **290**

For a refreshingly cool dessert, prepare these pears in advance and serve them chilled.

16 fl oz (475ml) red or white wine

Grated rind 1 lemon

Juice ½ lemon

6 oz (175g) sugar

½ teaspoon ground cinnamon

4 firm, ripe pears

1. Combine the **wine, lemon rind, lemon juice, sugar** and **cinnamon** in a large saucepan. Bring to the boil, reduce the heat, and simmer until the sugar has melted.

2. Meanwhile, peel, halve and core the **pears.** When the sugar has dissolved, drop the pears into the syrup. Add more wine or water, if necessary, to cover the pears. Simmer, covered, for 8 minutes, turning the pears once, until they are just tender. Cool for 20 minutes, and serve with the syrup.

> **Tip:** *Substitute peaches for the pears, if you like.*

Strawberries with Raspberry Sauce

Preparation: **10 min**   Serves **6**   Cals per portion: **45**

12 oz (350g) raspberries (or frozen raspberries, thawed)

1 lb (450g) strawberries, washed, hulled and halved

> **Tips: 1.** *You may wish to sweeten the strawberries with a few teaspoons of sugar.* **2.** *This sauce is very good over vanilla ice cream.*

Try the raspberry sauce with fresh pineapple or peaches, too.

1. Purée the **raspberries** in an electric blender or food processor at low speed for 30 seconds. Press the raspberries and juice through a sieve. Discard the seeds.

2. Divide the **strawberries** among 6 dessert dishes, and spoon the raspberry sauce over them.

Raspberry and Redcurrant Cheese

Preparation: **6 min**   Serves **4**   Cals per portion: **140**

8 oz (225g) fromage frais

1 oz (25g) caster sugar

2 tablespoons redcurrant jelly

3 tablespoons thick natural yoghurt

8 oz (225g) raspberries

1. Beat the **fromage frais** with the **caster sugar** and **redcurrant jelly;** mix in the **yoghurt.**

2. Fold in the **raspberries.**

3. Spoon into small glass dishes and serve with small sponge biscuits.

> *Tip: The fromage frais can be blended with the sugar and redcurrant jelly in a liquidiser or food processor.*

Middle Eastern Style Figs

Preparation: **10 min**   Serves **4**   Cals per portion: **185**

12 fresh figs

1 oz (25g) shelled pistachios, chopped

2 oz (50g) dates, chopped

2 oz (50g) raisins, chopped

Finely grated rind ½ orange

1 tablespoon sweet sherry

7 fl oz (200ml) natural yoghurt

Generous pinch mixed spice

1. Make a criss-cross cut in the stalk end of each **fig,** and carefully open out.

2. Mix the **pistachios, dates, raisins, orange rind** and **sherry** together; place a little in the centre of each split fig.

3. Serve the stuffed figs on small plates, allowing three per portion. Serve with the **yoghurt** flavoured with **mixed spice.**

Baked Ginger Pears

Preparation: **8 min**   Cooking: **25 min**   Serves **4**   Cals per portion: **170**

4 large pears, just ripe

Juice and grated rind 1 lemon

2 tablespoons dark soft brown sugar

Small piece cinnamon stick, flaked

3 tablespoons ginger wine

1 oz (25g) butter

4 tablespoons soured cream

1. Preheat the oven to 190°C (375°F, gas mark 5).

2. Peel, halve and core the **pears;** place rounded sides uppermost in a shallow ovenproof dish with the **lemon rind** and **juice, brown sugar** and flaked **cinnamon stick.**

3. Spoon over the **ginger wine** and dot with **butter.** Bake in the oven for 20 minutes, basting once or twice with the juices.

4. Spoon over the **soured cream** and return to the oven for a further 5 minutes.

5. Serve piping hot.

DESSERTS

Banana Pudding

Preparation: **8 min**   Cooking: **25 min**   Serves **4**   Cals per portion: **350**

4 medium-sized ripe bananas, cut into ¼ in (5mm) slices

Juice ½ lemon

4 fl oz (115ml) soured cream

3 oz (75g) dark soft brown sugar

Pinch ground nutmeg

1½ oz (40g) fresh breadcrumbs

1 oz (25g) butter or margarine

1½ oz (40g) chopped walnuts or pecans

1. Preheat the oven to 180°C (350°F, gas mark 4). Arrange a layer of sliced **bananas** on the bottom of a greased, shallow ovenproof dish. Sprinkle with half of the **lemon juice,** spread with half of the **soured cream,** then sprinkle with half of the **sugar,** a few grains of the **nutmeg** and half of the **breadcrumbs.**

2. Repeat with another layer, using the remaining ingredients. Dot with the **butter,** and bake for 25 minutes until golden. Sprinkle with the **walnuts,** and serve warm or cold.

> **Tip:** You can substitute desiccated coconut for the walnuts.

Bread and Butter Pudding

Preparation: **8 min**   Cooking: **25 min**   Serves **4**   Cals per portion: **460**

3 oz (75g) raisins

5 slices day-old white bread

2 oz (50g) butter or margarine, softened

16 fl oz (475ml) milk

3 oz (75g) sugar

1 teaspoon vanilla essence

2 eggs

> **Tips: 1.** Sprinkle ⅛ to ¼ teaspoon ground nutmeg or cinnamon over the top of the pudding after removing it from the oven. **2.** Use wholemeal or raisin bread instead of the white bread. **3.** If you don't have day-old bread, toast fresh bread very lightly.

1. Preheat the oven to 180°C (350°F, gas mark 4). Place the **raisins** in 8fl oz (225ml) of hot water, and let them soak for 5 minutes. Meanwhile, trim the crusts from the **bread,** spread one side of each slice with the **butter,** then cut the slices in half. Put the bread, buttered side uppermost, into a greased, shallow ovenproof dish. Drain the raisins and sprinkle them over the bread.

2. Heat the **milk** and **sugar** until just hot. Remove from the heat and stir in the **vanilla essence.**

3. In a mixing bowl, beat the **eggs** lightly, then gradually stir the hot milk into the eggs. Pour the mixture over the bread slices. Bake for 25 minutes, or until the top is brown and a knife inserted into the centre of the pudding comes out clean.

Quick Rice Pudding ½

Preparation: **5 min**   Cooking: **18 min**   Serves **6**   Cals per portion: **455**

You can do most of the preparation while the rice cooks. Or use about 12oz (350g) leftover cooked rice, and assemble the pudding in 5 minutes.

½ teaspoon salt

16 fl oz (475ml) water

4 oz (115g) rice

4 oz (115g) raisins

2 oz (50g) dark soft brown sugar

3 oz (75g) chopped walnuts

8 fl oz (225ml) soured cream

¼ teaspoon ground cinnamon

Generous squeeze lemon juice

1. Bring the **salt** and **water** to the boil in a large saucepan. Add the **rice,** stir once, reduce the heat, cover, and simmer for 18 to 20 minutes, or until all the water has been absorbed, and the rice is tender. Drain thoroughly.

2. Meanwhile, in a mixing bowl, combine the **raisins, sugar, walnuts, soured cream, cinnamon** and **lemon juice.** Add the warm rice, stir to mix, and serve warm or cold.

Tips: 1. You can substitute natural yoghurt for the soured cream and chopped dried apricots or dried figs for the raisins. 2. You can also substitute brown rice for the white rice, but it will take about 40 minutes for the brown rice to cook.

Fudge Delight ½

Preparation: **5 min**   Cooking: **5 min**   Serves **8–12**   Cals per portion: **435**

9 oz (250g) dark, plain chocolate, broken into small pieces

9 oz (250g) unsalted butter, cubed

9 oz (250g) plain, semi-sweet biscuits

9 oz (250g) assorted dried fruits, finely chopped

3 oz (75g) mixed nuts, chopped

2 eggs, beaten

Tips: 1. Use a mixture of the dried fruits you have available, such as raisins, apricots, pears, lemon and orange peel; but make sure they are finely chopped. 2. If you like, add a slice of fresh fruit such as kiwi fruit or a strawberry to each serving to add colour contrast.

This dessert can be made well in advance – whenever you have 10 minutes to spare. The quantities given produce a rich and luxurious 1½in (40mm) deep cake which can be cut into narrow wedges, with ample leftovers for second helpings.

1. Put 1in (25mm) depth of water into the bottom of a double saucepan and bring to simmering point. Place the **chocolate** and the **butter** in the top half and stir occasionally until completely melted. Make sure the mixture does not get too hot. Remove from the heat.

2. Meanwhile, crush the **biscuits** coarsely in a plastic bag, with a rolling pin, or a mallet. Put them into a bowl with the **dried fruit** and the **nuts.** Add the **eggs** and stir thoroughly. Add the chocolate and mix well.

3. Turn the mixture into a greased and lined, 8in (200mm) loose-bottomed tin and refrigerate for 2 hours. Cut into narrow wedges and serve with cream.

DESSERTS

Lemon Pudding Cake

Preparation: 15 min   Cooking: **35 min**   Serves **4**   Cals per portion: **325**

While baking, the pudding sinks to the bottom and the cake rises to the top. Note that the cooking time is unattended baking and that you can make the cake a day or two in advance and refrigerate it.

3 eggs, separated

2 oz (50g) butter or margarine

3 oz (75g) sugar

Grated rind 1 lemon

2½ fl oz (75ml) lemon juice

8 fl oz (225ml) milk

1 oz (25g) plain flour

1. Preheat the oven to 180°C (350°F, gas mark 4). In a mixing bowl, beat the whites of the **eggs** until stiff, and cover with plastic film or foil.

2. In a separate bowl, cream the **butter** and **sugar** until light and fluffy. Beat in the **lemon rind, lemon juice** and the egg yolks, one at a time, until well mixed. Beat in the **milk,** then the **flour** until blended.

3. Fold the beaten egg whites into the lemon mixture, then pour into a greased, 8in (200mm), shallow ovenproof dish. Set the dish in a large pan; pour hot water into the pan to come halfway up the sides of the dish. Bake for 35 minutes. Serve warm or cold.

Pecan Pie

Preparation: 15 min   Cooking: **30 min**   Serves **6**   Cals per portion: **400**

4 oz (115g) crushed digestive biscuits

3 oz (75g) butter or margarine, melted

2 eggs

2½ fl oz (75ml) double cream

2½ fl oz (75ml) golden syrup

Pinch salt

¼ teaspoon ground cinnamon

3 oz (75g) dark soft brown sugar

½ teaspoon vanilla essence

3 oz (75g) chopped pecans

1. Preheat the oven to 180°C (350°F, gas mark 4). In a mixing bowl, combine the **crushed biscuits** with 2oz (50g) of the **butter.** Turn the mixture into an 8in (200mm) pie plate, and press the crumbs firmly and evenly over the bottom and sides (but not the rim) of the dish. Put aside.

2. In a mixing bowl, combine the **eggs, cream, golden syrup, salt, cinnamon, sugar, vanilla essence** and the remaining butter, and mix well. Add the **pecans** and stir.

3. Pour the mixture into the crust, and place the pie plate on a baking tray. Bake for 30 minutes, or until the top of the pie is brown and puffy. Watch carefully towards the end of the baking to prevent burning. The filling will set as it cools.

> **Tip:** *The pie can be topped with whipped cream flavoured with a little rum.*

Italian Custard ½

Preparation: **4 min**   Cooking: **5 min**   Serves **4**   Cals per portion: **200**

This dessert, also called zabaglione, is quick to make. You can prepare it while the coffee is brewing.

6 large egg yolks

3 tablespoons caster sugar

4 fl oz (115ml) Marsala wine

Pinch salt

Tips: 1. You can substitute dry sherry or Madeira for the Marsala. 2. This custard may be served over strawberries, peaches, puddings or sliced cake. 3. Freeze the egg whites for another use in ice-cube trays, then transfer the cubes to a plastic bag and return to the freezer.

1. Place the **egg yolks, sugar, wine** and **salt** in the top of a double saucepan set over gently simmering water.

2. Beat continuously with a whisk or electric beater at medium speed, until the custard mounds slightly when dropped from the whisk. Do not overcook or the custard will curdle.

3. Remove from the hot water immediately, and spoon the custard into 4 wine glasses or dessert dishes. Serve at once.

Quick Mandarin Trifle

Preparation: **20 min**   Serves **4–6**   Cals per portion: **410**

1 jam-filled swiss roll

1 x 11 oz (300g) can mandarin orange segments

3 tablespoons sweet sherry

2 oz (50g) glacé cherries, chopped

1 oz (25g) blanched almonds, chopped

2 egg yolks

2 oz (50g) caster sugar

½ pint (285ml) double cream

3 tablespoons toasted flaked almonds

Tip: For a change, try chocolate swiss roll and canned pear halves.

1. Cut the **swiss roll** into slices about ½in (15mm) thick; place in a decorative glass bowl.

2. Spoon 3 tablespoons of the juice from the **mandarin oranges** and the **sherry** over the swiss roll. Add the drained mandarin oranges, **cherries** and **almonds.**

3. Whisk the **egg yolks** and **caster sugar** until the mixture is thick, light and fluffy. Whip the **cream** until it holds its own shape and fold in the whisked egg mixture.

4. Pour over the sponge and sprinkle with the toasted **almonds.** Chill briefly if you have the time.

DESSERTS

245

Apple-Oatmeal Crunch

Preparation: **12 min**   Cooking: **30 min**   Serves **4**   Cals per portion: **755**

4 or 5 medium-sized cooking apples, cored, peeled and thinly sliced

5 tablespoons dark soft brown sugar

5 tablespoons granulated sugar

2 oz (50g) plain flour

3 oz (75g) rolled oats

4 oz (115g) butter, melted

4 fl oz (115ml) water

8 fl oz (225ml) whipped cream or vanilla ice cream

Simply prepared foods are often the most delicious, and this dessert is no exception.

1. Preheat the oven to 190°C (375°F, gas mark 5). Spread the sliced **apples** over the bottom of a greased, shallow baking dish.

2. In a mixing bowl, combine the **brown sugar, granulated sugar, flour** and **oats,** then stir in the melted **butter.** Spread this mixture over the apples. Pour the **water** evenly over the top.

3. Bake until the apples are tender – about 30 minutes. Serve warm or at room temperature with **whipped cream** or ice cream.

> **Tip:** *Prepare as above, but mix in ½ teaspoon of ground cinnamon and ¼ teaspoon of ground nutmeg with the sugar, flour and oats.*

Blender Chocolate Mousse

Preparation: **10 min**   Serves **6**   Cals per portion: **230**

This chocolate mousse requires at least 50 minutes' chilling time, but you can prepare it as much as a day in advance and refrigerate it. If you like, serve it with pouring cream or with Whipped Cream Topping, page 247.

4 eggs

7 oz (200g) semi-sweet chocolate

5 tablespoons hot strong black coffee

½ teaspoon vanilla essence

1. Separate the **eggs,** placing the whites in a small mixing bowl and the yolks in a cup. Beat the egg whites until stiff but not dry. Put aside.

2. Break the **chocolate** into small pieces and put them into an electric blender or food processor. Switch on and off to break up the pieces. Add the hot **coffee,** and blend until smooth.

3. Add the egg yolks and **vanilla essence.** Blend for 1 minute, or until thoroughly mixed. Pour the chocolate mixture slowly over the egg whites, and fold in gently until no white shows. Spoon into individual dessert dishes or a large serving dish. Refrigerate for 50 minutes, or until set and well chilled.

> **Tip:** *Instead of vanilla essence, you can add 1 tablespoon coffee liqueur such as Tia Maria.*

Whipped Cream Topping

Preparation: **10 min**   Makes about **1 pint (570ml)**   Cals per tablespoon: **70**

Whip cream according to this recipe, and it will keep as long as 4 days in the refrigerator without separating. Just be sure the cream is very fresh.

½ teaspoon gelatine

1 tablespoon cold water

8 fl oz (225ml) double cream

½ teaspoon vanilla essence

Pinch salt

1 tablespoon caster sugar

1. Sprinkle the **gelatine** over the **water** in a small bowl. Stand in a pan of simmering water and stir until the gelatine dissolves. Remove the bowl from the water, and let the mixture cool for about 1 minute.

2. Whip the **cream,** until floppy, then add the dissolved gelatine mixture, the **vanilla essence, salt** and **sugar,** and continue to whip until the cream is thick. Cover and refrigerate. Just before serving, beat with a spoon to blend.

> ***Tips: 1.*** *Add 1 tablespoon whisky or orange liqueur, or substitute ¼ teaspoon almond essence for the vanilla essence.* ***2.*** *As a variation, whip the cream with the gelatine as above, then add 2½fl oz (75ml) soured cream, 1 tablespoon sugar and ½ teaspoon vanilla essence. Blend well. Serve over fresh peaches or berries. The result is a French-style cream.*

Custard Sauce

Preparation: **8 min**   Cooking: **5 min**   Makes about **1 pint (570ml)**   Cals per tablespoon: **25**

Here is a sauce to serve over fresh or cooked fruit as well as cake, apple pie and puddings.

16 fl oz (475ml) milk

1½ oz (40g) sugar

Pinch salt

4 egg yolks

1 teaspoon vanilla essence, sherry or brandy

> ***Tip:*** *This sauce will keep for up to 3 days in the refrigerator.*

1. In a large, heavy saucepan over moderate heat, heat the **milk, sugar** and **salt** until the sugar has dissolved and the milk is very hot.

2. In a small bowl, beat the **egg yolks** lightly, then stir in a few tablespoons of the hot milk mixture. Blend the egg yolk mixture with the hot milk in the saucepan. Reduce the heat and cook, stirring continuously, until the mixture coats the spoon – about 5 minutes. Do not boil or the sauce will curdle.

3. Remove the pan from the heat and place it in cold water. Stir the sauce continuously for 2 minutes, then blend in the **vanilla essence.** Cool, then cover and refrigerate until serving time.

DESSERTS

Butterscotch Sauce

Preparation: **1 min**   Cooking: **5 min**   Makes about ½ **pint (285ml)**   Cals per tablespoon: **90**

Treat the family or guests to a sundae with home-made butterscotch sauce.

6 oz (175g) dark soft brown sugar

2 fl oz (50ml) double cream

1½ oz (40g) butter or margarine

2 tablespoons golden syrup

Bring the **sugar, cream, butter** and **golden syrup** slowly to the boil in a heavy saucepan over moderate heat, stirring occasionally. Serve warm over ice cream, waffles or cake.

> **Tip:** *This sauce will keep for several weeks in the refrigerator.*

Orange Cream Sauce

Preparation: **5 min**   Cooking: **3 min**   Makes about ½ **pint (285ml)**   Cals per tablespoon: **30**

Serve this quick sauce warm or cold over plain cake, sponge cake or simple puddings.

1 orange

1½ oz (40g) sugar

2 teaspoons cornflour

2 fl oz (50ml) double cream

1. Grate half the rind from the **orange,** and put aside. Squeeze the juice from the orange and strain into a measuring jug. Add enough water to make up to 6fl oz (175ml).

2. Pour the orange juice mixture into a saucepan. Combine the **sugar** and **cornflour,** and stir into the orange mixture. Cook over low heat, stirring frequently, until the sugar has dissolved and the mixture has thickened – about 3 minutes. Remove the pan from the heat, and stir in the reserved orange rind and **cream.**

Chocolate Sauce

Preparation: **2 min**   Cooking: **4 min**   Makes about ½ **pint (285ml)**   Cals per tablespoon: **110**

7 oz (200g) semi-sweet chocolate

4 fl oz (115ml) golden syrup

2 fl oz (50ml) double cream

½ oz (15g) butter or margarine

½ teaspoon vanilla essence

Hot chocolate sauce on vanilla or coffee ice cream makes a delicious dessert. For more sumptuous dishes, pour the sauce over cream puffs, sponge cake topped with preserved fruit, or canned pear halves filled with cream.

In a large heavy saucepan over low heat, melt the **chocolate** with the **golden syrup,** stirring continuously. Remove the pan from the heat, and stir in the **cream, butter** and **vanilla essence.**

> **Tips: 1.** *As variations, add ½ teaspoon finely grated orange peel; substitute 1 teaspoon rum or brandy for the vanilla.* **2.** *Top each serving with a teaspoon of finely chopped mixed nuts.* **3.** *This sauce will keep for at least a week in the refrigerator if tightly sealed. Reheat in a double saucepan.*

OVEN-
BAKED
DISHES

(See also recipes for Eggs and
Cheese as well as Desserts and
Sauces)

OVEN-BAKED DISHES

Oven cooking may take longer than other methods, but most of the cooking time is unattended. In addition, many of the recipes in this section are for one-dish meals that need to be accompanied by only a tossed salad, and then followed with some fruit.

Garden Casserole

Preparation: **15 min**   Cooking: **35 min**   Serves **4**   Cals per portion: **170**

9 oz (250g) courgettes

1 aubergine (about 9 oz/250g)

1 medium-sized onion, peeled

2 large, very ripe tomatoes

1 pepper, cored and seeded

1 teaspoon each dried basil and thyme

2 cloves garlic, finely chopped

1½ teaspoons salt

¼ teaspoon black pepper

3 tablespoons chopped parsley

4 tablespoons vegetable oil

This recipe is ideal for the busy cook; it takes only minutes to prepare for baking; it can be made in advance and reheated or served cold, and it is nourishing.

1. Preheat the oven to 200°C (400°F, gas mark 6). Thinly slice the **courgettes, aubergine, onion, tomatoes** and **pepper.** In a dish, combine the **basil, thyme, garlic, salt, black pepper** and **parsley.**

2. Grease the bottom of a deep, ovenproof dish with half the **oil.** Layer the courgettes, then the aubergine, onion, tomatoes and pepper in the dish, sprinkling each layer with the herb mixture. Sprinkle the remaining oil over the top, and bake, covered, for 35 minutes, or until the vegetables are tender.

Broccoli au Gratin

Preparation: **15 min**   Cooking: **30 min**   Serves **6**   Cals per portion: **250**

2¼ lb (1kg) broccoli

½ teaspoon salt

¼ teaspoon black pepper

1 red pepper, seeded and chopped

3 eggs, lightly beaten

4 oz (115g) grated strong cheese

3 oz (75g) fine fresh breadcrumbs

8 fl oz (225ml) milk

½ oz (15g) butter

1. Preheat the oven to 180°C (350°F, gas mark 4). Trim the leaves and coarse stem ends from the **broccoli** and break into florets. Bring about 2in (50mm) of water to the boil in a large saucepan, add the broccoli and cook, covered, for 5 minutes. (If using frozen broccoli, cook, covered, for 2 minutes.)

2. In a deep casserole mix the broccoli, **salt, black pepper, red pepper, eggs, cheese,** three-quarters of the **breadcrumbs** and the **milk.** Dot with the **butter,** sprinkle with the remaining breadcrumbs and bake for 30 minutes, or until just set.

Green Beans with Mushrooms and Water Chestnuts

Preparation: **15 min**   Cooking: **20 min**   Serves **6**   Cals per portion: **310**

1½ lb (700g) green beans

3 oz (75g) butter or margarine

1 large onion, peeled and chopped

4 oz (115g) thinly sliced mushrooms

2 tablespoons plain flour

8 fl oz (225ml) milk

2½ oz (65g) grated Cheddar cheese

½ teaspoon salt

¼ teaspoon black pepper

4 oz (115g) canned water chestnuts, drained and sliced

1½ oz (40g) flaked blanched almonds

1½ oz (40g) fine dry breadcrumbs

1. Preheat the oven to 180°C (350°F, gas mark 4). Wash the **beans** and cut off the ends. Bring about ¾in (20mm) of lightly salted water to the boil in a large saucepan and add the beans. Cook, covered, for 5 to 7 minutes, or until just tender. Drain the beans and put aside.

2. Meanwhile, melt 2½oz (65g) of the **butter** in a medium-sized, heavy frying pan over moderate heat. Add the **onion** and **mushrooms,** and cook for 5 minutes, or until the onion is soft. Blend in the **flour,** and the **milk, cheese, salt** and **pepper,** and cook, stirring, until the cheese melts and the sauce thickens – about 5 minutes.

3. In a greased, shallow ovenproof dish combine the cheese mixture, the beans, and the **water chestnuts.** Top with the **almonds** and **breadcrumbs,** and dot with the remaining butter. Bake for 20 minutes, or until bubbling.

> *Tips: **1.** You can use frozen beans instead of fresh; thaw but do not cook them. **2.** You can also substitute broccoli spears for the beans.*

Sweet Carrots and Potatoes

Preparation: **20 min**   Cooking: **25 min**   Serves **4**   Cals per portion: **320**

This sweet vegetable dish goes well with roast pork, chicken or turkey – it tastes even better when made in advance and reheated.

4 medium-sized carrots, peeled and diced

3 large potatoes, peeled and diced

1 orange

1 oz (25g) butter or margarine

¼ teaspoon black pepper

4 oz (115g) pitted prunes, chopped

4 tablespoons clear honey

1. Preheat the oven to 200°C (400°F, gas mark 6). Bring ¾in (20mm) of lightly salted water to the boil in a large saucepan. Add the **carrots** and **potatoes** and cook, covered, for 5 minutes, then drain.

2. Meanwhile, grate the rind from the **orange,** then squeeze out the juice. Place the rind and juice in a greased casserole.

3. Add the drained carrots and potatoes, half the **butter,** the **pepper** and **prunes,** and mix well. Drizzle the **honey** over the top, and dot with the remaining butter. Cover and bake for 25 minutes.

Sweetcorn and Cheese Casserole

Preparation: **20 min**   Cooking: **30 min**

Serves **4**   Cals per portion: **390**

12 oz (350g) frozen sweetcorn kernels, thawed, or canned sweetcorn, drained

4 oz (115g) whole green chillies, seeded and chopped

3½ oz (90g) grated strong Cheddar cheese

8 fl oz (225ml) soured cream or natural yoghurt

1 egg, lightly beaten

½ teaspoon salt

1 oz (25g) butter or margarine, melted

Serve this as a side dish with roast beef, lamb or chicken, or as a main course for a light lunch with a lettuce and tomato salad.

1. Preheat the oven to 200°C (400°F, gas mark 6). In a mixing bowl, combine the **sweetcorn, chillies, cheese, soured cream, egg, salt** and **butter.**

2. Pour the mixture into a greased, shallow ovenproof dish, and bake for 30 to 35 minutes, or until a knife inserted in the centre of the casserole comes out clean.

> **Tip:** *To make the dish more substantial, add 4oz (115g) chopped lean ham.*

Aubergine with Cheese and Tomatoes

Preparation: **20 min**   Cooking: **15 min**

Serves **4**   Cals per portion: **280**

1 small aubergine (about 9 oz/250g), peeled and cut into ¾ in (20mm) slices

3 tablespoons vegetable oil

1 teaspoon salt

¾ teaspoon black pepper

1 large onion, peeled and chopped

1 clove garlic, peeled and finely chopped

4 medium-sized tomatoes, peeled and chopped

Pinch dried thyme

3 tablespoons finely chopped parsley

2 oz (50g) soft fresh breadcrumbs

4 oz (115g) grated Swiss, or strong Cheddar cheese

Here is an economical main-course casserole that can be made in advance. Cook the recipe up to the end of Step 2, refrigerate overnight, and bake just before serving.

1. Preheat the grill. Place the **aubergine** slices on a greased baking sheet and brush with 1 tablespoon of the **oil.** Sprinkle with ½ teaspoon of the **salt** and ½ teaspoon of the **pepper.** Grill for 5 minutes on each side and remove from the grill. Preheat the oven to 180°C (350°F, gas mark 4).

2. While the aubergine is grilling, heat the remaining oil in a medium-sized, heavy frying pan over moderate heat. Add the **onion,** and cook until soft – about 5 minutes. Add the **garlic,** and cook for 1 minute longer, then add the **tomatoes** and cook, stirring, until the mixture thickens slightly – about 8 minutes. Stir in the **thyme, parsley** and **breadcrumbs** and the remaining salt and pepper.

3. Place the aubergine in a greased, shallow ovenproof dish, spoon the tomato mixture over, top with the **cheese,** and bake until the cheese has melted – about 15 minutes.

Mushroom and Barley Casserole

Preparation: **15 min**   Cooking: **35 min**   Serves **4**   Cals per portion: **285**

This makes a tasty vegetarian dish served simply with an accompanying salad and grated cheese.

3 oz (75g) butter or margarine

1 large onion, peeled and finely chopped

4 oz (115g) mushrooms, thinly sliced

4 oz (115g) medium pearl barley

½ teaspoon salt

¼ teaspoon black pepper

16 fl oz (475ml) chicken or beef stock

1. Preheat the oven to 180°C (350°F, gas mark 4). Melt the **butter** in a medium-sized, heavy frying pan over moderate heat. Add the **onion,** and cook for 3 minutes. Add the **mushrooms** and **barley,** and cook for 4 minutes, stirring occasionally.

2. Add the **salt, pepper** and **stock,** and bring to the boil. Pour the mixture into a greased casserole, cover, and bake for 35 minutes.

> **Tip:** *Try adding 2oz (50g) of currants and ¼ teaspoon of allspice before adding the stock.*

Spinach, Noodle and Cheese Casserole

Preparation: **15 min**   Cooking: **30 min**   Serves **4**   Cals per portion: **560**

4 oz (115g) egg noodles

1 lb (450g) fresh spinach

3 oz (75g) butter or margarine

1 small onion, peeled and chopped

2 eggs

8 fl oz (225ml) soured cream

¾ teaspoon salt

Pinch black pepper

4 oz (115g) grated strong Cheddar cheese

> **Tip:** *This dish can be prepared in advance. Simply cook the noodles, spinach and onions, mix the ingredients as directed, then cover and refrigerate. Before serving, mix again lightly, pour into the buttered dish, and bake.*

1. Preheat the oven to 180°C (350°F, gas mark 4). Cook the **noodles** according to packet directions, drain thoroughly in a colander, and put aside.

2. Meanwhile, trim the fresh **spinach** of coarse stems and blemished leaves, wash it, and shake dry. Place the spinach in a large saucepan with just the water that clings to the leaves, and cook, covered, for 5 minutes, or until the spinach is just limp. Drain thoroughly. (If you are using frozen spinach, cook according to packet directions, drain well, and press out as much liquid as you can.)

3. In a mixing bowl, combine the noodles and spinach. Melt the **butter** in a small frying pan over moderate heat. Add the **onion,** and cook until soft – about 5 minutes. Stir the onion and butter into the noodle mixture.

4. Beat the **eggs** with the **soured cream, salt** and **pepper.** Add to the noodle mixture along with the **cheese.** Mix well.

5. Pour into a greased shallow casserole and bake for 30 minutes.

Potato, Stilton and Onion Pie

Preparation: **20 min**   Cooking: **25 min**   Serves **4**   Cals per portion: **410**

3 large potatoes (about 1½ lb/700g)

2 leeks, cut into rings

1 medium-sized onion, peeled and thinly sliced

1 tablespoon vegetable oil

4 oz (115g) curd cheese

4 oz (115g) Stilton cheese, crumbled

2 tablespoons chopped chives

6 tomatoes, seeded and chopped

1 clove garlic, peeled and chopped

¼ teaspoon salt

¼ teaspoon black pepper

4 tablespoons chicken stock

2 tablespoons grated Parmesan cheese

1. Preheat oven to 190°C (375°F, gas mark 5).

2. Bring water to the boil in a large saucepan, add the **potatoes,** and cook, covered, for 10 minutes. In another pan, parboil the **leeks** for 5 minutes and drain. Drain the potatoes, allow them to cool a little, then peel and thinly slice.

3. While the potatoes are cooling, fry the **onion** gently in the **oil** for 4 to 5 minutes; layer in a greased ovenproof dish with the potatoes, leeks, knobs of **curd cheese,** crumbled **Stilton cheese** and **chives.**

4. Mix the chopped **tomatoes, garlic, salt, pepper** and **chicken stock;** spoon over the vegetables and sprinkle with the **Parmesan cheese.**

5. Bake in the oven for 25 minutes until golden. Serve piping hot with a tossed salad.

> **Tip:** *A great recipe for using leftover cooked vegetables – and this means the cooking time is cut too. Instead of the leeks you can use halved, cooked Brussels sprouts, cauliflower florets, roughly chopped carrots or peas.*

Pumpkin with Bacon

Preparation: **20 min**   Cooking: **35 min**   Serves **4**   Cals per portion: **180**

2 rashers bacon, cut into ¾ in (20mm) strips

1¼ lb (575g) pumpkin, peeled and chopped

1 medium-sized onion, peeled and chopped

2½ fl oz (75ml) water

1 oz (25g) butter or margarine, softened

½ teaspoon salt

¼ teaspoon black pepper

2 teaspoons sugar

1 egg, lightly beaten

2 oz (50g) soft fresh breadcrumbs

1. Preheat the oven to 180°C (350°F, gas mark 4). Cook the **bacon** in a medium-sized, heavy frying pan over moderately high heat until crisp – about 5 minutes. Transfer the bacon to absorbent paper and put aside.

2. Add the **pumpkin** and **onion** to the bacon fat, and cook for 2 minutes. Add the **water,** cover, and cook until the vegetables are tender – about 15 minutes.

3. Remove the pan from the heat and mash the vegetables with a potato masher. Add the **butter, salt, pepper, sugar, egg** and **breadcrumbs,** and mix well. Pour into a greased casserole. Crumble the reserved bacon, sprinkle it over the pumpkin mixture, and bake for 20 minutes.

Chicken and Broccoli Bake

Preparation: **20 min**   Cooking: **15 min**   Serves **4**   Cals per portion: **445**

Here is a good way to use leftover chicken or turkey.

1¼ lb (575g) broccoli

1¾ oz (45g) butter or margarine

1 small onion, peeled and finely chopped

2 tablespoons plain flour

½ teaspoon salt

Pinch black pepper

16 fl oz (475ml) milk

8 oz (225g) diced cooked chicken

4 oz (115g) grated Cheddar cheese

1. Preheat the oven to 180°C (350°F, gas mark 4). Trim the leaves and coarse stem ends from the **broccoli,** and cut the remaining stems and florets into bite-sized pieces. Bring about ¾in (20mm) of lightly salted water to the boil in a large saucepan. Add the broccoli and cook, covered, for 5 minutes, or until just tender. Drain thoroughly, then transfer to a greased, ovenproof casserole dish.

2. Meanwhile, melt the **butter** in a saucepan over moderate heat. Add the **onion,** and cook until soft – about 5 minutes.

3. Blend in the **flour, salt** and **pepper** to form a smooth paste. Gradually add the **milk,** and cook over moderate heat, stirring, until thickened – about 5 minutes.

4. Add the **chicken,** then pour the mixture over the broccoli. Sprinkle the **cheese** over the top and bake for 15 minutes. Serve with Cherry Tomatoes in Brown-Butter Sauce, page 83.

Chicken Gratinée

Preparation: **15 min**   Cooking: **25-30 min**   Serves **6**   Cals per portion: **500**

6 small cooked chicken joints

6 slices lean ham

1 tablespoon French mustard

14 fl oz (400ml) dry white wine

10 oz (275g) grated Gruyère cheese

1 teaspoon cornflour

1 tablespoon water

¼ teaspoon salt

¼ teaspoon black pepper

2 oz (50g) wholemeal breadcrumbs

1. Preheat the oven to 190°C (375°F, gas mark 5).

2. Wrap each **chicken joint** in a slice of **ham** spread with **mustard;** place in a greased ovenproof dish.

3. Put the **wine** into a saucepan with the grated **cheese,** and the **cornflour** blended with the **water;** stir over a gentle heat until the cheese has melted and is like fondue. Season with **salt** and **pepper.**

4. Pour the cheese mixture over the chicken and sprinkle with the **breadcrumbs.**

5. Bake in the preheated oven for 25 to 30 minutes. Serve hot with a salad.

> *Tip: Instead of using complete joints of chicken, you can wrap several chunky pieces of cooked chicken in each slice of ham.*

Santa's Pie

Preparation: **25 min**   Cooking: **30 min**   Serves **4**   Cals per portion: **350**

1 lb (450g) potatoes, peeled and cut into chunks

8 oz (225g) cooked and boned chicken

1 x 15 oz (425g) can baked beans

1 x 11 oz (300g) can sweetcorn kernels, drained

2 tablespoons sweet chutney

1 eating apple, cored and grated

1 tablespoon salted peanuts

1 tablespoon raisins

2 egg yolks

¼ teaspoon salt

¼ teaspoon black pepper

¾ oz (20g) butter

1. Preheat the oven to 190°C (375°F, gas mark 5). Bring water to the boil in a large saucepan and cook the **potatoes** for about 10 minutes or until they are tender.

2. Meanwhile, cut the cooked **chicken** into small chunks and mix with the **baked beans, sweetcorn, chutney, apple, peanuts** and **raisins;** put the mixture into a greased, shallow ovenproof dish.

3. Mash the cooked potatoes with the **egg yolks, salt, pepper** and **butter;** fork onto the chicken and bean filling.

4. Bake in the oven for 30 minutes, until the potato topping is deep golden-brown.

5. Serve piping hot with a salad.

> *Tips: 1. The pie can be assembled ready for baking the night before. 2. Other leftover cooked meats can be used, such as roast lamb or beef.*

Hot Chicken Salad

Preparation: **15 min**   Cooking: **15 min**   Serves **4**   Cals per portion: **550**

12 oz (350g) diced cooked chicken

2 oz (50g) chopped almonds

8 fl oz (225ml) mayonnaise

Juice 1 lemon

2 large stems celery, thinly sliced

1 small onion, peeled and finely chopped

1 teaspoon salt

¼ teaspoon black pepper

2 oz (50g) soft fresh breadcrumbs

½ oz (15g) butter or margarine, melted

2 oz (50g) grated Swiss cheese

1. Preheat the oven to 180°C (350°F, gas mark 4). In a mixing bowl, combine the **chicken, almonds, mayonnaise, lemon juice, celery, onion, salt** and **pepper.** Place the mixture in a greased, shallow casserole.

2. Combine the **breadcrumbs** with the melted **butter.** Top the casserole with the buttered breadcrumbs, and sprinkle with the **cheese.** Bake for 15 minutes.

> *Tips: 1. As a variation, use cooked turkey instead of the chicken and add 2 tablespoons of snipped fresh dill. 2. You can make this dish a day in advance and refrigerate it, or reheat any leftovers.*

Chicken Risotto ⊘

Preparation: **12 min**   Cooking: **20 min**   Serves **4**   Cals per portion: **390**

2 oz (50g) butter or margarine

1 medium-sized onion, peeled and chopped

1 clove garlic, peeled and finely chopped

1 large stem celery, chopped

4 oz (115g) rice

6 oz (175g) diced cooked chicken

1 pint (570ml) chicken stock

½ teaspoon salt

¼ teaspoon black pepper

Pinch dried rosemary

4 oz (115g) frozen peas, thawed

3 oz (75g) grated Parmesan cheese

1. Preheat the oven to 200°C (400°F, gas mark 6). Melt the **butter** over moderately high heat in a large saucepan with an ovenproof handle. Add the **onion, garlic** and **celery,** and cook for 3 minutes.

2. Add the **rice** and **chicken,** and cook for another 2 minutes. Add the **chicken stock, salt, pepper** and **rosemary,** and bring to the boil. Cover and put in the oven.

3. Bake for 15 minutes, then add the **peas** and **cheese,** cover again, and bake 5 minutes longer. When done, the rice should be just tender, but not soft.

> **Tips: 1.** *If you do not have a covered saucepan with an ovenproof handle, use a medium-sized frying pan until you are ready to bake the dish. Then transfer to a medium casserole and cover.* **2.** *You can make this dish a day in advance and refrigerate it, or reheat any leftovers.*

Creamed Chicken and Rice ⊘

Preparation: **7 min**   Cooking: **15 min**   Serves **4**   Cals per portion: **510**

Here is a fast way to give leftover chicken and rice a freshly made taste.

12 fl oz (340ml) single cream

1¾ oz (45g) butter or margarine

1 tablespoon cornflour

6 tablespoons dry sherry

1 teaspoon curry powder

¾ teaspoon salt

Pinch cayenne pepper

12 oz (350g) diced cooked chicken

8 oz (225g) cooked rice

1. Preheat the oven to 180°C (350°F, gas mark 4). Put the **cream** and **butter** into a saucepan over moderate heat and bring to the boil.

2. In a small bowl, combine the **cornflour** and **sherry,** and slowly add to the saucepan, stirring vigorously. Add the **curry powder, salt** and **cayenne pepper,** and cook until the sauce has boiled and thickened – about 3 minutes. Add the **chicken,** stir, and remove from the heat.

3. Cover the bottom of a greased shallow casserole with the **rice,** and pour in the chicken mixture. Bake for 15 minutes.

> **Tip:** *You can increase the amount of cayenne pepper to ¼ teaspoon and add 3 peeled and chopped shallots.*

Beef and Tomato Bake

Preparation: **15 min**   Cooking: **20 min**   Serves **4**   Cals per portion: **365**

1 tablespoon olive oil

1 medium-sized onion, peeled and finely chopped

1 clove garlic, peeled and crushed

1¼ lb (575g) lean minced beef

½ teaspoon ground coriander

¼ teaspoon ground ginger

4 medium-sized tomatoes, peeled and chopped

1 teaspoon brown sugar

2 tablespoons finely chopped parsley

1½ oz (40g) chopped stuffed olives

½ teaspoon salt

Pinch black pepper

1. Preheat the oven to 180°C (350°F, gas mark 4). Heat the **oil** in a medium-sized, heavy frying pan over moderate heat. Add the **onion** and **garlic,** and cook for 5 minutes, or until the onion is soft. Push to one side, add the **beef,** and cook, stirring occasionally, until browned – about 5 minutes.

2. Add the **coriander, ginger, tomatoes, brown sugar, parsley, olives, salt** and **pepper,** and mix well. Transfer to a greased ovenproof dish, and bake for 20 minutes. Serve with rice and a green salad.

Tip: For a creamy topping to this dish, spread 4 tablespoons of soured cream evenly over the top as soon as it comes out of the oven.

Spiced Beef

Preparation: **15 min**   Cooking: **20 min**   Serves **4**   Cals per portion: **355**

1 tablespoon vegetable oil

1 medium-sized onion, peeled and chopped

1 clove garlic, peeled and crushed

1 teaspoon grated fresh root ginger or ¼ teaspoon ground ginger

1¼ lb (575g) lean minced beef

¼ teaspoon dried red chilli flakes

1 medium-sized pepper, seeded and cut into thin strips

3 shallots, peeled and cut into ¾ in (20mm) pieces

1 teaspoon salt

Pinch paprika

1. Preheat the oven to 200°C (400°F, gas mark 6). Heat the **oil** in a medium-sized, heavy frying pan over moderate heat. Add the **onion, garlic** and **ginger,** and cook until the onion is golden – about 6 minutes.

2. Add the **beef** and **chilli flakes,** and cook, stirring occasionally, until the beef has browned – about 5 minutes. Add the **pepper, shallots, salt** and **paprika,** stir, and transfer the mixture to a greased, shallow ovenproof dish. Cover with foil and bake for 20 minutes. Before serving, tilt the dish and skim off the fat. Serve with steamed rice.

Tips: 1. You can substitute minced lamb or pork for the beef. 2. Add sliced mushrooms to the beef while it is browning.

Beef and Cabbage Casserole

Preparation: **10 min**   Cooking: **35 min**   Serves **4**   Cals per portion: **335**

1¼ lb (575g) lean minced beef

1 medium-sized onion, peeled and finely chopped

4 tablespoons tomato purée

4 fl oz (115ml) beef stock

Pinch ground cinnamon

Pinch ground cloves

1 teaspoon salt

½ teaspoon black pepper

½ small head cabbage, shredded

1. Preheat the oven to 180°C (350°F, gas mark 4). Place the **beef** and **onion** in a medium-sized, heavy frying pan over moderate heat. Cook, stirring occasionally, until the beef has browned – about 5 minutes. Pour off and discard the fat from the pan. Add the **tomato purée, beef stock, cinnamon, cloves, salt** and **pepper** to the beef, and stir to blend.

2. Place half the **cabbage** in a greased casserole, and top with half the beef mixture. Repeat the layers. Cover and bake for 35 minutes. Serve with buttered noodles, and Green Beans with Garlic and Cheese, page 62.

Tips: 1. You can make this dish a day in advance and refrigerate it, or reheat leftovers. 2. As a variation, use minced pork instead of beef, and shredded Chinese leaves in place of the cabbage. Add 1 teaspoon caraway seeds for extra flavour.

Beef and Noodles with Two Cheeses

Preparation: **15 min**   Cooking: **30 min**   Serves **6**   Cals per portion: **485**

Make this casserole when convenient and reheat and serve it when you are ready.

6oz (175g) wide egg noodles

1¼ lb (575g) lean minced beef

1 small onion, peeled and chopped

1 teaspoon salt

¼ teaspoon black pepper

3 tablespoons tomato purée

6 oz (175g) cottage cheese

6 oz (175g) cream cheese

3 tablespoons soured cream

1 small pepper, seeded and chopped

3 shallots, peeled and chopped

1. Preheat the oven to 180°C (350°F, gas mark 4). Cook the **noodles** according to packet directions, drain thoroughly in a colander, and put aside.

2. Meanwhile, heat a medium-sized, heavy frying pan over moderate heat. Add the **beef** and **onion,** and cook, stirring occasionally, until the beef has browned – about 5 minutes. Add the **salt, black pepper** and **tomato purée,** stir, and simmer slowly while preparing the remaining ingredients.

3. In a mixing bowl, combine the **cottage cheese, cream cheese, soured cream, pepper** and **shallots.**

4. Place half the noodles in a greased casserole. Cover with the meat mixture, then with the remaining noodles. Pour the cheese mixture over the top. Bake for 30 minutes. Serve with a crisp salad.

Curried Beef Casserole

Preparation: **12 min**   Cooking: **20 min**   Serves **4**   Cals per portion: **615**

2 oz (50g) butter or margarine

1 large onion, peeled and finely chopped

2 slices white bread

6 fl oz (175ml) milk

1¼ lb (575g) lean minced beef

1½ oz (40g) raisins

2 oz (50g) chopped blanched almonds

4 apricots, stoned and chopped

Juice 1 lemon

1 tablespoon curry powder

Pinch dried oregano

¼ teaspoon salt

Pinch black pepper

1 egg

1. Preheat the oven to 160°C (325°F, gas mark 3). Melt the **butter** in a medium-sized, heavy frying pan over moderate heat. Add the **onion,** and cook for 5 minutes, or until soft. Meanwhile, soak the **bread** in a third of the **milk.**

2. When the onion is soft, add the bread, **beef, raisins, almonds, apricots, lemon juice, curry powder, oregano, salt** and **pepper.** Cook for 5 minutes, stirring continuously. Transfer to a greased, shallow ovenproof dish.

3. In a small bowl, beat the remaining milk with the **egg,** and pour over the beef mixture. Bake for 20 minutes. Skim any fat from the top of the dish before serving.

> **Tip:** *If you have time, you can substitute finely chopped dried apricots. Soak in water for 4 hours.*

Baked Cheeseburger Casserole

Preparation: **15 min**   Cooking: **25 min**   Serves **4**   Cals per portion: **610**

1 oz (25g) butter

6 slices white bread, toasted

1¼ lb (575g) lean minced beef

1 small onion, chopped

2 stems celery, chopped

1 tablespoon prepared English mustard

1 teaspoon salt

4 oz (115g) grated strong Cheddar cheese

1 egg

6 fl oz (175ml) milk

Pinch dry mustard

¼ teaspoon paprika

1. Preheat the oven to 180°C (350°F, gas mark 4). Spread the **butter** on both sides of the **bread,** cut the slices in half diagonally, and put aside.

2. Heat a medium-sized, heavy frying pan over moderate heat. Add the **beef, onion, celery, prepared mustard** and ½ teaspoon of the **salt,** and cook, stirring occasionally, until the beef has browned – about 5 minutes.

3. In a greased shallow casserole, place alternate layers of toast, beef and **cheese.**

4. In a small bowl, beat the **egg,** then stir in the **milk, dry mustard** and the remaining salt. Pour over the cheese, sprinkle with the **paprika,** and bake for 25 minutes.

Pork and Sweetcorn Pie

Preparation: **20 min**   Cooking: **20 min**   Serves **4**   Cals per portion: **565**

2 fl oz (50ml) vegetable oil

1 medium-sized onion, peeled and chopped

8 oz (225g) diced cooked pork

5 tablespoons plain flour

2 teaspoons chilli powder

8 fl oz (225ml) chicken stock

12 oz (350g) frozen or canned sweetcorn kernels

2 oz (50g) raisins

1½ oz (40g) pitted black olives, chopped

½ teaspoon salt

Juice ½ lemon

8 fl oz (225ml) milk

3 oz (75g) cornmeal

1 egg, lightly beaten

2 teaspoons baking powder

½ teaspoon bicarbonate of soda

1. Preheat the oven to 220°C (425°F, gas mark 7). Heat 3 tablespoons of the **oil** in a medium-sized, ovenproof frying pan or shallow, flameproof casserole over moderate heat. Add the **onion,** and cook for 5 minutes. Add the **pork,** and cook until lightly browned – about 2 minutes.

2. Blend in 1 tablespoon of the **flour,** the **chilli powder** and the **chicken stock.** Add the **sweetcorn, raisins, olives** and ¼ teaspoon of the **salt.** Stir until the mixture thickens – about 4 minutes.

3. In a small bowl, stir the **lemon juice** into the **milk,** and let stand for a few minutes. In a mixing bowl, combine the **cornmeal** with the remaining flour and salt. In the order listed, gradually stir in the milk mixture, **egg, baking powder, bicarbonate of soda** and the remaining oil.

4. Stir the topping mixture and pour over the pork. Bake for 20 minutes, or until the topping is set and just firm to the touch.

Ham and Egg Casserole

Preparation: **17 min**   Cooking: **20 min**   Serves **4**   Cals per portion: **225**

1 oz (25g) butter or margarine

1 medium-sized onion, peeled and thinly sliced

2 tablespoons plain flour

8 fl oz (225ml) milk

1 tablespoon French mustard

¼ teaspoon black pepper

12 oz (350g) diced cooked ham

2 hard-boiled eggs, sliced

1. Preheat the oven to 180°C (350°F, gas mark 4). Melt the **butter** in a saucepan over moderate heat. Add the **onion,** and cook for 5 minutes, or until soft.

2. Reduce the heat to low. Blend in the **flour,** slowly add the **milk,** and cook, stirring continuously, until the mixture has thickened and is smooth – about 3 minutes. Remove the pan from the heat, and stir in the **mustard** and **pepper.**

3. Pour half the sauce into a greased casserole. Add a layer of the **ham,** then a layer of half the sliced **eggs.** Repeat the layers of ham and eggs, then pour the remaining sauce over all. Bake for 20 minutes, or until the sauce is bubbling.

Golden Ham Casserole

Preparation: **15 min**   Cooking: **20 min**   Serves **4**   Cals per portion: **465**

4 oz (115g) medium egg noodles

1 tablespoon cider vinegar

8 fl oz (225ml) milk

6 oz (175g) diced cooked ham

2 eggs, lightly beaten

½ teaspoon salt

¼ teaspoon black pepper

4 oz (115g) grated Cheddar cheese

1 small onion, peeled and finely chopped

2 stems celery, sliced

1 small pepper, seeded and chopped

4 oz (115g) cooked peas

2 oz (50g) soft fresh breadcrumbs

½ oz (15g) butter or margarine

1. Preheat the oven to 190°C (375°F, gas mark 5). Cook the **noodles** according to packet directions and drain thoroughly in a colander. Meanwhile, stir the **vinegar** into the **milk,** and let stand for a few minutes. The milk will sour.

2. In a mixing bowl, combine the milk, **ham, eggs, salt, black pepper, cheese** and the noodles. Add the **onion, celery, pepper** and **peas,** and mix well. Pour the mixture into a greased casserole.

3. Sprinkle the **breadcrumbs** over the casserole, and dot with the **butter.** Bake for 20 minutes. Serve with a starter of Cream of Tomato Soup, page 32, and a green salad.

> **Tip:** *Try blue cheese in place of the Cheddar – the flavour blends very well with the ham.*

Sausage Casserole

Preparation: **15 min**   Cooking: **45 min**   Serves **4**   Cals per portion: **640**

1¼ lb (575g) Bratwurst sausages, thickly sliced

2 medium-sized potatoes, peeled and thinly sliced

1 medium-sized onion, peeled and thinly sliced

1 large carrot, peeled and thinly sliced

1 teaspoon dried basil

4 medium-sized tomatoes, peeled and chopped

⅓ pint (190ml) tomato juice

1 teaspoon salt

Pinch black pepper

1. Preheat the oven to 180°C (350°F, gas mark 4). Place the **sausages** in a medium-sized, heavy frying pan over moderate heat and cook, stirring frequently, until browned – about 5 minutes. Pour off and discard the fat from the pan.

2. Layer the sausages, **potatoes, onion** and **carrot** in a greased casserole. Repeat the layers. Add the **basil, tomatoes, tomato juice, salt** and **pepper,** and bake, covered, for 45 minutes.

> **Tip:** *You can use pork sausages or sausage meat instead of the Bratwurst; sage instead of the basil.*

Sweetcorn and Sausage Casserole 🐖

Preparation: **12 min**   Cooking: **20 min**   Serves **4**   Cals per portion: **560**

1¼ lb (575g) sausage meat

12 oz (350g) frozen sweetcorn kernels, thawed, or canned sweetcorn, drained

2 eggs, lightly beaten

¼ teaspoon salt

Pinch black pepper

3 oz (75g) soft fresh breadcrumbs

Tip: *If you like black pudding, use half pork sausage meat and half black pudding (crumbled).*

1. Preheat the oven to 200°C (400°F, gas mark 6). Place the **sausage meat** in a medium-sized, heavy frying pan over moderate heat, and cook, stirring frequently, until browned – about 5 minutes. Spoon off any excess fat.

2. Meanwhile, in a small bowl, combine the **sweetcorn, eggs, salt** and **pepper,** and place half the mixture in a greased casserole.

3. Using a slotted spoon, transfer the sausage mixture from the pan to the casserole, and arrange evenly on the sweetcorn mixture. Top with the remaining sweetcorn mixture.

4. Add the **breadcrumbs** to the frying pan, stir to coat them with the sausage meat juices, and spread over the top of the casserole. Bake for 20 minutes, or until the mixture has set and browned. Serve with a lettuce and tomato salad.

Moussaka ½

Preparation: **20 min**   Cooking: **35 min**   Serves **6**   Cals per portion: **370**

2 large, firm aubergines

4 tablespoons olive oil or vegetable oil

2 large onions, peeled and chopped

2 cloves garlic, peeled and crushed

1 lb (450g) cooked lamb, minced

4 large tomatoes, peeled, seeded and chopped

2 eggs

1 tablespoon plain flour

½ teaspoon salt

½ teaspoon black pepper

8 fl oz (225ml) soured cream or natural yoghurt

1. Preheat the oven to 190°C (375°F, gas mark 5). Top and tail the **aubergines** and cut them lengthways into ½in (15mm) slices. Heat the **oil** in a large frying pan over moderate heat and fry the aubergines until soft. Line the bottom of a deep rectangular dish with half the slices and put the remaining slices aside.

2. Add the **onions** and **garlic** to the pan and cook until soft but not browned – about 3 minutes. Add the minced **lamb** and stir. Tip the contents of the pan into the dish and cover the aubergines. Spread the **tomatoes** and their juices evenly over the meat and cover with the remaining aubergines.

3. Beat the **eggs,** then blend in the **flour, salt** and **pepper** and whisk in the **soured cream.** Pour the topping over the casserole and bake until the top is a deep golden-brown – about 35 minutes. Serve with a salad.

Lentil and Sausage Stew

Preparation: 25 min Cooking: **25 min**   Serves **4**   Cals per portion: **665**

1 lb (450g) dried red lentils
2 tablespoons vegetable oil
1 medium-sized onion, peeled and chopped
1 clove garlic, peeled and finely chopped
4 medium-sized tomatoes, peeled and chopped
12 oz (350g) smoked sausage or frankfurters, cut into ¾ in (20mm) pieces
1 bay leaf
¼ teaspoon dried thyme
¼ teaspoon dried marjoram
1 teaspoon salt
¼ teaspoon black pepper

This is a very economical and satisfying main dish. It tastes even better when reheated.

1. Preheat the oven to 200°C (400°F, gas mark 6). Rinse and sort the **lentils,** and put them into a large saucepan. Cover the lentils with water; bring to the boil, cover, and simmer for 20 minutes, or until the lentils are tender. Do not drain.

2. Meanwhile, heat the **oil** in a large, heavy frying pan over moderate heat. Add the **onion** and **garlic,** and cook until the onion is soft – about 5 minutes. Stir in the **tomatoes.**

3. Pour the lentils and their cooking liquid into a large, greased casserole. Stir in the **sausage,** the tomato mixture, the **bay leaf, thyme, marjoram, salt** and **pepper.** Cover and bake for 20 minutes. Remove the lid and bake for a further 5 minutes.

Fish Casserole

Preparation: 20 min Cooking: **10 min**   Serves **4**   Cals per portion: **380**

1¼ lb (575g) mullet or mackerel fillets
3 oz (75g) plain flour
3 tablespoons olive oil or vegetable oil
1 large onion, peeled and thinly sliced
2 medium-sized carrots, peeled and thinly sliced
Juice 2 limes or 1 lemon
1 bay leaf, crumbled
¾ teaspoon salt
¼ teaspoon black pepper

> **Tip:** *This dish has a better flavour if you use a mixture of fish; for example, a third each of mullet, mackerel and trout.*

1. Preheat the oven to 220°C (425°F, gas mark 7). Slice the **fish fillets** crosswise into ¾in (20mm) strips. Put the **flour** onto a plate or a sheet of waxed paper, and coat the strips evenly. Shake off any excess flour.

2. Heat 2 tablespoons of the **oil** in a flameproof casserole over moderately high heat. Cook the fish strips for 1 minute on each side. Using a slotted spoon, transfer the fish to a plate and put aside.

3. Add the remaining oil and the **onion** and **carrots** to the casserole, and cook, stirring, for 2 minutes. Reduce the heat to moderate, cover, and cook for 5 minutes.

4. Remove the casserole from the heat, and add the fish, **lime juice, bay leaf, salt** and **pepper.** Stir gently. Bake, covered, for about 10 minutes. If the fish flakes easily when tested with a fork, it is done. Serve hot with steamed rice.

Fish and Potato Casserole ⟩

Preparation: **20 min**   Cooking: **8 min**   Serves **4**   Cals per portion: **285**

4 rashers bacon, cut into ¾ in (20mm) strips

3 medium-sized potatoes, peeled and diced

1 large stem celery, finely chopped

1¼ lb (575g) firm, white fish fillets cut into ¾ in (20mm) pieces

4 fl oz (115ml) fish stock

1 teaspoon salt

¼ teaspoon black pepper

1. Preheat the oven to 220°C (425°F, gas mark 7). Cook the **bacon** in a saucepan over moderate heat for 3 minutes. Add the **potatoes** and **celery,** and cook for 5 minutes, stirring often.

2. Transfer the mixture to a greased casserole, and stir in the **fish fillets, fish stock, salt** and **pepper.** Bake, covered, for 8 to 10 minutes, depending on the thickness of the fish. If the fish flakes easily when tested with a fork, it is done.

Salmon and Mushroom Casserole

Preparation: **15 min**   Cooking: **20 min**   Serves **4**   Cals per portion: **385**

4 oz (115g) wide egg noodles

2 oz (50g) butter or margarine

1 medium onion, peeled and chopped

4 oz (115g) mushrooms, thinly sliced

2 tablespoons plain flour

1 x 7 oz (200g) can salmon

8 fl oz (225ml) milk

2 tablespoons water or chicken stock

¼ teaspoon salt

Pinch black pepper

2 oz (50g) fine dry breadcrumbs

> **Tip:** *Instead of using canned salmon, you can use flaked, smoked mackerel; use a little white wine to make up for the salmon liquid.*

1. Preheat the oven to 220°C (425°F, gas mark 7). Cook the **noodles** according to packet directions, drain thoroughly in a colander, and put aside.

2. Meanwhile, melt half the **butter** in a medium-sized, heavy frying pan over moderate heat. Add the **onion** and **mushrooms,** and cook until the onion is soft – about 5 minutes. Blend in the **flour** and put aside.

3. Drain the **salmon,** reserving the liquid. Remove any skin and bone, mash, and put aside. Add the reserved salmon liquid and the **milk** and **water** to the onion-mushroom mixture, and cook, stirring continuously, until thickened – about 3 minutes. Season with the **salt** and **pepper.**

4. In a greased casserole, combine the sauce, salmon and noodles. Top with the **breadcrumbs,** and dot with the remaining butter. Bake for 20 minutes. Serve with a green salad.

Mussel and Sweetcorn Pudding

Preparation: **10 min**   Cooking: **20 min**   Serves **4**   Cals per portion: **350**

1 x 8.8 oz (250g) can cooked mussels

3 oz (75g) savoury biscuits, crumbed or crushed

4 fl oz (115ml) milk

2 eggs, lightly beaten

12 oz (350g) frozen or canned sweetcorn kernels

2 tablespoons finely chopped parsley

1½ oz (40g) butter, melted

1 small onion, finely chopped

½ teaspoon Worcestershire sauce

¼ teaspoon salt

¼ teaspoon black pepper

2 oz (50g) grated Cheddar cheese

1. Preheat the oven to 200°C (425°F, gas mark 7). Drain the **mussels,** reserving their juices. Chop the mussels. In a mixing bowl, combine the **biscuit crumbs, milk, eggs,** chopped mussels and their juices, **sweetcorn, parsley, butter, onion, Worcestershire sauce, salt** and **pepper.**

2. Transfer the mixture to a greased casserole, and top with the **cheese.** Bake for 20 minutes. Serve with Coleslaw, page 46, or Grated Carrots with Herbs and Lemon, page 47.

> ***Tips: 1.*** *To add colour, halve the quantity of sweetcorn and add 6oz (175g) frozen peas, thawed.* ***2.*** *Parmesan cheese can be used instead of the Cheddar.*

Mussel and Noodle Bake

Preparation: **15 min**   Cooking: **15 min**   Serves **4**   Cals per portion: **390**

4 oz (115g) medium egg noodles

2 x 8.8 oz (250g) cans cooked mussels

2 oz (50g) butter or margarine

3 shallots, peeled and finely chopped

1 stem celery, finely chopped

2 tablespoons plain flour

8 fl oz (225ml) milk

½ teaspoon salt

Pinch black pepper

Pinch ground cardamom

2 oz (50g) fine dry breadcrumbs

> ***Tip:*** *You can use pasta shapes such as shells or bows, or cut macaroni instead of the noodles.*

1. Preheat the oven to 220°C (425°F, gas mark 7). Cook the **noodles** according to packet directions, drain, and put aside.

2. Meanwhile, drain the **mussels,** reserving the juices, and put both aside. Melt three-quarters of the **butter** in a saucepan over moderate heat. Add the **shallots** and **celery,** and cook for 5 minutes, or until soft.

3. Blend in the **flour** with a wire whisk, then add the **milk,** and stir vigorously until the mixture is thickened and smooth – about 3 minutes. Add the mussel juices, **salt, pepper** and **ground cardamom.**

4. Place half the noodles in a greased, deep ovenproof dish, cover with the mussels, then add the remaining noodles. Pour the sauce over all, top with the **breadcrumbs,** dot with the remaining butter, and bake for 15 minutes, or until brown and bubbling.

Upside-Down Tuna Pie

Preparation: **20 min**   Cooking: **20 min**   Serves **4**   Cals per portion: **530**

1 lemon, very thinly sliced

1½ oz (40g) butter or margarine

1 oz (25g) plain flour, plus
2 tablespoons

16 fl oz (475ml) milk

¾ teaspoon salt

Pinch black pepper

2 x 7 oz (200g) cans tuna in
brine, drained and flaked

1 small onion, peeled
and chopped

1½ oz (40g) soft fresh
breadcrumbs

3 oz (75g) cornmeal

1½ teaspoons baking powder

1 egg

2 fl oz (50ml) vegetable oil

1. Preheat the oven to 220°C (425°F, gas mark 7). Line a shallow dish or a deep pie plate with greased greaseproof paper and with the **lemon** slices. Put aside.

2. Melt the **butter** in a large saucepan over moderate heat. Stir in 2 tablespoons of the **flour,** then add 12fl oz (340ml) of the **milk,** ¼ teaspoon of the **salt,** and the **pepper.** Cook, stirring continuously, until the mixture thickens – about 3 minutes. Fold in the **tuna, onion** and **breadcrumbs.** Pour over the lemon slices.

3. Into a mixing bowl, put the **cornmeal,** the remaining flour, salt and **baking powder.** Beat the **egg,** the remaining milk, and the **oil** with a hand beater, and blend thoroughly into the dry ingredients.

4. Spoon over the tuna mixture. Bake for 20 minutes, or until just firm to the touch. Remove from the oven and cool for 10 minutes. Loosen the edges with a knife, cover with a serving plate, and carefully unmould onto the plate.

Noodles with Soured Cream and Cottage Cheese

Preparation: **10 min**   Cooking: **30 min**   Serves **4**   Cals per portion: **310**

4 oz (115g) medium egg noodles

8 oz (225g) cottage cheese

8 fl oz (225ml) soured cream

½ teaspoon salt

Pinch black pepper

2 tablespoons chopped fresh
chives or 2 teaspoons dried
chives

½ oz (15g) butter or margarine

Tip: *For a sweet variation, omit the pepper and chives, and add 1 teaspoon ground cinnamon, 1 grated apple, 2oz (50g) raisins and 2 lightly beaten eggs.*

You can prepare this dish in the morning, cover and refrigerate it, and bake it for the evening meal.

1. Preheat the oven to 190°C (375°F, gas mark 5). Cook the **noodles** according to packet directions and drain thoroughly in a colander.

2. In a greased, shallow casserole dish, combine the noodles with the **cottage cheese, soured cream, salt, pepper** and **chives.** Dot with the **butter,** and bake for 30 minutes, or until the top starts to brown. Serve with a mixed green salad tossed with Oil and Vinegar Dressing for Green Salads, page 52.

COOKING FOR ONE

Vegetables

Poultry

Meat

Pasta

Fish

Desserts

COOKING FOR ONE

When you eat alone, you want to get out of the kitchen as quickly as possible. Most of these dishes take less than 20 minutes to prepare, and they can be doubled for another serving.

Peas with Watercress Butter Sauce

Preparation: **3 min**   Cooking: **7 min**   Cals per portion: **490**

1¾ oz (45g) butter	Melt the **butter** in a saucepan over moderate heat. Add the **watercress, onion, salt** and **pepper.** Cover, and cook for 5 minutes. Add the **peas** and **vinegar,** and stir. Cover, and cook for 2 minutes.
1 small bunch watercress, chopped	
½ small onion, peeled and chopped	
Pinch salt	
¼ teaspoon black pepper	
4 oz (115g) frozen green peas	
1 teaspoon cider vinegar	

Tip: *Prepare a salad the next day with any unused watercress and an oil and vinegar dressing.*

Savoury Courgettes

Preparation: **8 min**   Cooking: **6 min**   Cals per portion: **320**

2 rashers bacon, cut into ¾ in (20mm) strips

1 small onion, peeled and finely chopped

8 oz (225g) courgettes, cut into ½ in (15mm) slices

1 tablespoon chopped walnuts

½ teaspoon dried basil

Pinch salt

¼ teaspoon black pepper

1. Cook the **bacon** in a medium-sized, heavy frying pan over moderately high heat for 3 minutes. Pour off all but 2 tablespoons of the bacon fat. Add the **onion** and **courgettes,** and cook for 3 minutes.

2. Add the **walnuts, basil, salt** and **pepper,** and cook, stirring occasionally, for 3 minutes or until the courgettes are just tender.

Tip: *You can omit the bacon and use 1oz (25g) butter or margarine and 2oz (50g) of diced cooked ham.*

Broccoli with Tarragon Chicken Sauce

Preparation: **15 min**   Cooking: **10 min**   Cals per portion: **330**

6 oz (175g) broccoli spears

⅓ oz (9g) butter

⅓ oz (9g) flour

7 fl oz (200ml) chicken stock

¼ teaspoon dried tarragon

¼ teaspoon salt

¼ teaspoon black pepper

1 egg yolk

1 tablespoon thick natural yoghurt

3 oz (75g) cooked chicken, chopped

1. Preheat the oven to 190°C (375°F, gas mark 5). Cook the **broccoli spears** in boiling, salted water until just tender. Drain thoroughly.

2. Meanwhile, melt the **butter;** stir in the **flour** and cook for 1 minute.

3. Gradually stir in the **stock** and bring to the boil, stirring until slightly thickened.

4. Add the **tarragon, salt** and **pepper, egg yolk, yoghurt** and **chicken.**

5. Put the broccoli into a greased ovenproof dish and spoon over the prepared sauce.

6. Bake in the oven for 10 minutes.

> **Tip:** *1oz (25g) crumbled blue cheese can be added to the sauce.*

Chicken Breast Parmesan

Preparation: **10 min**   Cooking: **8 min**   Cals per portion: **675**

1 chicken breast, skinned and boned

Salt and black pepper

1½ tablespoons fine dry breadcrumbs

1½ tablespoons grated Parmesan cheese

¼ teaspoon dried oregano

1 egg, lightly beaten

½ oz (15g) butter or margarine

2 tablespoons tomato sauce or ketchup

2 thin slices mozzarella or Swiss cheese

1. Preheat the grill. Pound the **chicken breast** between two sheets of waxed paper to a thickness of about ¼in (5mm). Season with the **salt** and **pepper.**

2. Combine the **breadcrumbs, Parmesan cheese** and **oregano** on a sheet of waxed paper. Dip the chicken breast into the **egg,** then press into the breadcrumb mixture to coat evenly on both sides.

3. Heat the **butter** in a medium-sized, heavy frying pan over moderate heat until bubbling. Add the chicken and cook for 3 minutes on each side, or until no longer pink when pierced with a knife. Do not overcook.

4. Line the rack of the grill pan with foil and place the chicken on it. Spoon the **tomato sauce** over the chicken, and top with the **mozzarella cheese,** trimmed to fit. Grill 3in (75mm) from the heat for about 2 minutes, or until the cheese melts. Serve with Peas with Watercress Butter Sauce, page 271.

Tropical Hamburger

Preparation: **13 min**   Cooking: **6 min**   Cals per portion: **520**

6 oz (175g) minced beef

1 small onion, peeled and finely chopped

Pinch salt

Pinch black pepper

½ clove garlic, peeled and finely chopped

1 tablespoon soya sauce

Pinch ground ginger

½ teaspoon sugar

1 tablespoon vegetable oil

> *Tip: You can substitute minced lamb, pork, chicken or veal for the beef.*

1. In a small bowl, combine the **beef, onion, salt** and **pepper,** and shape the mixture into a ¾in (20mm) thick patty. Place the patty on a small plate.

2. In the same bowl, combine the **garlic, soya sauce, ginger** and **sugar,** and pour over the patty. Leave to stand for 10 minutes to marinate, then remove the patty from the marinade.

3. Heat the **oil** in a small, heavy frying pan over moderate heat for about 1 minute. Add the patty and cook about 3 minutes on each side for rare, 4 for medium, and 6 for well done.

Oriental Beef and Green Beans

Preparation: **12 min**   Cooking: **11 min**   Cals per portion: **460**

4 oz (115g) topside, cut crosswise into thin strips, 2 in (50mm) long

1½ teaspoons soya sauce

4 oz (115g) green beans

2 tablespoons vegetable oil

1 clove garlic, peeled and finely chopped

¼ teaspoon salt

Pinch black pepper

2 tablespoons beef stock

1. Put the **beef** strips into a small bowl, add the **soya sauce,** and toss to mix. Let the beef stand for 10 minutes to marinate. Meanwhile wash the **beans,** cut off the ends, and break into 2in (50mm) lengths.

2. Heat the **oil** in a medium-sized, heavy frying pan over moderate heat for about 1 minute. Add the **garlic, salt,** and **pepper,** and cook, stirring, for 30 seconds. Do not let the garlic brown. Add the beans to the pan and cook, stirring, for 3 minutes. Add the **stock,** cover, reduce the heat, and cook for 3 more minutes.

3. Raise the heat to moderately high, cook until the stock has boiled away, then add the beef and marinade. Cook, stirring continuously, for 4 minutes. The beef should be pink; do not overcook or it will be tough. Serve with rice.

Beef, Tomato and Noodle Supper

Preparation: **12 min**   Cooking: **20 min**   Cals per portion: **700**

½ oz (15g) butter or margarine

6 oz (175g) minced beef

1 medium-sized onion, peeled and chopped

3 small tomatoes, peeled and chopped

1 stem celery, finely chopped

½ teaspoon salt

Pinch black pepper

¼ teaspoon dried basil

¼ teaspoon dried oregano

7 fl oz (200ml) beef stock

2 oz (50g) egg noodles or elbow macaroni

Heat the **butter** in a medium-sized, heavy frying pan over moderate heat until bubbling. Add the **beef** and **onion,** and cook, stirring occasionally, for 5 minutes, or until the beef has browned and the onion is soft. Add the **tomatoes, celery, salt, pepper, basil, oregano** and **stock.** Cover, and simmer for 15 minutes. Cook the **noodles** in boiling water until just tender. Drain well; heat through with the meat.

Tips: 1. You can substitute minced lamb, pork, veal or chicken for the beef. 2. You can make this dish a day in advance and refrigerate it. You may need to add a few tablespoons of extra stock when reheating if the mixture seems too dry.

Chicken Livers with Mushrooms and Tomato

Preparation: **7 min**   Cooking: **11 min**   Cals per portion: **570**

Serve this dish with buttered noodles, or rice and a green salad, and you will enjoy a tasty, complete meal. To save time, prepare the tomato and mushrooms while the onion is cooking.

1¾ oz (45g) butter or margarine

1 small onion, peeled and chopped

1 medium-sized tomato, peeled and chopped

4 medium-sized mushrooms, chopped

½ teaspoon dried rosemary

Pinch salt

Pinch black pepper

4 oz (115g) chicken livers, sinews removed, and drained

1. Melt two-thirds of the **butter** in a small frying pan over moderate heat until bubbling. Add the **onion,** and cook for 5 minutes or until soft.

2. Add the **tomato, mushrooms, rosemary, salt** and **pepper,** and cook for 3 minutes. Push the vegetables to one side of the pan.

3. Add the remaining butter and the **chicken livers** to the pan, and cook them for 2 minutes on each side. Stir the livers in with the vegetables, and cook for 4 more minutes.

Curried Tomato

Preparation: **3 min**   Cooking: **4 min**   Cals per portion: **250**

2 medium-sized tomatoes, halved

Pinch salt

¼ teaspoon black pepper

1 oz (25g) butter, softened

½ teaspoon curry powder

¼ small onion, peeled and finely chopped

1. Preheat the grill. Sprinkle the **tomato** halves with the **salt** and **pepper.** Combine the **butter, curry powder** and **onion,** and spread the tops of the tomato halves with this mixture.

2. Place the tomato halves on the rack of the grill pan, or in an individual baking tin. Grill 4in (100mm) from the heat for 4 or 5 minutes, until the tomatoes are just tender.

Grilled Fish with Cucumber Sauce

Preparation: **5 min**   Cooking: **8 min**   Cals per portion: **390**

1 oz (25g) butter, melted

2 tablespoons seeded and grated cucumber

½ small onion, peeled and finely chopped

2 dashes Tabasco sauce

Juice ½ small lemon

1 tablespoon chopped parsley

6 oz (175g) white, firm-fleshed fish fillet

Salt and black pepper

Serve with new potatoes sprinkled with dried dill.

1. Preheat the grill. In a small bowl, combine the **butter, cucumber, onion, Tabasco sauce, lemon juice** and **parsley.** Spread about one-third of this mixture on the bottom of a small, shallow casserole dish. Place the **fish fillet** in the dish, and top with the remaining mixture. Sprinkle with **salt** and **pepper** to taste.

2. Grill 4in (100mm) from the heat for about 8 minutes. Baste the fish twice with the juices in the dish. If the fish flakes easily when tested with a fork, it is done.

Baked Fish with Tomatoes and Tarragon

Preparation: **7 min**   Cooking: **15 min**   Cals per portion: **310**

6 oz (175g) white, firm-fleshed fish fillet

3 small tomatoes, peeled and chopped

1 small onion, chopped

½ small red pepper, seeded and chopped

¼ teaspoon dried tarragon

Pinch salt

½ oz (15g) butter

1. Preheat the oven to 200°C (400°F, gas mark 6). Place the **fish** in a greased, shallow casserole dish. If the fillet is very thin, fold it in half.

2. In a small bowl, combine the **tomatoes, onion, red pepper, tarragon** and **salt.** Sprinkle the mixture over the fish, then dot with the **butter.**

3. Bake for 15 minutes until the fish flakes easily when tested with a fork. Serve with rice and Peas with Watercress Butter Sauce, page 271.

Smoked Fish and Ginger Stir-fry

Preparation: **5 min**   Cooking: **3 min**

Cals per portion: **440**

3 spring onions, chopped diagonally

2 tablespoons olive oil

1 clove garlic, peeled and finely chopped

Thin slice fresh root ginger, chopped

Pinch ground coriander

1 small yellow pepper, seeded and cut into thin strips

Generous pinch salt

Generous pinch black pepper

Grated rind ¼ lemon

6 oz (175g) smoked haddock, coarsely flaked

Tip: Use fresh coriander, chopped when available.

1. Fry the **spring onions** in the **olive oil** in a deep frying pan over a moderate heat for 2 minutes.

2. Add the **garlic, ginger, coriander, yellow pepper, salt, pepper** and **lemon rind;** stir-fry for a further 2 minutes.

3. Add the flaked smoked **haddock** and stir-fry for 3 minutes.

4. Serve piping hot, with a salad and rice.

Sausage Fried Rice

Preparation: **10 min**   Cooking: **20 min**

Cals per portion: **565**

4 oz (115g) sausage meat

2 oz (50g) rice

1 small onion, peeled and finely chopped

4 medium-sized mushrooms, thinly sliced

½ clove garlic, peeled and finely chopped

3 small tomatoes, peeled and chopped

7 fl oz (200ml) chicken stock

½ teaspoon salt

Pinch black pepper

2 or 3 drops Tabasco sauce

1 tablespoon chopped parsley

To complete the meal, serve this with a green salad, which you can prepare while the sausage and rice are cooking.

1. Cook the **sausage meat** in a medium-sized, heavy frying pan over moderate heat for 3 minutes, stirring occasionally. Add the **rice, onion** and **mushrooms,** and cook for 3 minutes, stirring frequently.

2. Add the **garlic, tomatoes, stock, salt** and **pepper.** Cover, and simmer for 20 minutes or until the rice is tender. Stir in the **Tabasco sauce** and **parsley,** and serve.

Ham and Mushroom Steaklet

Preparation: **15 min**   Cooking: **7 min**   Cals per portion: **565**

1 small onion, peeled and finely chopped

1 tablespoon vegetable oil

2 oz (50g) mushrooms, chopped

1 clove garlic, peeled and crushed

1 tablespoon flour

4 tablespoons milk

1 hard-boiled egg, shelled and chopped

2 tablespoons chopped parsley

3 oz (75g) finely chopped ham

1 egg, beaten

2 tablespoons dry breadcrumbs

¾ oz (20g) butter

1. Fry the **onion** in the **oil** for 2 minutes; add the **mushrooms** and **garlic,** and fry for a further 2 minutes.

2. Stir in the **flour** and cook for 1 minute; add the **milk** and stir over the heat until the mixture has thickened.

3. Mix in the **hard-boiled egg, parsley** and **ham;** shape into an oval patty.

4. Dip into the beaten **egg** and then into the **breadcrumbs** to coat evenly.

5. Place the steaklet on the rack of the grill pan and dot with a quarter of the **butter;** grill for 3 minutes. Turn the steaklet, dot with a further quarter of the butter and grill for 4 minutes.

6. Meanwhile, melt the remaining butter in a small saucepan, add the remaining beaten egg, and scramble lightly over a low heat.

7. Serve the grilled steaklet topped with the scrambled egg, and with a side salad.

COOKING FOR ONE

Macaroni with Bacon, Tomato and Pepper

Preparation and cooking: **17 min**   Cals per portion: **720**

4 oz (115g) elbow macaroni

2 rashers bacon, cut into ¾ in (20mm) strips

3 shallots, peeled and cut into ½ in (15mm) slices

½ small red pepper, cored, seeded and chopped

2 small tomatoes, peeled and chopped

2 tablespoons chopped parsley

Pinch dried basil

Pinch salt

Pinch black pepper

2 tablespoons grated Parmesan cheese

Prepare the onions, red pepper, tomatoes and parsley before you start the recipe. If the sauce is done before the macaroni, keep it warm over a very low heat.

1. Cook the **macaroni** according to packet directions. Meanwhile, cook the **bacon** in a medium-sized frying pan over moderately high heat for 3 minutes, or until almost crisp. Pour off all but 2 tablespoons of the bacon fat. Add the **shallots** and **red pepper,** and cook for 2 minutes. Add the **tomatoes, parsley, basil, salt** and **black pepper,** and cook for 3 more minutes. Remove from the heat and put aside.

2. When the macaroni is done, drain it thoroughly in a colander and add it to the pan with the bacon and vegetables. Toss to mix over low heat. Add the **cheese,** and toss again.

Pasta Custard Cheese

Preparation: **10 min**   Cooking: **25 min**   Cals per portion: **820**

3 oz (75g) pasta shells

2 eggs

7 fl oz (200ml) milk

2 oz (50g) grated Cheddar cheese

½ teaspoon French mustard

¼ teaspoon salt

Generous pinch black pepper

¼ teaspoon caraway seeds

1 small onion, peeled and very thinly sliced

1. Preheat the oven to 180°C (350°F, gas mark 4). Cook the **pasta shells** in boiling salted water until just tender. Drain thoroughly.

2. Meanwhile, beat the **eggs** with the **milk, cheese, mustard, salt, pepper** and **caraway seeds.**

3. Place the drained pasta in a small, greased ovenproof dish; pour on the milk mixture, and scatter the sliced **onion** over the top.

4. Bake in the oven for 25 minutes until just set.

Butterscotch Peach Crisp

Preparation: **5 min**   Cooking: **15 min**   Cals per portion: **420**

1 large ripe peach, peeled, halved, stoned and sliced

2 tablespoons dark soft brown sugar

1 tablespoon plain flour

Pinch ground cinnamon

Small pinch ground nutmeg

1 oz (25g) butter or margarine

1. Preheat the oven to 180°C (350°F, gas mark 4). Place the sliced **peach** in a buttered individual ovenproof dish.

2. In a small bowl, combine the **sugar, flour, cinnamon** and **nutmeg.** Cut in the **butter** with a fork until the mixture resembles coarse crumbs. Sprinkle over the peach slices, and bake for 15 minutes.

> *Tip: Try apple or pear, peeled and sliced, in place of the peach.*

Strawberries in Snow

Preparation: **5 min**   Cals per serving: **150**

4 tablespoons thick natural yoghurt or soured cream

1 level tablespoon icing sugar, or to taste

¼ teaspoon finely grated orange rind

4 oz (115g) strawberries, hulled

Fresh mint sprig (optional)

Mix together the **yoghurt, sugar** and **orange rind.** Spoon the mixture onto dessert plates and then arrange the **strawberries** on top. Garnish with a sprig of **mint,** if used.

> *Tip: You can substitute many kinds of fresh or canned fruit for strawberries, for example: seedless green grapes, raspberries, sliced peaches, pitted cherries or sliced bananas.*

BREAKFASTS

Fruits and Cereals

Cooked Breakfasts

Breads and Pancakes

BREAKFASTS

Since breakfast sets the scene for the day, it should be good. If you are tired of packaged cereal or bacon and eggs, vary your breakfasts with some of the recipes in this section.

Make your own nutritious muesli. Branch out with a spectacular Giant Pancake, the spiciness of Grandma's French Toast or a hearty Ginger Waffle, or add a fresh fruit dish.

Muesli

Preparation: **5 min**   Makes **1¾ lb (800g)**   Cals per 5 tablespoons: **275**

6 oz (175g) oatmeal

3 oz (75g) wheatgerm

3 oz (75g) bran or bran cereal

3 oz (75g) raisins

3 oz (75g) diced dried fruit – apricots, apples, prunes, figs or a mixture

3 oz (75g) chopped nuts, such as walnuts, pecans, cashews, hazelnuts or almonds

3 oz (75g) sunflower seeds

2 oz (50g) sesame seeds

1½ oz (40g) flaked coconut

Make your own muesli, and enjoy a fast and nutritious breakfast. All the ingredients should be available in your local supermarket or health food store.

Combine all the ingredients and store in an airtight container in the refrigerator. (It will keep for at least 2 weeks.) Serve with milk or natural yoghurt, and sugar or honey.

> *Tip: If you like, you can cook the muesli like porridge. For each serving, bring 6fl oz (175ml) of water to the boil; add 5 tablespoons of muesli and a pinch of salt, and cook over moderate heat for 5 minutes. Remove from the heat, cover, and let the muesli stand for 3 minutes. Sweeten, if desired, with brown sugar or honey.*

Apples in Brown Sugar Sauce ½

Preparation: **5 min**   Cooking: **7 min**   Serves **4**   Cals per portion: **175**

2 oz (50g) butter or margarine

4 medium-sized apples, cored, peeled and cut into thin slices

1 tablespoon moist dark brown sugar

¼ teaspoon ground nutmeg

2 fl oz (50ml) apple juice

These apples go perfectly with bacon and eggs or with pancakes.

1. Melt the **butter** in a medium-sized, heavy frying pan over moderate heat. Add the **apples,** and cook, stirring frequently, for 5 minutes.

2. Sprinkle the apples with the **sugar, nutmeg** and **apple juice.** Continue to cook, shaking the pan, until the sugar melts and the mixture comes to the boil.

> *Tip: Firm pears can be cooked in the same way.*

Baked Bananas ½ 🐷

Preparation: **3 min**   Cooking: **15 min**   Serves **4**   Cals per portion: **145**

4 bananas, peeled and halved
lengthwise

Juice ½ lemon

1½ oz (40g) butter or
margarine, melted

Preheat the oven to 180°C (350°F, gas mark 4).
Lay the **bananas** over the bottom of a buttered
baking dish. Sprinkle with the **lemon juice**
and brush with the **butter.** Bake for
15 minutes, turning the bananas once about
halfway through the cooking.

Peach Ambrosia ½

Preparation: **7 min**   Serves **4**   Cals per portion: **210**

1 medium-sized grapefruit

2 medium-sized peaches

1 x 8 oz (225g) can pineapple
pieces in natural juice, drained

2 oz (50g) seedless green grapes

Juice ½ small lemon

1½ oz (40g) flaked coconut

2 fl oz (50ml) soured cream or
natural yoghurt

2 tablespoons chopped toasted
almonds

*Commonly thought of as a side dish or dessert, ambrosia
makes a nutritious, appetising breakfast. Allow time to
chill the ambrosia after assembling it, or start with cold
ingredients.*

1. Peel and segment the **grapefruit,** removing
all the pith. Peel and slice the **peaches,** and
remove the stones.

2. In a mixing bowl, gently fold together the
grapefruit segments, peaches, **pineapple,
grapes, lemon juice, coconut** and **soured
cream.** Just before serving, sprinkle the fruit
and soured cream mixture with the **almonds.**

Melon, Orange and Grapefruit Cocktail

Preparation: **16 min**   Serves **4**   Cals per portion: **80**

1 small ripe melon (or half a
larger one)

2 oranges

1 pink grapefruit

Juice 2 oranges

Juice 1 grapefruit

2 tablespoons caster sugar

1. Halve the **melon** and remove the pips; cut
the flesh into cubes.

2. Peel and segment the **oranges** and **pink
grapefruit,** and put into a bowl.

3. Mix the **orange** and **grapefruit juices** with
the **sugar,** and spoon over the prepared fruit;
toss lightly together.

4. Serve in small bowls with natural yoghurt.

> **Tip:** *If you have the chance, prepare the fruit in
> advance; the cocktail tastes even better if chilled for
> an hour or two before serving.*

Ginger Waffles

Preparation: **5 min**   Cooking: **20 min**   Serves **4**   Cals per portion: **385**

6 oz (175g) plain flour

1½ teaspoons baking powder

½ teaspoon bicarbonate of soda

1 teaspoon ground ginger

¼ teaspoon ground nutmeg

1 teaspoon ground cinnamon

8 fl oz (225ml) buttermilk

2 eggs, lightly beaten

2 oz (50g) butter, melted

1 tablespoon golden syrup
or molasses

1½ oz (40g) moist dark
brown sugar

1. In a mixing bowl, combine the **flour, baking powder, bicarbonate of soda, ginger, nutmeg** and **cinnamon.** Stir in the **buttermilk, eggs, butter, golden syrup** and **brown sugar,** and mix until smooth.

2. Cook the waffles in a waffle iron according to manufacturer's directions. You should get 4 large waffles, about 8 x 8in (200 x 200mm), and they should take about 5 minutes each to cook.

> *Tip: You can use this batter to make large pancakes instead of waffles. Simply spoon a quarter of the batter at a time into a large, buttered frying pan and cook over moderate heat for 4 minutes on each side, or until browned.*

Giant Pancake

Preparation: **5 min**   Cooking: **16 min**   Serves **4**   Cals per portion: **310**

This pancake serves 4, but after you try it you may want to double the recipe for second helpings. If you do, use two pans, and put the second one into the oven as you take out and serve the first. If you do not have a pan with a heatproof handle, melt the butter in a small saucepan and pour into a shallow baking dish; then pour in the batter and bake as described.

2 eggs

2 oz (50g) plain flour

4 fl oz (115ml) milk

¼ teaspoon ground nutmeg

3 oz (75g) butter or margarine,
cut into small pieces

2 tablespoons icing sugar

Juice ½ lemon

1. Preheat the oven to 220°C (425°F, gas mark 7). In a mixing bowl, beat the **eggs** lightly with a whisk, then beat in the **flour, milk** and **nutmeg.**

2. Melt the **butter** over moderate heat in a large, heavy frying pan with a heatproof handle. When the butter is hot, immediately pour in all the batter. Bake for 15 to 20 minutes, or until golden-brown and puffed.

3. Sift the **icing sugar** over the pancake and return it to the oven for 1 or 2 minutes. Remove the pancake from the oven and sprinkle it with the **lemon juice.** Cut into wedges, and serve with fruit syrup, jam, honey or maple syrup.

> *Tips: 1. The pancake will puff while baking, but when taken from the oven it will fall, resembling a large crêpe. 2. As a variation, after heating the butter, add 1 apple that has been cored, peeled and sliced tissue thin, and cook for 1 minute. Spread the apple slices out to cover the bottom of the pan, then pour the batter over the apples and bake for 15 minutes. Omit the icing sugar and lemon juice, but sprinkle the finished pancake with a mixture of 2 tablespoons brown sugar and 1½ teaspoons ground cinnamon.*

Herrings in Oatmeal

Preparation: **5 min**   Cooking: **6 min**   Serves **4**   Cals per portion: **445**

4 small herrings, filleted

2 tablespoons plain flour

½ teaspoon dry mustard

¼ teaspoon salt

¼ teaspoon black pepper

1 egg, beaten

2 oz (50g) fine oatmeal

1½ oz (40g) butter

2 tablespoons olive oil

Juice 1 lemon

1. Dust the **herring fillets** in a mixture of **flour, mustard, salt** and **pepper.**

2. Dip the fish fillets into the beaten **egg** and coat evenly with the **oatmeal.**

3. Heat the **butter** and **olive oil,** and fry the fish fillets for 3 minutes on each side. (It is important not to overcook them.)

4. Drain quickly on absorbent paper and serve piping hot with **lemon juice** squeezed over the top.

> **Tip:** As an accompaniment to the Herrings in Oatmeal, try serving scrambled egg with a little coarse-grained mustard added.

Black Pudding with Apple ½

Preparation: **11 min**   Cooking: **2 min**   Serves **4**   Cals per portion: **395**

1 small onion, peeled and thinly sliced

¾ oz (20g) butter

2 dessert apples, cored and thinly sliced

Juice ½ lemon

1 tablespoon brown sugar

¼ teaspoon salt

¼ teaspoon black pepper

3 rashers lean bacon, chopped

12 oz (350g) black pudding, sliced

1 tablespoon chopped sage

1. Fry the **onion** gently in the **butter** in a large frying pan for 3 minutes. Add the **apples** and fry gently for a further 3 minutes, adding the **lemon juice, brown sugar, salt** and **pepper** for the last minute.

2. Remove the apple mixture to a plate and keep warm.

3. Add the **bacon** to the pan and fry for 1 minute; add the **black pudding** and fry for 4 minutes, turning once.

4. Return the apple mixture to the pan, sprinkle with the **sage,** and cook gently together for 2 minutes.

5. Serve immediately with a coarse-grained bread.

Kipper Scramble

Preparation: **5 min** Cooking: **3 min**   Serves **4** Cals per portion: **425**

4 eggs

¼ teaspoon salt

¼ teaspoon black pepper

1 teaspoon anchovy essence

Juice ¼ lemon

1½ oz (40g) butter

12 oz (350g) kipper fillet, flaked

3 tablespoons single cream

Triangular toast croutons

1. Beat the **eggs** with the **salt, pepper** and **anchovy essence;** add **lemon juice** to taste.

2. Melt the **butter** in a pan (preferably non-stick); add the flaked **kipper,** and stir for 2 to 3 minutes over gentle heat.

3. Add the egg mixture and cook, stirring continuously, until the mixture starts to form soft, creamy flakes.

4. Stir in the **cream** and continue cooking for 30 seconds.

5. Serve piping hot with the **croutons.**

Quick Eggs Benedict ½

Preparation: **15 min** Cooking: **5 min**   Serves **4** Cals per portion: **620**

Eggs Benedict is a popular dish for Sunday brunch. Try this quick, simple version using a foolproof, mock hollandaise sauce.

3 oz (75g) butter or margarine

4 thin slices cooked ham

2 English muffins, split

1¼ pints (725ml) water

1 tablespoon cider vinegar

½ teaspoon salt

4 eggs

Juice ½ lemon

8 fl oz (225ml) mayonnaise

1. Melt ½oz (15g) of the **butter** in a medium-sized, heavy frying pan over moderate heat. Add the **ham,** and cook for 1 minute on each side, or until lightly browned. Meanwhile, toast the **muffins** and butter them with ½oz (15g) of the butter. Arrange the muffins on serving plates and top with the ham. Put aside and keep warm.

2. Combine the **water, vinegar** and **salt** in a medium-sized frying pan, and bring to the boil, then reduce the heat until the water simmers. Break the **eggs** one at a time into a saucer and carefully slide each egg into the water. Cook until the eggs are done as you like them – 3 to 5 minutes. Remove the eggs with a slotted spoon, let them drain, then place them on the muffins.

3. While the eggs cook, melt the remaining butter in a saucepan over low heat. Gradually beat in the **lemon juice** and **mayonnaise** with a wire whisk. Continue to beat for 2 minutes. Remove from the heat and spoon over the eggs.

Egg in a Hole ⊙ ½ 🐷

Preparation: **6 min**   Cooking: **4 min**   Serves **4**   Cals per portion: **230**

Cook your egg and toast together for a breakfast treat. You can substitute wholemeal or mixed-grain bread for the white bread.

4 slices white bread

2 oz (50g) butter or margarine

4 eggs

¼ teaspoon salt

Pinch black pepper

> *Tip: This recipe can be reduced proportionally to serve 1, 2 or 3.*

1. Using a 2¼in (60mm) diameter pastry cutter or the rim of a glass, cut a hole in the centre of each slice of **bread.** Melt half of the **butter** in a large, heavy frying pan over moderately high heat. Add the bread (including the cut-out centres) and cook until browned lightly – about 3 minutes.

2. Turn the bread over, add the remaining butter, and reduce the heat to moderately low. Break an **egg** into each hole, and season with the **salt** and **pepper.** Cover, and cook until the eggs are set – about 4 minutes. Serve with the cut-out toast centres on the side.

Eggs in Sausage Rings ½

Preparation: **5 min**   Cooking: **8 min**   Serves **4**   Cals per portion: **400**

Here is a novel way of cooking sausage and eggs that makes an attractive dish you can serve for lunch as well as breakfast. Try it with potatoes and Baked Stuffed Tomatoes, page 83.

1 lb (450g) pork sausage meat, cut into 4 equal pieces and flattened slightly

4 eggs

1 tablespoon chopped fresh chives, or 1 teaspoon dried chives

¼ teaspoon salt

Pinch black pepper

> *Tip: If you do not have a pastry cutter, use the rim of a glass.*

1. Place the pieces of **sausage meat** 4in (100mm) apart on a sheet of waxed paper. Cover with a second sheet and, using a rolling pin, roll the meat out into circles about 4in (100mm) in diameter. They will be about ½in (15mm) thick.

2. Remove the top sheet of paper. Using a 2¼in (60mm) diameter round pastry cutter, cut a hole in the centre of each patty, and remove the centre circles. Place the sausage rings and the circles in a large frying pan.

3. Turn the heat to moderately high and cook the sausage for 3 minutes. Flip the sausage rings and circles with an egg slice, then break an **egg** into the centre of each ring. Sprinkle with the **chives, salt** and **pepper.**

4. Cook for 5 to 8 minutes, depending on how firm you want the eggs to be. Top with the sausage circles and serve.

Spanish Scrambled Eggs ½

Preparation: **8 min**   Cooking: **6 min**   Serves **4**   Cals per portion: **330**

Try this version of scrambled eggs for a change. You can add more chillies, if you like, or leave them out completely. To save time, chop the pimentos, chillies, shallots and tomato while the bacon is cooking.

6 rashers bacon, cut into ¾ in (20mm) strips

6 eggs, lightly beaten

2 oz (50g) canned pimentos, drained and chopped

1 or 2 canned whole green chillies, rinsed, seeded and chopped

Pinch salt

1 oz (25g) butter or margarine

6 to 8 shallots, trimmed and finely chopped

1 large tomato, peeled and chopped

1. Cook the **bacon** in a medium-sized frying pan over moderately high heat for 5 minutes, or until crisp. Using a slotted spoon, remove the bacon from the pan and drain on absorbent paper. Discard the bacon fat.

2. In a small bowl, combine the **eggs, pimentos, chillies** and **salt,** and put aside.

3. Melt the **butter** in the pan over moderate heat. Add the **shallots** and **tomato,** and cook for 3 minutes, or until the shallots are tender.

4. Add the egg mixture and continue to cook, stirring, for 3 to 4 minutes, or until the eggs are firm but still moist. Spoon onto a serving dish and crumble the bacon over the top.

> *Tips: 1. As a variation, omit the bacon and add 4oz (115g) of pork sausage meat to the onions to brown. 2. Instead of scrambling the eggs, let them set into an omelette-style pancake; when it has browned on the bottom, cut into wedges and serve.*

Oven-Baked Tomatoes ½

Preparation: **7 min**   Cooking: **15 min**   Serves **4**   Cals per portion: **135**

12 firm tomatoes, halved

1 oz (25g) butter

1 tablespoon olive oil

1 clove garlic, peeled and finely chopped

2 tablespoons chopped parsley

¼ teaspoon salt

Large pinch black pepper

2 tablespoons Worcestershire sauce

2 oz (50g) chopped ham

1. Preheat the oven to 190°C (375°F, gas mark 5).

2. Put the **tomatoes** into an ovenproof dish, cut sides uppermost.

3. Heat the **butter** and **oil** gently in a pan; add the **garlic, parsley, salt, pepper, Worcestershire sauce** and chopped **ham.**

4. Spoon evenly over the tomatoes and bake for 15 minutes.

5. Serve piping hot.

Grandma's French Toast ½

Preparation: **15 min**   Cooking: **8 min**   Serves **4**   Cals per portion: **310**

Use up day-old bread and give the family a treat at the same time.

8 fl oz (225ml) milk

2 tablespoons sugar

2 or 3 drops vanilla essence

½ teaspoon grated lemon rind

¼ teaspoon ground nutmeg

8 slices day-old French bread, cut ¾ in (20mm) thick

½ oz (15g) butter or margarine

1 tablespoon vegetable oil

4 eggs

Pinch salt

1. In a large bowl combine the **milk, sugar, vanilla, lemon rind** and **nutmeg.** Soak the **bread** in the mixture for 10 minutes, or until all the mixture is absorbed.

2. Meanwhile, heat the **butter** with the **oil** in a large, heavy frying pan over moderately high heat. Beat the **eggs** with the **salt.**

3. Dip each slice of bread into the beaten eggs, then place in the pan and cook for 4 minutes on each side, or until golden-brown.

Tips: 1. You can use sliced hard rolls, raisin bread or firm-textured white bread instead of the French bread in this dish. If you use raisin bread, substitute cinnamon for the nutmeg. 2. If the bread will not fit into the pan in 1 batch, cook in 2 batches, adding another ½oz (15g) each of butter and oil to the pan for the second batch. 3. Omit the sugar and vanilla and serve with grilled bacon rashers.

Blintz Pancakes ½

Preparation: **5 min**   Cooking: **24 min**   Serves **4**   Cals per portion: **295**

Blintzes are pancakes that are usually stuffed with soft cheese and topped with soured cream. In this variation, the cheese and soured cream are added to the batter.

4 oz (115g) plain flour

1 tablespoon sugar

½ teaspoon salt

8 fl oz (225ml) soured cream or natural yoghurt

8 oz (225g) cottage cheese

4 eggs, lightly beaten

1 tablespoon vegetable oil

1. Mix the **flour, sugar** and **salt** together in a mixing bowl. Add the **soured cream, cottage cheese** and **eggs.** Fold the ingredients together until the flour is barely moistened.

2. Heat the **oil** in a large, heavy frying pan over moderate heat. Drop enough batter into the pan to form 4 pancakes – about 3 tablespoons of batter per pancake. Cook for 3 or 4 minutes, until browned on the bottom, then turn the pancakes and cook for another 3 or 4 minutes.

3. Transfer the pancakes to a plate and place in a warm 120°C (250°F, gas mark ½) oven, while you make 3 more batches of pancakes in the same way. Add more oil to the pan if necessary.

Tips: 1. You can cut the cooking time of this dish in half if you use two pans. 2. Making these pancakes with natural yoghurt instead of soured cream reduces the calories per portion.

SANDWICHES AND SNACKS

Salads

Sandwiches

Hot Snacks

Whole Loaf Sandwiches

SANDWICHES AND SNACKS

Don't fall into the boring sandwich trap – a cheese and tomato today and a corned beef and pickle tomorrow. Add variety to packed lunches with the recipes in this section. To save time, keep a few hard-boiled eggs on hand for the recipes that call for them.

High-Protein Vegetarian Salad

Preparation: **8 min**

Serves **4** Cals per portion: **385**

3 tablespoons natural yoghurt

2 tablespoons vegetable oil

Pinch salt

¼ teaspoon ground cumin

2 x 15 oz (425g) cans chickpeas, rinsed and drained

2 medium-sized peppers, seeded and chopped

1 small onion, peeled and chopped

2 tablespoons sunflower seeds

Put this salad in tightly sealed plastic containers and pack, along with fresh fruit, for a school or office lunch.

In a mixing bowl, combine the **yoghurt, oil, salt** and **cumin.** Add the **chickpeas, peppers, onion** and **sunflower seeds,** and toss to mix. Taste for seasoning, and add more salt and cumin if desired.

Tips: 1. *Use chopped walnuts in place of the sunflower seeds if you like.* **2.** *You can substitute soured cream for the yoghurt, but remember that you will increase the number of calories.*

Chinese Chicken Salad ½

Preparation and cooking: **20 min**

Serves **6** Cals per portion: **295**

4 skinned and boned chicken breasts

½ teaspoon salt

1 x 8 oz (225g) can crushed pineapple, drained

2 stems celery, chopped

2 shallots, peeled and finely chopped

2 tablespoons vegetable oil

2 tablespoons soya sauce

2 teaspoons white wine vinegar

1. Put the **chicken breasts** in a large saucepan with just enough water to cover. Add the **salt.** Bring to the boil, lower the heat, cover, and simmer about 15 minutes. Transfer the chicken to a plate to cool. Save the chicken stock for another use.

2. Meanwhile, in a large mixing bowl, combine the **pineapple, celery, shallots, oil, soya sauce** and **vinegar.** Put aside.

3. When the chicken is cool enough to handle (in about 5 minutes), cut it into thin strips. Add the chicken to the pineapple mixture, and toss to mix thoroughly.

Golden Ham Salad Sandwiches ½

Preparation: **22 min** Cooking: **8 min**   Serves **4** Cals per portion: **430**

6 oz (175g) finely chopped or minced cooked ham

2 hard-boiled eggs, chopped

Squeeze of lemon juice

1 teaspoon French mustard

2 teaspoons Worcestershire sauce

½ teaspoon salt

½ small pepper, seeded and finely chopped

3 tablespoons mayonnaise

2 tablespoons finely chopped dill pickle or gherkin

8 slices bread

1 egg

2 fl oz (50ml) milk

2 oz (50g) butter or margarine

If you like, serve this as a salad on lettuce leaves instead of bread, and omit Steps 2 and 3. The preparation time includes 15 minutes for hard-boiling the eggs.

1. In a mixing bowl, combine the **ham, hard-boiled eggs, lemon juice, mustard, Worcestershire sauce, salt, pepper, mayonnaise** and **pickle.** Spread the ham mixture on 4 slices of the **bread,** and top with the remaining bread. Press together.

2. In a shallow bowl or pie plate, beat together the **egg** and **milk.** Carefully holding each sandwich to keep the filling intact, dip it quickly on each side into the egg and milk mixture.

3. Melt the **butter** in a large, heavy frying pan over moderate heat. Place the sandwiches in the pan, and cook for 4 or 5 minutes on each side, or until golden-brown.

> **Tips: 1.** *The ham mixture can be made in advance and refrigerated for 1 or 2 days.* **2.** *You can substitute leftover cooked pork, beef, lamb or chicken for the ham.*

Steak Sandwich ⟩

Preparation: **5 min** Cooking: **10 min**   Serves **4** Cals per portion: **510**

2 tablespoons vegetable oil

2 onions, peeled and thinly sliced

4 thin tender steaks

1½ oz (40g) butter, softened

8 slices white or wholemeal bread

½ teaspoon salt

Pinch freshly ground black pepper

1 teaspoon Worcestershire sauce

1. Heat the **oil** in a large frying pan over a moderate heat, add the **onions** and cook until lightly browned. Remove the onions from the pan with a slotted spoon and keep warm.

2. Turn up the heat and fry the **steaks** in the remaining oil for 2 minutes each side. Meanwhile, toast and **butter** the **bread.**

3. Place a steak on a slice of buttered toast, season with the **salt, pepper** and a dash of **Worcestershire sauce.** Top each steak with a spoonful of fried onions, and cover with the remaining buttered toast.

Tuna Melt ½

Preparation: **12 min**   Cooking: **3 min**   Serves **4**   Cals per portion: **540**

4 muffins, split, or 8 slices wholemeal bread

1 x 7 oz (198g) can tuna, drained and flaked

½ small pepper, seeded and finely chopped

½ small onion, peeled and finely chopped

5 tablespoons mayonnaise

1 teaspoon French mustard

4 teaspoons Worcestershire sauce

¼ teaspoon black pepper

8 oz (225g) extra strong Cheddar cheese, thinly sliced

1 canned pimento, cut into 8 strips

Melted cheese on tuna salad may seem unusual, but the combination is a good one.

1. Preheat the grill. Toast the **muffins,** and put aside.

2. Meanwhile, in a mixing bowl, combine the **tuna, pepper, onion, mayonnaise, mustard, Worcestershire sauce** and **black pepper.** Spread the tuna mixture on the 8 muffin halves, and top with the **cheese** slices.

3. Grill for 3 minutes, or until the cheese melts and browns lightly. Top each half with a **pimento** strip. Serve with a lettuce and tomato salad.

> **Tips: 1.** *The tuna mixture can be made a day in advance, but do not spread it on the muffins until just before grilling.* **2.** *Cut each muffin into 8 wedges and serve as hors d'oeuvres.*

Baked Tomato Avocado ½

Preparation: **15 min**   Cooking: **15 min**   Serves **4**   Cals per portion: **215**

2 large, slightly under-ripe avocados

Juice ½ lemon

1 clove garlic, peeled and crushed

4 tomatoes, seeded and chopped

3 oz (75g) smoked ham, chopped

1 tablespoon chopped fresh chives

4 tablespoons single cream

Few drops Tabasco sauce

¼ teaspoon salt

2 tablespoons fine, crisp breadcrumbs

1. Preheat the oven to 190°C (375°F, gas mark 5). Halve and stone the **avocados,** and using a small spoon (a serrated grapefruit spoon is ideal), scoop out the flesh.

2. Brush the hollowed avocado 'shells' with **lemon juice,** and toss the scooped-out avocado flesh in the remaining lemon juice.

3. Mix the avocado with the **garlic, chopped tomatoes, ham, chives, cream, Tabasco** and **salt;** spoon back into the avocado 'shells', and top with the **breadcrumbs.**

4. Bake in the preheated oven for 15 minutes, and serve piping hot.

Sweetcorn Rarebit

Preparation: **15 min**   Cooking: **5 min**   Serves **4**   Cals per portion: **495**

½ oz (15g) butter or margarine

1 small pepper, seeded and chopped

1 medium-sized tomato, peeled and chopped

8 oz (225g) sweetcorn kernels

2 whole canned green chillies, rinsed, seeded and chopped

¼ teaspoon salt

12 oz (350g) grated strong Cheddar cheese

4 slices toast

1 canned pimento, sliced

1 tablespoon finely chopped parsley

Try this variation of cheese on toast for brunch or a television snack. You can grate the cheese while the pepper is cooking, but you must prepare the remaining ingredients before you start the recipe.

1. Melt the **butter** in the top of a double saucepan set directly over moderate heat. Add the **pepper,** and cook until soft – about 5 minutes. Meanwhile, bring about 1½in (40mm) of water to a simmer in the bottom of the double saucepan.

2. Place the top of the double saucepan over the hot water, and add the **tomato, sweetcorn, chillies, salt** and **cheese.** Stir until the mixture is well blended and the cheese has melted – about 5 minutes. Serve over the **toast,** and garnish with the **pimento** and **parsley.**

Tip: Instead of serving the rarebit on toast, try it with tortillas that have been warmed in the oven, or over toasted muffins or crumpets.

Blue Rarebit

Preparation: **12 min**   Cooking: **4 min**   Serves **4**   Cals per portion: **530**

10 oz (275g) blue cheese, crumbled

4 tablespoons mayonnaise

2 eggs, separated

1½ oz (40g) chopped walnuts

3 spring onions, chopped

¼ teaspoon salt

¼ teaspoon black pepper

4 slices crusty wholemeal bread

1 oz (25g) butter

1. Mix the **blue cheese** with the **mayonnaise, egg** yolks, **walnuts, spring onions, salt** and **pepper.**

2. Whisk the egg whites until stiff but not dry, and fold lightly but thoroughly into the cheese mixture.

3. Spread the **bread** with **butter** on one side only, and grill until pale golden. Turn the slices over.

4. Pile the cheese mixture onto the untoasted sides.

5. Place under the preheated grill and cook until the topping is puffed, melted and golden. Serve immediately.

Sardine Stacks ½

Preparation: 22 min	Serves **6** Cals per portion: **400**

4 fl oz (115ml) mayonnaise

Juice 1 small lemon

2 tablespoons sweet chilli sauce or tomato sauce

12 slices rye or wholemeal bread

6 hard-boiled eggs, sliced

2 x 6 oz (175g) cans sardines, drained and boned

12 lettuce leaves

In a small mixing bowl, combine the **mayonnaise, lemon juice** and **chilli sauce.** Spread this mixture on 6 slices of the **bread,** then evenly distribute the **eggs, sardines** and **lettuce leaves** in layers over the slices. Top with the remaining bread.

*Tips: Omit the egg and substitute: **1.** 3 large tomatoes, thinly sliced. **2.** 1 tablespoon each finely chopped shallot, celery and pepper. **3.** ½ small cucumber, thinly sliced.*

Shrimps in a Basket ½

Preparation: 15 min Cooking: **10 min**	Serves **4** Cals per portion: **410**

4 large, round, crusty brown bread rolls

2 tablespoons melted butter

¼ teaspoon salt

¼ teaspoon black pepper

4 small tubs potted shrimps

4 lemon wedges

1. Preheat the oven to 190°C (375°F, gas mark 5).

2. Take a slice off the top of each **roll,** about ½in (15mm) thick. Carefully scoop out most of the centre, leaving hollowed bread 'shells' about ½in (15mm) thick.

3. Brush inside with melted **butter,** sprinkle with the **salt** and **pepper** and warm in the preheated oven for 5 minutes.

4. Carefully unmould a tub of **potted shrimps** into the centre of each hollowed roll, and place the bread 'lids' back on top.

5. Bake in the oven for 10 minutes, and serve immediately with the **lemon wedges.**

Date Cream Cheese Sandwiches ◎ ½

Preparation: 8 min	Serves **4** Cals per portion: **540**

6 oz (175g) cream cheese

1 tablespoon milk or cream

8 slices buttered wholemeal or rye bread

1½ oz (40g) chopped walnuts or pecans

2 oz (50g) chopped dates

1. In a small bowl, soften the **cream cheese** with the **milk.**

2. Spread the **bread** with the cream cheese. Top 4 of the slices with the **walnuts** and **dates** and sandwich with the remaining bread.

*Tips: **1.** For a heartier sandwich, add a slice of ham or crisp bacon to each sandwich. **2.** Add lettuce to each sandwich if you like.*

Exotic Cheese Sandwiches ½

Preparation: **8 min**   Cooking: **8 min**   Serves **4**   Cals per portion: **470**

4 rashers lean bacon, cut into ¼ in (20mm) strips

6 oz (175g) grated Swiss cheese

½ small pepper, seeded and chopped

2 fl oz (50ml) sweet chilli or tomato sauce

2 teaspoons Worcestershire sauce

8 slices buttered bread

1. Preheat the oven to 220°C (425°F, gas mark 7). Cook the **bacon** in a medium-sized, heavy frying pan over moderately high heat for 5 minutes, or until crisp. Using a slotted spoon, transfer the bacon to absorbent paper to drain.

2. In a mixing bowl, combine the **cheese, pepper, chilli sauce, Worcestershire sauce** and bacon. Spread the mixture on 4 slices of the **bread,** and top with the remaining bread. Place the sandwiches on a baking sheet and bake for 8 minutes.

Chilli Cheddar Sandwiches ⬦ ½ 🐷

Preparation: **10 min**   Serves **4**   Cals per portion: **675**

12 oz (350g) grated strong Cheddar cheese

3½ oz (90g) butter or margarine, softened

4 oz (115g) whole green chillies, rinsed, seeded and chopped

1 small onion, peeled and finely chopped

½ teaspoon ground cumin

8 slices wholemeal bread

Moderately hot and decidedly tasty, these sandwiches will add zest to a packed lunch.

In a mixing bowl, combine the **cheese** and **butter,** then mix in the **chillies, onion** and **cumin.** Spread the cheese mixture on 4 slices of the **bread,** and top with the remaining bread.

> ***Tips: 1.*** *Add tomato and lettuce to each sandwich if you like.* ***2.*** *The cheese mixture can be made in advance; it will keep for a week in the refrigerator.*

Apple Cream Cheese Sandwiches ⬦ ½ 🐷

Preparation: **10 min**   Serves **4**   Cals per portion: **380**

1 medium-sized cooking apple, cored and cut into thin slices

Juice ½ small lemon

4 oz (115g) cream cheese, softened

1 tablespoon honey

8 slices buttered plain or toasted rye bread

Fruit sandwiches? Yes, and they are nutritious and fresh tasting. Pack these sandwiches and take them to work if you have access to a refrigerator or a cool storage space.

1. In a mixing bowl, toss the **apple** slices with the **lemon juice,** and put aside.

2. Mix the **cream cheese** with the **honey** in a small bowl, and spread the mixture on 4 slices of the **bread.** Drain the apples, and place them on the cream cheese. Top with the remaining bread.

Summer Loaf Sandwich ½

Preparation: **15 min**

3 medium-sized carrots, peeled and grated

2 fl oz (50ml) mayonnaise

½ teaspoon salt

¼ teaspoon black pepper

Juice 1 small lemon

8 oz (225g) alfalfa sprouts (optional)

1 large ripe avocado, peeled, stoned and halved lengthwise

1 loaf French bread (about 17 in/430mm long)

4 oz (115g) thinly sliced cooked ham

8 oz (225g) mozzarella or mild Cheddar cheese, thinly sliced

1. In a mixing bowl, combine the **carrots, mayonnaise, salt, pepper,** half the **lemon juice,** and the **alfalfa sprouts** if used. Cut the **avocado** halves lengthwise into thin slices. In a small bowl, toss the slices with the remaining lemon juice.

2. Cut the **bread** in half lengthwise and scoop out the centre of the bottom half, leaving a shell ¾in (20mm) thick. Save the centre to make breadcrumbs.

3. Place half the carrot mixture in the scooped-out half, and cover with the avocado slices, **ham** and **cheese.** Top with the remaining carrot mixture and the other half of the bread. Cut into 4 portions.

Crunchy Indian-style Sandwiches ⊙

Preparation: **8 min**   Cooking: **about 2 min**

10 oz (275g) cooked chicken, pulled into strips

3 tablespoons mango chutney

2 teaspoons curry paste

1 firm banana, sliced

2 tablespoons chopped toasted peanuts

1 red pepper, seeded and chopped

3 spring onions, chopped

8 small poppadoms

¼ cucumber, thinly sliced

1. Mix the **chicken** with the **mango chutney, curry paste, banana, peanuts, red pepper** and **spring onions.**

2. Carefully toast the **poppadoms** on both sides (not too close to the grill), until golden and crisp.

3. Quickly sandwich together in pairs with the prepared chicken mixture and sliced **cucumber,** and serve immediately.

Tip: You can serve with a bowl of natural yoghurt for dunking crisp bits of 'sandwich' in.

SANDWICHES AND SNACKS

Pizza Loaf

Preparation: **10 min**   Cooking: **15 min**   Serves **6**   Cals per portion: **415**

2 tablespoons olive oil or vegetable oil

1 medium-sized onion, peeled and chopped

1 lb (450g) lean minced beef

4 tablespoons tomato purée

½ teaspoon dried oregano

½ teaspoon dried basil

¼ teaspoon dried rosemary

½ teaspoon salt

¼ teaspoon black pepper

1 loaf French bread (about 17 in/430mm long)

8 oz (225g) grated mozzarella or mild Cheddar cheese

1. Preheat the oven to 180°C (350°F, gas mark 4). Heat the **oil** in a medium-sized, heavy frying pan over moderate heat for about 1 minute. Add the **onion** and **beef,** and cook, stirring occasionally, for 5 minutes, or until the onion is soft and the beef has browned. Stir in the **tomato purée, oregano, basil, rosemary, salt** and **pepper.** Cook for 1 minute.

2. Cut the **bread** in half lengthwise and scoop out the centre of each half, leaving a shell ¾in (20mm) thick. Save the centre to make breadcrumbs for future use.

3. Place half the beef mixture in each half loaf, then sprinkle with the **cheese.** Place on a greased baking sheet and bake for 15 minutes, or until the cheese melts. Cut into 6 portions and serve hot.

Pan Bagna

Preparation: **15 min**   Serves **6**   Cals per portion: **220**

1 long French loaf

1 clove garlic, halved

4 tablespoons olive oil

2 teaspoons vinegar

Pinch black pepper

1 small cucumber, thinly sliced

3 large tomatoes, thinly sliced

3 canned pimentos, chopped

1 x 2 oz (50g) can anchovies, drained and rinsed

10 black olives, pitted and chopped

Whole-loaf sandwiches are ideal for lunchtime or picnic fare, and when cut into slices or wedges can provide a snack for 6 or a pre-barbecue appetiser for 8 to 10 people. They are best made the night before so that the juices have time to soak into the bread.

1. Halve the **loaf** lengthwise. Rub the cut sides with the **garlic** and sprinkle with the **olive oil, vinegar** and **pepper.**

2. On one half arrange the **cucumber, tomato, pimentos, anchovies** and **olives.** Put the two halves together and wrap the whole sandwich in foil. Place it between two flat plates, or two baking tins, with a weight on top. Refrigerate until needed.

> **Tips: 1.** *For a stronger flavour, add thinly sliced raw onion and fresh herbs such as basil, marjoram or thyme.* **2.** *Use chopped capers or gherkins and omit the vinegar.* **3.** *Change the filling to suit your taste; try celery, mushrooms, canned artichoke hearts, pickled herrings or tuna; if using tuna, increase the olive oil by a tablespoon.*

SAUCES

Uncooked Sauces

Blender Mayonnaise, page 301
Soured Cream Cucumber Sauce,
    page 303
Soured Cream Horseradish Sauce,
    page 303
Soured Cream Mustard Sauce,
    page 303
Aioli, page 306
Green Sauce, page 306
Pesto, page 307
Lumpfish Roe Mousseline, page 307

Cooked Sauces

Easy White Sauce, page 301
Hollandaise Sauce, page 302
Jiffy Cheese Sauce, page 302
Soured Cream Cheese Sauce,
    page 303
Soured Cream Curry Sauce, page 303
Creole Sauce, page 303
Lemon Sauce for Vegetables,
    page 304
All-Purpose Barbecue Sauce,
    page 304
Olive and Nut Sauce, page 305
Rouille, page 305
Apricot and Mint Sauce, page 307
Red Butter Sauce, page 308
Mushroom and Marsala Sauce,
    page 308

(See also Dessert Sauces, pages 247
and 248)

SAUCES

These sauces have been selected not only for ease and speed of preparation (all but two take less than 12 minutes), but because they can be used to enhance many different foods, from vegetables, eggs and pasta to poultry, meats and seafood.

Blender Mayonnaise

Preparation: **4 min** Makes ½ **pint (285ml)** Cals per tablespoon: **135**

Why not make your own mayonnaise for a change? It takes only 4 minutes in a blender, it is cheaper than bought mayonnaise, and it has a far superior flavour. You can make this recipe in advance and refrigerate it, covered, for 1 week.

1 egg

½ teaspoon salt

¼ teaspoon black pepper

½ teaspoon Dijon or other French mustard

Juice ½ small lemon

8 fl oz (225ml) olive oil at room temperature

1. Put the **egg, salt, pepper, mustard, lemon juice** and a quarter of the **oil** into the blender. Cover and blend on high speed for 30 seconds. Add the remaining oil, pouring it in a very slow, thin, steady stream with the blender running at moderately high speed.

2. Turn off the blender occasionally and clean the sides with a rubber spatula. Add more lemon juice and salt to taste, if necessary.

> *Tips: Try one of the following variations:* **Horseradish** *Mix in 1 to 2 tablespoons creamed horseradish for meat and seafood salads.* **Dill** *Fold in ½ teaspoon dried dill for seafood.* **Curry** *Blend in 1 teaspoon or more curry powder for chicken, meat and egg salads.*

Easy White Sauce ½

Preparation and cooking: **8 min** Makes ½ **pint (285ml)** Cals per tablespoon: **40**

Try this easy method of making white sauce without lumps. Use it in casseroles, over vegetables and for making creamed soups or creamed fish dishes.

8 fl oz (225ml) milk

1½ oz (40g) butter or margarine, softened

2 tablespoons plain flour

¼ teaspoon salt

Pinch black pepper

1. Bring the **milk** to simmering point in a saucepan over moderate heat. Meanwhile, in a small bowl, blend the **butter** and **flour** together with a spoon to form a smooth paste.

2. Add the butter and flour mixture, a teaspoonful at a time, whisking it into the hot milk. Cook, stirring continuously, over moderate heat for 2 to 3 minutes, or until the sauce has thickened and is smooth. Season with the **salt** and **pepper.**

> *Tip: For a thinner sauce, reduce the butter and flour by half; for a thicker sauce, increase the butter by ¾oz (20g) and the flour by 1 tablespoon.*

Hollandaise Sauce ⊘ ½ 🐷

Preparation: **5 min**   Cooking: **5 min**   Makes ⅓ **pint (190ml)**   Cals per tablespoon: **125**

If you don't have a double saucepan, place a trivet or small cooling rack in a larger pan. Make the sauce in a heat-proof bowl or smaller saucepan, standing it on the trivet or rack.

2 large egg yolks

Pinch salt

Pinch black pepper

1 tablespoon tepid water

5 oz (150g) butter or margarine, cut into small cubes

Juice ½ lemon

1. Put 1in (25mm) of water into the bottom of a double saucepan and heat until just below simmering. Make sure the top section does not touch the water and, if necessary, turn the heat down to keep the water just below simmering point. Meanwhile, mix the **egg yolks, salt** and **pepper** with the **tepid water.** Place in the top saucepan and whisk until the mixture just begins to thicken.

2. Whisk in the **butter cubes,** 2 or 3 at a time, letting them melt and blend in before adding more. Whisk continuously until all the butter is incorporated. Turn off the heat and continue to whisk while adding the **lemon juice.** Serve with vegetables, fish or poached eggs.

> *Tips: 1. Use 1 tablespoon white wine vinegar instead of the lemon juice. 2. To make a Maltaise Sauce, use lemon juice instead of the tepid water and whisk in the juice and 1 teaspoon grated rind of a small blood orange after all the butter has been incorporated. 3. For Mustard Sauce, stir in 1 or 2 teaspoons of freshly made English mustard at the last moment.*

Jiffy Cheese Sauce ⊘ ½ 🐷

Preparation: **4 min**   Cooking: **4 min**   Makes **14 fl oz (400ml)**   Cals per tablespoon: **50**

Serve this sauce over cooked vegetables, eggs, pasta or buttered toast.

8 fl oz (225ml) milk

4 oz (115g) grated strong Cheddar cheese

2 tablespoons plain flour

¼ teaspoon salt

Pinch black pepper

Pinch cayenne pepper or paprika

1 oz (25g) butter or margarine, cut into small pieces

Bring the **milk** to simmering point in a saucepan over moderate heat. Reduce the heat, add the **cheese,** and cook, stirring occasionally, until the cheese melts. Do not let the milk boil, and do not stir too much after the cheese melts or the cheese may become stringy. Blend in the **flour** with a wire whisk and stir until smooth. Season with the **salt, black pepper** and **cayenne pepper.** Add the **butter,** and stir until it melts.

> *Tips: 1. When the cheese melts, the mixture may seem curdled, but it will become smooth again when the flour is whisked in. 2. To vary the sauce, substitute 2oz (50g) blue cheese for 2oz (50g) of the Cheddar cheese, or add 2 teaspoons French mustard, 1 teaspoon Worcestershire sauce and 3 to 4 drops Tabasco sauce after whisking in the flour.*

Easy Soured Cream Sauces 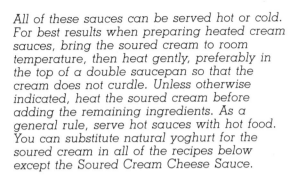 ½

All of these sauces can be served hot or cold. For best results when preparing heated cream sauces, bring the soured cream to room temperature, then heat gently, preferably in the top of a double saucepan so that the cream does not curdle. Unless otherwise indicated, heat the soured cream before adding the remaining ingredients. As a general rule, serve hot sauces with hot food. You can substitute natural yoghurt for the soured cream in all of the recipes below except the Soured Cream Cheese Sauce.

Soured Cream Cheese Sauce

Melt 4oz (115g) finely grated Cheddar cheese with 2fl oz (50ml) milk and 1 teaspoon Worcestershire sauce in the top of a double saucepan over simmering water. Blend in 8fl oz (225ml) soured cream. Add salt and pepper to taste. Serve with fish, baked potatoes and green vegetables. Makes **14 fl oz (400ml)**; Cals per tablespoon: **50**

Soured Cream Cucumber Sauce

Combine 8fl oz (225ml) soured cream with ½ cucumber peeled, seeded and diced, 2 tablespoons white wine vinegar, 1 tablespoon snipped fresh dill or ½ teaspoon dried dill, and salt and pepper to taste. Serve with fish or ham. Makes **14 fl oz (400ml)**; Cals per tablespoon: **25**

Soured Cream Curry Sauce

In a small saucepan over low heat, melt ½oz (15g) butter with 1 teaspoon curry powder; add 1 tablespoon finely chopped onion and fry for 2 to 3 minutes. Blend in 8fl oz (225ml) soured cream, and add salt and pepper to taste. Serve with meat or fish. Makes **9 fl oz (250ml)**; Cals per tablespoon: **40**

Soured Cream Horseradish Sauce

Combine 8fl oz (225ml) soured cream with 2 tablespoons cider vinegar and 2 tablespoons creamed horseradish. Add salt and pepper to taste. Serve with beef, ham or pork. Makes **½ pint (285ml)**; Cals per tablespoon: **30**

Soured Cream Mustard Sauce

Combine 8fl oz (225ml) soured cream with 2 to 3 tablespoons of any type of prepared mustard and 1 tablespoon cider vinegar. Add salt and pepper to taste. Serve with beef, ham or pork. Makes **½ pint (285ml)**; Cals per tablespoon: **30**

Creole Sauce

Preparation: **15 min**   Cooking: **25 min**   Makes **12 fl oz (340ml)**   Cals per tablespoon: **30**

3 tablespoons vegetable oil

1 medium-sized onion, peeled and chopped

1 clove garlic, peeled and finely chopped

1 small green pepper, seeded and finely chopped

3 oz (75g) mushrooms, thinly sliced

4 medium-sized tomatoes, peeled and chopped

⅓ pint (190 ml) tomato juice

¼ teaspoon salt

Here is a versatile, tomato-based sauce. Serve it with fish, shellfish, meat, poultry, omelettes, rice or spaghetti.

Heat the **oil** in a large saucepan over moderate heat; add the **onion,** and cook for 2 minutes. Add the **garlic, pepper** and **mushrooms,** and cook for 2 more minutes. Add the **tomatoes, tomato juice** and **salt** and simmer for 25 minutes.

> **Tip:** You can make this sauce in advance and refrigerate it for 1 or 2 days, or freeze it.

Lemon Sauce for Vegetables ◯ ½ 🐷

Preparation: **5 min**　Cooking: **7 min**　　　Makes **12 fl oz (340ml)**　Cals per tablespoon: **20**

8 fl oz (225ml) chicken stock

½ oz (15g) butter or margarine

1 tablespoon cornflour

2 fl oz (50ml) cold water

2 egg yolks

Juice and grated rind medium-sized lemon

*Tips: 1. You can make this sauce in advance and refrigerate it for 1 or 2 days. **2.** Freeze the egg whites in ice-cube trays (one egg white per division); when frozen, transfer the egg whites to a plastic bag and return to the freezer. Use the whites to make angel food cakes, macaroons, and icing.*

1. Heat the **chicken stock** and **butter** in a saucepan over moderate heat. Meanwhile, in a small bowl, combine the **cornflour** and **water,** and stir into the heated stock. Cook for 3 minutes, stirring continuously.

2. Using the same bowl, beat together the **egg yolks, lemon juice** and **lemon rind** until frothy. Gradually stir a quarter of the hot stock into the egg-yolk mixture, then pour slowly back into the hot stock, stirring continuously. Be careful not to let the sauce boil or the eggs will curdle. Serve over cauliflower, broccoli, spinach, courgettes and other vegetables.

All-Purpose Barbecue Sauce ½ 🐷

Preparation: **5 min**　Cooking: **20 min**　　　Makes **½ pint (285ml)**　Cals per tablespoon: **50**

2 fl oz (50ml) cider vinegar

4 fl oz (115ml) water

2 tablespoons sugar

1 tablespoon prepared English mustard

½ teaspoon black pepper

1½ teaspoons salt

¼ teaspoon paprika

1 slice lemon, about ½ in (15mm) thick

1 small onion, peeled and thinly sliced

3 oz (75g) butter or margarine

4 fl oz (115ml) tomato or chilli sauce

2 tablespoons Worcestershire sauce

1. Combine the **vinegar, water, sugar, mustard, pepper, salt, paprika, lemon, onion** and **butter** in a saucepan. Simmer for 20 minutes, stirring occasionally.

2. Remove the saucepan from the heat, and stir in the **tomato sauce** and **Worcestershire sauce.** Remove and discard the lemon slice. Use the sauce as a baste when grilling or barbecuing beef, lamb, chicken or fish.

Tip: You can make this sauce in advance and refrigerate it for 2 or 3 days; make it slightly thicker in consistency by using a little less water. It also freezes well.

Olive and Nut Sauce ⊘

Preparation: **4 min**   Cooking: **7 min**   Makes **1¼ pints (725ml)**   Cals per tablespoon: **20**

2 tablespoons olive oil

1 small onion, peeled and finely chopped

1 lb (450g) tomatoes, skinned, seeded and chopped

2 tablespoons tomato purée

1 large clove garlic, peeled and crushed

½ pint (285ml) red wine

¼ pint (150ml) dry sherry

2 red chilli peppers, finely chopped

2 oz (50g) raisins

½ teaspoon ground cinnamon

¼ teaspoon salt

¼ teaspoon black pepper

2 oz (50g) stuffed olives, sliced

1 tablespoon chopped blanched almonds

1. Heat the **oil** in a large pan and fry the **onion** for 3 minutes; add all the remaining ingredients, apart from the olives and almonds, and simmer steadily for 7 minutes.

2. Stir in the **olives** and **almonds** and heat through for 1 minute.

3. Serve with grilled and barbecued meats.

> *Tip: Spoon the sauce over a whole chicken during roasting.*

Rouille ⊘

Preparation: **8 min**   Cooking: **10 min**   Makes **½ pint (285ml)**   Cals per tablespoon: **35**

14 fl oz (400ml) fish stock

3 cloves garlic, peeled and roughly chopped

1 medium-sized red pepper, seeded and finely chopped

1 thick slice white bread, moistened with cold water and squeezed

3 tablespoons olive oil

¼ teaspoon salt

¼ teaspoon black pepper

1. Boil the **fish stock** rapidly until reduced by half (to about ⅓ pint/190ml).

2. Pound the **garlic** with the **red pepper** and squeezed-out **bread;** this can be done in a liquidiser or food processor.

3. Beat in the **olive oil** and reduced fish stock and add the **salt** and **pepper.**

> *Tip: This is traditionally served as an accompaniment to many Mediterranean fish soups – it also goes well with soft-boiled eggs and poached eggs.*

SAUCES

Aioli ½

Preparation: **6 min**   Makes **½ pint (285ml)**   Cals per tablespoon: **110**

2 cloves garlic, peeled
and crushed

2 teaspoons Dijon mustard

Generous squeeze lemon juice

¼ teaspoon salt

¼ teaspoon black pepper

2 egg yolks

⅓ pint (190ml) olive oil

2 tablespoons Marsala

1. Mix the **garlic, mustard, lemon juice, salt**
and **pepper** in a bowl; beat in the **egg yolks.**

2. Gradually whisk in the **olive oil,** drop by
drop at first, and then in a thin, steady stream.

3. Stir in the **Marsala.**

> **Tip:** *This sauce is delicious with cold cooked chicken,
> fish or veal.*

Green Sauce

Preparation: **2 min**   Makes **½ pint (285ml)**   Cals per tablespoon: **85**

6 anchovy fillets, chopped

3 tablespoons chopped parsley

2 tablespoons chopped capers

1 large clove garlic,
peeled and crushed

1 teaspoon coarse-grain mustard

Juice ½ lemon

¼ pint (150ml) olive oil

1 tablespoon tarragon vinegar

2 teaspoons Pesto sauce

Pinch salt

¼ teaspoon black pepper

1. Mix all the ingredients thoroughly together,
using a small balloon whisk (alternatively,
blend ingredients briefly in a food processor or
liquidiser).

2. Serve with fried vegetable fritters, poached
fish or over fried eggs.

> **Tip:** *This sauce contains several highly flavoured
> ingredients, and you can economise by using
> vegetable oil instead of olive oil.*

Pesto ⊘

Preparation: **2 min** Makes **⅓ pint (190ml)** Cals per tablespoon: **150**

1 large bunch basil leaves

3 cloves garlic, peeled

2 oz (50g) pine kernels

¼ teaspoon salt

¼ teaspoon black pepper

¼ pint (150ml) good quality olive oil

1. Put all the ingredients into a liquidiser or food processor and blend until smooth.

2. Keep in a screw-top jar in the refrigerator for up to 10 days.

> *Tips: 1. Pesto is added to a variety of different Italian-style dishes. Next time you cook pasta, stir 2 teaspoons of Pesto into the strained, cooked pasta. 2. To vary the Pesto, add 2 to 3 tablespoons grated Parmesan cheese.*

Lumpfish Roe Mousseline

Preparation: **2 min** Makes **⅓ pint (190ml)** Cals per tablespoon: **35**

¼ pint (150ml) soured cream

1 teaspoon grated lemon rind

1 tablespoon finely chopped parsley

2 oz (50g) orange lumpfish roe

¼ teaspoon salt

¼ teaspoon black pepper

1. Mix together all the sauce ingredients.

2. Use as a 'centre sauce' for half avocados, or as a dipping sauce for large peeled prawns.

Apricot and Mint Sauce

Preparation: **3 min** Cooking: **10 min** Makes **¾ pint (450ml)** Cals per tablespoon: **20**

1 small onion, peeled and finely chopped

2 tablespoons olive oil

1 lb (450g) fresh, ripe apricots, stoned and chopped

2 tablespoons chopped fresh mint

¼ pint (150ml) dry white wine

Juice ½ lemon

1 tablespoon clear honey

1. Fry the chopped **onion** gently in the **olive oil** for 2 minutes.

2. Add the remaining ingredients and simmer gently for 10 minutes.

3. Beat the sauce with a wooden spoon until smooth.

4. Serve with roast lamb, grilled kebabs, etc.

> *Tip: Drained, canned apricot halves can be used in place of fresh ones.*

SAUCES

307

Red Butter Sauce

Preparation: **8 min**   Cooking: **3 min**   Makes ¼ **pint (150ml)**   Cals per tablespoon: **120**

2 shallots, peeled and
finely chopped

1 teaspoon crushed peppercorns
(preferably pink ones)

5 tablespoons full-bodied
red wine

5 tablespoons chicken stock

4 oz (115g) unsalted butter

Salt

1. Put the **shallots, peppercorns, red wine**
and **chicken stock** into a pan; bubble briskly
over a high heat until reduced to about
3 tablespoons.

2. Strain the reduced liquid into a clean pan
and reheat. Gradually add the **butter** in small
knobs, whisking well between each addition.
Keep the heat low, and do not allow the sauce
to boil, or it will curdle.

3. Season to taste with a little **salt.** This sauce
is delicious with firm-textured white fish, such
as monkfish, and with speciality shellfish such
as lobster.

> **Tip:** *To ensure that the sauce does not curdle, it can be
> made in the top of a double saucepan.*

Mushroom and Marsala Sauce

Preparation: **10 min**   Cooking: **15 min**   Makes ⅔ **pint (380ml)**   Cals per tablespoon: **60**

1 oz (25g) butter

2 tablespoons olive oil

1 medium-sized onion, peeled
and finely chopped

1 large clove garlic, peeled
and crushed

3 rashers lean bacon, chopped

4 oz (115g) mushrooms, chopped

2 oz (50g) chopped chicken livers

1 tablespoon flour

Finely grated rind ½ orange

⅓ pint (190ml) red wine

3 tablespoons Marsala

1. Heat the **butter** and **oil** and fry the **onion,
garlic** and **bacon** for 5 minutes over a
moderate heat; add the **mushrooms** and
chicken livers and cook for a further
2 minutes.

2. Stir in the **flour** and cook for 30 seconds;
add the **orange rind** and gradually stir in the
red wine and **Marsala.**

3. Bring to the boil and simmer for 15 minutes.

4. Serve with grilled steaks or chops.

Index

ACKNOWLEDGMENTS

Grateful acknowledgment is made for permission to use and adapt recipes from the following sources. Note that when the recipe title differs from the title under which the recipe originally appeared, the original title is given in brackets.

Anne Ager Lamb in Ham and Pesto Sauce, Lamb in Tomato and Wine Sauce, Peppered Lamb Fillet, Lamb and Feta Kebabs, Lamb in Lemon and Basil Sauce, Lamb, Pepper and Almond Meatballs; Baked Sole Knots, Italian Sweet-Sour Fish, Chilled Fish Curry, Creamed Smoked Haddock, Herrings with Mustard Cream, Baked Sardines with Cucumber, Grilled Prawns with Basil Butter, Lettuce, Egg and Prawn Cocottes; Soft Eggs with Watercress Sauce, Spinach Eggs, Picnic Tortilla, Rolled Chicken Omelette, Cheddar and Nut Loaf, Eggs with Chicken and Asparagus Cream (Oeufs en Cocotte Crème de Volaille), Crisp Curried Eggs, Parmesan and Basil Roulade, Watercress and Walnut Tartlets, Lettuce and Chicory Soufflé, Cheese Crêpes, Eggs with Black Butter Sauce; Pasta with Avocado and Smoked Mackerel, Farfalle with Spiced Olive Sauce, Gazpacho Noodles, Brunch Pasta; Fruit Shortcake, Lemon Tart, Orange and Chocolate Biscuits, Prune and Nut Tart, Apricot Pie, Aniseed Biscuits; Bananas Romanoff, Cassis Peaches, Middle-Eastern-Style Figs, Baked Ginger Pears, Quick Mandarin Trifle; Santa's Pie, Chicken Gratinée, Potato, Stilton and Onion Pie; Broccoli with Tarragon Chicken Sauce, Smoked Fish and Ginger Stir-Fry, Ham and Mushroom Steaklet, Pasta Custard Cheese, Kipper Scramble, Herrings in Oatmeal, Black Pudding with Apple, Melon, Orange and Grapefruit Cocktail, Oven-Baked Tomatoes, Crunchy Indian-Style Sandwiches, Shrimps in a Basket, Baked Tomato Avocado, Blue Rarebit; Aioli, Olive and Nut Sauce, Green Sauce, Mushroom and Marsala Sauce, Pesto, Rouille, Apricot and Mint Sauce, Lumpfish Roe Mousseline, Red Butter Sauce. **Anne Ager/B.C.I.S.** Chicken Ratatouille, Chicken Escalopes with Garlic and Mint, Chicken and Mozzarella Kebabs, Grilled Citrus Chicken, Stir-Fried Chicken with Avocado and Cashews, Marinated Chicken in Olive and Tomato Sauce, Tagliatelle with Chicken and Asparagus Sauce, Chicken with Watercress Sauce, Madras-Style Chicken Livers. **Atheneum Publishers** Richard Olney, Bread and Pumpkin Soup (Bread and Squash Soup), from *Simple French Food*. Copyright © 1974 by Richard Olney. Reprinted by permission of Atheneum Publishers and John Schaffner Associates Inc. **The Bach Cookbooks** Lentil and Sausage Stew (Conductor's Stew), from *Bach's Lunch – Picnic and Patio Classics*. Egg Chutney Madras, from *Bach for More – Fireside Classics*. Reprinted by permission of the Junior Committee of the Cleveland Orchestra. **Better Homes & Gardens Books** Spicy Pork Tacos, Turkey Jambalaya, from *Better Homes and Gardens Pork, Sausage, and Ham Cookbook*. **Canadian Government Publishing Centre** Maritime Oatcakes, Minced Pork Pie (Tortière), from *Food à La Canadienne*. Reproduced by permission of the Minister of Supply and Services – Canada. **The Canadian Home Economics Association** Fish and Potato Pancakes (Acadian Fish Pancake), from *A Collage of Canadian Cooking*. **Contemporary Books, Inc.** Spaghetti Florentine (Baked Spaghetti Florentine), Macaroni and Cheese (Macaroni and Cheese Casserole), Spaghetti with Oil Garlic and Cheese (Spaghetti, Oil and Garlic), from *Shortcut Cooking* by Charlotte Erickson. Copyright © 1981 by Charlotte Erickson. **Crown Publishers, Inc.** Beef and Potato Stew (Picadillo-Spicy Beef), Quick Chilli Con Carne (Speedy Chili Con Carne), from *Jane Butel's Tex-Mex Cookbook* by Jane Butel. Copyright © 1980 by Jane Butel. Used by permission of Harmony Books, a division of Crown Publishers, Inc. Chicken and Sausage with Sage (Chicken Fricassee), from *The Talisman Italian Cookbook* by Ada Boni, translated by Matilde La Rosa. Copyright © 1950, 1977 by Crown Publishers. **David and Charles Limited**

Green Beans in Egg Sauce, from *Customs and Cookery in the Périgord and Quercy*. **Delair Publishing Co., Inc.** Minced Beef and Vegetable Chowder (Vegetable and Hamburger Chowder), from *250 Delicious Soups*. **Dell Publishing Co., Inc.** Mexican Chicken, excerpted from *Michele Evans' All Poultry Cookbook* by Michele Evans. Copyright © 1974 by Michele Evans. **Doubleday & Company, Inc.** Exotic Cheese Sandwiches, from *Best Loved Recipes of the American People* by Ida Bailey Allen. Copyright © 1973 by Ruth Allen Castelli. Macaroni Salad (Basic Macaroni Salad), Beef Croquettes, Sweet and Sour Fruit Dressing, Spinach Dressed with Oil and Vinegar, Superb Cheese Cake (The Very Best Cheese Pie), All-Purpose Barbecue Sauce, Easy Soured Cream Sauces (Some Easy Sour Cream Sauces), from *The Doubleday Cookbook* by Jean Anderson and Elaine Hanna. Copyright © 1975 by Doubleday & Company, Inc. Grilled Sole (Flounders Flanagan), from *Hook 'Em and Cook 'Em* by Bunny Day. Copyright © 1962 by Eleanor F. Day. Chicken Oriental (Three Cups Chicken), from *The Joy of Wokking* by Martin Yan. Copyright © 1982 by Martin Yan. Sweetcorn Rarebit (Corn Rarebit), from *San Francisco à la Carte* by the Junior League of San Francisco. Copyright © 1979 by the Junior League of San Francisco, Inc. Creamed Cod and Potatoes (Codfish Hash), Haddock Chowder, Creamed Onions, from *Recipes from America's Restored Villages* by Jean Anderson. Copyright © 1975 by Jean Anderson. Reprinted by permission of Doubleday & Company, Inc. and McIntosh and Otis, Inc. Chicken in Apple and Onion Sauce (Shaker Chicken Pudding), from *365 Ways to Cook Chicken* by Carl Lyren. Copyright © 1974 by Carl Lyren. Reprinted by permission of Doubleday & Company, Inc., and JCA Literary Agency, Inc. **Dover Publications Inc.** Curried Fillets (Madras Fish, Gowanus Bay), from *Long Island Seafood Cook Book* by J. George Frederick. **E. P. Dutton Co., Inc.** Oriental Noodle Salad, Cucumber Salad with Soya and Sesame Dressing (Pan Huang Kua), from *Florence Lin's Chinese Regional Cookbook* by Florence Lin. Copyright © 1975 by Florence Lin. **The Entre Nous Club, Inc.** Pumpkin with Bacon (Bacon-Squash Casserole), Chicken and Broccoli Bake (Chicken Broccoli Bake), from *Sunshine Sampler*. **M. Evans and Company**, Fried Rice, Singapore Rice, from *American Home All-Purpose Cook Book*, edited by the Food Staff of American Home. Copyright © 1966 by the Curtis Publishing Company. Revised copyright © 1972 by Downe Publishing, Inc. Reprinted by permission of M. Evans and Company, Inc., 216 East 49th Street, New York, N.Y. 10017. Curried New Potatoes, Quick Rice Pudding, from *The Quick and Easy Vegetarian Cookbook* by Ruth Ann Manners and William Manners. Copyright © 1978 by Ruth Ann Manners and William Manners. Reprinted by permission of M. Evans and Company, Inc., and International Creative Management. **Fairchild Publications** Spiced Beef (Beef and Indonesian Rice), from *Greenwich Village Cookbook* by Vivian Kramer. **Fannie Farmer Cookbook Corp.** Orange Cream Sauce, from *The Fannie Farmer Cookbook*, revised by Wilma Lord Perkins. Copyright © 1979 by the Fannie Farmer Cookbook Corp. **Farm Journal Inc.** Upside-Down Tuna Pie from *Complete Pie Cookbook*, Edited by Nell B. Nichols. Reprinted by permission of Farm Journal Inc. Beef and Noodles with Two Cheeses (Beef-Cheese Casserole), from *The Busy Woman's Cookbook*. **Harper & Row, Publishers, Inc.** Buttermilk Gazpacho, Sweetcorn Chowder (Cherokee Chowder), Creamed Diced Carrots with Green Pepper (Creamed Diced Carrots with Green Capsicum), from *Half a Can of Tomato Paste and Other Culinary Dilemmas* by Jean Anderson and Ruth Buchan. Copyright © 1980 by Jean Anderson and Ruth Buchan. Spicy Oriental Beef (Chungking Beef Shreds – Hot), from *Joyce Chen Cookbook*, J. B. Lippincott. Copyright © 1962 by Joyce Chen. Beef with Curry Sauce (Beefsteak in Curry Sauce), from *Jim Lee's*